STALIN'S EMPIRE OF MEMORY:
RUSSIAN-UKRAINIAN RELATIONS IN THE SOVIET
HISTORICAL IMAGINATION

Based on declassified materials from eight Ukrainian and Russian archives, *Stalin's Empire of Memory* offers a complex and vivid analysis of the politics of memory under Stalinism. Using the Ukrainian republic as a case study, Serhy Yekelchyk elucidates the intricate interaction between the Kremlin, non-Russian intellectuals, and their audiences.

Yekelchyk posits that contemporary representations of the past reflected the USSR's evolution into an empire with a complex hierarchy among its nations. In reality, he argues, the authorities never quite managed to control popular historical imagination or fully reconcile Russia's 'glorious past' with national mythologies of the non-Russian nationalities.

Combining archival research with an innovative methodology that links scholarly and political texts with the literary works and artistic images, *Stalin's Empire of Memory* presents a lucid, readable text that will become a must-have for students, academics, and anyone interested in Russian history.

SERHY YEKELCHYK is an assistant professor in the Department of Germanic and Russian Studies and the Department of History at the University of Victoria.

Stalin's Empire of Memory

Russian-Ukrainian Relations in the Soviet Historical Imagination

Serhy Yekelchyk

UNIVERSITY OF TORONTO PRESS
Toronto Buffalo London

© University of Toronto Press 2004
Toronto Buffalo London
www.utppublishing.com

Reprinted in paperback 2014

ISBN 978-0-8020-8808-6 (cloth)
ISBN 978-1-4426-2846-5 (paper)

Library and Archives Canada Cataloguing in Publication

Yekelchyk, Serhy
    Stalin's empire of memory : Russian-Ukrainian relations in the
Soviet historical imagination / Serhy Yekelchyk.

    Includes bibliographical references and index.
    ISBN 978-0-8020-8808-6 (cloth). – ISBN 978-1-4426-2846-5 (pbk.)

    1. Patriotism – Ukraine – History – 20th century.   2. Ukraine –
Historiography.   3. Russia – Historiography.   4. Soviet Union –
Relations – Ukraine.   5. Ukraine – Relations – Soviet Union.
6. Patriotism in literature.   7. Patriotism in art.   8. Ukraine – History –
20th century.   9. Soviet Union – History – 1925–1953.   I. Title.

DK508.813Y44 2004   947.7'0842   C2003-905133-1

University of Toronto Press acknowledges the financial assistance to its publishing
program of the Canada Council for the Arts and the Ontario Arts Council, an agency
of the Government of Ontario.

Canada Council   **Conseil des Arts**
for the Arts   **du Canada**

ONTARIO ARTS COUNCIL
CONSEIL DES ARTS DE L'ONTARIO
an Ontario government agency
un organisme du gouvernement de l'Ontario

This book has been published with the help of a grant from the Canadian Federation
for the Humanities and Social Sciences, through the Aid to Scholarly Publications
Programme, using funds provided by the Social Sciences and Humanities Research
Council of Canada.

University of Toronto Press acknowledges the financial support for its publishing
activities of the Government of Canada through the Canada Book Fund.

For Olia and Yulia

Contents

Illustrations follow p. xiv

Acknowledgments

Looking back at the time when I first developed my interest in Stalinism as a graduate student, I can now fully appreciate the guidance and encouragement of my professors at the University of Alberta. My adviser, John-Paul Himka, counselled me over the years on a wide array of problems, ranging from the intricacies of modern Ukrainian history to the beneficial properties of red wine during times of uncertainty. He donated a 1982 IBM computer, which I used (and abused) to write my thesis, and his clan helped me and my family in meeting the myriad small and big challenges that every immigrant faces. If it were not for John-Paul, I would never have come to North America, let alone have completed my dissertation. Other Albertans who were generous with their advice and support include David Marples, Zenon Kohut, Oleh Ilnytzkyj, Lesley Cormack, Ann MacDougal, Stephen Slemon, and Nicholas Wickenden. The Department of History and Classics and the Canadian Institute of Ukrainian Studies (CIUS) provided a hospitable and stimulating environment for thinking and writing. My studies and research at the University of Alberta were made possible by a string of scholarships: the Alberta Ukrainian Centennial Graduate Scholarship, the Izaak Walton Killam Memorial Doctoral Fellowship, the Ivan Lysiak Rudnytsky Memorial Doctoral Fellowship in Ukrainian History and Political Thought, the Dissertation Fellowship, and a research grant from the John Kolasky Memorial Endowment Fund at the CIUS.

No matter how much I liked the thesis at its defence in March 2000, a year spent as a postdoctoral fellow at the University of Michigan opened my eyes to the manuscript's innumerable shortcomings. I am grateful to Bill Rosenberg and Fran Blouin for making me part of their excellent Sawyer seminar on archives and institutions of social memory, and to Jane Burbank, Geoff Eley, Debbie Field, Madina Goldberg, Val Kivelson, Brian Porter, and Ron Suny for stimulating conversations over many lunches and coffees. It was in Ann Arbor that this book acquired its main argument and new conceptual apparatus.

Most of the present text, however, was written during the summer of 2001 in my parents' apartment in Kiev and in the fall of the same year during my first semester at the University of Victoria. I thank the colleagues in my two departments, History and Germanic and Russian Studies, for their support and kind words of encouragement during the last stages of work. Most of all, I am grateful to them for having trusted me enough to give me a job – and the peace of mind that helped greatly in putting the finishing touches on the manuscript.

This book is the product of my archival research in Ukraine and Russia. Of the very helpful archivists at the eight institutions where I worked I owe a special debt of gratitude to Iryna Leonidivna Komarova, Viktor Oleksandrovych Tykhomyrov, Valentyna Vasylivna Serhiienko, and Antonina Lukivna Kraskivska at the Ukrainian Central State Archive of Civic Organizations (TsDAHO, former Party Archive) and to Lesia Klymivna Zabarylo and Olena Zinoviivna Rachkivska at the Ukrainian State Archive and Museum of Literature and the Arts (TsDAMLM). My research at TsDAHO furnished most of the materials for this book, while the files in TsDAMLM somehow seem to better preserve the unmistakable air of Stalinist culture.

Hiroaki Kuromiya and Myroslav Shkandrij, who have since confessed to having served as anonymous reviewers of my manuscript, provided a number of helpful suggestions. Many other colleagues and friends have commented on the work in progress or helped in other ways, in particular Mark Baker, Jeffrey Burds, Michael David-Fox, Diane Koenker, Yoshiko Mitsuyoshi, Don Raleigh, Oleksandr Serhiiovych Rublov, Roman Serbyn, Stephen Velychenko, Amir Weiner, and Myroslav Yurkevich. Special thanks are due to David Brandenberger and Marko Pavlyshyn, who read the entire text and most articles derived from it. Susan Ingram, Peter Klovan, and Alan Rutkowski kindly suggested numerous stylistic improvements. At the University of Toronto Press, Suzanne Rancourt took an early interest in my project and encouraged its completion, while Catherine Frost has carefully copyedited my manuscript.

Parts of this book have previously appeared in a different form and are reprinted here with the kind permission of the following publishers: '*Diktat* and Dialogue in Stalinist Culture: Staging Patriotic Historical Opera in Soviet Ukraine, 1936–1954,' *Slavic Review* 59, no. 3 (2000): 597–624, © 2000 by the American Association for the Advancement of Slavic Studies; 'How the "Iron Minister" Kaganovich Failed to Discipline Ukrainian Historians: A Stalinist Ideological Campaign Reconsidered,' *Nationalities Papers* 27, no. 4 (1999): 579–604, © 1999 by Taylor and Francis (http://www.tandf.co.uk); Condensation of 'Celebrating the Soviet Present: The *Zhdanovshchina* Campaign in Ukrainian Literature in the Arts' in *Provincial Landscapes: Local Dimensions of Soviet Power, 1917–1953*, ed. Donald J. Raleigh, © 2001 by University of Pittsburgh Press. Used by permission of the

University of Pittsburgh Press. In addition, this book incorporates the text of my article 'Stalinist Patriotism as Imperial Discourse: Reconciling the Ukrainian and Russian "Heroic Pasts," 1939–45,' *Kritika: Explorations in Russian and Eurasian History* 3, no. 1 (2002): 51–80, © 2002 by Serhy Yekelchyk.

My greatest, broadest, and oldest debt is to my parents and grandparents, whose stories gave me a sense of personal connection to Stalin's era and who – against many odds – made my school years in the Soviet Union under Brezhnev a time to remember. My wife, Olga, has been more than patient and supportive during all the years it took me to see this work to completion. Our daughter, Yulia, who started and almost finished elementary school as I was writing this book, never made me feel guilty for not spending enough time with her – although she should have.

Abbreviations

Agitprop	Department or Administration of Propaganda and Agitation of the VKP(b) Central Committee
IMEL	Institute of Marx, Engels, and Lenin
KP(b)U	Communist Party (Bolshevik) of Ukraine
KPSS	Communist Party of the Soviet Union (after 1952)
KPU	Communist Party of Ukraine (after 1952)
OUN	Organization of Ukrainian Nationalists
RUP	Revolutionary Ukrainian Party
USSR	Union of Soviet Socialist Republics
VKP(b)	All-Union Communist Party (Bolshevik)

I.B. Romanytsky as Bohdan in Oleksandr Korniichuk's play *Bohdan Khmelnytsky* (Zankovetska Drama Company, Lviv, 1939–41). From Oleksandr Korniichuk, *Tvory v piaty tomakh* (Kiev, 1967), 2: 357.

Maksym Rylsky (left) and Oleksandr Dovzhenko during the war (1943). From Hryhorii Donets and Mykola Nahnybida, eds, *Nezabutnii Maksym Rylsky: Spohady* (Kiev, 1968), between pp. 96 and 97.

Dmytro Manuilsky (left) in conversation with Nikita Khrushchev (1945). From Borys Zavialov, *Dmytro Zakharovych Manuilsky* (Kiev, 1964), between pp. 112 and 113.

Black-and-white reproduction of Hryhorii Melikhov's *Young Taras Shevchenko Visiting the Artist K.P. Bruillov* (1947). From Bazhan, *Istoriia ukrainskoho mystetstrva v shesty tomakh*, 127.

A group of leading Ukrainian writers during the early 1950s. Left to right: Andrii Malyshko, Maksym Rylsky, Mykola Bazhan, Oleksandr Korniichuk, and Pavlo Tychyna. From Kyryliuk, *Istoriia ukrainskoi literatury u vosmy tomakh*, vol. 7, between pp. 96 and 97.

Black-and-white reproduction of Mykhailo Khmelko's *Forever with Moscow, Forever with the Russian People* (2d variant, 1954). From Bazhan, *Istoriia ukraïnskoho mystetstva v shesty tomakh*, 123.

STALIN'S EMPIRE OF MEMORY:
RUSSIAN-UKRAINIAN RELATIONS IN THE
SOVIET HISTORICAL IMAGINATION

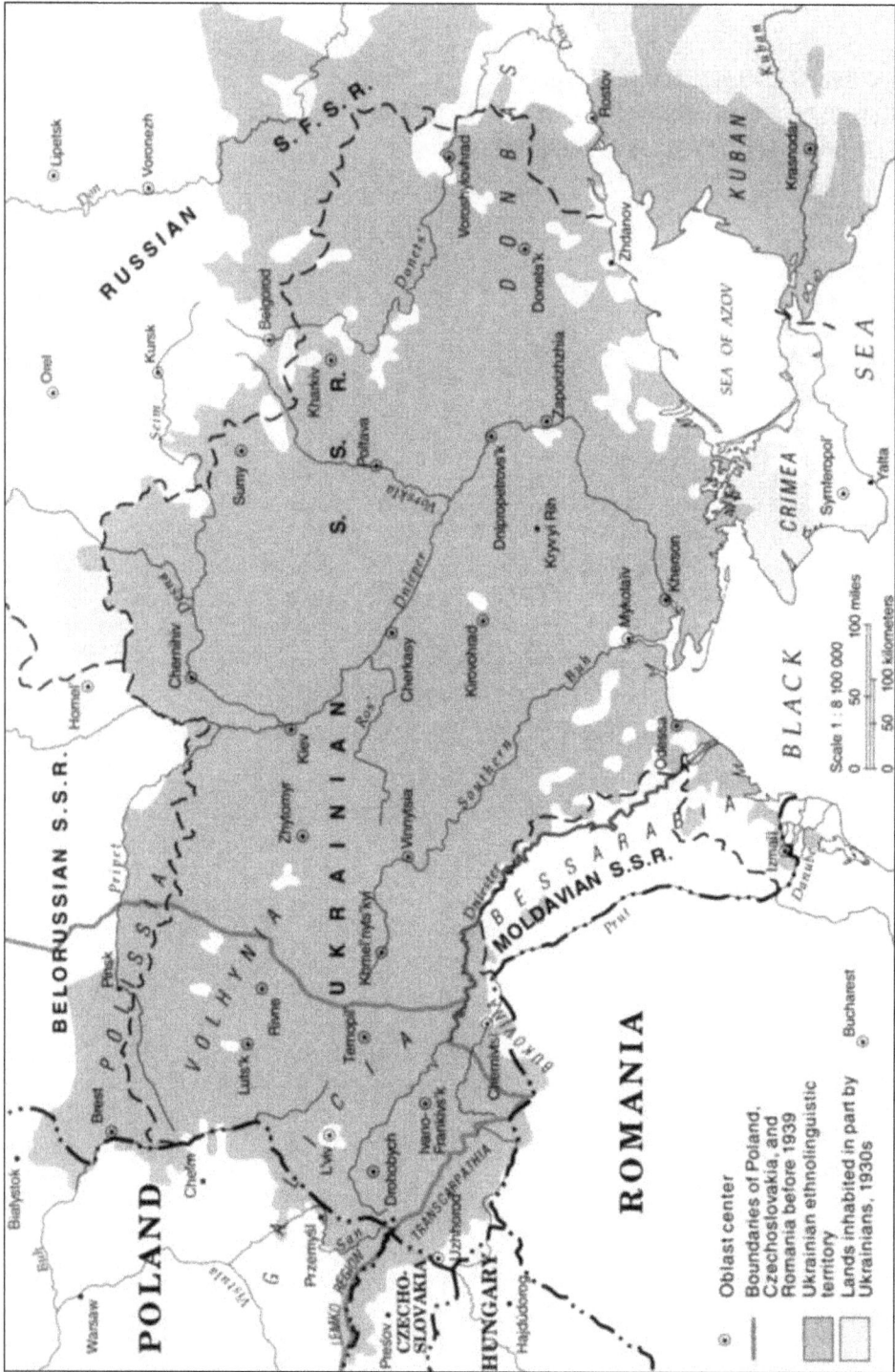

Map of Ukraine, 1945. From Paul Robert Magocsi, *A History of Ukraine* (University of Toronto Press, 1996), p. 640.

Introduction

The spectacular ease with which the republics of the USSR converted themselves into nation-states in 1991 puzzled many western observers. Did this sudden transformation confirm the traditional view of the oppressive Soviet empire, which had imposed its ideology on pre-existing nationalities and was finally undone by its peoples' long-suppressed national stirrings?[1] Or did it corroborate the 'revisionist' vision of the Soviet Union as the creator of territorial nations with their own modern high cultures, political elites, and state symbols?[2]

Access to declassified Soviet archives allows researchers for the first time to examine in unprecedented detail the inner workings of Soviet nationality policy. The emerging picture of the USSR is that of a 'nation-builder,' albeit one that periodically cracked down on the national identities that it had previously fostered.[3] But the archival findings also suggest that the question could have been posed differently. Instead of pondering what the Soviet Union had been doing to its nations, scholars could have asked how interaction among Moscow ideologues, local bureaucrats, non-Russian intellectuals, and their audiences had shaped national identities within the USSR.

Empire and Its Nations

The Soviet experiment in constructing socialism in a multinational state consisted of at least two stages with markedly different imagery and vocabularies. The original Bolshevik project laid claim to a kind of global universality based on class. Reconfigured by this core project, the essentially imperialist undertaking of keeping the nations of the Russian Empire in the new state resulted in a program of nativization, endowing the toilers of various nationalities with presumably equal and full-fledged national institutions.[4] However, Stalin's 'construction of socialism in one country' weakened the class ethos of Soviet ideology, and the emerging void was gradually filled by the default imagery of modern nations and nation-states.

A departure from Soviet identification with proletarian internationalism was an aspect of the general Stalinist turn towards conservative social and cultural values that the émigré sociologist Nicholas Timasheff famously diagnosed in 1946 as the 'Great Retreat' from communism. Later scholars of the revisionist generation did not share Timasheff's concept of communism, but adopted his term, albeit interpreting the process as the 'Big Deal' between the Stalinist authorities and the new Soviet middle class.[5] It is interesting, however, that practically all accounts of the 'Great Retreat' ignore the contemporary developments in non-Russian republics. Nevertheless, as Yuri Slezkine has recently noted, High Stalinism did not reverse the policy of nation-building in non-Russian regions. In the mid-1930s ethnicity became reified, and all officially recognized Soviet nationalities were to possess their own 'Great Traditions' – founding fathers, literary classics, and folkloric riches.[6] In other words, indigenous cultural agents were allowed, and often encouraged, to articulate their people's heritage.

Still, the message of the central media was unmistakably Russocentric. In a recent, fundamental study of the Kremlin's embrace of Russian nationalism, David Brandenberger argues that Stalin and his associates accepted 'Russocentric etatism' as the most effective way to promote state-building, popular mobilization, and legitimacy among the masses of ethnic Russians, who had been poorly educated and were finding it difficult to relate to more abstract Marxist ideas.[7]

The 'Stalin Constitution' of 1936 announced that exploiting classes no longer existed in the USSR. In fact, the notion of 'class' had long been losing its utility for the state as a classification tool precisely because the Bolsheviks had recast this sociological category to define individuals' relationship to the state, as well as their political rights and obligations.[8] In a 'workers' and peasants' state' populated exclusively, at least on paper, by workers and kolkhoz peasantry, the category 'class' lost its taxonomic value. Nationality, then, became the only universal label for classifying – and ruling – the Soviet populace.[9] It is not surprising that nationalities ceased to be considered equal: those less important lost their territorial and cultural privileges; the remaining major peoples could be ranked in a hierarchy headed by the 'great Russian people'; and a new category, 'enemy nations,' became possible.[10] While in the 1920s the USSR was a state of equal nationalities and unequal classes, by the late 1930s it had become a state of equal classes and unequal nationalities, in which a party-state increasingly identified with the Russian nation.

The question of whether or not the Stalinist and post-Stalinist USSR was an empire has generated considerable debate. Most commentators agree that the Soviet Union was a composite state in which the centre dominated many distinct ethnic societies, and that the relations of control, inequality, and hierarchy be-

tween the centre and the periphery qualified the USSR as an empire. Never having
been an ethnically 'Russian empire,' the Soviet Union nevertheless pursued familiar imperial strategies for ruling and exhibited recognizable imperial attitudes.[11]
Although debate continues on the question of whether the USSR was a typically
modern colonial empire, recent scholarship is more interested in finding out what
new knowledge historians can generate by comparing the Soviet Union with other
modern empires and what fundamental characteristics of the Soviet system they
can reveal by comparing the ways in which it and other empires sought to 'civilize'
their dominions.[12] Such an approach transcends the contradiction between the
traditional view of the USSR as fitting some objective definition of an empire and
more recent suggestions that Soviet specialists use 'empire' as a subjective category
of analysis.[13] In fact, literary scholars Marko Pavlyshyn and Myroslav Shkandrij
have made a similar argument about the Russian-Ukrainian cultural interaction.
Regardless of whether Ukraine had ever been Russia's classic colony in economic
and political sense, they show that the relations between the two literatures are best
analysed with the tools from post-colonial literary criticism.[14]

In this study of the Stalinist politics of memory I take the discussion a step
further by drawing on the insights of post-colonial theory to interpret Soviet
national ideology as an imperial discourse and to analyse the complex entanglement of the Kremlin, local bureaucrats, non-Russian intellectuals, and their
audiences in the shaping of the Stalinist historical imagination.

Recent work on empires and nationalism suggests that, far from being an
assimilatory enterprise, an empire allows for the articulation of ethnic difference.
Moreover, imperial rule necessitates the development of homogenizing and
essentializing devices such as 'India' or 'Ukraine' that are useful both for imperial
definitions of what is being ruled and for indigenous elites who can claim a broad
domain that their cultural knowledge qualifies them to govern.[15] Thus, Ukraine
and the other non-Russian republics remained distinctly different, albeit decidedly
'junior brothers,' in a Soviet family of nations. Soviet Ukrainian ideologues and
intellectuals both guarded their own historical mythology and promoted the meta-
narrative of Russian guidance. In other words, understanding Stalinist historical
memory as a subspecies of imperial discourse allows us to make sense of the
hierarchy of national pasts within it.

Such an approach also throws new light on the question of agency in Stalinist
cultural production. In spite of claims throughout post-Soviet Ukrainian historiography,[16] the Stalinist variety of Ukrainian culture did not result from Moscow's
diktat and suppression of the local intelligentsia's 'natural' national sentiment.
Bureaucrats and intellectuals in the republics who interpreted the vague yet
powerful signals from the Kremlin emerge as major players in the shaping of the
Stalinist historical imagination. It was their interaction with Moscow, rather than
simply the centre's totalizing designs, that produced the official line on non-

Russian identities and national patrimonies. Furthermore, the local ideologues and intelligentsia occupied the ambiguous position of mediator between the Kremlin and their non-Russian constituencies, and their survival and well-being depended on producing a socialist 'national ideology' specific to their republic.[17] This social group's complicated relationships with the centre and their audiences, as well as the resulting cultural products, defy explanation based solely on familiar models of totalitarian control or patron-client links. Insights from post-colonial theory are particularly helpful in making sense of the limits and possibilities in the promotion of non-Russian historical memory under Stalinism.

New archival evidence reveals that holding the party hierarchy in Moscow solely responsible for all ideological mutations in Ukraine has been an oversimplification; for the republic's bureaucrats and intellectuals played an active role in developing and revising the official politics of memory. Nor can the material sustain an opposition between local 'servants of the regime' and cultural agents presumably promoting their national cause. Many, like Mykola Bazhan, Oleksandr Korniichuk, and Pavlo Tychyna, alternated between ministerial positions and creative writing – and between elevating the national patrimony and denouncing it as nationalistic deviation. In many respects, Ukrainian cultural agents of the time acted as classic indigenous elites who defined their difference and protected their cultural domain without challenging (and, in fact, facilitating and justifying) imperial domination itself.

Although the party leaders would like to have seen them as simple cogs in the Stalinist ideological machine, many Ukrainian intellectuals in Stalin's time (with the exception of the recently 'reunited' Western Ukrainians) were of the 1920s generation, for whom the construction of socialism and Ukrainian nation-building were potentially compatible projects. Both the private diary of the great filmmaker Oleksandr Dovzhenko, who was denounced in 1944 as a Ukrainian nationalist, and the later memoirs of the poet Volodymyr Sosiura, who suffered a similar fate in 1951, testify to their authors' sincere belief in socialism – as well as their strong devotion to Ukraine.[18] From scattered anecdotal evidence on scores of other, less prominent Ukrainian intellectuals of the time, one can safely say that while some faked their devotion to communist ideas, others internalized Stalinist ideology.[19] Significantly, though, they were not expected to choose between Ukraine and socialism, since these two allegiances were compatible in the official discourse as well.

Communities of Memory

Modern students of nationalism have little patience with older scholars who saw nations as organic entities with unique, objective characteristics. Ever since Karl

Deutsch, it has not been possible to analyse nation-building without emphasizing the role of print media; over time, Eric Hobsbawm's and Benedict Anderson's once revisionist notions of modern nations as 'invented' and 'imagined' rallied overwhelming support in the profession.[20] Ernest Gellner contributed an influential proposal: although national high culture is a recent invention, nationalists always insist on its primordial character and folk roots.[21] Taken to the extreme, the idea of a nation as a 'discursive construct' ignores the historically specific character of the nation-building process as well as the need for historical myths that resonate with the current needs and inherited perceptions of the nation's potential members.[22]

Without rejecting the nation's 'discursivity,' in this study of Stalinist historical memory I suggest that nations are always imagined through the concrete social and cultural practices of their given societies. States and intellectuals do not have a free hand to invent or manipulate national traditions and memories because, as Arjuna Appadurai noted back in 1981, history is not 'a limitless and plastic symbolic resource.'[23] The continuous veneration of the glorious Cossack past in Ukraine since the seventeenth century only confirms that national myths can have deep historical roots and a long tradition of collective remembrance before they are mobilized in the modern process of identity construction. Nineteenth- and twentieth-century intellectuals thus had limited cultural space for their social engineering: they were evoking narratives, objects, and images that were already associated with certain inherited notions or emotions.[24]

Even if granted a free hand in their manipulation of historical narratives, modern nation-builders (and empire-builders) still have difficulty enforcing their interpretation outside the public domain. Prasenjit Duara suggests that '[n]ationalism is rarely the nationalism of *the nation*, but rather marks the site where different representations of the nation contest and negotiate with each other.'[25] Stalinist ideologues could, at a price of considerable effort, impose uniformity on public representations of the past – but not on individual readings of those representations. In addition, they were frustrated by the ambiguous, changeable nature of national identity, which was in constant interplay with other identifications and, as Duara shows in his work on Modern China, could 'be as subversive of the nation-state as it has been supportive.'[26]

Memory has proved no less elusive and difficult to regiment. The obsession with interpreting the past, characteristic of all nationalism, reflects the nature of modern national identity, which relies on the prescription of 'natural' continuity among a people's collective past, present, and future. This nationalist obsession is only reinforced by the fact that remembering is an individual act, a consideration forcing some social scientists to see the term 'collective memory' as nothing more than a problematic metaphor.[27] Much more constructive was the contribution of Maurice Halbwachs, the early twentieth-century French sociologist, who suggested that individuals cannot retain and activate pure personal memories unless they are constructed in certain social frameworks (such as family, religion, and nation) and sustained by these groups.[28] Halbwachs's emphasis on the social contextualization of individual memories affected influential twentieth-century students of social memory, such as Pierre Nora and Yosef Yerushalmi, both of whom also perpetuated Halbwachs's distinction between collective memory and history.

According to Halbwachs, '[G]eneral history starts only when tradition ends and the social memory is fading or breaking up,' that is, historical memory represents a more distant past, which no longer exists as collective memory and with which living contact has been lost. In addition, collective memory consists of the multiple voices of different groups, whereas historical narrative is unitary.[29] In his famous *Lieux de mémoire* series, Nora attempted to describe a variety of French monuments, places, and images as 'sites' of memory, which were once a living collective memory but had long been institutionalized as historical memory. Likewise, Yerushalmi laments the loss of living collective memory under an assault of modern historical representations, including the production of scholarly history and preservationist discourse.[30] In this interpretation, present-day collective memory incorporates both historical memory as our knowledge of the past and social memory of our lived experience, but the latter is bound to disappear and be replaced in the next generations by the learned historical memory about our time.

One major element missing from this scheme is the moment when historical memory is internalized by an individual. This individual practice of remembering, which shapes private memories in the framework of contemporary public knowledge of the past, is also a moment of defining one's sense of self, because an awareness of history forms the basis of a modern national identity. Recently, there have been two interesting attempts to recover individual agency in this process. Amos Funkenstein has proposed use of the term 'historical consciousness' to connote individuals' desire to understand their experiences historically. Susan A. Crane has further suggested that individuals can internalize public historical memory as their collective memory through their lived experience of learning about the past.[31] In other words, one does not have to witness one's ancestors' great deeds. A person can simply read a history book and develop his or her personal (or shared with peers) understanding of a distant past, which does not have to coincide with the book's interpretation but which a reader would defend passionately based on his/her personal experience of learning.

If individual conscious participation in the practice of remembering and forgetting is a requirement for a society's 'historical consciousness,' then the Stalinist project of memory was disadvantaged from the beginning by the state's inability to control individual interpretations of historical narratives. But this was not its only problem. Although the terms 'historical memory' and 'historical consciousness' occurred only occasionally in post-war Soviet scholarly literature, Lenin, Stalin, and scores of lesser ideologues repeatedly addressed the issue of the various Soviet nations' 'national pride' and 'patrimony.' This was because official identification with certain historical movements and personalities changed noticeably as Soviet socialism evolved, often confusing both intellectuals and common people in the process. When in the 1930s the Stalinist USSR became the self-conscious successor of the Russian Empire, it had to incorporate into its narrative the story of tsarist conquests and territorial acquisitions but never quite reconciled it with the previous notion of 'class history' or with the separate historical mythologies of the non-Russian peoples. In addition, residual counter-memories of pre-Bolshevik nationalist historical narratives survived in Ukraine long after the Second World War, which also brought into the Stalinist fold Western Ukrainians who had been exposed to a nationalist version of their past until 1939. The German occupation further undermined the Soviet authorities' control over public memory. The Kremlin sought to prescribe and homogenize social memory, but internal tensions within the Stalinist historical narrative and its inability to prescribe only one possible reading of cultural products undermined their efforts. The authorities could not fix the meaning of the past from which the Soviet nations supposedly got their sense of orientation for the future. In the end, the Stalinist empire of memory was kept together by state intimidation – and began disintegrating as soon as the threat of political violence was removed.

Stalin's Ukrainians

Using previously classified Soviet archives, in this book I examine the Stalinist politics of memory in the Ukrainian Soviet Socialist Republic. Paying special attention to the portrayal of Russian-Ukrainian relations, I look at how the pre-revolutionary past of the USSR's second largest nation was represented in scholarly works, political pronouncements, novels, plays, operas, paintings, monuments, and festivals during Stalin's time. Since only the major landmarks of pre-1917 Ukrainian history are considered, it is assumed that the protagonists – Stalinist ideologues, intellectuals, and general public – had no first-hand personal recollections of Kievan Rus', the Cossack epoch, or the poet Taras Shevchenko (1814–61). Some individuals still alive in 1945 might actually have met the writer Lesia Ukrainka (d. 1913) or the composer Mykola Lysenko (d. 1912), but the vast majority of the population derived their images of these classical figures from later historical narratives. In other words, this work is not concerned with contrasting historical memory and living collective memory of more recent events, but represents an attempt to uncover the mechanisms of (and glitches in) the institutionalization of official historical memory.[32]

Ukrainian history is particularly well suited for a study of imperial myth-making because it is intertwined so closely with Russian history. Both Ukrainians and Russians are Eastern Slavic peoples with common origins and mutually comprehensible languages; both national histories claim medieval Kievan Rus' as their people's first polity. When in the seventeenth century the Ukrainian Cossacks under the leadership of Bohdan Khmelnytsky overthrew Polish dominion over their lands, they soon asked Muscovy for protection. Although historical interpretations of the 1654 Pereiaslav Treaty vary widely, its final result was Ukraine's incorporation into Russia (with considerable, if decreasing autonomy during the first 120 years). While the western third of the Ukrainian ethnic lands remained under Polish, then Austro-Hungarian, and again Polish rule until 1939, Eastern Ukrainians experienced the process of modern nation-building within the Russian Empire. The greatest national bard, Taras Shevchenko, became the embodiment of what the contemporary intelligentsia understood as the Ukrainian 'national revival.' Following a brief interlude of independent statehood in 1918–20, Eastern Ukraine was forcibly incorporated into the Bolshevik multinational state, subsequently in the form of the Ukrainian SSR. In 1939 the Soviet Union occupied Eastern Poland and arranged for the Ukrainians' reunification within their republic.

In the seven chapters that follow, the book's argument is developed with chronological and subject analysis of policies, texts, and images. In chapters 1 and 2 the ideological evolution during the war years is discussed, and postwar ideological retrenchment is analysed in chapters 3 and 4. In the next three chapters I look, in turn, at the production of historical texts, codification of national heritage, and creation of artistic representations of the past during the late 1940s and early 1950s. The epilogue carries the narrative to Stalin's death and beyond, to the collapse of the USSR, thus tracing to its end the story of the Soviet historical memory.

This book shows that, during the late 1930s and early 1940s, when the USSR accomplished the transition from an unqualified condemnation of tsarist colonialism to an increasing identification with the Russian imperial past, the Stalinist reinstatement of the 'nation' as a subject of history resulted in the rehabilitation of both Imperial Russian and Ukrainian national patrimony. Following signals from above, individual writers, historians, and filmmakers accomplished this change in public discourse, but not without an internal debate on the relative importance of 'class' and 'nation' within the new Soviet historical memory. When the tension between class and national narratives of Russian-Ukrainian relations was suppressed during the war, another contradiction surfaced, namely, between Russian and Ukrainian patriotic national histories. Before the Kremlin could issue any directives on this subject, the republic's own ideologues and intellectuals were already reconciling Ukrainian historical mythology with the Russian grand narrative within a framework of a Russian-dominated 'friendship of peoples.'[33] In watching Moscow's reaction, the republic's intelligentsia soon came to understand that they could valorize Ukraine's 'Great Tradition' as long as it complemented, but did not undermine, the story of the Russian imperial past.

During the immediate post-war years Moscow was concerned with checking the growth of non-Russian national ideologies. After initial confusion over either returning to a class vision or strengthening the imperial hierarchy of national pasts, the central authorities ultimately used the post-war ideological campaigns to denounce the Ukrainian national interpretation of the past. However, the local elites were reluctant to follow the Kremlin's call to reinstall class struggle as the core of historical narratives. Instead, they soon worked out a revised and acceptable version of the Ukrainian national past that emphasized historical and ethnic ties to Russia. As they were doing so, Ukrainian intellectuals also proved that they could successfully exploit the official idiom to defend themselves during ideological campaigns. In the end, an uneasy symbiosis between ideologues and intellectuals revealed the entanglement of control, denunciation, and collaboration that allowed both parties to survive in the oppressive atmosphere of late Stalinism and produce 'ideologically sound' narratives of Russian-Ukrainian relations. Yet both parties were painfully aware of their failure to fashion a Soviet Ukrainian historical memory completely separate from the nationalist myth of origins.

In the final analysis, Soviet authorities never fully reconciled the Soviet peoples' multiple national histories. Although Ukrainian bureaucrats periodically suppressed 'nationalist deviations' in scholarship and culture through the late 1980s, their views on Ukrainian national memory remained deeply ambiguous. With reified ethnicity as a principal category of Soviet political taxonomy, historical narratives of the post-war period remained in essence 'national histories' disguised by the superficial rhetoric of class and amalgamated into the imperial grand story. Tracing the various nations' historical trajectories as leading into the Russian Empire and the Russian-dominated Soviet Union thus inescapably involved the constant affirmation of the peoples' ethnic difference – at once a cornerstone of and a time bomb built into all imperial ideologies.

In conclusion, I do not claim to have recovered the mentality of Ukrainians in Stalin's time. A collection of anecdotal evidence from the popular historical memory of the period does not allow for the comprehensive reconstruction of the actual collective memory. Throughout the book, however, numerous indications of the varied reception of official historical memory do suggest that the Stalinist collective memory remained frustratingly ambiguous. The production of official discourse on the past did not lend itself to total regimentation: republic-level ideologues constantly adjusted the Kremlin's guidelines to local realities, intellectuals often deviated from the prescribed course, and audiences could read differently even the most impeccable cultural product. Given the totalizing nature of the Stalinist project of memory, anything less than a unitary collective memory would have been considered a failure by contemporary ideologues. And a failure it was: far from being a coherent community of memory, the Stalinist Soviet Union remained a conglomerate of nations with loosely coordinated and internally unstable national memories.

This book is based on the materials in eight Ukrainian and Russian archives.[34] Most of the documents became available to researchers only in the early 1990s. Nevertheless, during the 'pre-archival age,' western scholars produced many insightful studies of Stalinism in Ukraine[35] and of Soviet attempts to redefine Ukrainian history to fit the evolving official vision of Russian-Ukrainian relations.[36]

After ideological control over scholarship disintegrated at the beginning of the 1990s and declassification of the party archives began, a number of western scholars visited Ukrainian archives, subsequently producing several influential works that take Ukraine as a case study for their analysis of Stalinist political and social life.[37] Amir Weiner's *Making Sense of War* is especially relevant for my argument about the role of indigenous intellectuals and bureaucrats. While concentrating on the war experience as a new centrepiece of the Soviet legitimizing myth, he also stresses that Ukrainian elites used the war narratives to articulate their ethnic difference. Ukrainian historians also started studying the Stalinist period and, in particular, the relations between Stalinist authorities and the Ukrainian intelligentsia. During the last decade, Ukrainian historians have produced two helpful documentary collections,[38] as well as several books and numerous articles relevant to my topic.[39] Unfortunately, most of these valuable studies subscribe to the traditional western view of Stalinism as a triumphant totalitarian dictatorship in which the state completely dominated society, and the focus is on the black deeds of Stalin and his envoys, who are presumed to have successfully terrorized the Ukrainian public into complying with the official party line.

This work offers a different, more complicated picture of Stalinist ideology and culture in the most important non-Russian republic of the Soviet Union. Further problematizing the traditional narratives of monolithic Stalinism, I attempt to reveal the subtle techniques of collaboration and resistance that defined the texture of Stalinist cultural life.

Ukrainian, Russian, and Polish personalities and place names are transliterated according to their respective spellings in these three languages. Exceptions have been made for places with common English forms, such as Moscow, the Kremlin, Kiev, Odessa, Sevastopol, Warsaw, and the Dnieper.

Chapter One

Soviet National Patriots

'The workers have no fatherland,' declared Marx and Engels in the *Communist Manifesto*. The founders of Marxism did not ignore the existence of nation-states or nationalism, but they considered them secondary and transitional phenomena. Marx understood the grand design of human history as the succession of distinctive 'modes of production' determining the forms of social organization: primitive, slave, feudal, capitalist, and communist. For the traditional nineteenth-century narrative of the rise of nation-states, Marx substituted the story of the struggle between exploited classes and their exploiters. According to the *Communist Manifesto*, 'The history of all hitherto existing society [was] the history of class struggles.'[1]

Early Soviet ideology discarded the historical narratives and commemorative rituals of the Russian Empire. Moreover, it rejected the very notion of 'national history.' The new regime went as far as declaring history irrelevant, dropping it from the Soviet school curriculum and replacing it with subjects such as 'social science' and 'political literacy.' The Bolsheviks identified with a past represented by the revolutionary movements of all peoples and in all times, from Spartacus and the Paris Commune to the Russian Revolutions of 1905 and 1917. The leading official historian of the time, Mikhail Pokrovsky (1868–1932), produced several Marxist surveys of Russian history, emphasizing economic structures, class struggle, and the tsarist empire's reactionary colonial policies. Yet until approximately 1928 the state did not enforce the Pokrovskian concept of history. The authorities tolerated non-Marxist historical scholarship, which flourished in the relaxed cultural atmosphere of the time. The 'socialist offensive' in history began simultaneously with industrialization, the collectivization of agriculture, and a cultural revolution, resulting in a purge of 'old specialists' during the period 1928–32. The practitioners of Pokrovskian class history emerged triumphant, if only briefly.[2]

By the early 1930s Stalin's pragmatic doctrine of 'building socialism in one country' firmly replaced the early ideal of the world revolution as the core of Soviet ideology. In February 1931 Stalin publicly revised the *Communist Manifesto*'s famous dictum in his address to the conference of industrial managers: 'In the past, we did not have and could not have had a fatherland. But now that we have overthrown capitalism and power belongs to the workers, we do have a fatherland and will defend its independence.'[3] Soviet ideologues proceeded to rehabilitate the notion of 'patriotism.' While the early Soviet encyclopedias defined it as an 'extremely reactionary ideology,' serving the needs of imperialists, newspapers in the 1930s hailed and promoted 'love for the Fatherland.'[4]

A part of the Stalinist 'Great Retreat' to traditional social and cultural values, the new patriotism restored to Soviet historical memory the ideas of statehood and nationhood. In 1931 the authorities reintroduced history as a school subject. In 1934 the party leadership specified that it expected teachers to offer a more traditional political history in which 'historical events were presented in historical, chronological succession and the memorization of important historical phenomena, historic figures, and chronological dates was mandatory.'[5] Beginning in 1936, the official press began denouncing the late Pokrovsky and his students for their preoccupation with 'abstract sociologism.' The authorities restored surviving old specialists to their positions, and university history departments returned to their traditional structure and curricula.

The state-sponsored rehabilitation of Russian patriotism, national pride, and tsarist heroes became perhaps the most visible aspect of the Stalinist 'Great Retreat.' From 1937 official propaganda elevated Russians to the status of the 'great Russian people.' Russian classical music and literature, previously labelled 'of the gentry' or 'bourgeois,' were also endorsed by the regime. An unprecedentedly extravagant commemoration of the 100th anniversary of Pushkin's death (1937) marked the official appropriation of Russian national culture, while the former canonical tsarist opera, Mikhail Glinka's *Life for the Tsar*, was edited and staged in 1939 as a Stalinist patriotic spectacle entitled *Ivan Susanin*, a pompous celebration of Russian national pride. Often acting on direct hints from the Politburo, Russian writers, filmmakers, and historians reinstalled as national heroes Prince Aleksandr Nevsky, Tsar Ivan the Terrible, and Emperor Peter the Great. Princes, tsars, and generals, previously condemned in the press as defenders of their class interests and exploiters of the people, were now praised as great statesmen, patriots, and military leaders.[6]

During Stalinism, there was a gradual transition from a revolutionary notion of time, implying a radical break with the past to an official historical memory valuing the continuity of great-power traditions. In the new historical narratives, the state and the nation increasingly replaced classes as subjects of history. However, students of the 'Great Retreat' in Stalinist ideology have generally ignored the multinational nature of this transformation. For Ukrainians and other Soviet nationalities, restoring the nation as the subject of history posed a question: Which nation?

Between Class and Nation

During the first years of the Soviet ideological mutation, Ukrainian ideologues, historians, and writers remained perplexed. Was a retreat from class analysis a new official line? If so, were they supposed to join the Moscovites in composing paeans to the Russian 'elder brother,' or were they to glorify their own national traditions and national heroes? Moscow could issue authoritative pronouncements only on major ideological issues arising in non-Russian republics. Moreover, the official denunciation in the late 1920s of both the dean of 'bourgeois nationalist' Ukrainian historiography, Mykhailo Hrushevsky, and the republic's leading Marxist historian, Matvii Iavorsky, produced confusing signals from above in Soviet Ukrainian intellectual life.

The Ukrainian republic had its equivalent of Pokrovsky in the person of Iavorsky, a highly placed scholar-bureaucrat who served as the party's mouthpiece on questions of history. Iavorsky authored several Marxist surveys of Ukrainian history focusing on economic processes and class struggle. Just as Pokrovsky did on the all-Union level, Iavorsky attacked 'bourgeois historians,' represented in the Ukrainian case primarily by the former president of the 'counter-revolutionary' Ukrainian People's Republic, Mykhailo Hrushevsky, who had returned from emigration in 1924.

As was the case elsewhere in the Soviet Union, Ukrainian historical scholarship flourished in the 1920s. Following Hrushevsky, the non-party historians of the time endorsed the integrity and continuity of Ukrainian history, working within the master-narrative of the nation. They produced numerous valuable studies of Kievan Rus', the Cossack period, and nineteenth-century Ukraine. Most of these scholars expressed their sympathy for the 'exploited masses,' a trope that was, after all, not a Marxist invention but part of the pre-revolutionary Ukrainian populist tradition.

Meanwhile, Iavorsky and other party historians were developing a new official narrative of Ukraine's past concentrating on class struggle. In his popular textbook, *A Short History of Ukraine*, Iavorsky unequivocally proclaimed, 'We do not care what princes we once had and what hetmans fought against Poland. We need to know how our people lived and worked and how they struggled against the lords who exploited them, both the Ukrainian and foreign ones.'[7] While rejecting the nation as a frame of historical analysis, Iavorsky was decidedly negative about the Ukrainians' experiences within the Russian Empire. If 'the Ukrainian toiling masses had not known then that life [under the tsars] would be worse than under the Polish lords,' the peasants soon learned to hate Hetman Bohdan Khmelnytsky, who brought Ukraine under the tsars. Iavorsky is neutral in his description of Hetman Ivan Mazepa's attempt to separate from Russia but condemns this Ukrainian ruler for having introduced corvée. Disapproving of nationalistic worship of Taras Shevchenko as a 'national idol,' Iavorsky paints the nineteenth-century bard as a 'great poet of revolution.'[8]

Although cast in the terms of class struggle, Iavorsky's Ukrainian history remains a distinct historical process, with even the 1917 Revolution presented as being radically different from the events in Russia because of the hegemony of the 'petit-bourgeois' peasantry in the Ukrainian revolutionary movement. This approach to Ukrainian history made Iavorsky one of the primary targets during the crackdown on 'national communists' in the late 1920s.[9] The fierce campaign against Iavorskyism continued until 1931, running hand in hand with the purge of Ukrainian non-party historians. Iavorsky himself had launched the latter campaign in 1928 by accusing Hrushevsky of construing a classless Ukrainian historical process and stressing the national factor over the social one. Subsequent attacks, including those by KP(b)U Central Committee Secretary Andrii Khvylia and by the young historian Mykhailo Rubach, openly denounced Hrushevsky as a 'bourgeois nationalist.' At the time, Hrushevsky had just published volume 9, part 1 of his multi-volume history of Ukraine, dealing with the Khmelnytsky Uprising. Although the populist Hrushevsky did not stress the importance of the war for Ukrainian state-building, he was accused of doing so with the aim of diminishing the significance of this seventeenth-century 'peasant revolution.' In the early 1930s his views were already reclassified by official historians as 'national-fascist.' In 1930 authorities transferred Hrushevsky to Russia, where he died four years later. Many of his students were arrested for participating in the Ukrainian National Centre, the nebulous underground organization that he supposedly headed, and disappeared into the Gulag.[10]

Iavorskyism, too, was officially condemned – Iavorsky himself was arrested in 1933 for his alleged participation in the subversive Ukrainian Military Organization[11] – but class history and the condemnation of Russian colonialism still predominated in Ukrainian history writing. In 1932 the Ukrainian Association of Marxist-Leninist Institutes published the collectively written *History of Ukraine: The Precapitalist Age*, in which it claimed to have undone the nationalistic theories of both Hrushevsky and Iavorsky. Nevertheless, the interpretation of events prior to the emergence of the revolutionary movement in Ukraine remained thoroughly Iavorskian.[12]

Shaken by the official denunciation of 'nationalism' in history, the republic's intellectuals did not hasten to rehabilitate the state and military traditions of Kievan Rus' or those of the Cossacks. The events potentially connecting Ukrainian

and Russian national mythology, the seventeenth-century Cossack war with Poland and the resulting union with Muscovy, were still interpreted in the spirit of
class history. In 1930 the rising authority on the period, the historian Mykola
Petrovsky, argued that, contrary to what was said in the *Eyewitness Chronicle*, the
Ukrainian people could not rejoice at the news of the union. Oleksandr Sokolovsky's
novel *Bohun* (1931) presented Khmelnytsky as an archetypal feudal warlord,
opposed by Colonel Ivan Bohun, a spokesman for the masses. Naturally, union
with the Russia of the boyars and serfs was not an option for Sokolovsky's Bohun;
instead, he advocated dependence on Ukraine's 'own forces.'[13] The authoritative
Great Soviet Encyclopedia endorsed this essentially Pokrovskian view as late as 1935
and characterized Khmelnytsky as 'A traitor and ardent enemy of the Ukrainian peasantry after the uprising. Kh[melnytsky] was a representative of the top
Ukrainian feudal Cossack officers, who strove to obtain the same rights as the
Polish feudal lords.' The 1654 Pereiaslav Treaty 'marked the union between the
Ukrainian and Russian feudal lords and, in essence, legalized the beginning of the
Russian colonial domination in Ukraine.'[14]

It is not surprising that in the mid-1930s the Soviet authorities saw the 1888
equestrian statue of Khmelnytsky in Kiev's St Sophia Square as an embarrassment.
During mass celebrations of Soviet holidays, the monument was boarded up with
wooden panels and the local bosses even considered demolishing it altogether. As
late as 1936 the republic's ideologues ordered Ukrainian museums to stop 'idealizing Cossack history.' In 1937 the ideological establishment denounced *The
Manhunters* by Zinaida Tulub as a 'subversive novel.' In this epic work about
Ukraine in the 1610s Tulub allegedly worshipped the Cossacks, ignored the plight
of the toiling peasantry and glorified the superior character of Polish culture.
Subsequently, she disappeared into the Gulag for almost two decades.[15]

However, the signals from above remained confusing. In the same year that the
authorities castigated Tulub for her harmful fascination with the Cossack past,
newspapers criticized a Kievan production of Mykola Lysenko's classic opera *Taras
Bulba* (1890) as an attempt to belittle Ukraine's heroic history. Left unedited by
Lysenko at his death in 1912, this first national historical opera ended with the
Cossack assault on the Polish fortress of Dubno, but the director of the 1937
production chose to be faithful to Gogol's famous story, closing the opera with the
scene in which the Cossack colonel Bulba is burned alive by the Poles. However,
Pravda used the tragic finale of *Taras* to dismiss the work as an 'anti-popular
production' exuding a 'spirit of doom.'[16]

Nor did professional historians have a clear idea of the shape a new official
politics of memory should take. Following the all-Union reform, Ukrainian
authorities abolished the Association of Marxist-Leninist Institutes and the Institute of Red Professors in 1936–7, concentrating the study of history in the

Institute of Ukrainian History of the republic's Academy of Sciences.[17] Neverthe-less, this centralizing effort did not lead to the production of a truly Bolshevik survey of Ukrainian history, which the party had urgently demanded. Frightened by the growing tide of repressions, the historians were in no position to respond to the contradictory signals from above. The institute began preparing a draft of a survey that did not survive but seems to have followed the Iavorskian line, at least in the interpretation of the Khmelnytsky Uprising and the tsarist colonial policies in Ukraine.[18]

Before work on the survey could advance far, the 1937 Great Purge hit the institute hard. Its first director, Professor Artashes Kharadzhev, Acting Director Hryhorii Sliusarenko, and researchers K. Hrebenkin, V. Hurystrymba, T. Skubytsky, and M. Tryhubenko were arrested and shot in 1937. The charges against them included Trotskyism, Rightism, Ukrainian nationalism, and terrorist intentions – crowned by participation in a 'counter-revolutionary terrorist rightist-leftist organization, headed by the Ukrainian Centre' that worked closely with both 'Trotskyist terrorists and Ukrainian nationalists.'[19] Their practical subversive work, confessed the accused, consisted of idealizing the national past in a forthcoming textbook on Ukrainian history. The arrested 'nationalist' Hurystrymba described his counter-revolutionary activities as follows:

> In one of our conversations in June 1935, Hrebenkin told me openly that the Ukrainians who work at the institute should take the initiative in editing the *History of Ukraine* to make this textbook a true document of history reflecting the glorious past of the Ukrainian people. I agreed willingly and asked him what concrete steps we could take to accomplish this. ... While visiting the Kharkiv Party Archive in 1935, I met with Iesypenko. During our conversation, I told him that we, a group of Ukrainian researchers at the Institute of History, had started working on a textbook on the *History of Ukraine*, and that we needed more people. I stressed that our aim was to make this textbook completely accessible and understandable to the Ukrainian masses. We needed to show the heroic past of the Ukrainian people in its entirety, their struggle for independence, and their colossal creative potential, in order to show that Ukrainians have always striven for independence. That is, I made clear to him that we had decided to write this textbook in the spirit of idealizing Ukraine. Iesypenko agreed to participate in assembling the textbook with this goal in mind.[20]

Thus, while the central press was extolling the great Russian people and their greatest national poet, Pushkin, Ukrainian intellectuals remained, at best, con-fused about how to appraise their national past and, at worst, silenced by undis-criminating repression.

Remembering the Nation

When the terror subsided in 1938–9 and the new Ukrainian party leader, Nikita Khrushchev, began consolidating the republic's elites, authorities encouraged the local intelligentsia to valorize the Ukrainian past. Khmelnytsky's spectacular rehabilitation in 1938 cleared the way for the restoration of other 'great ancestors,' such as the Ukrainian equivalent of Aleksandr Nevsky, Prince Danylo of Halych (1200–64). The peasant-born Ukrainian bard Taras Shevchenko (1814–61) had always been a Soviet icon as a 'poet of rebellion,' but during the late 1930s he was increasingly cast as the greatest national poet and the father of his nation. Ukrainian media, literature, and the arts began teaching the population to identify with their great ancestors: warriors of Kievan Rus', the Cossacks, and nineteenth-century nation-builders. In so doing, Soviet Ukrainian ideologues and intellectuals subscribed to the modified version of national memory that the nationalistic Ukrainian intelligentsia had created in the late nineteenth century.

The rehabilitation of national heroes was carried out not by decree, but through the efforts of individual Ukrainian writers and historians sensitive to the new ideological currents, whose vision was open to public discussion.[21] Initially, debates centred on the contradiction between the Marxist principle of class analysis and the ethno-patriotic criteria by which the new great ancestors were chosen. The ideological reversal began with Bohdan Khmelnytsky, the Cossack leader who had created the first modern Ukrainian polity and, conveniently enough, presided over its union with Muscovy in 1654. As a 'gatherer of Russian lands,' the hetman had belonged to the old tsarist pantheon of great historical figures, but as a founder of the Cossack state, Khmelnytsky was also a hero for Ukrainian nationalists. His ambiguous profile in the narratives of nation-building, however, was largely irrelevant for the class history of the 1920s, which denounced him as a feudal seigneur who sold out the Ukrainian peasantry to the Russian tsar and landowners.

Moscow first signalled the possible rehabilitation of Khmelnytsky in an official communiqué on history textbooks in August 1937. The Politburo commission had detected the following major flaw in the manuscripts submitted to a textbook competition:

> The authors do not see any positive role in Khmelnytsky's actions in the seventeenth century, in his struggle against Ukraine's occupation by the Poland of the lords and the Turkey of the Sultan. For example, the fact of Georgia's passing to the protectorate of Russia at the end of the eighteenth century, as well as the fact of Ukraine's transfer to Russian rule, is considered by the authors as an absolute evil, without regard for the

concrete historical circumstances of those times. The authors do not see that Georgia faced at the time the alternative of either being swallowed up by the Persia of the Shah and the Turkey of the Sultan, or coming under a Russian protectorate, just as Ukraine also had at the time the alternative of either being absorbed by the Poland of the lords and the Turkey of the Sultan, or falling under Russian control. They do not see that the second alternative was nevertheless the lesser evil.[22]

Introduced here for the first time, the 'lesser evil' formula would enjoy a long life in Stalinist official discourse on the past. According to the contemporary Soviet historian Militsa Nechkina, Stalin himself added the paragraph about Ukraine and Georgia while editing the text of the communiqué.[23] The 'lesser evil' paradigm represented a compromise between the traditional Marxist condemnation of imperial Russian colonialism and a new emphasis on continuity in state tradition between the Russian Empire and the Soviet Union. But the 1937 pronouncement did not yet define the imperial annexation of Ukraine and Georgia as historically progressive, as would later Soviet ideological documents.

The winning textbook, *A Short Course on the History of the USSR*, under the editorship of A.V. Shestakov, became a standard elementary-school history text for almost twenty years. However, this text rehabilitated the Russian imperial tradition rather cautiously. In discussing Khmelnytsky and the incorporation of Ukraine, the authors quoted the revisionist 'lesser evil' formula, but the class vision of history still reigned supreme. As a result of joining Russia, the Ukrainian people substituted one form of social oppression for another. Khmelnytsky himself appeared to have been concerned only with the interests of the landowner class, and his turn to Russia was supposedly determined by political conjuncture rather than any ethnic or religious affinity between the two peoples.[24]

In hindsight, one can see that the 1937 communiqué allowed historians much more leeway in the rehabilitation of Khmelnytsky and even reprimanded them for underestimating him as a military leader and patriot. Yet, as had occurred with Peter the Great and Ivan the Terrible, writers took the lead in reinstalling the hetman as a national hero. The young Ukrainian playwright Oleksandr Korniichuk, whose dramas had already demonstrated his party loyalty, quickly completed a historical play, *Bohdan Khmelnytsky*, in which the hetman was portrayed as a great statesman and military leader, an essentially ethnic hero who had liberated Ukraine from Polish oppression and created the Cossack state. (Significantly, the play did not stress the subsequent union with Muscovy.)[25] But precisely because the ideological turn had been hinted at rather than prescribed, Korniichuk's vision of Khmelnytsky caused a debate.

In 1938, when the prestigious Malyi Theatre company in Moscow accepted the play and went ahead with dress rehearsals, Korniichuk was suddenly summoned to

Moscow to answer accusations that he had distorted history. The reviewer of the drama, the Moscow historian Vladimir Picheta,[26] found that the text contained fictional characters and events and, more important, that the author did not portray Khmelnytsky as a defender of landowners' class interests. Discussion of the play in the Malyi Theatre on 16 October 1938 turned into a veritable battle over Khmelnytsky. Defending his emphasis on national liberation rather than internal class struggle, Korniichuk presented his work as a Soviet Ukrainian answer to Polish historical mythology. He reminded the audience about the famous nineteenth-century novel that had enshrined the Polish stereotype of the Ukrainian Cossacks, Henryk Sienkiewicz's *With Fire and Sword*: 'That book argued that Ukrainians were beasts, infidels, that Poland was the master of Ukraine and that Ukraine once again belonged under its yoke ... It is not for nothing that the Polish fascists made that book a school text.' The likelihood of a new war with Poland and/or Germany justified the promotion of Ukrainian national patriotism: 'What other ideas do you want? And what kind of ideas are needed now, when the Polish gentry and the German fascists again intend to invade Ukraine, when the Ukrainian people might have to fight for their independence?'[27]

Korniichuk prevailed over his opponents. A further attempt by the literary critic Vladimir Blium to derail *Bohdan Khmelnytsky* by informing Stalin that it ignored the class approach to history failed. The VKP(b) Central Committee's Department of Propaganda and Agitation concluded that Blium had misunderstood the notion of Soviet patriotism.[28] In the spring of 1939 both the Malyi Theatre and several leading Ukrainian companies premiered the play. The republic's newspapers hailed *Bohdan Khmelnytsky* as a work that evoked in the spectator a 'deep love, respect, and interest in our people's heroic past.' The play earned official approval and was staged by theatre companies throughout the Soviet Union, including almost every theatre in Ukraine. In 1941 *Bohdan Khmelnytsky* received the highest Soviet artistic accolade, the Stalin Prize, First Class.[29]

Other Ukrainian writers followed Korniichuk's lead. In 1939 Petro Panch published excerpts from his new historical novel, *The Zaporozhians*, which glorified the Cossack struggle against Poland in the decades immediately before the Khmelnytsky Uprising. Iakiv Kachura promptly completed the novel *Ivan Bohun* (1940), which followed the plot of Sokolovsky's earlier work without placing the colonel in opposition to Khmelnytsky. The composer Kost Dankevych wrote music to Korniichuk's play and was contemplating an opera about the hetman. However, the management of the Kiev Opera Company secured the consent of a much bigger celebrity: in the spring of 1939 it announced that Dmitrii Shostakovich had agreed to write an opera, *Bohdan Khmelnytsky*, based on Korniichuk's libretto.[30]

Historians were slower to adopt the new patriotic paradigm. While the Learned

Council of the Ukrainian Academy of Sciences' Institute of Ukrainian History debated the new appraisal of Khmelnytsky, the resourceful Moscow writer Osip Kuperman (pen name, K. Osipov) stole the historians' thunder by producing the first positive biography of the hetman, though the book's lionization of Khmelnytsky remained conditional. Throughout the text, Osipov stressed the hetman's 'class interests' as a landowner and his cruel treatment of the Ukrainian toiling masses. Portrayed as a progressive event, the union with Russia was still labelled the 'lesser evil.'[31] In 1940 the Ukrainian historian Mykola Petrovsky published the first scholarly revisionist account of the Khmelnytsky Uprising, *The Ukrainian People's War of Liberation against the Oppression by the Poland of the Gentry and Ukraine's Incorporation into Russia (1648–1654)*. The book downplayed the internal class struggle, speaking of the Ukrainian people in general and portraying Khmelnytsky as the leader of the nation. At the same time, Petrovsky presented the union with Russia as something like the teleological outcome of Ukrainian history: 'The entire historical process, the entire history of Ukraine led in inevitable, logical succession to the Ukrainian people's War of Liberation, to Ukraine's incorporation into Russia, to the unification with the fraternal Russian people.'[32] Unlike Korniichuk, Petrovsky belonged to the so-called old specialists; the ideas that appeared revisionist to Soviet-educated scholars were to him simply a blend of Ukrainian nationalism with familiar pre-revolutionary historical models.

In retrospect, this strategy of rehabilitating Ukrainian national history as part of a larger imperial discourse by connecting it with the Russian grand narrative appears as a precursor of later Soviet dogma. However, the leading historical journal, *Istorik-marksist*, published a dismissive review of the monograph. Himself a Ukrainian historian, reviewer A. Baraboi plainly announced that Petrovsky's theory 'could not be characterized as Marxist.' He doubted Cossack officers' early commitment to the union with Russia and, more important, saw the book as failing to provide a Marxist critique of this class. According to Baraboi, class struggle was the 'mainspring of all historical developments in 1648–1654,' whereas Petrovsky turned a blind eye to the 'class tensions' between Khmelnytsky and the leader of the peasant masses, Colonel Kryvonis. The reviewer concluded by recommending that the book be completely rewritten.[33]

While advocates of the concept of class history were fighting back in scholarly journals, those of national history were triumphing in the mass media. In 1939–40, the director Ihor Savchenko shot at the Kiev Film Studios a full-length movie *Bohdan Khmelnytsky* based on Korniichuk's play. Two prominent apologists for the hetman collaborated in the film's production; Korniichuk wrote the script, while Petrovsky served as scholarly consultant. Savchenko announced that his main aim was to 'purify the image of Khmelnytsky from the lies he had been coated in and to show him as a leader of the people.'[34] The film, which shared much of its plot with

Korniichuk's play, indeed provided a powerful portrayal of Khmelnytsky as the nation's leader in its struggle against Polish oppression, whereas the theme of the subsequent union with Russia remained undeveloped. When leading Soviet film-makers gathered in Leningrad in March 1941 to discuss the finished work, almost all stressed the topic's importance for Soviet Ukrainian historical memory. L. Arnshtam observed that 'Savchenko proved himself a real Ukrainian,' while Fridrikh Ermler suggested that 'this historical film will elaborate and promote the patriotic feeling that is now growing in Soviet society.' Savchenko himself dismissed minor criticisms with a statement that 'this movie was shot in Ukraine and is perceived differently there.'[35]

Bohdan Khmelnytsky was released in April 1941 and became a major event in Ukrainian cultural life. With the beginning of the Soviet-German war in June, the film was mobilized as an important propaganda movie and was shown to the troops immediately before their departure for the front. (Conveniently, Savchenko and Korniichuk had presented the 'enemies' as both Polish landowners and their mercenaries, the German dragoons.) It is interesting, however, that reviews of the film did not emphasize the resulting union with Muscovy. The critics and, likely, the general public understood *Bohdan Khmelnytsky* primarily as a film about the 'Ukrainian people's heroic struggle against the Polish gentry,' a picture promoting 'patriotism, love for the Fatherland, and hatred of the enemy.'[36]

The film had a profound impact on contemporary collective memory. Millions of Ukrainians repeatedly saw this last pre-war blockbuster of Soviet cinematography. In the early 1950s, when discussing Dankevych's opera about the hetman, even the republic's bureaucrats and intellectuals would time and again refer to Savchenko's film as a true or proper depiction of the Ukrainian past. In 1952 the historian Vadym Diadychenko would explain to an audience of party functionaries, 'People as a whole rarely read special sociological or historical books, but many are acquainted with Bohdan Khmelnytsky on account of the well-known movie.'[37]

The paradigm shift soon involved other historical personalities and periods. In March 1939 Soviet Ukraine celebrated the 125th anniversary of the birth of Taras Shevchenko on a scale unheard of since the Pushkin festivities in Moscow in 1937. The republic's authorities renamed Kiev University and the Kiev Opera House after the poet, published a complete edition of his works, and erected no less than three majestic monuments to Shevchenko. The unveiling of a statue in Kiev was accompanied by a mass rally with some 200,000 participants and speeches by Khrushchev and other dignitaries from the highest echelons. While the previous Soviet canon had included Shevchenko as the 'poet of peasant rebellion,' official texts from 1939 glorified him as the 'great son of Ukraine' – the founder of its national literature and the father of the nation.[38] If it were not for the emphasis on Shevchenko's 'revolutionary-democratic' views, this interpretation could have been mistaken for a piece of Ukrainian nationalist propaganda. Mykola Rudenko, a writer who was in his late teens at the time, testifies that the impressive monuments to the poet and the renewed cult of Shevchenko had a profound effect on his becoming a conscious Ukrainian.[39]

In 1940 the Institute of Ukrainian History finally published a 400-page collectively written survey, *History of Ukraine: A Short Course*. Released simultaneously in Ukrainian and Russian, this work marked the beginning of the rehabilitation of the national narrative. In it the thirteenth-century Prince Danylo of Halych and Khmelnytsky appear as great patriots and military leaders, although their social profile as exploiters is also mentioned. In a remarkable return to tsarist historical interpretation, Hetman Mazepa is branded a traitor for his rebellion against Peter I. The story of the Cyril and Methodius Brotherhood (1845–7) as the first Ukrainian underground political organization is shortened and subordinated to the glorification of one of its members, the great national bard, Taras Shevchenko. The authors attempt to strike a balance between the grand narrative of the nation and class analysis, but the final chapter's last section affirms the story of the Ukrainian people as the book's interpretive framework. The solemn account of the 'great Ukrainian people's reunification within a single Ukrainian socialist state' (with the Soviet annexation of Eastern Poland in September 1939) portrays this event as the apogee of Ukrainian history.[40]

The Great Ukrainian People

The Soviet invasion of Poland in August 1939 profoundly influenced the shaping of a new Soviet Ukrainian historical memory. Like many other imperial undertakings, this conquest reinforced the local population's distinct ethnic identity and generally confirmed ethnicity as the fundamental category of Stalinist ideological discourse.[41] The Red Army's westward march was accompanied by a propaganda campaign structured along ethnic, rather than class, lines. In his radio address on 17 September 1939 People's Commissar of Foreign Affairs Viacheslav Molotov presented the invasion as protection of 'our brothers of the same blood' in Western Ukraine and Belarus. *Pravda*'s editorial on 19 September referred to the defence of 'our brothers of the same nation [*natsii*],' while Marshal Semen Timoshenko, the commander of the Soviet invading troops, issued a proclamation ending with the appeal 'Long live the great and free Ukrainian people!'[42]

As the contradiction between class and national narratives of the Ukrainian past was being suppressed, a tension surfaced within the new imperial discourse between the Ukrainian and Russian grand narratives of national history. In addition to numerous newspaper articles, two brief surveys of the history of Western Ukraine were published in 1940 in Moscow and Kiev. These pamphlets reveal that the Soviet historians in the centre and in the Ukrainian capital understood the new politics of memory differently – and confirm that there was some room in official Soviet pronouncements for subtle interpretative debate. In Kiev, Serhii Bilousov and Oleksandr Ohloblyn presented the newly incorporated Western Ukraine as the 'age-old Ukrainian land.' In Moscow, Vladimir Picheta announced in the very first sentence of his pamphlet that Western Ukraine and Belarus were 'primordial Russian lands that had been part of the Rurikids' empire.'[43] Notwithstanding the apparent, though not irreconcilable, opposition between Russian imperialism and Ukrainian national patriotism, both pamphlets adopted a new term already widely used by the press: the 'great Ukrainian people.'

This term represented a remarkable addition, and one completely overlooked by scholars of Stalinism, to the previous only 'great' nation of the Soviet Union, the Russians, who were promoted to this status in 1937.[44] The official newspaper of the Ukrainian Communist Party, *Komunist*, first used this designation on 15 November 1939, in the text of the Supreme Soviet's letter to Stalin: 'Having been divided, having been separated for centuries by artificial borders, the great Ukrainian people today reunite forever in a single Ukrainian republic.' The letter also referred to the Ukrainians' homeland as 'their mother, Great Ukraine.' As well, the text of the law on the incorporation of Western Ukraine was peppered with the epithet 'great.'[45] Mykola Petrovsky freely used the adjective in his Russian-language pamphlet, *The Military Past of the Ukrainian People*, commissioned by the Ministry of Defence and published in 1939 in the mass series 'Library of the Red Army Soldier.' According to Petrovsky, the Polish lords and their German mercenaries 'were always beaten by our heroic ancestors. The secret of their victories was in their patriotism, in the spirit of independence and freedom that always characterized our great people.'[46]

References to the great Ukrainian people decreased in official discourse during 1940 and mushroomed again with the German invasion in June 1941, only to disappear, this time completely and for a long time, in about 1944. This curious episode of Stalinist semantics reflected the authorities' attempt to use Ukrainian patriotism as a mobilization tool, but without abandoning the new imperial vocabulary. In a state with one dominant 'great nation,' the only way to boost the national pride of the largest non-Russian people was to promote them, temporarily, to 'greatness' alongside the Russian elder brother.

In 'reunited' Western Ukraine, the Soviet administration similarly promoted the national heritage in its Stalinized version. The authorities 'Ukrainized' Jan Kazimierz Lviv University, renaming it after the nineteenth-century Ukrainian writer Ivan Franko. The institutes of history, archaeology, literature, linguistics, folklore, and economics of the republic's Academy of Sciences set up branches in Lviv. As the Soviet administration closed down the Shevchenko Scientific Society, the local 'bourgeois-nationalist' equivalent of the Academy, and two Ukrainian 'nationalistic' military-patriotic museums, the university and the branch of the Institute of Ukrainian History gave jobs to practically all established West Ukrainian historians. The leading local specialist on the Cossack period, Ivan Krypiakevych, although no Marxist and a former student of Hrushevsky, became both the chair of Ukrainian history at the university and the head of the institute's branch in addition to being elected a deputy to the oblast Soviet. In 1941 a then rare and highly prestigious Soviet doctoral degree in history was conferred on Krypiakevych without defence.[47]

At the beginning of the German-Soviet war in June 1941 historical memory emerged as an even more important referent in Soviet ideology. In his famous first radio address to the population on 22 June Molotov designated the war Patriotic (*otechestvennaia*), alluding to the tsarist name for the 1812 war with Napoleon. The central press freely evoked Russian pre-revolutionary martial traditions. In December *Pravda* published an unprecedentedly Russocentric article by Iemelian Iaroslavsky, 'The Bolsheviks Are the Heirs of the Russian People's Best Patriotic Traditions.' On 7 November 1941 Stalin concluded his Revolution Day speech by appealing to the Soviet people to draw inspiration from the 'brave example of our great ancestors, Aleksandr Nevsky, Dmitrii Donskoi, Kuzma Minin, Dmitrii Pozharskii, Aleksandr Suvorov, and Mikhail Kutuzov.'[48] Notable for the absence of revolutionaries and Civil War icons, this list of Russian princes, defenders of the monarchy, and tsarist military leaders seems to have provided the multinational Soviet state with a single heroic past to identify with: the familiar Russian tsarist historical mythology.

Although the Ukrainian press duly reprinted *Pravda*'s lead articles, local functionaries and intellectuals did not simply proceed to glorify Nevsky and Kutuzov. Instead, the republic's media intensified the promotion of the Ukrainian national heritage. References to Danylo of Halych, who had defeated the Teutonic knights, and to the Cossacks, who had prevailed over German mercenaries, appeared in the press from the very first days of the war.[49] Moreover, just as the Russians had fought a Patriotic War against Napoleon in 1812, so too had the Ukrainians fought their Patriotic War against the Poles and their German legionnaires in the mid-seventeenth century. As the Ukrainian writers stated in their open letter to Stalin, 'It will not be the first time that the Ukrainian people smash the insolent German hordes. Danylo of Halych beat the German mongrel-knights and, during the sixteenth-century Great Patriotic War, the barbarous German mercenary cavalry learned well the strength of the Cossack sabre.'[50] As early as 2 July Petrovsky published a lengthy newspaper article, 'The Martial Prowess of the Ukrainian People,' which traced Ukrainian military traditions back to tenth-century Prince Sviatoslav. The historian also coined a definition of Ukrainian history that did not refer to class struggle: 'The entire history of Ukraine is filled with the people's heroic struggle for their freedom and independence against every kind of foreign aggressor.' The Institute of Ukrainian History announced on 28 June that its researchers were preparing a pamphlet series about Ukraine's heroic past. The first pamphlet was to glorify Prince Danylo's battles and the last the inevitable Soviet victory in the present war.[51]

Although it was designed to imitate and supplement the Russian catalogue of great ancestors, the new canon of the republic's historic heroes actually asserted a concurrent claim to the foundation of the Russian grand narrative, namely, Kievan Rus'. No writer claimed this large medieval empire of Eastern Slavs exclusively for Ukrainian national memory, but the thirteenth-century Prince Danylo of Halych and his Galician-Volhynian Principality could be designated publicly as the patrimony of the Ukrainian people. Given the principality's prominence in na-tionalist theories tracing the Kievan heritage though Galicia-Volhynia to the Great Duchy of Lithuania to Cossack Ukraine, the valorization of Danylo was fraught with controversy. Could Ukrainians glorify the southwestern princes of Galicia-Volhynia if the Russians were extolling the northeastern princes of Vladimir-Suzdal as the heirs to Kievan grand princes? If Kievan Rus' was a common heritage of the Russians and Ukrainians, where did their separate historical mythologies begin? For the moment, though, nobody objected to the 'Ukrainization' of Prince Danylo.

On 7 July the republic's government, parliament, and party leadership issued an appeal to the Ukrainian people, affirming the new pantheon of great ancestors, a pantheon modelled after the Russian one, yet unmistakably separate: 'The fighters of Danylo of Halych cut the German knights with their swords, Bohdan Khmelnytsky's Cossacks cut them down with their sabres, and the Ukrainian people led by Lenin and Stalin destroyed the Kaiser's hordes in 1918. We have always beaten the German bandits.'[52] Disproving this statement, the German advance, the hurried evacuation that it precipitated, and the Kiev catastrophe in September left the republic's ideologues no time to refine the new canon of national memory. The next time the authorities were able to organize a major ideological rally, the First Meeting of the Representatives of the Ukrainian People, was in Saratov, Russia, on 26 November 1941. The meeting adopted a manifesto for the Ukrainian people that spoke of the 'sacred Ukrainian land' and appealed to 'freedom-loving Ukrainians, the descendants of the glorious defenders of our native land, Danylo of Halych and Sahaidachny, Bohdan Khmelnytsky and Bohun, Taras Shevchenko and Ivan Franko, Bozhenko and Mykola Shchors' never to submit themselves to German slavery.[53]

As the Russocentric undertones of the central press matured during 1942–3, Ukrainian patriotic propaganda in the local media was not suppressed but actually intensified. The Second (30 August 1942) and the Third (16 May 1943) Meetings of the Representatives of the Ukrainian People adopted manifestos that the war historians would be reluctant to reprint in 1948 because 'they did not mention the Bolsheviks.'[54] 'The great Ukrainian people' endured as a legitimate term in public discourse, forming the title of the editorial the official *Radianska Ukraina* published after the Third Meeting. Moreover, the 1943 pamphlet survey of Ukrainian history (discussed below) bore the title *The Unshakable Spirit of the Great Ukrainian People*. 'The freedom-loving Ukrainian people have always striven toward the unification [of the Ukrainian ethnic lands], toward the creation of their mighty state (*derzhavy*) on the banks of the Dniester and the Dnieper, without lords and slaves,' wrote the poet Maksym Rylsky in *Radianska Ukraina* in May 1943.[55]

During 1942 the Ukrainian State Publishing House in Saratov unveiled a series in Ukrainian of pocket-size pamphlets on 'Our Great Ancestors,' beginning with Danylo of Halych, Petro Sahaidachny, and Bohdan Khmelnytsky. Other pamphlets then in preparation featured portaits of Khmelnytsky's colonels Ivan Bohun and Maksym Kryvonis, the leaders of anti-Polish peasant rebellions Semen Palii and Ustym Karmaliuk, writers Shevchenko and Franko, and Civil War heroes Shchors and Oleksandr Parkhomenko.[56] Late in 1942 a 200-page collectively written *Survey of the History of Ukraine* was published in Ukrainian in Ufa. The book picked up the rhetorical device of the 'great Ukrainian people,' further downplaying the class approach and emphasizing state and nation building. Prince Danylo is characterized as a 'courageous and talented military leader and a patriot of his fatherland,' while Khmelnytsky in addition is celebrated as an 'exemplary Cossack officer and a progressive figure of his time.' The narrative especially exalts the Cossacks; the authors designate the Khmelnytsky Uprising as a 'War of National Liberation,' which resulted in Ukraine's incorporation into Russia – a 'lesser evil' that was not originally in the rebels' plans. The *Survey* earned a positive review in Moscow's *Istoricheskii zhurnal*.[57]

The *Survey* was intended to serve as a popular reference book, unlike the four-volume *History of Ukraine*, which was explicitly conceived as a university textbook. Edited by the leading 'rehabilitationist' Mykola Petrovsky, volume 1 covered the period from ancient times until 1654. The book not only continued the valorization of the Cossacks; the chapter on Kievan Rus' also paid unprecedented attention to the princes, with separate sections devoted to Iaroslav the Wise and Volodymyr (Vladimir) Monomakh, primarily to their state-building efforts and the promotion of culture. The list of further reading contained many works by 'bourgeois-nationalist' historians of the nineteenth and early twentieth century: Mykola (Nikolai) Kostomarov, Oleksandr Lazarevsky, and Mykhailo Hrushevsky.[58]

The working conditions in Eastern Russia and Central Asia, where Ukrainian intellectuals spent the first two years of the war, hardly encouraged a serious elaboration of the historical genre in literature and the arts. Not a single historical novel was written there; the authorities 'planned' to arrange the writing of two patriotic historical operas, *Danylo of Halych* and *Bohdan Khmelnytsky*, but work apparently never moved beyond the planning stage.[59] Some Ukrainian artists, however, proceeded to explore new historical topics. At the exhibition of Ukrainian art in Ufa in the summer of 1942, Ivan Shulga presented the sketch of his painting *The Pereiaslav Council*, the first attempt by a Soviet artist to portray the 1654 act of union with Russia. As early as 1942 the Artists' Union planned to organize a major art exhibition to celebrate the republic's imminent liberation. The exhibition's theme was to be 'The Great Patriotic War and the Heroic Past of the Ukrainian People.'[60]

In 1942 the poet Mykola Bazhan published a long patriotic poem, 'Danylo of Halych,' depicting the prince as a great warlord and popular leader. Although the poet typically referred to the thirteenth-century ancestors of Ukrainians as Rus' or Slavs, twice Bazhan used the word 'Ukraine': 'All of Ukraine hears the tread of [Danylo's] troops' and 'As the first warrior in the Ukrainian fields.' Apparently, at the war's mid-point the poet's ideological supervisors deemed acceptable such appropriation of the Galician-Volhynian principality to Ukrainian historical memory. Subsequently, Bazhan received the Stalin Prize, Second Class, for 'Danylo of Halych' and his other wartime poems.[61]

Noticeable since the mid-1930s, the elevation of the Ukrainian 'classical cultural heritage' constituted another significant dimension of the new politics of memory. During the war, the party ideologues organized widely publicized celebrations of Shevchenko and the founder of the modern Ukrainian musical tradition, Mykola Lysenko, in Ufa and Samarkand in 1942–3. The republic's Academy of Sciences in 1943 considered the study of Ukrainian cultural patrimony – the legacy of Shevchenko, Franko, Lysenko, the writer Mykhailo Kotsiubynsky, the eighteenth-century philosopher Hryhorii Skovoroda, and the nineteenth-century philologist Osyp Bodiansky – its primary aim. As soon as the republic's opera companies had moved to Central Asia, they were ordered to start working immediately and stage 'as their first priority' Ukrainian classical works such as Semen Hulak-Artemovsky's *The Zaporozhian Cossack beyond the Danube* (1863) and Lysenko's *Natalka from Poltava* (1889).[62]

The patriotic writings of Shevchenko, Franko, and Lesia Ukrainka continued to be published in mass editions even when all the territory of Ukraine was under German occupation. Indeed, Shevchenko's poems and Franko's short stories appeared in special editions 'for [distribution in] the occupied territories.' In May 1943 the Ukrainian State Publishing House (then operating in Russia), released a new edition of Shevchenko's canonic collection of poems, *Kobzar*, in a run of 20,000 copies. The tribulations of war notwithstanding, the Moscow printing presses ensured what a contemporary reviewer called 'a luxurious quality of print.'[63] During 1942–3, the celebrated artist Vasyl Kasiian produced a poster series, 'Shevchenko's Wrath Is the Weapon of Victory,' combining portraits of Shevchenko and lines from his poetry with background imagery of warfare. The series was reprinted as leaflets and dropped from aeroplanes over the occupied Ukrainian territories.[64]

The Soviet Ukrainian ideologues and intelligentsia had been well aware that their version of national memory faced competition from the nationalist narratives of the past that were circulating in the occupied territories. The activities of the Western Ukrainian historian Ivan Krypiakevych particularly bothered the Soviet authorities. Having been a darling of the Soviet administration in Lviv before the war, he now published a *Brief History of Ukraine*, which was hailed as a nationalist alternative to Soviet textbooks. A cursory exposition of Ukrainian history in its national interpretation, the *Brief History* acquired political significance primarily because of its promotion in nationalist newspapers published with the permission of the German administration. Thus, *Vinnytski visti* concluded its publication of the book with a statement summarizing the anti-Russian and anti-Soviet variant of Ukrainian memory:

> The time has finally come when the Soviet Union, that terrible prison and torture-house of peoples, is weakened, primarily by the Ukrainian national-liberation movement, and is collapsing under the mighty pressure of the forces of revolution and liberation, as well as under the strong blows of German arms. Bolshevism is collapsing and our Fatherland is obtaining new freedom. We must now build our life anew, proceeding along the path of our ancient heroes who constantly fought for Ukraine's freedom. From Sviatoslav and Volodymyr to Khmelnytsky and Mazepa, from Shevchenko and Franko to Mykola Mikhnovsky, Symon Petliura, Ievhen Konovalets and many others, all of whom sacrificed their efforts for the Ukrainian cause ... We will follow in their footsteps, and we will win freedom, independence, and unity for Ukraine![65]

It is not clear whether the quoted paragraph was written by Krypiakevych himself or was added by the newspaper's editors. Later émigré editions of his *Brief History of Ukraine* contain a similar conclusion with a nationalist canon of great ancestors.

Besides this small book, the nationalist Ukrainian Publishing House based in Cracow and Lviv issued *The History of Ukraine from Ancient Times to the Present* by I. Petrenko (Krypiakevych) and reprinted his 1929 short *History of Ukraine for the People* under the title *History of Ukraine*. While Krypiakevych was also preparing a more substantial book under the same title, the publisher reprinted Dmytro Doroshenko's *Survey of the History of Ukraine*, a work by a revered Ukrainian activist who was foreign minister of the short-lived Hetman State in 1918. In all these works the Ukrainian nation was treated as a subject of history and the negative effects of Russian domination were stressed.[66]

Radianska Ukraina was disturbed enough by the nationalist competition in the construction of memory to ridicule it in a special article. In July 1943 the paper mocked the nationalist historian Ivan Pohanko (literally, the 'Rascal'), who was allegedly writing a Ukrainian history in response to Goebbels's orders. Unfortunately for Ivan, the paper reported, a certain older nationalist, Doroshenko, had already published an anti-Soviet account of Ukraine's past. The article ended with a satirical description of Ivan walking unhappily to report to his master, *Reichskommissar* Erich Koch, that his attempts at being a good little lackey had not been successful.[67] The publishers might not have known that 'Pohanko' was actually Krypiakevych, who carefully used different pen names for his publications.

Fighting on two fronts, Ukrainian Soviet intellectuals also had to rebuff their nationalist compatriots in Canada. In April 1943 the Soviet All-Slavic Committee learned that a 'pro-fascist nationalist organization,' the Canadian Ukrainian Committee, presented Prime Minister W.L. Mackenzie King with a memo expressing the Ukrainians' desire to obtain 'their own independent state in Europe.' The Moscow-based Slavic Committee enlisted leading Ukrainian scholars and writers to prepare rebuttals for publication in both Ukraine and Canada. The poet Pavlo Tychyna wrote a particularly amusing article, 'Keep Your Dirty Hands off Ukraine,' trying to prove that 'one cannot create a fully independent state in such a geographical setting.' Even Danylo of Halych had had to ally himself with Hungary and Poland. The Ukrainian Central Rada of 1918 did not last long as an independent government before inviting the Germans in. The Soviet Union, Tychyna implied, was by far the best deal for the geopolitically challenged Ukrainians.[68]

Serious concern with concurrent nationalist propaganda surfaced in the Soviet Ukrainian press and ideological documents during late 1942 and early 1943. However, neither the actual activities of Ukrainian nationalists (who were discouraged and harassed by the Germans) nor the Soviet authorities' information about 'nationalist propaganda' (as evidenced by the archives of the KP(b)U Central Committee) seems to have justified such alarm. Perhaps Stalinist ideologues denounced Ukrainian nationalism so strongly precisely because they had been aware of the tensions within their own historical imagination, where 'nation' sat uneasily with 'class' and the 'great Ukrainian people' competed for the citizens' allegiance with the 'great Russian people.' A fierce anti-nationalist rhetoric reflected the inability of Ukrainian functionaries and intellectuals to fashion a Soviet Ukrainian historical memory that would be completely separate from a nationalist understanding of national memory.

The simultaneous and poorly coordinated promotion of the Russian and

Ukrainian national patrimonies in the first period of the war soon led both the ideologues and the Ukrainian intelligentsia to realize that their work was beginning to threaten certain basic structures of imperial ideology. In November 1942 the writer Iurii Ianovsky reported from Ufa to Moscow, to Kost Lytvyn, the secretary for ideology of the Ukrainian Central Committee, a fragment of a conversation among unidentified Ukrainian scholars: 'Ukrainian nationalism passes during the war for patriotism, but after the war [the authorities] will square accounts with it.'[69] This lapidary political language of the time disguised a major problem with Soviet Ukrainian historical memory: the Ukrainian national history had come dangerously close to completeness as a self-sufficient story of the nation's heroic trials and victories. But imperial narratives, by definition, should stress the incompleteness of indigenous historical experiences, casting the indigenous past as a story of transition to normalcy under the tutelage of the empire's dominant people.[70] As the rhetoric of Ukrainian patriotism exploded again with the Red Army's counter-offensive in the republic's territory in the autumn of 1943, Ukrainian elites realized the need to modify their vision of the past by the doctrine of Russian guidance.

Chapter Two

The Unbreakable Union

The Stalinist retreat from proletarian internationalism reached its climax in December 1943, when the Kremlin dropped the 'Internationale' as the Soviet anthem. Reflecting the new official blend of Russian and Soviet patriotism, the new anthem began with the line, 'Great Rus' forever joined together the unbreakable union of free republics.' Significantly, the non-Russian republics soon proceeded to create their own anthems. As early as 21 February 1944 the Ukrainian authorities announced a competition for the best text and music. Most entries were variations of the all-Union anthem with two or three local themes added: the great and free Ukraine, the Ukrainians' reunification in one state, and their historical friendship with the Russians. Tychyna contributed a poem with the refrain: 'Glory to brotherhood! Glory to freedom! / The Ukrainian land is reunited again. / In concord with the fraternal Russian people / The Ukrainian people have achieved happiness.' The first stanza of Bazhan's entry read: 'Live, O Ukraine, blossoming and mighty / In the union of fraternal Soviet peoples. / Equal among equals, free among free, / Live, O Ukraine, forever and ever.'[1]

Increasingly wary of allowing the excessive glorification of Ukraine, however, the republic's bureaucrats dragged the competition out until mid-1946, when they finally submitted the text and music to Moscow for approval. With the first signs of the post-war ideological freeze already in the air, Georgii Aleksandrov, the head of Agitprop, suggested that the anthem should 'show more clearly that Ukraine is a Soviet socialist republic.' Only after the purge of Soviet literature and the arts abated in 1948 did the Ukrainian ideologues inaugurate the republic's anthem with a text co-authored by Tychyna and Bazhan.[2]

Another official announcement in early 1944 was even more groundbreaking than separate anthems for the republics. On 1 February amendments to the Soviet Constitution gave the union republics the right to establish their own armies and to maintain diplomatic relations with foreign states. The most likely motivation for this metamorphosis was Stalin's intention to claim seats at the United Nations for each republic, although eventually he had to settle for three seats: for the Union itself, Ukraine, and Belarus.[3] Nevertheless, recent studies by Ukrainian scholars reveal that the republic's establishment took the constitutional amendments very seriously. Local newspapers interpreted the announcement as a 'new step in Ukrainian state-building.' While the other republics established only tiny People's Commissariats of Foreign Affairs, Ukraine created its own Commissariat of Defence. In the summer of 1944 Khrushchev and the people's commissar of defence, Lt-General V.P. Herasymenko, developed a plan for a full-fledged ministry with impressive prerogatives and power. The ministry, however, was quietly disbanded soon after the war. The first commissar of foreign affairs, the writer Oleksandr Korniichuk, likewise began building a bona fide ministry before being replaced by Dmytro Manuilsky in July 1944.[4] The Ukrainian Foreign Ministry existed in an emasculated, rudimentary form until the end of the Soviet Union.

In November 1944 Ukrainian authorities announced another major nation-building project, the preparation of a twenty-volume *Ukrainian Soviet Encyclopedia*. Manuilsky, the designated editor-in-chief, cleared this local initiative with Moscow, through 'Comrade Aleksandrov, who expressed not only his opinion but also the opinion of Comrade Malenkov that such a Ukrainian Soviet encyclopedia was needed.'[5] A joint decree of the Ukrainian party and government directed that the encyclopedia 'portray comprehensively the heroic past and the cultural heritage' of Ukrainians, as well as highlight 'the unbreakable union of the Russian and Ukrainian people.' The republic's bureaucrats developed an ambitious plan to complete the twenty volumes by 1955, but they had to discontinue the project in 1947 because of a lack of financing from Moscow.[6] (The encyclopedia was subsequently issued in seventeen volumes from 1959 to 1965.)

These three enterprises illustrate how patriotic projects conceived or developed locally during the war suffered serious, if not always fatal, setbacks during the mid- to late 1940s. More important, they demonstrate how local initiatives, ambiguous signals from above, and changing interpretations of the party line all influenced Stalinist 'nation-building' in Ukraine. The emerging official version of national memory was likewise produced by the interaction between the centre and the periphery, when the Ukrainian ideologues and intellectuals attempted to reconcile their people's historical mythology with the imperial grand narrative of Russian guidance.

The Unifying Past

Ukrainian patriotic propaganda reached its wartime heights in the autumn of 1943 when the Red Army quickly advanced into the republic's territory. Although the national past remained paramount propaganda material, the Soviet notion of Ukrainian historical memory underwent a significant configuration. The creation of the Order of Bohdan Khmelnytsky, the only Soviet military order named after a non-Russian historical personality, best symbolizes this development.

Declassified archival documents and recently published memoirs reveal that Ukrainian intellectuals and functionaries initiated the establishment of this order, and that the idea itself can be traced to the prominent film director and writer Oleksandr Dovzhenko. Apparently mindful of the creation of the orders of Aleksandr Nevsky, Mikhail Kutuzov, and Aleksandr Suvorov in mid-1942, Dovzhenko talked to Khrushchev on 29 August 1943 about establishing an Order of Bohdan Khmelnytsky. According to Dovzhenko's diary, the Ukrainian Communist Party's first secretary accepted the idea 'with delight.'[7] The archives have preserved Khrushchev's original telegram to Stalin of 31 August concerning this matter:

> In connection with the liberation of Ukraine that has now begun, I think it would be expedient to establish a military Order of Bohdan Khmelnytsky, to be awarded to officers and generals of the Red Army [stricken out: for services in liberating Ukrainian territory from the German aggressors]. The news that such an order has been established will raise the morale of Red Army fighters, especially Ukrainians. The Ukrainian people [and] the Ukrainian intelligentsia will greet the news that an Order of Bohdan Khmelnytsky has been created with particular pleasure and enthusiasm. Bohdan Khmelnytsky is a statesman and military leader who is very popular and very much loved in Ukraine. He fought for Ukraine's liberation, as well as its union [with Russia] and the union of the Ukrainian and Russian peoples. In this sense, establishing an order named after him would be desirable politically.[8]

Thus, the republic's elites evoked the notion of Russian-Ukrainian friendship in order both to promote the national patrimony and to coordinate it with an overarching imperial mythology. In the best tradition of colonial narratives, they presented Ukrainian national history as culminating in union with Russia.

On 2 September Khrushchev advised one of his deputies of Stalin's approval: 'I have received Comrade Stalin's consent in principle to establish the military Order of Bohdan Khmelnytsky.'[9] During September two groups of Ukrainian artists in Kharkiv and Moscow worked around the clock to prepare sketches of the order. It is interesting that the Ukrainian leadership instructed them to use the Ukrainian, rather than the Russian, spelling of the hetman's name on this all-Union order. The winning design, by the Moscow-based Ukrainian graphic artist Oleksandr Pashchenko, consisted of a richly ornamented six-point star with Khmelnytsky's portrait in the centre and the hetman's name in Ukrainian, with two soft signs instead of one (as in Russian) beneath.[10]

Before the order was unveiled, however, Stalin decided to magnify its propagandist effect by simultaneously renaming the city of Pereiaslav Pereiaslav-Khmelnytsky.[11] Aware that this site of the 1654 Russian-Ukrainian treaty was about to be taken by the Red Army, Khrushchev instructed *Pravda*'s editor, Petr Pospelov, to have a group of leading Ukrainian writers then in Moscow prepare the proper propaganda materials on Khmelnytsky in advance: Tychyna, Bazhan, Rylsky, and Dovzhenko. Although he himself was one of the highest ideological bureaucrats, Pospelov learned of the renaming from a handwritten note that Khrushchev dictated to his aide, Lt-Colonel Pavlo Hapochka, for delivery to Pospelov. At the mid-point of the war, Stalin and his Ukrainian viceroy, Khrushchev, decided on Ukrainian issues themselves without involving the apparatus of the VKP(b) Central Committee.[12]

As soon as the Red Army took Pereiaslav, the central and Ukrainian newspapers unveiled a series of decrees and propaganda articles. On 11 October *Pravda* published a decree (dated the previous day) establishing the Order of Bohdan Khmelnytsky. Written by or with the participation of Ukrainian writers, the accompanying editorial stressed Khmelnytsky's role in uniting Ukraine with Russia:

> The Ukrainian people hold sacred the name of Bohdan Khmelnytsky, the Russian people revere his name, and all the peoples of the Soviet Union know his name and pronounce it with the greatest respect and love because his name is linked inseparably with the Ukrainian people's struggle for liberation from the foreign yoke, with the history of the reunification of the Russian and Ukrainian peoples, and with the fraternal union of the Ukrainian and Russian peoples ... The greatest statesman of his time, [Khmelnytsky] understood well that the Ukrainian people could survive only in union with the fraternal Russian people ... Uniting two fraternal peoples, the Russians and the Ukrainians, was Bohdan Khmelnytsky's greatest historical service.[13]

Ukrainian newspapers offered a similar interpretation. Writing in *Radianska Ukraina*, Petrovsky exalted Khmelnytsky as a national hero, the 'great military leader and the liberator of all Ukrainian lands from Poland.' The historian condemned the previously popular view that Khmelnytsky considered the Pereiaslav Treaty a temporary diplomatic manoeuvre and intended to break with Muscovy in his later years. According to Petrovsky, the hetman sought from the very beginning of the war to unite with Russia, and this desire reflected the age-old strivings of the Ukrainian people.[14]

The archives reveal that the new official interpretation of Ukraine's incorporation into Russia as a fraternal union and the 'only right path,' instead of a 'lesser evil,' was developed in the apparatus of the KP(b)U Central Committee and relied heavily on the writings of Mykola Petrovsky, the court historian of the Khmelnytsky Uprising and the leading 'rehabilitationist.' Moreover, the USSR Supreme Soviet Presidium's draft decrees creating the Order of Khmelnytsky and renaming the city of Pereiaslav, as well as much of the accompanying propaganda materials, were prepared in Kiev, and all these texts featured the 'only right path' theme.[15] By confirming that the Ukrainian national mythology was subordinate to its Russian counterpart, the republic's ideologues constructed an acceptable version of Ukrainian Soviet historical memory. For creative intelligentsia, this meant a licence to continue with their patriotic propaganda. On 13 October both the central and the republican press announced the rechristening of Pereiaslav as Pereiaslav-Khmelnytsky 'in memory of the great son of the Ukrainian people, statesman and military leader Bohdan Khmelnytsky.' While stressing the hetman's services in uniting Ukraine and Russia, *Radianska Ukraina* featured a particularly frenetic sample of patriotic rhetoric, elevating Khmelnytsky to the stature of the father of his nation: 'Bohdan Khmelnytsky's ardent blood streams through and wells up in our people's veins.'[16]

During the war, the Soviet military command awarded over 9,000 Orders of Bohdan Khmelnytsky.[17] The creation of the order confirmed that the rehabilitation of Cossack mythology was irreversible. At the same time, however, the image of Khmelnytsky in official discourse was evolving: the liberator of Ukraine was becoming Ukraine's unifier with Russia.

At the beginning of September 1943, as the Red Army was taking one Ukrainian city after another, *Radianska Ukraina* featured articles on these cities' historical role. Historians and journalists filled their writing with references to the 'traditions of our freedom-loving ancestors,' the princes of Kievan Rus' and the Cossack leaders.[18] On 31 October the same authoritative newspaper allotted its entire page 3 to Petrovsky's long article 'The Unshakable Spirit of the Great Ukrainian People.' Also published as a pamphlet, the article scanned the entire history of Ukraine from Kievan Rus' to the Great Patriotic War. The work designated princes Sviatoslav, Volodymyr Monomakh, Roman Mstyslavych, and Danylo of Halych as 'great leaders' (*vozhdi*); presented the Zaporozhian Host as the 'beginning of a new Ukrainian state' (implying that Kievan Rus' had been the *old* Ukrainian state); and dropped any mention of the 'lesser evil' theory in favour of a more optimistic construct: 'In 1654 Ukraine concluded with Russia an unbreakable fraternal union.' Finally, in the opening sentence of the article, Petrovsky coined a new crypto-Hegelian definition of Ukrainian *Volksgeist*, a statement to be reworded often in subsequent Ukrainian scholarship and political pronouncements: 'The history of the Ukrainian people is a history of the long and fierce struggle against various foreign invaders, against social and national oppression, for unification within the Ukrainian state, and for the establishment of an unbreakable union with the fraternal Russian people.'[19]

After the Red Army took Kiev on 6 November, Khrushchev and other Ukrainian leaders issued a manifesto, 'To the Ukrainian People,' celebrating the liberation of the 'glorious and ancient capital of Ukraine' and referring to the 'glory of Bohdan Khmelnytsky, Petro Sahaidachny, Taras Shevchenko, and Mykola Shchors' – an abbreviated, familiar Soviet Ukrainian canon of great ancestors. As Dovzhenko's diary discloses, a group of Ukrainian writers headed by Iurii Ianovsky prepared the appeal.[20] In Moscow a prominent Ukrainian poet, Maksym Rylsky, gave a speech titled 'Kiev in the History of Ukraine' at a special convention of the All-Union Academy of Sciences. A carry-over from pre-1943 Ukrainian patriotic rhetoric, Rylsky's speech was nothing less than a comprehensive survey of the development of Ukrainian culture from ancient times to the present. Downplaying the Bolshevik Revolution as a turning point, Rylsky spoke of the 'uninterrupted development of Ukrainian culture' across the centuries. He praised the Cossacks as 'Ukraine's sharp sword' and exalted the 'brilliant representatives of Ukrainian historical scholarship': nineteenth-century Ukrainian historians Kostomarov, Kulish, Antonovych, Lazarevsky, Levytsky, the collaborators of the Shevchenko Scientific Society, and Hrushevsky, with his 'monumental' *History of Ukraine-Rus'* – all of whom had been stigmatized before the war as nationalists. *Radianska Ukraina* dutifully reported the speech in full.[21]

The Ukrainian elites continued to promote this version of national memory for a variety of reasons: from a sense of duty (since each Soviet nation had to cherish its ethnic patrimony), in order to justify their positions, and in many cases because of a genuine allegiance to the nation. Yet they were well aware of the need to reconcile the propaganda about the Ukrainian heritage with Moscow's increasingly strident praise of Russian historical greatness. In addition, the Ukrainian ideologues and intellectuals felt obliged to stress that their version of national memory differed from the nationalistic variant to which the population in the occupied territories was exposed. To map the direction of ideological change, the Ukrainian party apparatus used an otherwise insignificant occasion, the 290th anniversary of the Pereiaslav Treaty in January 1944. In late October 1943 Khrushchev wrote to Stalin: '18 January 1944 will mark the 290th anniversary of Ukraine's incorporation [*prisoedineniia*] into Russia according to the terms of the Pereiaslav Treaty that Bohdan Khmelnytsky concluded in the city of Pereiaslav-Khmelnytsky [*sic*]. The KP(b)U Central Committee requests that the celebration of this anniversary be permitted, given the furious anti-historical propaganda against the union of the Russian and Ukrainian people that the German fascists and Ukrainian-German nationalists have conducted in Ukraine ... This would be the first time the anniversary of this event was commemorated during the entire period that the Soviet power has existed in Ukraine.'[22] The plans for this unprecedented celebration of a non-round number of years were quite modest and limited mainly to articles, leaflets, and rallies in major cities. Stalin apparently approved the plan, and the Ukrainian authorities celebrated the 290th anniversary of Pereiaslav on 18 January 1944. While the rehabilitation of Khmelnytsky reinstalled in historical memory national liberation and statehood, the renewed cult of Pereiaslav symbolized the dominant presence of the Russian elder brother. The media no longer stressed that in 1654 Ukraine had joined *tsarist* Russia, and editorials with titles like 'The Sacred Union' seemed to revise irrevocably the 'lesser evil' theory.[23]

On 8 July 1944 the Ukrainian Academy of Sciences held a festive convention and concert to commemorate an even less 'round' jubilee than that of the 290th of Pereiaslav: the 235th anniversary of the Battle of Poltava. Poltava, where in 1709 Peter I and the Ukrainian Cossacks who were loyal to him defeated Charles XII of Sweden and his ally Hetman Mazepa, ideally suited the contemporary ideological requirements. Speakers praised the unbreakable union of Russians and Ukrainians and condemned the 'Ukrainian fascist nationalists.'[24] In October 1944 *Radianska Ukraina* published a landmark editorial, 'Great Rus',' elaborating on the first line of the new Soviet anthem and pledging 'our love' for Great Rus', a term clearly connoting historical Russia. In November the newspaper carried a long article by Moscow historian Anna Pankratova, 'The Historical Friendship of the Russian and Ukrainian Peoples.'[25] By late 1944 most public pronouncements on the Ukrainian past firmly incorporated the idea of Russian guidance. In an interesting modification of what Jeffrey Brooks has called the Stalinist moral economy of 'gift,'[26] expressions of gratitude to the great Russian people supplemented the pages of Ukrainian press devoted to the ritualistic thanks to Stalin, the party, and the state.

Ranking Friends and Brothers

Although Ukrainian bureaucrats and intellectuals played the principal roles in subordinating Ukrainian national mythology to its Russian counterpart, Moscow was not uninvolved in the process. After regaining the strategic initiative in the war by late 1943, party leaders indicated their displeasure with the proliferation of non-Russian national memories by denouncing the *History of the Kazakh SSR*, but the press did not report the incident until 1945.[27] The centre objected primarily to the cult of Kazakh national heroes who had fought against tsarist Russia, a crime that Danylo of Halych and Bohdan Khmelnytsky had never committed; however, Moscow also demonstrated its dissatisfaction with the growth of Ukrainian historical mythology.

After the liberation of Kiev, the Ukrainian authorities enlisted a group of writers to compose an open 'Letter from the Ukrainian People to the Great Russian

People' for publication in *Pravda*. It is significant that the text does not designate Ukraine as a second 'great' nation of the USSR, although it claims that the two fraternal peoples achieved all their historic victories together. A paean to Russian-Ukrainian friendship and Russian guidance, the letter attempts to present all the Ukrainian 'great ancestors' as comrades-in-arms of the contemporary Russian heroes. Aleksandrov, however, interpreted the text as presuming that there were 'two leading peoples in the Soviet Union, the Russians and the Ukrainians,' while it was 'known and universally accepted that the Russian people [were] the elder brother in the Soviet Union's family of peoples.' As well, the head of Agitprop dismissed as fictitious Ukrainian claims that Danylo of Halych had somehow assisted Aleksandr Nevsky in his victories over the German knights during the early 1240s. In the end, *Pravda* published a report on a mass rally in the newly liberated Kiev, rather than the letter itself.[28]

Nonetheless, the signals from Moscow remained confusing. Just as Aleksandrov criticized the unfortunate letter for insufficiently worshipping the great Russian people, Dovzhenko learned on 26 November that Stalin had banned his novel and film script, *Ukraine in Flames*. In January 1944 the Politburo convened in the Kremlin with a group of Ukrainian functionaries and leading writers to discuss the faulty work. During the meeting, Stalin personally accused Dovzhenko of 'revising Leninism' by emphasizing national pride over the principle of class struggle. Although the excessive national pride in question was Ukrainian, Stalin did not claim that it detracted from the Russians' greatness; instead, he resented the opposition of Ukrainian patriotism and allegiance to the working class, party, and the kolkhoz system.[29] This intervention (discussed in more detail in the next chapter) for a short time obscured the actual direction of ideological change: ahead to the empire, rather than back to class solidarity.

Watching for further signals from above, Ukrainian bureaucrats and intellectuals groped their way to a new official interpretation of their national past. Striking the right balance between national history and class analysis, as well as between Ukrainian national pride and kowtowing to the Russian elder brother, proved no easy task.

Thus, the Ukrainian ideologues themselves discarded the first major attempt at a new history text as a failure. The KP(b)U Central Committee archives preserve the 1943 typescript of a school textbook of Ukrainian history that was never published. No party resolutions on this book's preparation or abandonment can be traced, and its existence in itself is a puzzle, since there was no such school discipline as Ukrainian history. (Instead, the republic's pupils studied the history of the USSR.) Given that the manuscript was written by Petrovsky, the top Ukrainian historian, edited by Rylsky, one of the republic's leading poets, and read by the powerful Korniichuk, however, it does not seem untoward to surmise

official sponsorship of the project. Although the Ukrainian party's wartime archives are incomplete, one can reasonably conclude that during 1942–3 Ukrainian
leaders entertained the idea of introducing national history into the curriculum.
Two surviving pieces of correspondence support this hypothesis. In November
1942 Petrovsky reported to the secretary for ideology, Kost Lytvyn, that work on
the textbook was almost completed, and in March 1943 Lytvyn informed him that
the question of the textbook 'would be definitively resolved in the nearest future.'[30] Exactly why the project was abandoned is not clear. The file contains a
rather negative review by Mykola Bazhan proving that by 1943 the author of the
patriotic 'Danylo of Halych' considered national history suspicious and sought a
new orthodoxy in class analysis. Bazhan underlined in red pencil statements like
'We, the free children of the great Ukrainian people, are proud of [our ancestors']
great deeds' and faulted Petrovsky's discussion of the Pereiaslav Treaty for forsaking
'Stalin's notion of the "lesser evil."'[31] Thus, the project could have been discontin-
ued because of its patriotic, national spirit, but also simply because the Ukrainian ideologues had decided that the political situation was not favourable for
Ukrainian history's introduction into the curriculum, or because Moscow had
torpedoed the project with a phone call, about which no records survived.

A new brief survey of Ukrainian history, Mykola Petrovsky's *The Reunification of
the Ukrainian People within a Single Ukrainian State*, appeared in early 1944, when
the Red Army had crossed the old Polish border and entered Western Ukraine.
The official party journal, *Bolshevik* (circulation 100,000), published a shortened
version in Russian, while the complete text appeared in Ukrainian in the republic's
major newspaper, *Radianska Ukraina*. As well, the work was published in Ukrainian as a separate pamphlet printed in a run of 42,000 copies, and in Moscow a
Russian edition followed, with a print run of 25,000.[32] Petrovsky offered a slightly
revised definition of Ukrainian history: 'The history of the Ukrainian people is a
history of the masses' age-old struggle against social and national oppression, for
reunification within a Ukrainian state, and for union with the fraternal and blood-
related Russian people.' The new definition seemingly restored social struggle to
its prominent position, yet in the text itself, the author highlighted three main
themes: Ukrainian statehood, Western Ukraine as age-old Ukrainian patrimony,
and Ukraine's historical ties with Russia. As the unabridged pamphlet version
explained, union with Muscovy did not contradict the interests of Ukrainian state-
building. Although Khmelnytsky's Ukraine was an 'independent state' in the form
of a Cossack republic, 'by joining Russia, Ukraine preserved its statehood.' However, neither union with Russia nor the Revolution represented a teleological
outcome of Ukrainian history. Petrovsky reserved this role for the Ukrainians'
historic reunification within their own nation-state, which the USSR accomplished in 1939.[33] All references to class struggle notwithstanding, the author cast

Ukrainian history as the grand narrative of the nation, albeit a nation that found its Hegelian-Stalinist self-realization within a multinational empire.

Petrovsky strengthened his reputation as the premier Ukrainian historian with one more influential publication. In 1944 a major Moscow publisher issued his pamphlet *Bohdan Khmelnytsky*, which exalted the Khmelnytsky Uprising as a 'National War of Liberation,' and the Cossacks as 'bearers of the best heroic traditions of the Ukrainian people.' As well, Petrovsky presented the union with Muscovy as having been the hetman's intention from the very beginning of the war. It is interesting that the historian's description of Khmelnytsky must have resonated profoundly for contemporary readers: 'the greatest statesman of his time,' and 'a prominent military leader, a skilful organizer, and an eminent diplomat.' The people revered Khmelnytsky 'as a leader [*vozhdia*],' his enemies organized an unsuccessful 'act of terror [*terakt*]' to kill him, he guided his armies with 'iron consistency,' he 'crushed [an] oppositional group [*oppozitsionnuiu gruppu*]' of Cossack officers and executed its leaders, and finally, he 'suppressed any opposition to his power and authority.' The language itself sent a powerful signal to Petrovsky's readers. Although no one used the abbreviation *terakt* or the idiom *oppozitsionnaia gruppa* in Khmelnytsky's time, they were intimately familiar to Stalin's contemporaries. If one adds Khmelnytsky's alleged plans to reunite all Ukrainian ethnic lands and unite Ukraine with Russia in an early modern 'Soviet Union' of sorts, the analogy between the Cossack hetman and Stalin becomes complete.[34] Under Stalinism, the Ukrainian past had to be 'remembered' in the language and images of the present.

Despite all efforts to subordinate it to the new Russian imperial mythology, this most recent version of Ukrainian national memory often competed with the Russian interpretation of the same events. In *Istoricheskii zhurnal* in 1943 the Russian historian Vladimir Pashuto presented Danylo of Halych as a 'Russian [*russkii*] prince' reigning over 'Russian' people in 'South Russian' lands. The writer Aleksei Iugov similarly designated Danylo and his people as 'Russian' in his 1944 pamphlet on the prince, claiming, moreover, that 'the people of Galicia, Bukovyna, and Volhynia preserved and passed on as sacred their Russian language, fathers' faith, and unquenchable ardent love for Great Rus' through the crucible of all their historical ordeals.' Boris Grekov wrote on the Polish period of Galician history without ever referring to the formation of Ukrainian, or at least proto-Ukrainian, nationality.[35]

The Ukrainian historians and writers simultaneously advanced their interpretations, often on the pages of the same journals. Their publications never directly challenged the Russian claims, but the archives preserve the traces of their subtle struggle to affirm Ukraine's ethnic difference and historical separateness from Russia. Actually, these two notions did not undermine the central myth of the new official historical memory, that of the beneficial union with Russia. Historical Ukraine *had* to be a separate and distinct entity in order to be able to conclude a union treaty with fraternal Muscovy. Moreover, it had to preserve its ethnic distinctiveness after Pereiaslav so that it could provide a historical foundation for Ukrainian Soviet nationality. These considerations permitted Ukrainian intellectuals to defend 'their' national memory against the extremes of new Russian historical aggrandizement.

Thus, Korniichuk in 1944 dismissed the manuscript of Picheta's pamphlet on Bohdan Khmelnytsky. In his review, the Ukrainian playwright demanded the revision of 'South-Western Rus'' and 'Russian' in the text to 'Ukraine' and 'Ukrainian' throughout, a more inspiring portrayal of Khmelnytsky as a great military leader and statesman, and the exaltation of the Pereiaslav Treaty. In his conclusion, Korniichuk added sarcastically, 'Comrade Picheta not long ago publicly argued that Khmelnytsky was a feudal lord and an ardent enemy of the people. Now he has changed his point of view.' Instead of Picheta, the influential writer recommended Mykola Petrovsky, the 'best Ukrainian specialist on this period,' as an author.[36]

During the Ukrainian historians' conference with the local party ideologues in early 1945 Professor Kost Huslysty raised the issue of the 'Russification' in the central press of Danylo of Halych. He particularly castigated Pashuto's article in *Istoricheskii zhurnal* and Iugov's pamphlet for seeing the Galician-Volhynian Principality 'through the lens of the "indivisible Russian people" and not connecting it directly with the history of Ukraine.' Both Ukrainian party bureaucrats and fellow historians listened without objection to Huslysty's statement that 'Danylo of Halych was one of the great ancestors of the Ukrainian people in the same way as Aleksandr Nevsky was one of the great ancestors of the Russian people.'[37]

In literature and the arts, the evolving understanding of the national memory also gave rise to new interpretations of the past. In literature, by far the most important development occurred in drama. Korniichuk's *Bohdan Khmelnytsky* remained *the* Ukrainian historical play for official purposes. The Shevchenko Kharkiv Ukrainian Drama Company, the first theatre company to return to Ukraine, on 11 January 1944, opened its season in Kharkiv with *Bohdan*, and on 6 April the Kharkivans took the play to Kiev to open the theatre season there.[38] Nevertheless, Korniichuk's classic no longer possessed its previous political topicality, especially because it did not celebrate Ukraine's union with Russia and embodied the now-obsolete anti-Polish animus. In early May 1945 Ukrainian authorities suspended performances of *Bohdan* in Kharkiv because a delegation of the allied Polish Provisional Government had arrived in Moscow, and rallies to celebrate Polish-Ukrainian friendship were being organized in major Ukrainian cities. Furious, Korniichuk complained in vain to Khrushchev that in Moscow nobody had suspended the notoriously anti-Polish opera *Ivan Susanin*. At the same time, the 1938 play no longer satisfied the changing cultural tastes of High Stalinism. When the Kharkiv company presented *Bohdan* in Moscow in 1945, the critics in the capital saw 'too much intrigue and too little grandeur' in the play.[39]

Ivan Kocherha wrote *Iaroslav the Wise*, the play that would soon replace *Bohdan Khmelnytsky* as the most popular Ukrainian historical drama. Writing only in Ukrainian and mainly in verse, Kocherha was well known in the republic but lacked Korniichuk's all-Union fame. However, the antiquarian genre of the verse play apparently resonated well with High Stalinism's aesthetic monumentalism. The play's topic, the life of the great statesman of Kievan Rus', Grand Prince Iaroslav the Wise (who reigned from 1019 to 1054), also meshed well with the emerging Stalinist cult of medieval princes as 'great ancestors.' Yet a drama in Ukrainian about Kievan Rus' was ideologically risky, because the Russian elder brother also claimed this state as the foundation of his historical tradition.

No wonder that the Ukrainian ideologues paid extraordinary attention to Kocherha's work. The only copy of the play's final draft, dated 27 September 1944, survived not in the writer's archives, but in the archives of the KP(b)U Central Committee. Dmytro Manuilsky, the foreign minister and ideological *éminence grise*, took time to read the play, making numerous notes on the characters' historical and psychological credibility and demanding additional reviews by historians. Having found nothing suggestive of Ukrainian nationalism, Manuilsky's notes reveal his concern with the 'proper' exalted portrayal of Iaroslav the Wise as a great statesman.[40]

Yet another copy of the manuscript from the party repositories shows what was edited out of the writer's text. Beginning with the author's preface, Kocherha repeatedly emphasizes Iaroslav's Varangian (Norman) background; his hero struggles with the contradiction between his foreign origin and princely status and the interests of Rus', of the common people. To be sure, the play's main character finally chooses the latter over the former, but the party censors found it undesirable to highlight the dilemma and downgraded Iaroslav's struggle with his 'Varangianness' from the drama's principal focus to a mere passing reference. Other deletions concern the incorrect glorification of 'our stately and sacred Kiev' as the centre of Rus'; for in Stalinist historical memory this site now belonged to Moscow, despite the fact that Moscow did not exist in Iaroslav's time. The play also included an untimely reminder about the ruler's duties to the people, whom Iaroslav 'served faithfully / And only lived by their wisdom. / Nobody is wise by his own insight, / Only the people always take the true path.' The anonymous ideologue's red pencil eliminated these lines as unnecessary.[41]

In late 1944 *Iaroslav the Wise* appeared in a literary journal, and the republic's newspapers carried excerpts from the work. *Radianska Ukraina* selected a longer scene containing the topical appeal for a 'united Rus'.' The play's somewhat belated premiere in Kharkiv in September 1946 occurred in a much colder ideological climate, yet it proved to be a success, earning Stalin Prizes for both Kocherha and the company.[42]

As had occurred previously, the figures of Khmelnytsky and Shevchenko often appeared on posters, inspiring their 'descendants' to free the native land, but several more serious artistic representations of the past also materialized. Working in 1943 in Moscow, Ivan Shulha painted the canvas *Muscovite Ambassadors Present Charters to Bohdan Khmelnytsky* for the Central Historical Museum. In 1944 the artist returned to his native Kharkiv to complete two other epic paintings, *The Pereiaslav Council* and *The Zaporozhians' Song*. Shulha professed monumentalism in historical paintings, a style that would flourish in the post-war Soviet Union. Less epic and more romantic is Mykhailo Derehus's vision of the War of Liberation in his series of small oil paintings, *The Khmelnytsky Uprising*. As well, Derehus completed an unusual 'psychological' portrait of the hetman.[43]

During the Eighth Exhibition of Ukrainian Art in November 1945 critics and the press paid special attention to historical paintings. Shulha's *The Zaporozhians' Song*; the painting by Lviv artist H. Rozmus, *Khmelnytsky at Lviv*; and Derehus's series *The Khmelnytsky Uprising* and his portrait of the hetman were among the most discussed works. Of these, the critics found the 'psychological' portrait of Khmelnytsky clearly out of line. As one of them wrote, Derehus 'quite unnecessarily stressed the nervousness, exhaustion, and even the physical sickliness [of the hetman]. This is not the image that lives in the masses' imagination of the popular leader, strong-willed Bohdan Khmelnytsky.' Although the official press claimed authority over what the popular historical memory was or should be, it was concerned with developing the historical genre in Ukrainian art in a way that would have a desirable educational impact on the popular imagination. An editorial in *Radianske mystetstvo* claimed that the works presented at the exhibition 'did not reflect even a small part of the Ukrainian people's history, which is so rich in glorious events.'[44]

Stalinism's ideological mutation into the self-acknowledged successor of the Russian Empire involved the rehabilitation of the legacy of prominent pre-revolutionary Russian historians such as Sergei Solovev and Vasilii Kliuchevsky. During the war, Ukrainian intellectuals likewise proceeded to reinstall Mykhailo Hrushevsky to the stature of patriarch of Ukrainian historiography, although in the 1930s he had been denounced as a bourgeois nationalist and even a 'fascist.' Khmelnytsky's official status provided Petrovsky with an opportunity in 1943 to clear his teacher's name. Writing in *Radianska Ukraina* the day after the Order of Khmelnytsky had been unveiled, Petrovsky announced that Hrushevsky's works were 'of great importance' for the study of the hetman's time. Hrushevsky allegedly concluded in volume 9, part 1, of his *History of Ukraine-Rus'* that the Cossack leader had no intention of ever breaking the union with Muscovy (as the Ukrainian nationalist historians claimed), a conclusion that would support Petrovsky's own idea that Khmelnytsky had always sought a union with the fraternal Russian people. In another article, Petrovsky claimed that Hrushevsky made this important conclusion in volume 9, part 2, and volume 10, which was never published and the manuscript of which was subsequently lost.[45]

Ukrainian intellectuals also pushed for the rehabilitation of the confirmed nineteenth-century 'reactionary,' Panteleimon Kulish, whose 125th anniversary was celebrated in August 1944. A Ukrainian nationalist in his youth and a Russian monarchist in his senior years, Kulish was beyond redemption as a historian, but he re-emerged as the revered author of the first Ukrainian historical novel, which was also the first novel in Ukrainian, *The Black Council* (1857).[46] In 1945 a Ukrainian literary critic suggested that the 'time has come to reevaluate the legacy' of another nineteenth-century Romantic writer who was also a 'reactionary' historian, Mykola (Nikolai) Kostomarov: 'Under [tsarist] colonial oppression, the awakening of national consciousness, which the Romantic writers promoted in their work, was a progressive phenomenon of public life.'[47] Even more unexpectedly, the Ukrainians claimed the famous Russian 'reactionary' writer of Ukrainian descent, Nikolai Gogol (Mykola Hohol). On the 135th anniversary of his birth in April 1944 *Radianska Ukraina*'s headline proclaimed Gogol a 'great son of Ukraine.'[48]

Late in the war, the republic's ideologues and intelligentsia established cults around some nineteenth-century Ukrainian cultural figures. The centenary of the founder of national music, Mykola Lysenko, was commemorated in April 1942 with a modest meeting and a concert in Ufa. The authorities found it desirable to honour Lysenko again after the liberation of Ukraine, but on a larger scale. In January 1945 the republic's government announced the construction of a monument to Lysenko in Kiev, the renaming of the Lviv Conservatory and the Kharkiv Opera Theatre after him, and the plan to publish the thirty-one volumes of his oeuvre before the composer's 105th anniversary in March 1947. On the eve of Lysenko's 103rd anniversary in 1945 one article elaborated on the renewed cult of the National Composer: 'All of Ukraine, united under the great banner of Lenin and Stalin, honours Lysenko's memory'; 'In their own house, the Ukrainian people cherish their own invaluable treasures.'[49]

At the height of the 'national heritage' campaign, in the summer of 1945, the KP(b)U Central Committee gathered the writers, critics, and managers of the republic's publishing houses to discuss the grandiose project of a 'Golden Treasury' of Ukrainian literature. This three-year plan envisaged the publication of 148 volumes by twenty-one pre-revolutionary Ukrainian writers, while plans were also made for the immediate release of one-volume selected works of major literary figures.[50] This drive to promote Ukraine's national history and cultural heritage continued unabated in Ukraine until mid-1946.

As the republic's establishment propagated the Soviet version of Ukrainian national memory among the population, it also struggled to restrict public access to alternate narratives of the past. The war destroyed the Soviet centralized book trade, leading to the revival of uncontrolled book bazaars. As the writer Petro Panch testified, pre-revolutionary books on Ukrainian history, especially works about separatist hetmans Mazepa and Petro Doroshenko, were in strong demand at the bazaars. Panch particularly singled out the works of pre-Soviet Ukrainian historians Mykola Kostomarov, Hrytsko Kovalenko, and Mykola Arkas, as well as historical novels by Adrian Kashchenko: '[People] pay ten times more for these books than for our Soviet histories. Why is it so?' Panch would not venture anything beyond the explanation that poorly educated peasants read Arkas's one-volume illustrated *History of Ukraine* (1912) 'with great pleasure because it is written in an overly popular style.' In December 1944 the authorities began enforcing the state monopoly on the book trade, at least in big cities. Many books discovered at the bazaars reportedly were 'politically harmful.'[51] Overall, however, during and immediately after the war the Ukrainian ideologues and intellectuals often felt insecure about the popular reception of their variant of historical memory.

Ukraine Reunited

With the westward advance of the Red Army in late 1943 and 1944 Soviet propaganda again highlighted the theme of a reunited Western Ukraine. The initiative in raising this issue belonged to the Ukrainian establishment. Soon after the liberation of Kharkiv in February 1943 *Radianska Ukraina* published Korniichuk's long article, 'The Reunification of the Ukrainian People within Their Own State.' In an unprecedented move, *Pravda* reprinted the article in Russian the very next day, and other central newspapers followed suit the following day. Korniichuk's aim was ostensibly to rebuff some unnamed Polish émigré newspapers that allegedly laid claim to Ukrainian territories 'up to the Dnieper and the Black Sea,' although the article's real importance was as an indication of the Soviet position on Eastern Galicia (Western Ukraine), annexed from Poland in 1939. Korniichuk's statements left no doubt that the Soviet Union would stand by its territorial acquisitions. To defend the pre-war annexations, the influential playwright referred to the ethnic and historical unity of the Ukrainian lands, Khmelnytsky's campaigns in Western Ukraine, and the nineteenth-century national revival in Galicia, personified by Ivan Franko.[52]

The Ukrainian leadership was also looking forward to annexing from Poland and Czechoslovakia the remaining territories with Ukrainian populations and was preparing historical arguments to support its plans. In March 1944 Khrushchev gave a report to the first wartime session of the republic's Supreme Soviet. After the traditional opening statements on the party's leading role and before moving on to discuss the heroic war effort and the requirements for economic recovery, Khrushchev gave his audience an authoritative definition of Ukrainian history suspiciously similar to that of Petrovsky: 'The history of the Ukrainian people is a history of the age-old struggle against social and national oppression [and] a history of continuous struggle for the reunification of all Ukrainian lands in a united Ukrainian state.' Having praised Stalin and the party for recovering Western Ukraine, Khrushchev announced: 'The Ukrainian people will seek to complete the great historic reunification of their lands in a single Soviet Ukrainian state. (Stormy applause.) The Ukrainian people will seek to include in the Ukrainian Soviet state such primordial Ukrainian lands as the Kholm region, Hrubeshiv, Zamostia, Tomashiv, [and] Iaroslav. (Stormy applause.)'[53] The territories Khrushchev referred to had once been part of the Galician-Volhynian Principality and, with the exception of Iaroslav, between 1832 and 1917 had belonged to the Russian Empire, but after the Revolution they had once again fallen under Polish control. The USSR did not claim these lands, located beyond the Curzon Line, before the war, nor did it try to occupy them in 1939.[54] Petrovsky speedily produced an article, 'The Primordial Ukrainian Lands,' which appeared in *Radianska Ukraina*. The historian noted that Danylo of Halych had died and was buried in Kholm, that Khmelnytsky had claimed this land, and that, according to the 1897 census, the majority of the local population was Ukrainian.[55] Nevertheless, after prolonged negotiations with the western allies and the Polish government in exile, Stalin settled for the Curzon Line as the border between Ukraine and Poland. Kholm was to remain in Polish hands.[56]

Somewhat embarrassed, Ukrainian politicians and intellectuals turned to another candidate for 'reunification': Transcarpathia. This pocket of East Slavic highlanders, ruled since the eleventh century by Hungary and after the First World War by Czechoslovakia, presented Ukrainian ideologues with a challenge. What historical arguments could they muster to support the designation of contemporary Transcarpathians as Ukrainian? Turning to the land's pre-Hungarian past risked endorsing the nationalist idea that the population of eleventh-century Rus' was 'Ukrainian.' (From this it followed that the Russian nationality emerged later and possibly as an offshoot of the great Ukrainian people.)

Nevertheless, as the Red Army approached the Carpathian mountains in the late summer of 1944, *Radianska Ukraina* published an article by two historians who proclaimed Transcarpathia 'the westernmost outpost of the Ukrainian people' and the land of 'our dear blood brothers,' who for 1000 years had suffered from national oppression and yet preserved their identity. In early November Khrushchev visited Transcarpathia incognito, allegedly observed mass enthusiasm for reunification with Ukraine, and secured Stalin's consent to begin organizing the appropriate petitions from the local population.[57] On 27 November the Congress of the People's Committees of Transcarpathia adopted a reunification manifesto. The text unambiguously identified Ukraine as 'our mother from whom we have been separated for centuries.' The attendant letter to Stalin explained to 'our dear father, Joseph Vissarionovich' that 'in times immemorial, our ancestors lived in one united and strong family with the multi-million Ukrainian people.'[58] Thus, in the frenzy of the wartime propaganda campaign, modern Ukrainian nationhood was telescoped as far back as the tenth century.

After the Soviet-Czechoslovak treaty in June 1945 legitimized the transfer of Transcarpathia, Bazhan wrote a more cautious propaganda piece on this event, the article 'Our Primordial Land.' Bazhan announced that Transcarpathians, although of 'Ukrainian kin,' were related to both Ukrainians and Russians. His article wisely stressed the Russian brother's seniority within the Soviet family into which Eastern Ukrainians were bringing their Transcarpathian brethren: 'For one thousand years, this small stream of people preserved their faith in reunification with the great Ukrainian sea, with the great ocean of Rus'. For a thousand years – could one imagine, for a millennium – half a million people of Ukrainian kin, taken by history south-west beyond the peaks of the Carpathian mountains, did not lose the sense of unity with the mighty Eastern Slavic peoples, with the Russian and Ukrainian peoples.'[59] The authorities sponsored a 'Ukrainization' of Transcarpathian cultural life that included the opening of Uzhhorod State University,[60] but 'historical reunification' presented the Ukrainian bureaucrats with all kinds of problems. On the one hand, those Transcarpathian teachers who welcomed the union were surprised to discover that Ukrainian history was not being taught in the schools of the united Ukrainian state. On the other, Kiev had to deal with local cultural separatists like the folklorist Professor Petro Lintur, who 'avoided' the name Ukraine and used instead the traditional designation 'Transcarpathian Rus'.'[61]

In addition, the republic's authorities had to ensure the ideological re-appropriation of Western Ukraine, which had been 'reunited' in 1939 but soon had been occupied by Germany. Khrushchev arrived in Lviv the day after the Soviet Army took the city on 27 July 1944; in early August and again in October-November the first secretary toured Western Ukraine. In his secret reports to Stalin, Khrushchev focused on the fighting with the nationalist Ukrainian Insurgent Army, and this struggle, rather than the economic recovery of the region, would occupy the attention of the republic's authorities for the next two years.[62]

Replanting the Soviet version of Ukrainian historical memory in the region, however, was high on the Ukrainian ideologues' agenda. Within a few years, 44,000 teachers from Eastern Ukraine arrived to staff the schools in the Western part, and thousands of administrators and propagandists went westwards to oversee the new ideological flock.[63] Manuilsky attended a teachers' conference in Lviv in January 1945 to give a speech, *The Ukrainian-German Bourgeois National- ists at the Service of Fascist Germany.* The text, promptly released as a pamphlet, portrayed the Soviet Union as a vehicle of modernization for the economically backward region. According to Manuilsky, some Galicians idealized the Austro- Hungarian past for the empire's promotion of national autonomy, yet the Habsburgs had discouraged Eastern Galicia's economic development, whereas the Soviet power would 'turn Lviv into one of the biggest industrial centres of Soviet Ukraine.' Geopolitically, Ukraine could not be independent, nor could there be a union with 'weak' Poland. The nationalists talked of independence but in practice submitted to oppressive Nazi Germany, which did not allow for the free develop- ment of Ukrainian culture. Consequently, historically 'the Soviet Union [was] the only guarantor of Ukraine's freedom and independence.'[64]

The Soviet authorities worked hard to suppress the alternate, 'nationalistic' version of the national memory in Western Ukraine. During the first years after reunification, the bureaucrats were obsessed with fighting the cult of Hetman Mazepa in the West. Again and again at conferences, ideologues raised the problem of the proper blackening of this 'traitor' who had attempted to separate Cossack Ukraine from Russia. Another source of the Galicians' national pride, the Ukrainian Galician Army of 1918–20, was also labelled 'nationalistic' in new narratives of the past. Finally, when Stalin proceeded to destroy the foundation of Galician national identity, the Ukrainian Greek Catholic (Uniate) Church, the first public attack on it came in the form of a derogatory historical survey of the Church's 'anti-people' activities. The survey was part of Iaroslav Halan's infamous article, 'With a Cross or With a Knife?' which denounced the late head of the Church, Metropolitan Andrei Sheptytsky. The Lviv authorities reported on the public reaction to this 'bomb of enormous force' directly to Khrushchev.[65]

As the Ukrainian ideologues eliminated the residue of nationalist historical narratives from Western Ukrainian public discourse, they also commissioned reliable historians to write model lectures on the region's past. The resourceful Petrovsky promptly composed a pamphlet survey of Western Ukrainian history. Sensing the new ideological winds of the last years of the war, he imputed to Galicians the age-old desire to unite not only with Eastern Ukrainians but also with the 'fraternal [and] blood-related Russian people.' Petrovsky went even further in undoing wartime patriotic concepts when he criticized the Galician historians Mykhailo Hrushevsky and Stepan Tomashivsky for tracing 'Ukrainian' statehood from ancient Kiev to Galicia-Volhynia. Until the fourteenth century, wrote Petrovsky, there was no Ukrainian, Russian, or Belarusian nationality, just the common Rus' people. Moreover, even before 1917 both Eastern and Western Ukrainians supposedly wanted to unite within a single 'Ukrainian state, which would be part of Russia.' According to this scheme, little had changed since 1917; simply, the Soviet Union had replaced the Russian Empire in the process of carrying out the ultimate historical reunification of Eastern Slavs.[66]

While the republic's ideologues and intellectuals were promoting the myths of Russian-Ukrainian friendship and the elder brother's guidance, they vigilantly guarded the notion of Ukraine's historical and ethnic unity. Sometime late in the war, Manuilsky reviewed the manuscript of volume 2 of the *History of Diplomacy*, prepared by the Moscow scholars. The Ukrainian foreign minister was outraged to find a reference to the 'Ruthenian part of Galicia.' Ignoring the Galician Ukrainians' self-identification as 'Ruthenians' until the turn of the century, Manuilsky wrote indignantly: 'This is the German and Polish term, especially devised to prove that the Galician population is different from Ukrainians. Our Soviet political literature should not repeat this term, since there are no Ruthenians. There is, however, a Ukrainian population in Galicia.'[67]

In December 1944 the Moscow historian Boris Grekov received an anonymous letter from Lviv. The letter, composed in good Russian and signed by 'a Russian Galician,' appealed to the renowned scholar to stop the Ukrainization of the 'primordial Russian' Galicia and Transcarpathia. The author argued that history had given Soviet power a chance to complete the gathering together of Russian lands begun by the Muscovite prince Ivan Kalita. In 1946 'Ivan the Galician' (most likely the same person as 'a Russian Galician') wrote to the KP(b)U Central Committee's secretary for propaganda, Ivan Nazarenko,[68] that Russians, Ukrainians, Galicians, and Transcarpathians were all part of the same people, 'Rus'.' The author attached his typescript 'Open Questions to Professor Petrovsky' in which he accused the leading Ukrainian Soviet historian of falsifying the past, separating the Ukrainians from the Russians, and, by extension, of fuelling the insurgent movement in Western Ukraine.[69] The anonymous writer was an isolated survivor of Galician Russophiles, a political and cultural movement that the Russian Empire had once supported. Stalinist ideologues did not take him seriously, however, because their multinational empire was structured as a hierarchy of ' fraternal nations,' and they did not openly advocate assimilation.

Few of the established scholars in Lviv denied the Ukrainian ethnic character of their land, but other potential complications existed. In December 1944 Petrovsky went to Lviv on a special mission to sound out local historians and literary scholars. He reported the results directly to Lytvyn, who passed this apparently important document on to Khrushchev. The bulk of the report dealt with the ex-favourite of the Soviet authorities, Professor Krypiakevych, who was now eager to expiate his sins by producing ideologically correct works on Khmelnytsky. He allegedly told Petrovsky, 'In this question, I now see many things much more clearly since exploring Marxism and reading your, Nikolai Neonovich, works on Bohdan Khmelnytsky, especially on his gravitation to the Russian people.' Five other leading scholars were also most compliant, agreeing to write newspaper articles and read lectures on desirable topics. It is surprising that almost all declined the offer to come to Kiev with the lecture tour. The insightful Petrovsky surmised that the Galicians must have been afraid of being arrested in Kiev, where their disappearance would not embarrass the authorities, and subsequently exiled.[70]

To displace the nationalist tradition of revering Mazepa, Hrushevsky, and the Ukrainian Galician Army, the Soviet authorities encouraged the official cult of Ivan Franko in Western Ukraine as the local counterpart to Shevchenko, a forefather in two senses: as a proto-socialist and as the father of the nation. Eastern Ukrainian court poets Mykola Bazhan and Andrii Malyshko led the first official pilgrimage to Franko's tomb in Lviv just ten days after the city's takeover by the Soviet Army. The state Franko museums in Lviv and in the writer's native village were among the first cultural establishments to open immediately after the war. The Eastern Ukrainian writer Leonid Smilainsky promptly composed the play *The Peasants' Deputy*, devoted to Franko's unsuccessful bid for the Austro-Hungarian parliament during the 1890s. The Lviv Ukrainian Drama Company premiered the play as early as December 1945.[71]

Significantly, the more reliable creative intelligentsia from the East played a major role in the 'Sovietization' of Western Ukrainian commemorative practices. Not that Stalinist ideologues were somehow imposing Ukrainian national memory on the East Slavic population of Galicia as they were, to some degree, in Transcarpathia. Owing to a long history of Ukrainian political activism in Austria-Hungary and Poland, the level of national consciousness, social organization, and community ties among Galician Ukrainians far surpassed those of their compatriots in the East.[72] The difference, however, was the authorities' intention to educate the Galicians as citizens of *Soviet* Ukraine, an inseparable part of the Soviet Union. Western Ukrainians had yet to learn the new paradigm of memory defined by the doctrine of Russian guidance that dictated the subordinate position of Ukrainian historical mythology. Under Stalin, the Ukrainians could venerate their past as long as it complemented, but did not compete with, the story of Russian imperial pursuits.

Chapter Three

Reinventing Ideological Orthodoxy

Occasionally, a senior ideologue's rough notes can open exciting avenues for contextualizing Soviet ideological processes. In the case of the Ukrainian *Zhdanovshchina*, for instance, a file in the personal archives of Dmytro Manuilsky is very revealing.[1] This file combines his drafts of various anti-nationalist resolutions with extremely interesting handwritten notes on the question of 'national pride' – apparently the first draft of an article or speech. The notes reveal how the person who single-handedly wrote most of the era's principal ideological pronouncements in the republic agonized over the definition of Ukrainian Soviet historical memory. In one paragraph, Manuilsky begins by denouncing the worship of the national past but then recognizes it as one of the pillars of national identity: '*On the pride of history*. When a nation has nothing in the present to be proud of, it appeals to the greatness of its history. (Italian fascists [were proud] of Ancient Rome's greatness.) Frenchmen [are proud] of their bourgeois revolution. History is the cement that unites a people's past with their present. History embodies the idea of a people's immortality.'[2] The notes open with a statement that the foreign minister apparently intended to develop: 'What is "national pride"? What we are proud of: our socialist construction, the Great October Socialist Revolution, the Party, Lenin, and Stalin.' The title he gave the last section read, 'On the National Pride of the USSR's Separate Peoples and that of the Multinational Soviet People in General.' Manuilsky's main thesis was that 'love for one's country (Ukraine) should be developed on the basis of love for the whole Soviet Union,' but he did not work out how to reconcile pride in one's national history with love for the Russian-led USSR.[3]

Manuilsky's notes remain incomplete, but much contemporary ideological literature struggles precisely with this issue. For instance, I. Martyniuk's article 'To Develop and Cultivate Soviet Patriotism' and the editorial 'On the Thirtieth Anniversary of the Ukrainian Soviet Socialist Republic' confirm that during the period 1946–8 the Ukrainian ideologues attempted to suppress 'ethnic' historical memory and promote pride in the Soviet present. In both pieces it is stressed that the republic's population should pledge allegiance to Soviet Ukraine as a part of the Soviet Union, and in both there is silence on the issue of national patrimony. Reprimanding several writers for references to the glory of the Cossacks in their works about the war and post-war reconstruction, the literary critic Ievhen Iuriev announced: 'The idea of our vivifying Soviet patriotism does not come from the Zaporozhian Host.' He then traced the roots of Soviet Ukrainian identity to revolutionary struggle and the construction of socialism.[4]

The *Zhdanovshchina*, the post-war cultural-ideological purification campaign of 1946–8, which takes its name from VKP(b) Central Committee Secretary Andrei Zhdanov, is usually understood as a reassertion of the party's ideological control over culture in order to purge literature and the arts of western influences and 'apolitical subjects.' While intellectuals in Moscow and Leningrad did indeed experience the campaign as a crusade against liberalism and heterodoxy, Russian national mythology was rarely attacked. The Ukrainian *Zhdanovshchina*, however, from its very beginnings primarily targeted 'nationalism,' particularly in history. Evidence of the complex, multidimensional nature of Stalinist ideological processes, this difference determined both the unusual intensity and the ultimate inconclusiveness of cultural purges in the republic.

Confusing Signals from Above

On 31 January 1944 Oleksandr Dovzhenko, together with four Ukrainian leaders and three other prominent writers, was invited to a Politburo meeting in Moscow to discuss his novel and movie script *Ukraine in Flames*, during which Stalin made a lengthy speech accusing the writer of 'revising Leninism.'[5] Dovzhenko had allegedly discarded the principle of the class struggle, blackened the party line and the kolkhoz system in Ukraine, and overemphasized Ukrainian patriotism. In Dovzhenko's novel, indeed, a decisive ideological shift from proletarian internationalism to patriotism, history, and the nation is championed. Its characters repeatedly attack the ideological device of 'class struggle' and suggest substituting this principal paradigm of early Soviet ideology with that of 'national pride.' For instance, the red pencil of some Kremlin ideologue underlined the following words of the novel's two main protagonists, Zaporozhets and Kravchyna: 'Today I do not know class struggle and I do not want to know it. I know the Fatherland!'; 'We were bad historians, weren't we? We did not know how to forgive each other. National pride did not shine in our books [full of] class struggle'; 'We are fighting for Ukraine. For the only forty-million people that through the centuries of European history could not find for themselves a life worthy of humans on their own land.'[6]

During the meeting, Stalin quoted the fragment in which Zaporozhets tells the orthodox partisan commander: 'To hell with your [class] struggle ... You went mad, you grew addicted to class struggle as if to moonshine. Oh, it will be our doom.' He also cited tirades against the lack of patriotism in Soviet history books. Dovzhenko and his heroes saw the homeland and the national past as alternative foci of allegiance, but, according to Stalin, the novel failed to stress that 'precisely Soviet power and the Bolshevik party cherish the historical traditions and rich cultural heritage of the Ukrainian people and the other peoples of the USSR, as well as raising their national consciousness.'[7]

Together with Dovzhenko's failure to denounce the Ukrainian 'bourgeois na-tionalists' for their collaboration with the Germans, the writer's appeal to national memory enabled Stalin to accuse him of 'nationalism.' A public persecution campaign against Dovzhenko soon developed in Ukraine, where Khrushchev, who had imprudently approved the novel in August 1943, set an example by denounc-ing the writer for 'revising Leninism,' 'slandering the socialist way of life,' 'attack-ing the party,' and, finally, professing 'militant nationalism.'[8] At this stage, however, emphasizing Ukrainian national memory over class ancestry was understood as only one of Dovzhenko's serious mistakes rather than as the principal mortal sin he had committed. In a fit of bureaucratic fervor, KP(b)U Central Committee Secretary Lytvyn prepared an index of pages in *Ukraine in Flames* on which various 'deviations' surfaced. 'Slandering the party' came first, with three page references, followed by 'hatred of the idea of class struggle,' with six references, and 'slander-ing Bohdan Khmelnytsky,' with three references.[9]

This last accusation was particularly misleading, since Dovzhenko actually attempted, in the form of a conversation among four uneducated peasants, to show what he understood to be the corruption of popular collective memory under the influence of prewar 'class history':

CHUBENKO: Yes, it is said that not once in the past did they [the lords] impose a yoke on our brothers.

NEKHODA: Who do you mean – they?

CHUBENKO: Bohdan Khmelnytsky!

TOVCHENYK: Oh, he was a great villain. Before the war, the museum in Chernihiv displayed his sabre. And there was an explanatory note in big letters: 'This is the sabre of a well-known butcher of the Ukrainian people, Bohdan Khmelnytsky, who suppressed the popular revolution in sixteen hundred and something.' So his sabre was behind glass, while twelve of his portraits were locked in the basement. They were not shown to the people. It is said that they created a haze in people's heads. That's what they say.

NEKHODA: What a villain!

TSAR: But who is the one on the horse, in the square in front of the church in Kiev?

CHUBENKO: That's a different one.
TOVCHENYK: So it is not him?
NEKHODA: They are all the same![10]

Pretending not to recognize this mockery of their own past pronouncements, the Ukrainian bureaucrats accused Dovzhenko of slandering the hetman. Since the novel had not been published at the time, dozens of Ukrainian intellectuals blindly repeated the same accusation at denunciatory meetings, with the result, ironically, of reinforcing Khmelnytsky's place of honour in Ukrainian Soviet historical memory – precisely the aim Dovzhenko had had in mind when he proposed the establishment of the Order of Khmelnytsky and when he wrote *Ukraine in Flames*. This paradox aside, the critique of Dovzhenko seems to have signalled a renewal of emphasis on shared Soviet patriotism at the expense of separate national ancestries, as well as the possible restoration of class struggle as the essence of the historical process. Nothing indicated the Kremlin's unhappiness with, say, the inadequate portrayal of Russian guidance.

Moreover, the critique of Dovzhenko did not develop into a purge of 'nationalism' in Ukrainian literature, although the preconditions for such an outcome existed. In March 1944, when the official press began denouncing Dovzhenko, Fedir Ienevych, the director of the Ukrainian branch of the Institute of Marx, Engels, and Lenin (IMEL), submitted to the KP(b)U Central Committee a report accusing Rylsky of 'nationalism.' Ienevych singled out Rylsky's November 1943 speech, 'Kiev in the History of Ukraine' (discussed in the previous chapter), for critique. On the one hand, the professional Marxist philosopher charged the poet with interpreting Soviet Ukrainian culture as simply an extension of pre-revolutionary, 'non-Soviet' Ukrainian culture, and insufficiently stressing the radically different 'class character' of socialist Ukraine. On the other, Ienevych decried the insufficient homage Rylsky paid to the Russian elder brother in his national narrative: 'It was necessary to stress in this speech the significance of the union between the Russian and Ukrainian peoples and the most important, decisive role that the great Russian people played in liberating Ukraine from the German imperialists. Rylsky avoided all these questions and, in fact, devoted the greater part of his speech to idealizing the Ukrainian past, concealing the Russian culture's influence on Ukrainian culture, and obscuring Soviet power's role in the social and national liberation of the Ukrainian people – in the real revival of Ukraine.'[11] Leonid Novychenko, a literary critic and the Central Committee expert charged with verifying Ienevych's report, seconded most of the accusations. He found that Rylsky had idealized the Cossacks and had made uncritical use of the works of Ukrainian bourgeois-nationalist historians, particularly Hrushevsky. The text of the speech was 'imbued with a nationalist theory, according to which M. Rylsky sees in the history of Ukraine only a struggle for national independence, a struggle conducted, in the author's view, by the Cossack officers, the gentry, and the bourgeoisie. [He] glosses over in silence the toiling Ukrainian masses' struggle for their social and national liberation, which they pursued with the fraternal support of the great Russian people ... Rylsky hardly mentions the progressive historical importance of Ukraine's incorporation into Russia; instead, he stresses that, as a result of this incorporation, "Ukraine became a province of the Russian Empire, which Lenin has aptly called the 'prison of peoples.'"'[12]

The Rylsky affair remained, however, an instructive example of an abortive denunciation. Although both the initial 'signal from below' and its favourable assessment by the Central Committee apparatus were in place, a campaign against Rylsky was not set in motion. The Ukrainian leadership apparently did not consider the denunciation of another high-profile littérateur to be necessary at the time. While the Dovzhenko affair represented a warning to the intellectuals who identified with the wartime cult of national patrimony, a further incident of similar stature could have prompted Moscow to initiate a comprehensive purge of 'nationalists' in the republic, with possible unpleasant consequences for the Ukrainian leadership itself.[13]

Just as Ukrainian bureaucrats were able to ignore an 'initiative from below,' pronouncements from Moscow did not always define the politics of memory in the republic. To start with, the centre often failed to issue clear directives on the proper line on history. Although Agitprop's internal correspondence criticized the 1943 *History of the Kazakh SSR* as 'anti-Russian,' as explained in chapter 2, Moscow ideologues did not sponsor the book's public denunciation until 1945. In fact, the Central Committee's functionaries were extremely displeased to find out that the book's co-editor, Professor Anna Pankratova, had made the story public in letters to her students. Pankratova took the issue to Zhdanov and subsequently to Stalin, protesting not only the critique of the book but also the entire ideological trend towards the rehabilitation of the Russian imperial past at the expense of class analysis.[14]

Combined with previous calls to clarify the party line on history, Pankratova's protests resulted in a conference of leading Soviet historians and ideologues in Moscow. During the conference's six sessions on 29 May, 1, 5, 10, 22 June, and 8 July 1944 the proponents of imperial patrimony clashed with the defenders of class history. However, the party leadership failed to declare a winner. Zhdanov first appeared to support Pankratova's call for a return to the class approach, using it as a tool to restore his authority in Moscow (he had just returned to the capital from Leningrad) and as a weapon against his unfaithful client Aleksandrov. Zhdanov had spent several months writing and rewriting the draft decree 'On the Shortcomings and Mistakes in Scholarly Work in the Area of the History of the

USSR.' He consulted Stalin several times but ultimately abandoned the project. In the end, a minor resolution to close *Istoricheskii zhurnal* and start a new scholarly periodical, *Voprosy istorii*, became the only Central Committee decision resulting from the conference.[15]

Likewise, in his speech before a conference of departmental chairs in the social sciences on 1 August 1945 Aleksandrov did not call for a clear policy change. On the one hand, Agitprop's head reproached those trying to revise the Marxist-Leninist definition of tsarist Russia as the 'gendarme of Europe' and the 'prison of peoples.' On the other hand, he criticized works on the history of Kazakhs, Iakuts, Tatars, and Bashkirs for 'describing [events] that had opposed' them to the Russians and for glorifying national heroes who had revolted against the tsars. According to Aleksandrov, 'The history of the peoples of Russia was a history of overcoming this animosity and their gradual consolidation around the Russian people.'[16]

Ukrainian intellectuals did not feel the need to modify their approach in the light of these recent discussions in Moscow. Aleksandrov had mentioned volume 1 of the *History of Ukraine* (1943) approvingly, probably because of the fact that Ukrainian historians and writers were well ahead of their counterparts in the other republics in exalting the historical events that 'united' their people with the Russians.

Despite the peaceful mood within the Ukrainian history profession, the republic's bureaucrats resolved to follow the centre's example in organizing a conference of historians. (Unlike their Moscow superiors, Ukrainian party leaders officially recognized the importance of literary representations in the shaping of historical memory by inviting a group of local writers to the conference.) Yet by the time the first session convened on 10 March 1945 the Ukrainian functionaries themselves were disoriented by the Moscow meetings' inconclusive outcome. Lytvyn opened the proceedings with neither a call to denounce nationalist deviations, nor an appeal to return to the orthodox class approach. Instead, he noted with uncharacteristic tranquility that the conference was 'unusual' and invited the participants to discuss 'the differing points of view in our literature on the history of Ukraine.'[17] During the five sessions that followed in late March and early April, party ideologues rarely took the floor, encouraging, instead, the participants themselves both to ask questions and to seek answers. It is not surprising that the KP(b)U Central Committee would soon be disappointed with the conference's inconclusiveness.

In the words of a Central Committee internal memo, 'Initially, the conference was spiritless and the speakers hardly mentioned troubling and disputable questions of history.' Indeed, the first fifty-six pages of the minutes feature mainly banal suggestions to publish more historical documents and to research understudied problems of Ukrainian history.[18] Finally, Rubach accused Petrovsky of ignoring the class approach in his work on Bohdan Khmelnytsky and the 1939 reunification of Western Ukraine, but the ensuing discussion did not result in a clear victory for either side. Those who, like Rubach, advocated a return to class analysis soon discovered that this approach would undermine the myth of Russian-Ukrainian friendship that emphasized state-building and ethnic affinity as well as required tsars and hetmans to be positive protagonists. To resolve this difficulty, Rubach proposed the familiar 'lesser evil'[19] paradigm, but neither the ideologues nor the historians hastened to readopt this concept, which seemed to have been compromised by the canonization of Khmelnytsky.

The historian Vadym Diadychenko boldly attempted to address 'one of the most important, principal questions, that of Russian tsarist colonial policy.' 'It is no coincidence,' he stated, 'that the Moscow conference of historians discussed this question all the time.' In essence, however, Diadychenko's own comments reflected the trend towards balancing Russian colonial oppression with the advantages of being imperial subjects. He suggested that, although the rule of Peter I had been a 'burden' for Ukrainians, the tsar's armies had protected Ukraine from the Turko-Tatar invasions during the 1710s and 1720s. Fedir Los seconded his colleague's interpretation: 'When covering the second half of the seventeenth and the eighteenth century, we are stressing tsarism's colonial offensive against Ukraine. This is correct but we often do not point out the positive consequences of the union between the Russian and Ukrainian peoples.'[20]

The majority of participants did not heed the party's call for a theoretical debate. Instead, they spoke of the further promotion of the 'glorious national past' and cultural heritage, even within the confines of the master-plot of Russian-Ukrainian friendship. Both historians and writers advanced far-reaching plans for the study of national history and for the rehabilitation of more 'great ancestors.' The historian Kost Huslysty announced, 'I believe that studying the heroic past of the Ukrainian people remains one of the most important tasks of Soviet Ukrainian historical scholarship.' Then he called for more works on national heroes such as Danylo of Halych, Sahaidachny, and Khmelnytsky. During a later session, he resumed the floor to criticize the central press's portrayal of Danylo as a Russian prince.[21] The literary scholar Ievhen Kyryliuk insisted on including in the national pantheon the nineteenth-century non-Marxist social thinker Mykhailo Drahomanov and his contemporaries, 'bourgeois' historians and writers Kostomarov, Kulish, and Oleksandr Lazarevsky. The writer Ivan Senchenko supported the call to rehabilitate Drahomanov and suggested promoting more 'national heroes' from the period between Khmelnytsky (d. 1657) and the philosopher Hryhory Skovoroda (1722–94). The archaeologist Lazar Slavin attempted to defend Hrushevsky by confirming the late historian's views on the origins of Ukrainians: 'I think those who discard all of Hrushevsky's writings on this problem, the problem of ethnogenesis, are wrong. Actually, he was right on many points.'[22]

Moreover, at one point during the session, an unidentified voice from the audience shouted, 'You had better introduce a separate course on Ukrainian history at school!' The next speaker, a schoolteacher by the name of Skrypnyk, actually supported this proposal: 'There is an enormous interest in the history of Ukraine [in schools]. The students are attracted to matters relating to the history of Ukraine.' Skrypnyk explained that of the sixty-five hours of History of the USSR in grade 8, only three or four were devoted to Ukrainian material. The grade 9 curriculum gave the history teacher some two to four hours out of sixty-five to explain the major events of Ukrainian history, and the grade 10 curriculum, eight to ten out of one hundred and ten. To supplement Shestakov's (Russocentric) textbook, the teachers organized readings of Bazhan's 'Danylo of Halych' and Petro Panch's *The Zaporozhians*. 'Our Grade 9 and 10 students asked repeatedly why we were not studying the history of Ukraine,' concluded the teacher.[23]

At this point, the conference was clearly moving in a direction that party functionaries found undesirable to explore. During the session on 14 April Lytvyn first announced: 'We will be meeting on Saturdays from 12 to 4, as usual,' but then he disclosed that there would be no meeting on the next Saturday. In fact, the conference never resumed its work. Although the KP(b)U Central Committee apparatus was working to draft a resolution on the improvement of historical scholarship, the decree never moved beyond the drafting stage.[24] Trapped between the confusing signals from Moscow and subtle non-compliance on the part of the Ukrainian intelligentsia, the republic's bureaucracy preferred halting the discussion altogether to acknowledging to its superiors in the centre that there were any problems in ideological work.

A February 1946 incident at Lviv University reveals just how unwilling the Ukrainian party leadership was to initiate a crackdown on the 'nationalist' historians. At the time, its faculty was a blend of politically unreliable local older professors and highly reliable party types who had recently arrived from Eastern Ukraine. Like many other newcomers, Volodymyr Horbatiuk, the new dean of the Faculty of History, was eager to demonstrate his zeal in eliminating traces of nationalism within the university walls. Together with the new rector, Ivan Biliakevych, he chose to target the Department of Ukrainian History, then still dominated by Hrushevsky's students: professors Ivan Krypiakevych, Myron Korduba, and Omelian Terletsky. The university administration organized three departmental meetings to condemn Hrushevsky and his school. Rector Biliakevych gave an introductory speech denouncing Hrushevsky's 'bourgeois-nationalist concepts,' while the professors were expected to uncover Hrushevsky's mistakes and falsifications in the different periods of Ukrainian history. Krypiakevych obediently read a paper on Ukraine's union with Russia and its 'misrepresentation' in

Hrushevsky's works, Terletsky and Horbatiuk outlined Hrushevsky's 'distortions' in modern Ukrainian history, and the newcomer Osechynsky elaborated on how Hrushevsky's nationalist theories contradicted Russian historiography of the nineteenth and twentieth centuries. Osechynsky went as far as to blame Hrushevsky's students for the continuing armed resistance of the Ukrainian Insurgent Army.[25]

Professor Myron Korduba, the oldest member of the department and the instructor responsible for the survey of Ukrainian history, refused to comply. Dean Horbatiuk ordered him to read a paper with a title crafted in inimitable Soviet ideological parlance: 'The Bourgeois-Nationalist Interpretation of Ancient Times, in Particular Kievan Rus' and the Period of Feudal Fragmentation, in Hrushevsky's Works.' But Korduba began by saying that his topic would be 'Mykhailo Hrushevsky as a Student of the Princely Period of the History of Ukraine.' He continued: 'Mykhailo Hrushevsky unquestionably occupies a place of honor in Ukrainian historiography. He was the first to provide his people with a vision of their past [and] of their historical development from ancient to modern times, a vision based on critically verified facts compliant with the demands of modern scholarship. [In so doing, Hrushevsky] laid the new foundations of his people's national consciousness.' Later in his speech, Korduba attempted to deconstruct the Soviet idiom with the aim of restoring Hrushevsky to the official canon of memory:

> Hrushevsky is being called a nationalist. I have an impression that today this word has the same role that 'heretic' had during the Middle Ages. When one is to be compromised and defamed in the eyes of the public, in other words, destroyed, this person is labelled as 'nationalist' without considering the real meaning of this word, which can be diverse. If nationalism is understood as a firm consciousness of belonging to one's nation and the active struggle against national oppression, as well as against the assimilationist policies of aggressive peoples (and that is how we understood nationalism in Galicia before the First World War) then, indeed, Hrushevsky should be recognized as 'nationalist.' But then Taras Shevchenko, Ivan Franko, Mykhailo Kotsiubynsky, Vasyl Stefanyk and many other progressive patriots whose memory we revere were 'nationalists' as well. If 'nationalism' is understood in the meaning that it has acquired in recent decades, that is, as opium and as a morbid idea that one's people are superior and should dominate other peoples of the world by oppression and assimilation – this idea nurtures hatred and animosity among peoples, and Hrushevsky never was a nationalist of this kind.[26]

Seditious as it looked to contemporaries, Korduba's speech actually stressed the negotiable nature of Stalinist rhetorical devices such as 'nationalism' and 'patriotism.' The elderly professor rightly noted the blurred line between the healthy national patriotism of 'progressive thinkers' and the reactionary nationalism of their 'bourgeois-nationalist' contemporaries, who often expressed exactly the same views. A clear distinction could not be established, because the party line itself kept changing the balance between the notions of 'class' and 'nation' within the Soviet historical imagination. The classification of specific historical actors was therefore negotiable, as demonstrated by the changing Soviet views on the hetmans Bohdan Khmelnytsky and Petro Sahaidachny, as well as the nineteenth-century thinkers Mykhailo Drahomanov and Panteleimon Kulish. As a former political enemy of the Bolsheviks, Hrushevsky was probably beyond redemption, but the different reactions to Korduba's speech in Lviv and Kiev demonstrated a distinct lack of coordination in the Soviet project of reforming Western Ukrainian historical memory.

The Lviv party committee supported the university's initiative to prepare a city-wide conference of scholars where the 'Hrushevsky school' at the Faculty of History would be publicly denounced. The university also planned a separate meeting of its faculty and students under the slogan 'Hrushevsky's Bourgeois-Nationalist Theory Is a Weapon of Ukrainian Nationalist Counterrevolution.' Nevertheless, in March 1946 the KP(b)U Central Committee sent to Lviv a brigade of ideological inspectors, who ordered that the campaign be terminated. The brigade concluded that the departmental conferences had been ill prepared, that Rector Biliakevych's and Dean Horbatiuk's speeches had been weak, and that the campaign against the Hrushevsky school was generally 'untimely and unnecessary.' Moreover, the powerful inspectors also reassured local scholars who thought 'that after discussions like this one they would be sent to Siberia.' The brigade's report to the Central Committee recommended a degree of toleration towards the local historians, as 'ideological reeducation is a difficult thing for people who are in their 60s and 70s and who were brought up in the spirit of bourgeois ideology.' The brigade further suggested halting the critique of Western Ukrainian scholars who, like Krypiakevych and Terletsky, were reportedly trying to master the Marxist-Leninist historical method, and it recommended that Kievan historians be sent on lecture tours to Lviv.[27]

In the end, although the materials about the Lviv incident occupy three thick folders in the Central Committee archives, the republic's ideologues effectively suppressed the local initiative to purge Hrushevsky's students in Lviv. Apparently, in early 1946 the Ukrainian leadership did not plan to turn the critique of the 'Hrushevsky school' into a major ideological campaign. It had another initiative for that purpose.

The Ukrainian *Zhdanovshchina*

Beginning in June 1946, Ukraine became a testing ground for the *Zhdanovshchina*, the all-Union campaign of ideological purification led by VKP(b) Central Committee Secretary Andrei Zhdanov. The *Zhdanovshchina* was a reaction to widespread hopes for a freer and more prosperous life after the war, as well as for a more tolerant and liberal cultural climate. The campaign signalled a return to the strident pre-war party line, the reassertion of ideological control over culture, and the purging of literature and the arts of real and imaginary western influences. The beginning of the *Zhdanovshchina* is usually dated August 1946, when the Central Committee condemned two prominent Leningrad journals, *Zvezda* and *Leningrad*, for publishing ideologically harmful apolitical works and for disparaging Soviet values.[28]

A look at the new policy's refraction in a non-Russian republic provides a different perspective on the post-war ideological purging. Although the attack on Leningrad writers in the late summer of 1946 continues to be widely understood as the inauguration of the *Zhdanovshchina*, Werner G. Hann has long suggested that the campaign actually began in late June in the Ukrainian capital, Kiev, when, Petr Fedoseev, the deputy head of Agitprop, arrived to coordinate the first salvos of the ideological purge, which in Ukraine was aimed at 'nationalism' rather than at western influences.[29] No archival document directly explains this specificity of Ukraine, but its likely cause was the difficulties that the Sovietization of Western Ukraine was encountering, particularly in the form of a fierce nationalist guerilla resistance.[30]

During the republican conference on propaganda of 24–6 June, Lytvyn announced that 'softness' on nationalism could no longer be tolerated in Ukraine, where the ideological climate had already been contaminated by German wartime propaganda, private landholding in the Western provinces, population exchanges with Poland, and the return of POWs and *Ostarbeiter* from Germany. (He managed not to mention the nationalist Ukrainian Insurgent Army, but its activities were very much on the minds of those present.) Although all of these phenomena were manifestly recent, Lytvyn and other speakers concentrated almost exclusively on ideological mistakes in artistic and scholarly representations of the Ukrainian past. In contrast to the subsequent denunciations in Leningrad and Moscow, ideologues did not accuse intellectuals of succumbing to western influences or publishing ideologically harmful apolitical works. Instead, they concentrated on criticizing writers, artists, and composers for 'escaping from our socialist reality' into subjects from the Ukrainian past. This was said to reflect the lasting influence of the late patriarch of Ukrainian nationalism, Mykhailo Hrushevsky.[31]

Lytvyn dismissed a recent textbook, *A Survey of the History of Ukrainian Literature*, for ignoring class divisions in pre-revolutionary Ukrainian culture and for not paying sufficient attention to its ties with progressive Russian culture. Yet he saw the general state of Ukrainian historical scholarship as satisfactory. The secretary cited only one example of Hrushevsky's influence on historians, the Lviv incident with Korduba.[32]

The situation changed on 20 July, when the central Agitprop newspaper *Kultura i zhizn* carried the article 'To Correct Mistakes in the Coverage of Some Questions of the History of Ukraine.' Written by Agitprop official S. Kovalev, this piece reiterated earlier criticisms of the *Survey*, the Lviv incident, and other points made during the June conference. At the same time, Kovalev noted that volume 1 of the *History of Ukraine* (1943) also contained serious errors: in particular, its periodization allegedly rested more on the events of political history than on socio-economic formations. He suggested that the republic's scholars had not made satisfactory progress in preparing a 'scholarly history' of Ukraine.[33] Ukrainian bureaucrats immediately followed Moscow's cue. During the plenary session of the KP(b)U Central Committee on 15 August Khrushchev counted the first volume of the *History of Ukraine* among the faulty works imbued with nationalistic deviations.[34] Elaborating on this statement, Nazarenko announced that a 'Marxist history of Ukraine' had yet to be written. Volume 1 was based on Hrushevsky's theories: 'It does not reflect the concept of class struggle. The first chapter is entitled "The History of Ukraine before the Creation of the Kievan State." How could one speak of "Ukraine" at that time?'[35]

Nonetheless, the attack on historians remained a sideline in the ideological purification campaign of 1946. Most speakers at the August plenary session focused their critique on the 'nationalist deviations' in literature and the arts. Khrushchev, Lytvyn, and Nazarenko demanded that the intellectuals revise the public discourse of self-identification by emphasizing the common socialist present at the expense of a 'separate' national past. Nazarenko accused the republic's literary historians of 'nationalistic' exaltation of the pre-revolutionary Ukrainian classics. Lytvyn pounced upon Bazhan's 'Danylo of Halych' for referring to Ukraine as already existing in the thirteenth century: 'Historical scholarship proved that the Slavic peoples were still united at the time of Danylo of Halych and separate nationalities (*narodnosti*) did not yet exist.' Bazhan had presumably borrowed his ideas from Hrushevsky.[36] Lytvyn also mentioned the idealization of bourgeois Ukrainian culture in Rylsky's 1943 speech on the history of Kiev and Oleksa Kundzich's story 'The Ukrainian Hut,' which was declared guilty of celebrating the traditional peasant dwelling as the primordial cradle of the Ukrainian nation.[37]

While most speakers dwelt on various 'nationalist mistakes' in portraying the past, some, like Leonid Melnikov, the party boss in Stalino (Donetsk) province, complained that no Ukrainian writer properly celebrated the republic's industrial growth under Soviet power. 'I have not seen anything either,' added Khrushchev. When Bazhan finally took the floor to apologize for the errors of his historical poem, the first secretary interrupted him: 'No, you tell me why writers are opposed to the Donbas and to industrialization.' Then Khrushchev closed the proceedings with an appeal 'to heat the ground so that our enemies will burn their feet.'[38] The key to remedying all of these ideological problems appeared simple: dilute 'nationalistic' historical memory with a healthy dose of love for the Soviet present.

Ukrainian ideologues spelled out the campaign's message at several denunciatory meetings. During the writers' conference of 27–8 August, Lytvyn frankly defined the ideological turn in terms that did not appear in the official documents of the time:

> Why did the comrades make serious mistakes? Because they proceeded from the wrong assumption that the party had changed its policy during the war. To foster popular patriotism, much has been written about Aleksandr Nevsky, Suvorov, Kutuzov, and Bohdan Khmelnytsky. Several patriotic manifestos to the Ukrainian people paid great attention to the heroic traditions of our people's past. Shevchenko's *Kobzar* was published in a pocket-size format and smuggled beyond the front line [into the occupied territories] together with many leaflets that used Shevchenko's poetry for purely propagandistic purposes. Some people wrongly interpreted this to the effect that the liberation of Ukraine was going on under the banner of Shevchenko, under the banner of Kulish. Excuse me for the sharp words, but this is what happened. These comrades decided that all previous critique [of nationalism] could be abandoned because the party's policy had changed, because the party had conceded.[39]

The secretary for ideology suggested crudely that all Ukrainian intellectuals, especially writers, needed to 'air out their brains' (*provetrivanie mozgov*). 'Instead of infatuation with the reactionary romantics of the Zaporozhian Host, which differed from our times in so many respects, the past should be interpreted through its connections with the present.'[40]

Significantly, the Ukrainian equivalent of the principal ideological resolution of the *Zhdanovshchina*, Moscow's decree on the journals *Zvezda* and *Leningrad*, also differed from its model by its unusual sensitivity to the questions of history. The KP(b)U Central Committee resolution 'About the Journal *Vitchyzna*' denounced the periodical not for 'kowtowing to western culture' but for publishing 'nationalistic' articles on Ivan Kotliarevsky, the founder of modern Ukrainian literature, and on the Cyril and Methodius Brotherhood, the first modern Ukrainian political organization. The decree accused the editors of neglecting Soviet subjects and encouraging their authors to elaborate on the national past.[41]

Whereas Kievan historians survived the 1946 purge with no significant losses, their Lviv colleagues suffered somewhat more on account of their alleged Hrushevskian heresy. On 28 October 1946 Ukraine's Council of Ministers closed down the Lviv branches of the institutes of History, Literature, and Economics, leaving local scholars to find a new means of livelihood. Korduba died the following year. The authorities transferred Krypiakevych to Kiev as a senior researcher at the Institute of Ukrainian History, but not before he publicly acknowledged his nationalistic mistakes at a meeting of the Social Sciences branch of the Academy of Sciences.[42]

Meanwhile, the Lviv provincial party committee began a close examination of historical research in the region. Local functionaries soon discovered the troubling fact that 'During the last two years, not a single article was published on the history of the revolutionary movement in the Western provinces.' To counteract the lasting influence of 'bourgeois nationalists' on popular historical memory in the west, the committee proposed the creation of a brigade of Marxist historians, who would specialize in denouncing the Hrushevsky school. The next necessary steps were to be writing and publishing popular pamphlets on Bohdan Khmelnytsky, the Pereiaslav Treaty, the Battle at Poltava, and Mazepa's treason. (Significantly, these directives called for emphasis more on Russian-Ukrainian historical friendship, rather than on Soviet achievements.) The authorities also discovered that the Lviv Historical Museum did not have a display on the Battle at Poltava. Moreover, the museum's staff seemed unreliable. On 14 July 1946 a guide, Iatskevych, led a group of Soviet Army soldiers and students (most of them apparently Russians and Eastern Ukrainians) through the museum's exposition. Reaching the hall displaying materials about the union with Russia, Iatskevych announced: 'So that was our history, and here is where your history begins.'[43]

A traditional centre of Western Ukrainian political and intellectual life, Lviv was something of an extreme case, but here as elsewhere throughout the republic, even in the long-Sovietized Eastern and Southern provinces, which had no nationalist guerillas, ideologues were lecturing the intelligentsia and the media were educating the population on the new, proper version of Ukrainian Soviet historical memory.

Fashioning an Acceptable Past

On 26 August 1946 the VKP(b) Central Committee elaborated on the strategic aims of the *Zhdanovshchina* in a resolution 'On the Repertoire of Drama Theaters and Measures toward Its Improvement.' The decree called for a purge of theatre repertoire, which was 'littered' with apolitical plays, works idealizing the past, and western plays that 'popularized bourgeois morals.' The resolution, which was summarized in *Pravda* but not published at the time, categorically demanded the staging of more Soviet plays on contemporary subjects. Western scholars have previously interpreted this decree as simply 'demanding an end to laxity in the theatre and, in particular, an end to the presentation of Western plays in the Moscow repertory houses,' and this might well be the way readers in the Soviet capital understood the resolution.[44] However, the writer of the *Pravda* article also criticized plays that 'idealiz[ed] the life of tsarist lords and Asian khans' and named five faulty productions: four historical dramas from the past of Soviet Asian peoples and a nineteenth-century French comedy, Eugène Scribe's *Tales of the Queen of Navarra*. Although Soviet Russian playwrights had authored numerous dramas glorifying the lives of tsars, feudal lords, and military leaders, the resolution did not mention any of these works. Nor were they criticized during the ensuing campaign for the purity of Soviet theatre.[45] In Ukraine, the pronouncements from Moscow clearly were interpreted as being aimed primarily against the valorization of the non-Russian past.

The attendant resolution of the KP(b)U Central Committee displayed a peculiar refraction of Moscow's dictum. The Ukrainian ideologues did not dare to criticize the powerful Korniichuk, author of the best-known Ukrainian Soviet historical drama, *Bohdan Khmelnytsky*. This left only a few little-known historical plays for denouncing, such as Oleksandr Kopylenko's *Why the Stars Do Not Go Out* and Mykhailo Pinchevsky's *I Live*. Neither did the hunt for 'corrupting' western plays produce sufficient prey, and the republic's theatre companies seemed to perform well in the category of staging 'contemporary' Soviet plays, since Korniichuk wrote these with exemplary regularity.

In this light, the Ukrainian bureaucrats adopted a strategy different from that deployed in Moscow. They broadened the scope of the critique to include opera, a genre traditionally preoccupied with the past. The KP(b)U Central Committee's resolution 'On the Repertoire of Drama *and Opera* Theatres of the Ukrainian SSR and Measures toward Its Improvement' assailed Ukrainian opera companies for not having staged a single new opera on a Soviet topic during the preceding three years. As for drama companies, they were guilty of paying disproportionate attention to the pre-revolutionary Ukrainian classics, including numerous less valuable plays on manners. These works could 'only educate the spectator in the spirit of ethnic narrow-mindedness and alienation from urgent contemporary questions.'[46] The Ukrainian authorities' initiative demonstrates that local elites exercised considerable autonomy in shaping Stalinist ideological campaigns. The 'mainstream' *Zhdanovshchina* would not envelop musical life until the 1948 attack on Vano Muradeli's opera *The Great Friendship* and the subsequent campaign against 'formalism' in Soviet music.

In October 1946 the Kiev Opera Company premiered a new version of Mykola Lysenko's classic historical opera, *Taras Bulba*. The result of several years of work, the ill-fated premiere came just a month after the decree on the repertoire of drama and opera theatres. The Ukrainian authorities immediately shut down the production before any criticism could sound from Moscow. Reviewers announced that *Taras* did not create 'an impression of Ukraine suffering under the yoke of the

Polish lords,' for in act 1, Bulba and other Cossacks were seen to be drinking too cheerfully in the orchard. The colonel himself looked 'inactive' and the whole opera seemed 'unfinished.'[47] Oleksandr Kopylenko's historical play *Why the Stars Do Not Go Out* also suffered a harsh critique, both as a falsification presenting the heroic Cossacks as passive drunkards and as a work idealizing the national past and neglecting the class struggle within seventeenth-century Ukrainian society.[48]

In late 1946, as the Ukrainian press unveiled a campaign against historical topics, *Radianske mystetstvo*, the newspaper of the republic's Committee for the Arts, focused on uncovering the 'unhealthy glorification of the past' in contemporary paintings. Art critics denounced Ivan Shulha for expressing in his canvas *The Zaporozhians' Song* 'morbid nostalgia for the past.' Hryhorii Svitlytsky's painting *Native Land*, depicting a young woman in traditional peasant dress against the background of a beautiful country landscape, prompted them to ask, 'What does it have in common with our Soviet Ukraine?' Mykhailo Derehus's series *The Khmelnytsky Uprising* was pronounced 'clearly unfinished,' but not because of its morbid nostalgia: the artist 'did not pay appropriate attention' to the Pereiaslav Council and the historic union with Russia.[49]

Despite all the rhetoric, one of Ukraine's leading theatres premiered Ivan Kocherha's new, grand, historical drama, *Iaroslav the Wise* within weeks of the all-Union decree. At its inauguration in September 1946 the play seemed doomed. As Kocherha would recall two years later at the writers' congress, when the resolution 'On the Repertoire of Drama Theatres' appeared some two weeks before the premiere, the management of the Kharkiv Drama Theatre considered cancelling the performance.[50] Yet, while highly susceptible to the charge of fascination with the distant past, the play contained hardly any specifically Ukrainian historical references. Nothing identified the Rus' of the text as the predecessor of modern Ukraine, rather than that of Russia or even the Soviet Union. Indeed, only the language betrayed the drama as a product of a Ukrainian writer. Ultimately, the strong princely power and the 'united Rus'' that constituted the drama's principal ideological message seemed to reverberate mightily with High Stalinism's ideological convictions. At the very last moment, the Ukrainian authorities reluctantly allowed the premiere to proceed, albeit suggesting some eleventh-hour insertions regarding the 'class struggle' in Kievan times.

The play premiered in Kharkiv on 17 September 1946; reviews in Ukrainian newspapers appeared only after unprecedented delay: *Literaturna hazeta* published a lengthy positive assessment on 12 December, while *Radianske mystetstvo* hesitated until 12 March 1947. In the end, amid public attacks on the historical genre as such and the promotion of Soviet subjects, *Iaroslav* won full approval in Moscow. In June 1947 the general public learned that the Kharkiv production of the play had earned the company the Stalin Prize, First Class. Commenting on the award, a writer in *Literaturna hazeta* credited the drama with educating spectators 'to be proud of the Fatherland, of the people, and of the mighty united state.'[51] Kocherha's representation of Kievan Rus' resonated well with both the Stalinist image of the Soviet Union and the notion of Russian-Ukrainian historical friendship and unity. Thus, it fit perfectly into the official version of national memory.

The fate of *Iaroslav* highlights the ambiguous nature of the anti-historical campaign in Ukraine. The executive ideologues targeted works identifying with a 'separate' Ukrainian national past, while those engaging with a past common for Ukrainians and Russians were still welcome. At the same time, local functionaries had considerable authority to interpret the official policy and often did so more rigidly that their superiors. A curious episode underscores the lack of a single 'party line' in the post-war politics of memory in Ukraine: not long before *Iaroslav*, the play, received the highest Soviet accolade, the Kiev Film Studios cancelled their plans to shoot *Iaroslav*, the movie, because of its potentially problematic theme.[52]

The Ninth Exhibition of Ukrainian Art (November 1947) demonstrated a turn towards representations of Russian-Ukrainian friendship. While no picture celebrating an 'exclusive' Ukrainian past made it into the exhibition, Hryhorii Melikhov presented a large painting, *Young Taras Shevchenko Visiting the Artist K. P. Briullov* (2.89m × 2.95 m). The canvas portrayed a young peasant lad – the future Ukrainian national bard and professional artist – gazing admiringly at the great Russian painter, who would become his teacher at the Imperial Academy of Arts. Artistically accomplished as it appeared at the time, the work also served as a perfect illustration of the myth of the Ukrainian 'younger brother' being taught and guided by the Russian 'elder brother.' As the head of the Union of Ukrainian Soviet Artists, Oleksandr Pashchenko, announced, 'Melikhov's canvas is a serious blow to the Ukrainian bourgeois nationalists, who sought to isolate Ukrainian culture from the wholesome influence of Russian culture.' The painting won the Stalin Prize, Third Class, thus proving that not all non-Russian historical works were doomed under the *Zhdanovshchina*.[53] In fact, Melikhov's work was such a coup on the all-Union artistic scene that in 1950 the famous Tretiakov Gallery pressured the Museum of Ukrainian Art in Kiev to give up this painting in exchange for a less valuable canvas from the Moscow art gallery's collection. Kievans managed to defend their property rights with help from the KP(b)U Central Committee.[54]

Cultural agents were beginning to sense what would be acceptable according to the new version of Ukrainian Soviet historical memory. Although the *Zhdanovshchina* ostensibly prescribed a return to class history, the Russian neo-imperial grand narrative remained the kernel of Stalinist historical memory, allowing (or forcing) the Ukrainian elites to retain a similar 'national' approach to their past. Rather than abandoning the national past completely and promoting proletarian internationalism, the republic's bureaucrats and intellectuals again attempted to ascertain that Ukrainian historical mythology was safely subordinated to its dominant Russian counterpart in the foundational myth of the friendship of peoples.

The attack on the Ukrainian national vision of the past met with some opposition in the republic, although only scattered evidence of it is preserved in the archives. Open non-conformism, as in the cases of Professor Korduba or the museum guide Iatskevych, was rare. However, Stalinist subjects could also express their disagreement anonymously. In January 1947 the Ukrainian State Committee for the Arts announced a competition for the best play on a contemporary topic. The competition produced miserable results: the artistic quality of most entries was apparently very low, no first prize was awarded, and only one play was subsequently staged.[55] Moreover, a certain Ievhen Blakytny (apparently a pen name) submitted to the jury a treatise entitled 'Is the Ukrainian Nation Capable of Further Existence and of Actively Making Its History? A Reference for Those Studying the History of Ukraine.' Judging from his style and argumentation, Blakytny was an amateur non-conformist rather than a professional nationalist propagandist. Far from glorifying the Soviet present, he affirmed the nation as a principal agent of history and stressed that Ukrainians were not just 'Moscow's eternal appendage,' that his nation always had been and still was capable of independent existence.[56]

Another anonymous writer submitted a three-act farce, *Without an Idea*, mocking the campaign for contemporary topics itself. The plot depicts a theatre whose administration is preparing feverishly for the 1 May holiday. The representative of the provincial party committee, with the telling Jewish name of Itsyk Pshenicher, laments the absence of Soviet subjects among 'all those things historical or those from the decadent but not yet decaying west.' A patently Ukrainian artistic director, Solopii Artemovych Bevz, seconds Pshenicher: 'What are the censors looking for? How could they let in such contaminating capitalist poison as *Othello*, *Faust*, *Corneville Bells*, and so on?' The nameless director goes through a pile of plays, mumbling: 'A whole bunch of Ukrainian classics, mountains of paper but not a line anywhere about collective farms, about socialism.' Only a bold young actor, Vladyslav Chubar, asks ironically: 'Why don't you simply reorganize our theatre into a party school?' Here and there, the text pointedly reminds the reader of post-war realities not reflected in the official literature: arrests at the railway station, denunciations, a shortage of sugar, bread rationing, lining up at 5 a.m., burglaries, and so on.[57]

In the end, Pshenicher orders that the most 'ideologically correct' Russian Soviet play, Konstantin Trenev's *Liubov Iarovaia*, be staged on the evening of 1 May. At the very last moment, however, the party representative has second thoughts about the appropriateness of *any* artistic representation of the most glorious present. Instead of allowing the performance of the play, he himself goes on stage to read a speech with the deliberately awkward title, 'The Leading Role of Communist Ideas in the Laws of the Development of Contemporary Society.' As the public is leaving and as occurs in classical farce, a secondary comic character, the maintenance manager Mykyta Dohada, appears on the vacant stage to recite the rhyming moral: 'What of the strength of Stalinist ideas? / The theatre is empty. There are no people.'[58]

The Ukrainian authorities did not have enough leads to locate the anonymous author who, like 'the young actor Vladyslav Chubar,' apparently belonged to the new generation of the Ukrainian intelligentsia. Having grown up during the late 1930s and 1940s, when local intellectuals were allowed to cultivate their national patrimony, the author (or authors) wanted to protest the recent devaluation of Ukrainian history and its cultural heritage in favour of class struggle and the Soviet present. Submitting an anonymous farce to the Ukrainian Committee for the Arts represented both an original method of communicating this opposition to the authorities and an effective undermining of the official discourse through its 'carnivalization.'[59]

Far away from the capitals, then, the *Zhdanovshchina* looked very different than it had appeared in its the Moscow-Leningrad version. Intellectuals in the capitals understood the campaign as a crusade against liberalism and western influences in the arts, but their colleagues in Kiev and Lviv were taught to eulogize the Soviet present at the expense of the Ukrainian national past. Together, these approaches picture the *Zhdanovshchina* as an attempt to redefine the Soviet Union as a society identifying with the history of class struggle and the Soviet present. In practice, however, the campaign came down to re-educating the peoples of the USSR to identify with the Soviet present and the Russian imperial past.

Chapter Four

The Unfinished Crusade of 1947

By January 1947 the purification campaign in Ukraine had clearly ended. No new ideological resolutions had appeared since early October, and the wave of criticism in the media was dying out. The republic's ideologues and intellectuals seemed to have arrived at an understanding of what the new proper version of Ukrainian historical memory was to be. Neither the Ukrainian leadership nor its Moscow bosses spoke of further eradication of 'nationalist deviations.' Then, an unexpected turn in Khrushchev's political fortunes and Kaganovich's arrival in Ukraine changed the situation dramatically.

In late February 1947 Stalin's trusted trouble-shooter Lazar Kaganovich arrived in Kiev as the Communist Party of Ukraine's new first secretary. A Ukrainian-born Jew, the notoriously heavy-handed Kaganovich had headed the republic's party organization in 1925–8; he had served in Moscow consecutively as the people's commissar of railway transport, heavy industry, and construction materials, earning the epithet of *zheleznyi narkom* (iron minister). Kaganovich replaced Nikita Khrushchev as the Ukrainian party leader, the latter until then having held the positions of both first secretary and Ukrainian premier. (He retained the second office.)

Whatever the reason for Khrushchev's sudden demotion, it had little to do with any 'nationalist deviations' in the republic's intellectual life. Khrushchev himself claimed that his requests for food assistance for Ukraine during the 1946 famine had provoked Stalin's wrath. Scholars have argued in a similar vein that Khrushchev's powerful rival in Moscow, Georgii Malenkov, attempted to discredit the Ukrainian leader's agricultural policies in order to remove him from the line of succession.[1]

The formal pretext for Khrushchev's being removed from his party post was a simple one. The minutes of the Politburo meeting explain that the practice of combining the offices of Ukrainian first secretary and premier had been 'dictated by the specific conditions of the war' and no longer applied. A similar division of positions occurred in neighbouring Belarus, although Stalin himself 'temporarily' continued holding both positions at the all-Union level.[2] Whatever the reason, Khrushchev was 'out' and Kaganovich was 'in.'

Both Khrushchev and Kaganovich agree in their otherwise remarkably antagonistic memoirs that the latter's main task was to revitalize Ukrainian agriculture, which had not yet recovered from wartime destruction. However, the same Politburo decree also appointed a special secretary for agriculture of the KP(b)U Central Committee, Nikolai Patolichev, while agriculture was one of Premier Khrushchev's major areas of specialization. Lacking their expertise and eager to demonstrate to Moscow his ability to ferret out and solve problems, Kaganovich began looking for errors elsewhere, especially in ideology, where he had found them so successfully while purging the Ukrainian 'national communists' in the late 1920s. In Khrushchev's words, 'From the very beginning of his activities in Ukraine, Kaganovich looked for every opportunity to show off and to throw his weight around.'[3] This search soon led the new first secretary to the promising field of Ukrainian historiography.

The Enforced Dialogue

Materials available in the archives of the VKP(b) and KP(b)U Central Committees contain no hints regarding a possible command from the Kremlin to purge Ukrainian historians, nor do they confirm that Kaganovich arrived in the republic with any such intention. In fact, the first secretary's interest in historical scholarship first surfaced in a rather curious form in April 1947. As the KP(b)U Central Committee was reviewing the working plans of the Ukrainian Academy of Sciences, someone apparently brought to Kaganovich's attention the fact that the Academy's Institute of Ukrainian History planned to publish a collection of articles, 'A Critique of the Bourgeois-Nationalist Theory of Hrushevsky and His "School."' Listed among the collection's authors was Professor Ivan Krypiakevych, who not only had been Hrushevsky's student but had remained in Lviv under the German occupation. The indignant Kaganovich immediately arranged for an unusual resolution of the Central Committee. The Ukrainian party's highest body called for Krypiakevych's exclusion from the plan, denouncing him as 'a student and epigone of Hrushevsky,' as well as the 'author of the spiteful anti-Soviet fascist book *History of Ukraine*, which was published in Lviv under the German occupation.'[4]

Although the politically unreliable Krypiakevych continued working at the Institute after the resolution, the decree effectively buried the anti-Hrushevskian collection. While the Institute's working plan for 1947 lists most leading researchers as preparing related articles, the five-year report for 1946–50 does not even mention the project.[5] Unaware of this effect of his intervention, Kaganovich meanwhile decided to look more closely into the state of Ukrainian Soviet historical scholarship. On 27 April the KP(b)U Central Committee announced a forthcoming conference of leading Ukrainian historians, the aim of which was to 'discover the causes of bourgeois-nationalist deviations' in their recent works.[6]

The conference opened on 29 April with a two-day session and continued on 6 May. On the first day, Kaganovich joined the discussions eagerly, but he and other party ideologues had neither the primary sources nor the knowledge necessary to analyse what they had designated 'nationalist errors' in historical works. Knowing that the scholars could be expected to criticize themselves, they nonetheless initiated an unequal dialogue with them. Yet the Ukrainian historians present had their own interests in mind. Fedir Los and Mykola Petrovsky gave speeches condemning Hrushevsky's heresy but acknowledging only innocent shortcomings and mistakes in the Institute's publications that they did not label 'nationalistic.' The scholars were prepared to remedy the situation by relying more on the Marxist theory of socio-economic formations and emphasizing Ukraine's historical ties with Russia. At this point, Kaganovich grew tired of waiting for real confessions and interrupted the next speaker with the demand to uncover 'invisible threads' connecting contemporary historians to Hrushevsky and his school.[7]

The first secretary, however, did not receive a clear answer on the matter of ideological ties to the past. The closest the participants came to locating these frightening 'invisible threads' was in tracing their biographical connections and those of their colleagues to the Hrushevsky school and to other non-party historians. (All this information was, of course, noted in their personal files and known to the party bureaucracy.) Some speakers noted that Petrovsky's mistakes betrayed him as a former student of Hrushevsky. Kost Huslysty told the audience about his studies under non-Marxist Ukrainian professors Dmytro Iavornytsky and Dmytro Bahalii during the 1920s. Mykhailo Rubach confessed to having experienced the influences of the Pokrovsky school and even Trotskyism during the 1920s. Instead of coming up with invisible threads to Ukrainian nationalist historiography, several historians directly traced the Institute's 'mistakes' to wartime patriotism and the official elevation of national heroes, eliciting total silence from the party functionaries present.[8]

Amid all the anti-nationalist rhetoric, the Ukrainian scholars acknowledged only a few conceptual 'errors,' all characteristic of the patriotic version of national memory that the authorities had previously promoted. Huslysty admitted to having unwittingly 'followed bourgeois-nationalist historiography' in his wartime pamphlet on Danylo of Halych in which the prince is described as a 'Ukrainian monarch and head of the Ukrainian nation-state.' This interpretation, the historian confessed, contradicted the official view of Kievan Rus' as the common patrimony of all Eastern Slavs. A professor from Kiev University, Arsen Bortnikov, acknowledged idealizing the Cyril and Methodius Brotherhood as a progressive organization of Ukrainian intellectuals. Now he was aware of the class struggle within this first Ukrainian political organization and of the fact that it had had a 'bourgeois-nationalist wing.'[9]

The conference participants realized that the strategies of emphasizing the class struggle and historical ties with Russia in historical narratives were potentially contradictory. The historian Huslysty indicated to Lytvyn that this was particularly the case with Khmelnytsky, whose social origin as a feudal lord obviously constituted a liability:

> HUSLYSTY: The question of the class aspects of his activities has not been resolved. Our previous profile of Bohdan Khmelnytsky went as follows: a great son of the Ukrainian people, a person who organized the Ukrainian people in the struggle against foreign aggressors, who united Ukraine with Russia, and so on. When we started working to reveal the class aspect of his deeds, we encountered difficulties. Mykola Neonovych [Petrovsky] wrote a section about this, and the situation only became worse. When he began clarifying the class factor, Bohdan Khmelnytsky appeared to have been separated from the people. A number of questions became muddled. I believe we will resolve all these questions. First of all, we ought to abandon the old theory, which was based on nationalist theories, and move on to the correct Marxist concept.
>
> LYTVYN: Why are we, Ukrainian historians, debating the question of Bohdan Khmelnytsky and trying to define his role when the government has long since defined it? It is enough that we have the Order of Bohdan Khmelnytsky. Our soldiers wear the order, and we, the historians of Ukraine, raise the question of whether the role of Bohdan Khmelnytsky is unclear?[10]

The secretary for ideology made his audience understand that, if class analysis undermined the sacred story of Ukraine's union with Russia, it should be tacitly suppressed.

On less important issues, however, the historians openly challenged the secretary, showing that clear ideological prescriptions on historical problems were not always possible. Just before the conference, Lytvyn had published the article 'On the History of the Ukrainian People' in the authoritative Moscow journal *Bolshevik*. After dwelling on the sins of Hrushevsky and his school, Lytvyn provided a brief summary of the official model of Ukrainian history. He pontificated that medieval Kievan Rus' was the common cradle of Russians, Ukrainians, and Belarusians, and that since its demise 'the Ukrainian people have always striven to unite with the great Russian people.'[11] But for all its apparent clarity, this scheme did not specify when the Ukrainians had emerged from the cradle as a separate people. Following the critique of Bazhan's 'Danylo of Halych,' the seemingly scholastic problem of the emergence of Ukrainian nationality acquired ideological importance because the date would determine how much of the glorious Eastern Slavic past Ukrainians could claim.

Lytvyn's article disposed of the problem in one ambiguous sentence: 'The Ukrainian nationality [narodnost] began to shape itself in the fourteenth century, and by the sixteenth century the main features of the Ukrainian nation [naroda] (language, culture, etc.) had developed.' Huslysty, who had just pleaded guilty to claiming for Ukrainian history the thirteenth-century Galician-Volhynian Principality, pointed out that this pronouncement only obscured the problem. It also contradicted the assertion made earlier on the same page that 'Three closely related nations [naroda], Russians, Ukrainians, and Belarusians, began to take shape from a single root after the disintegration of Kievan Rus', meaning during the thirteenth century at the latest. In addition, Lytvyn's chronology dissented from the one in Shestakov's Politburo-approved textbook, which had dated the emergence of the three separate peoples in the thirteenth century, while other Moscow historians had proposed, variously, the fourteenth (S. Iushkov), the fifteenth (A. Pankratova), and the sixteenth (V. Picheta) centuries. When an embattled party ideologue snarled at his opponent, 'Do you want a date?' Hyslysty rebuffed him, 'I thought you would provide one.' (During this argument, the party secretary spoke Russian and the historian Ukrainian.)[12] On the evening of 6 May the conference ended in an impasse. No party functionary made a concluding speech, and no official resolution resulted from the meetings.

One possible reason for the stalemate was that Kaganovich had been contemplating an ideological purge on a much wider scale. The formerly top secret working files of the KP(b)U Politburo reveal that in May 1947 Kaganovich planned a major denunciatory session of the Ukrainian Central Committee. On 28 May the Politburo approved in principle a draft resolution entitled 'On Improving the Ideological and Political Education of the Cadres and the Struggle against Manifestations of Bourgeois-Nationalist Ideology.' According to a handwritten note in the file, the Ukrainian leadership sent this draft to the VKP(b) Central Committee on the same day. Another note in Kaganovich's hand reads, 'Do not send out [the draft to the members of the KP(b)U Central Committee]. Include in the agenda without the title.' Yet another note explains that on 10 June the Ukrainian Politburo decided to revise the draft, which itself had been removed from the file.[13] In the end, the plenary session was never convened. Apparently, Stalin and his advisers did not express the requisite enthusiasm for Kaganovich's plan for a comprehensive purge of 'nationalists' in Ukrainian culture and scholarship. According to a legendary account circulating at the time among the Ukrainian intelligentsia, Stalin dismissed Kaganovich's proposal with the words: 'Comrade Kaganovich, you will not embroil me in a quarrel with the Ukrainian people.'[14]

The Attack on Historians

Having lost his bid for a major ideological purge, Kaganovich initiated a surprise crackdown on Ukrainian historians. During July and August the apparatus of the KP(b)U Central Committee engaged in its usual languid 'political education' of scholars. On 16 and 18 August the Ukrainian Agitprop held a staff conference to discuss a number of pressing practical problems in their propaganda work, yet nothing in the minutes indicates serious concern with the state of history writing. Participants dwelt on a glitch in the work of IMEL, whose director, Fedir Ienevych, had just been fired.[15]

On 31 July 1947 the demoted Ienevych attempted to restore himself to the Politburo's favour by sending Kaganovich information compromising the poet Maksym Rylsky. Ienevych included a copy of Rylsky's 1943 speech on the history of Kiev, as well as the poet's introduction to a 1944 edition of Ukrainian historical folk songs and the 1946 autobiographical article, 'From Years Gone By.' All these texts allegedly idealized the Ukrainian past and did not discriminate between nationalistic and 'progressive' trends in Ukrainian culture. On 20 August, the Secretariat of the Ukrainian Central Committee adopted an unusual retroactive resolution, 'On M.T. Rylsky's Speech "Kiev in the History of Ukraine,"' declaring that the 1943 text 'in reality represents not a speech about Kiev but a statement on the history of Ukraine in which M. Rylsky defends nationalistic mistakes that the party had condemned.'[16]

More important, this incident impelled Kaganovich to go ahead with strict measures against historians. The first secretary enlisted Manuilsky to write an appropriate resolution, and on 29 August 1947 the Ukrainian Politburo adopted the Central Committee's decree 'On Political Mistakes and the Unsatisfactory Work of the Institute of Ukrainian History of the Ukrainian SSR Academy of Sciences.' The resolution condemned historians for failing to produce a 'scholarly, seasoned, Marxist-Leninist history of Ukraine.' Wartime publications of the Institute were judged to have been compiled in an 'anti-Marxist spirit' and to 'contain gross political mistakes and bourgeois-nationalist distortions.' While the document condemned historical narratives emphasizing the birth, growth, struggles, and victories of the Ukrainian nation, the party directives on the writing of Ukrainian history remained confusing. The resolution announced that 'instead of considering the history of Ukraine in close connection with the history of the Russian, Belarusian, and other peoples of the Soviet Union, [the scholars] follow

Ukrainian nationalists in treating the history of Ukraine in isolation from the history of other peoples.' In line with this statement, the decree demanded that historians eliminate all traces of exclusively Ukrainian claims to Kievan Rus' and stress historical ties with Russia. At the same time, the document's statement on the Khmelnytsky War suggested a return to class analysis: historians should have explained the War of Liberation as 'primarily the peasant masses' struggle against Polish aggressors and feudal oppression in general.' The resolution did not explain why, in this light, a union with the Russia of tsars and landlords was historically progressive, but requested further attention to Russian-Ukrainian fraternal co-operation in the revolutionary movement and in socialist construction.[17]

The decree explained Ukrainian historians' mistakes by pointing to the vestiges of 'bourgeois-nationalist' views among the Institute's researchers and singling out its director, Petrovsky. The party decision proclaimed the creation of a Marxist-Leninist 'Short Course on the History of Ukraine' as the scholars' most important task. By 15 October the Institute was to have delivered to the Central Committee the outline and theses of the 'Short Course.'[18]

Although the decree was not published in full until 1994, the official KP(b)U journal, *Bilshovyk Ukrainy*, carried a lengthy editorial, 'To Carry Through the Liquidation of Bourgeois-Nationalist Distortions in the History of Ukraine,' which closely followed the original text. In addition, *Radianska Ukraina* published an even more verbose editorial, 'To Create a Truly Scholarly, Marxist-Leninist History of Ukraine,' in which the decree's ideas were expounded on at greater length.[19] That said, Kaganovich wanted to make sure the republic's intellectuals had received his message. He requested detailed reports on party group meetings in all the institutes of the Academy of Sciences as well as on a historians' conference held on 16–19 September.[20] During this meeting, the historians of the Institute, IMEL, Kiev University, and the Kiev Pedagogical Institute discussed the party resolution.

Kaganovich apparently never read the minutes of this conference, which would have upset him greatly. While all participants dutifully repeated the general ideological formulae of the decree, many questioned their practical application. Petrovsky acknowledged some mistakes but rejected accusations that his views were anti-Marxist or nationalistic. The Institute's researchers Oleksandr Slutsky and Pylyp Stoian supported him, causing the Central Committee's Secretary for Propaganda, Ivan Nazarenko, to intervene: 'I do not agree with Comrade Slutsky, who devoted his speech to defending Comrade Petrovsky. The Central Committee wrote down [its decision], pointing out serious mistakes that resulted from both a weak Marxist-Leninist education and the complacency of the Institute's director, Professor Petrovsky. He made serious mistakes, he did not organize a struggle against the manifestations of bourgeois-nationalist trends, and he did not direct scholarly work on the history of Ukraine sufficiently. This would appear to be perfectly clear ... That is why I am bewildered by the speeches of comrades Slutsky and Stoian, who have attempted to underestimate and to water down the discussion of this historic document [of the Central Committee].'[21] There was, of course, a difference between the resolution, which charged Petrovsky personally with vestiges of nationalism and 'past serious mistakes of a bourgeois-nationalist character,' and Nazarenko's comments, where the historian appeared guilty of mere complacency, of not organizing a struggle against nationalism. The secretary himself seemed to have been captivated by the general tone of 'watering down' Kaganovich's resolution. However, Huslysty went further than other participants in challenging the authority of the ideologues: 'As you know, during the 1946 conference on propaganda, the work of our Institute of History received a positive appraisal. It was noted that the Institute had done considerable work, that it had published the *Short Course*, the first volume [of the *History of Ukraine*], and so on. That is, in June of 1946, nobody found any fault with historical scholarship in Ukraine.'[22] All of the participants knew full well that the party official who had spoken so highly of the Institute's work in 1946 was Nazarenko himself. In his concluding remarks, the embarrassed secretary of the Central Committee sounded a call for collaboration, referring to both historians and ideological functionaries as 'we': 'We need to compile the outline and theses of the "Short Course" before the 15th, to develop several methodological instructions for teachers, and to publish the plans that will help our instructors teach history properly ... We need to roll up our sleeves and get to work.' Neither the incident with Huslysty, nor the opposition from Petrovsky, Slutsky, and Stoian was recorded in Nazarenko's report to Kaganovich.[23]

On 22 and 23 September the Institute's party group held a special two-day meeting at which party members voted 'to ensure that all works on the history of Ukraine are imbued with the idea of unbreakable ties with the history of the Russian, Belarusian, and the other peoples of the Soviet Union.' Party meetings to discuss the historians' political mistakes were held at all the institutes of the Ukrainian Academy of Sciences.[24] In all Ukrainian provinces, authorities organized conferences and lectures for the intelligentsia to spell out the Central Committee resolution. *Radianska osvita*, the newspaper of the Ministry of Education, dutifully carried articles explaining to teachers the danger of 'nationalist deviation' in Ukrainian history. The ministry also forwarded to all universities and colleges a lengthy circular requesting that the course outlines on the history of Ukraine be revised by 1 October.[25]

Aside from the obligatory theoretical condemnations of nationalism, the local conferences produced little of interest for the authorities. Local historians and educational administrators claimed that they had not been involved in spreading erroneous concepts. At Uzhhorod University, instructors normally used the 1942 *Survey of the History of the Ukrainian SSR* as a text; when the resolution on the Institute of Ukrainian History appeared several days before the start of the classes, the department decided not to risk using a potentially faulty text and simply cancelled the course. Both Kirovohrad and Stalino Pedagogical Institutes also chose to play it safe, reporting that, although they offered a course in Ukrainian history, they allegedly had neither the designated text nor the outline. At Zaporizhzhia Pedagogical Institute, instructor Zhyvalov actually demanded more hours for his survey of Ukrainian history.[26]

Schoolteachers used the occasion to complain that a Moscow-approved standard history textbook did not reflect the changing official interpretations of events from the history of Ukraine. Speaking at a teachers' seminar in Poltava, the teacher Morhulenko noted that Pankratova's textbook for grade 8 was unsatisfactory: 'One cannot give this material to students. In the textbook, the description of Bohdan Khmelnytsky's personality is vague. Also, it does not say that Kievan Rus' was the cradle of three fraternal peoples, the Russians, Ukrainians, and Belarusians.' A fellow teacher, Meliavsky, seconded her complaint, saying that 'secondary schoolteachers are experiencing great difficulties in teaching' because 'the existing texts view many problems differently.'[27]

The School Department of the KP(b)U Central Committee inspected the teaching of history in several provinces and did not find any nationalist mistakes in the East. In the West, the Soviet version of historical memory was not yet firmly established; some students there referred to Kievan Rus' as 'Ukraine' and spoke highly of 'petite-bourgeois nationalist' parties in pre-1917 Ukraine, such as the Revolutionary Ukrainian Party (RUP) and the Ukrainian Social Democratic Workers' Party. Even the specialists at the Lviv Institute of Teachers' Professional Development proposed erroneous examination essay topics such as 'The Role of the Varangians in the Creation of the Kievan State' and 'The National Movement in Ukraine in 1905–7 and the Activities of the RUP.' Nonetheless, the School Department defended Western Ukrainians, who were 'insufficiently familiar with the demands and principles of Marxist historical science.' It was the Institute of Ukrainian History that was guilty of not developing model course outlines for schoolteachers.[28] The ideological circle was thus complete: teachers blamed the textbook authors, historians insisted that ideologues share the responsibility, and local functionaries downplayed the severity of the issues at hand.

Meanwhile, Kaganovich appeared frustrated with the absence of concrete denunciations. On 3 October the Secretariat of the Central Committee adopted yet another resolution on the progress of the discussion of the previous resolution concerning the Institute of Ukrainian History. The decree announced that the meetings at the republic's universities and colleges had reviewed the resolution only superficially, without uncovering the 'nationalist mistakes' of their own faculties. The decree demanded more denunciatory sessions in the capital and in major cities, as well as another conference at the Institute. (These directives were never implemented.)[29] Although the Institute submitted two versions of the future textbook's outline to Kaganovich in early October, the Ukrainian leadership fired Petrovsky as the Institute's director, replacing him with the loyal party type Oleksii Kasymenko. The new director had not yet published a single book; not until in 1954 would his first monograph, *The Reunification of Ukraine with Russia and Its Historical Significance*, appear.[30] This administrative solution might have satisfied Kaganovich's thirst for decisive measures, but the campaign never regained momentum.

However, the August attack on historians also triggered a renewed purge of writers.[31] The ideologues of the *Zhdanovshchina* were generally suspicious of non-Russians' identification with their own past rather than with the Soviet present and with Russian imperial history. In June 1947 Aleksandr Fadeev, the head of the Soviet Writers' Union, gave a highly publicized speech at a meeting of the union's Presidium, hammering out the thesis that no decisive turn to Soviet subjects had yet occurred in literature. Fadeev blamed the 'vestiges of bourgeois nationalism' as one of the causes of this problem. In particular, he criticized non-Russian historical novels for excessive blackening of the Russian Empire: 'In depicting the historical past, one should not show only tsarism's colonial deeds. It is much more important now to show those individuals in the past of your people who understood that your people should follow the lead of Russian culture.' In his speech at the same meeting, Korniichuk, the head of the Ukrainian Writers' Union, enumerated the nationalist mistakes of his fellow writers. Almost all of these errors were taken from the archives of the 1946 campaign, the only noteworthy addition being Petro Panch's novel *The Zaporozhians*, which had been published in late 1946.[32]

This first post-war Ukrainian historical novel, an epic narrative set in seventeenth-century Ukraine, soon came under critical fire for 'idealizing' the Cossacks. Panch allegedly did not stress the tension between rich and poor Cossacks sufficiently; instead, he portrayed the wealthy Cossack Veryha positively and had one of the characters, the noble Buzhinsky, utter the incriminating words: 'Cossacks have always fought for Ukraine, for our faith, for freedom!'[33]

From 15 to 20 September the Writers' Union held an extended session to uncover nationalist errors among its members. Most of the 'discoveries' repeated the accusations from 1946; Korniichuk in his speech went as far back as Dovzhenko's *Ukraine in Flames*. Aside from *The Zaporozhians*, the participants condemned only one short new historical novel, Fedir Burlaka's *Ostap Veresai*. (Its hero, a blind nineteenth-century peasant bard, performed before contemporary 'bourgeois nationalists' and even Tsar Alexander II.) Since the much-scrutinized historical genre provided no other material for critique, Ukrainian ideologues dismissed, for good measure, two novels that incorrectly interpreted contemporary topics: Iurii Ianovsky's *Living Water* and Ivan Senchenko's *His Generation*. Rylsky publicly acknowledged his sins. Mykola Bazhan, who had composed the patriotic 'Danylo of Halych,' gave a fierce speech against nationalism in history, denouncing Hrushevsky, the 'fascist' Krypiakevych, Petrovsky, and Rylsky. As soon as Bazhan finished a particularly angry tirade against Rylsky, the latter himself shouted, 'Right!'[34]

Later during the meeting, Panch took the floor to repent his errors and promise a 'party novel about Bohdan Khmelnytsky's time.' The writer quoted two letters of support received from his readers after *The Zaporozhians* had been criticized in the press. One reader from Lviv regretted that the witch-hunt would prevent Panch from writing interesting works. Another, a twenty-two-year-old disabled veteran, advised the writer not to bow before the ideological pressure: 'The novels they would like you to write would be of low artistic quality and would find sympathetic readers only in a certain historical period and exclusively among a small group of people.' Up to this point, Panch had seemed to be defending himself with evidence of his readers' support, yet the embattled writer suddenly shouted: 'Together with my critics, I will slap these "sympathizers" in the face!'[35]

On 19 September Kaganovich and Khrushchev met with a group of 105 leading Ukrainian writers, who discussed the 'nationalist mistakes' of their comrades and pledged loyalty to the party cause. Most speakers strongly condemned 'harmful nostalgia for the past,' but the well-known novelist Natan Rybak, who had just completed the first part of an ideologically sound historical novel about Ukraine's incorporation into Russia, decided to test the waters. Phrasing his defence of the historical genre to resonate with the official anti-nationalist rhetoric, he said: 'I do not know who could have a stake in the disappearance of historical novels ... We Soviet writers should not abandon a topic of such importance as our people's history [i.e., leave it for the émigré nationalists].' Rybak also mentioned that he had discussed the idea for his latest novel with Khrushchev as early as 1940 and that the then party leader had given him some helpful advice. Kaganovich and Khrushchev, however, made no comments in response, leaving the writer in uncertainty.[36]

Isolated and lacking the historical profession's claim to special knowledge, writers had little room to defend themselves when the press resumed its persecution of nationalism in literature. *Radianska Ukraina* soon published Ienevych's lengthy article 'On Maksym Rylsky's Nationalist Mistakes.' *Literaturna hazeta* followed with a salvo of denunciatory articles on Panch, Ianovsky, and others. Rylsky was forced to publish his confession, 'On the Nationalist Mistakes in My Literary Work.'[37] The measures taken against Western Ukrainian writers exceeded the relatively mild administrative reprimand of their Eastern counterparts. In Lviv, authorities expelled the 'nationalists' Petro Karmansky, Mykhailo Rudnytsky, and Andrii Patrus-Karpatsky from the Writers' Union and even arrested Patrus-Karpatsky.[38]

Novels about wartime heroism, industrial reconstruction, and the revival of agriculture came to constitute the bulk of Ukrainian literary production. In 1947 the young writer Oles Honchar received the Stalin Prize, Second Class, for part 1 of his war trilogy, *The Standard-Bearers*. The following year, the same award went to him for part 2 of the work, while Ivan Riabokliach received the Stalin Prize, Third Class, for a short novel about post-war collective farms, *A Golden Thousand*. Rybak's bulky historical novel, *The Pereiaslav Council*, was actually published, first in a literary journal and then in late 1948 separately, in due time earning the writer the Stalin Prize, Second Class.[39] Rybak's case established a precedent: as long as they celebrated Ukraine's eternal friendship with Russia, historical novels were welcome, even if they were based on the slippery ground of the glorious Cossack past.

Whatever the first secretary's intentions might have been, the drive for ideological purity under Kaganovich did not develop into a blanket cleansing of Ukrainian scholarly and cultural life. The republic's bureaucrats and intellectuals alike did not want a self-destructive ideological battle, and the Kremlin did not request one. In mid-December 1947 Stalin summoned Kaganovich to Moscow as suddenly as he had sent him to Ukraine earlier in the year. Kaganovich became deputy chairman of the USSR Council of Ministers, while Khrushchev resumed his duties as first secretary in Ukraine.[40] The campaign against 'nationalist errors' in Ukrainian historiography and literature faded out soon after Kaganovich's departure for the capital, although the ideological resolutions of 1947 were never formally revoked. Although the purge remained unfinished, the Ukrainian intellectuals had learned their lesson. For the next year or two, most writers stayed away from historical topics, while historians took extra care to highlight wherever possible both historical ties with Russia and class analysis – even if the simultaneous use of these two strategies did not add clarity to their narratives.

As happened elsewhere in the Soviet Union, aftershocks of the *Zhdanovshchina* recurred in Ukraine long after Zhdanov's death in August 1948. Local intellectuals, however, soon learned how to appropriate Moscow's ideological pronouncements to defend and promote their own agendas. For instance, they used the crusade against the (usually Jewish) 'rootless cosmopolitans' to dismiss some of the literary scholars who had participated in earlier attacks on the Ukrainian historical genre and pre-revolutionary classics. Liubomyr Dmyterko, the secretary of the Ukrainian Writers' Union, publicly denounced the 'cosmopolitan' critic Oleksandr Borshchahivsky, who had allegedly 'slandered *Bohdan Khmelnytsky* and other plays by O. Korniichuk.' He also accused Iukhym Martych (Finkelstein) of 'stigmatizing Kocherha's *Iaroslav the Wise* as "cloying."' *Bilshovyk Ukrainy* condemned 'a group of anti-patriotic theatre and literary critics' that included 'Borshchahivsky, Gozenpud, Stebun (Katsnelson), Adelheim, Starynkevych, Shamrai, Sanov (Smulson), and others' for maligning the Ukrainian classical heritage – 'our pride [and] our national treasure (*sviatynia*).'[41]

The Campaign's Nationalist Echoes

When the wave of anti-nationalist articles appeared in the press in the autumn of 1947, the official *Radianska Ukraina* started receiving anonymous letters of protest from its readers. After the August-September publication of a series of articles explaining the resolution on the Institute of History, the paper received several letters specifically on this topic. By early October *Radianska Ukraina* found it desirable to reply to its anonymous opponents with a spiteful article by L. Levchenko, 'Into the Dustbin of History!' The author defended the official view of the 'nationalist traitors' Mazepa, Hrushevsky, Dontsov, and Konovalets, who, according to the anonymous letters, actually 'brought Ukrainians [as a modern nation] to life.'[42] However, the newspaper soon received an unsigned letter from the Eastern Ukrainian industrial town of Dniprodzerzhynsk, arguing against Levchenko's article: 'Good man, you have the right to write [this] in the newspaper, but no matter how much you swear that "Hrushevsky always held the Ukrainian people in contempt," who will believe you? Whoever has raised a voice for our extremely oppressed people, you call this person a traitor and you would probably call me a traitor as well, although I am not one of the nobility ... And who are the "people" in whose name you speak and who "condemn" Mazepa, Hrushevsky, and other glorious but unfortunate sons of Ukraine?'[43] Not a good writer and probably not a member of the nationalist underground, the author was likely an isolated home-grown Ukrainian patriot, one of the many who had bought old history books at book bazaars during the war and who would be mobilized by the dissident movement a generation later. Another anonymous tract, signed by 'The Lviv Group of the Union for the Liberation of Ukraine,' displayed a more consistent nationalistic approach. The authors explained that the history of Ukraine as a state and as a nation could not be produced by the official historians, because they wrote 'from the colonizers' point of view.' Moreover, such a history was not really necessary, since 'the truly national history of Ukraine has long been created and written down in the way it should be by a prominent representative of Ukrainian scholarship, Citizen Hrushevsky.' In general, history writing 'should contribute to the future development of a truly free and independent Ukrainian state, which would emerge in the near future with the help of the western democracies.'[44]

When on 2 October *Radianska Ukraina* ran a lengthy article by Fedir Ienevych, 'On Maksym Rylsky's Nationalist Mistakes,' the newspaper soon received two very different anonymous responses from Western Ukraine: one defending wartime Soviet patriotism and another expressing outright anti-Soviet views. 'Ten students from Lviv' asked the editor to let Ienevych know that 'he is akin to that dog who killed Pushkin, without knowing at whom he was shooting. If Rylsky is a nationalist, then a non-nationalist is a person who has completely broken with his people.' Another 'youth circle from the Western provinces of Ukraine' took a rather bleak view of the poet: 'Rylsky sold his soul and was made "Stalin's laureate" for his black scribble.' Moreover, they felt that Rylsky had publicly renounced his Ukrainianness in favour of a Soviet identity when he coined the verse line, 'My fatherland is not the line of ancestors.' The authors insisted that Ukrainian nationalism had been born when the warriors of Kievan Rus' had raised their swords against their aggressors, that the Cossacks had fought for the nation rather than for any 'theory of production growth,' and that Khmelnytsky had signed the treaty with Muscovy in order to break with Poland and not 'sink into the Muscovite mire.'[45]

The Soviet authorities were extremely concerned with the propaganda activities of the organized nationalist movement. Although guerrilla resistance centred in the Western provinces, nationalist leaflets and pocket-sized pamphlets were regularly discovered in Eastern Ukraine, including the capital. On the morning of the December 1947 all-Union elections, for instance, a nationalist leaflet was found on the wall of St Volodymyr cathedral in the center of Kiev.[46] In July 1948 Leonid Melnikov, the second secretary of the KP(b)U Central Committee, received an alarmed report from a local party boss in Dnipropetrovsk province by the name of Leonid Brezhnev. Brezhnev reported that a railway car carrying wooden construction materials had arrived in his Eastern Ukrainian province from Western Ukraine and appeared to contain an additional cargo of nationalist literature. A disturbed Brezhnev assured his superiors that his ideological staff had 'intensified the [propaganda] work among the workers and the peasants of the province.'[47]

As is evident from the examples Brezhnev attached to his report and from other nationalist publications, the topics of national memory, Ukraine's historical nationhood, and Russian imperialism occupied a strategic place in nationalist propaganda. Moreover, nationalist writers seemed to have closely monitored the developments in official historical scholarship, often offering alternative readings to recent party pronouncements on history and identity. Thus, in a typewritten pamphlet from the Ternopil branch of the Organization of Ukrainian Nationalists (OUN) the notion of the elder brother, the great Russian people was attacked, in the process revealing a thorough knowledge of both the local Soviet press and articles in the party's main theoretical journal, *Bolshevik*. According to the analysis in the pamphlet after the war 'the Bolsheviks definitively returned to the old ways of Russian tsarist imperialism. They did so because the idea of prewar Bolshevik imperialism based on the so-called international proletarian revolution had exhausted itself. The Bolsheviks failed to establish [the rule of the proletariat] even in the USSR, not to mention the world. The peoples of the USSR did not merge into a "Soviet people" that became a prototypical nationless society, whereas the peoples of the world preferred to create and defend their nation-states.'[48] During the Second World War, the author continued, fighting had been not along class lines but along national lines, as the Bolsheviks themselves had recognized by spreading the cult of the Russian tsars and imperial generals during the war. Post-war Soviet nationality policy was compared to the colonizing efforts of the *ancien régime* in France and the Turkey of the Sultans. As well, the author appears to have followed the campaign against the Hrushevsky school closely. The recent party ideological decrees imposed a Bolshevik 'programmatic idea' on Ukrainian culture, but according to the nationalist propagandist, the Mongols, Pechenegs, Cumans, Turks, Tatars, Lithuanians, and Poles had come to Ukraine over the centuries with the same 'programmatic idea,' to destroy the Ukrainian nation, and had failed. Even today, the traditions of the Cossacks and the Ukrainian Revolution of 1917 lived on in the armed struggle of the OUN.[49]

In 1947 the OUN issued a leaflet commenting on the new composition of the republic's Supreme Soviet. The authors noted the absence of many criticized writers, most notably Panch and Rylsky, and observed, 'Among the historians, Petrovsky is not on the list of deputies. Once the Bolsheviks glorified him, but now he has fallen into disgrace for his *History of Ukraine*.'[50] Another OUN communiqué, released in the spring of 1947, commemorated the battle of Hurby, a village in the Kremianets region where nationalist forces had faced Soviet security detachments in 1944. Hurby was compared to Khmelnytsky's battles with Poles at Korsun, Zhovti Vody, Pyliavtsi, Zbarazh, and Berestechko; to Cossack action against Russians at Konotip in 1659 and Poltava in 1709; and to the twentieth-century encounter with Soviet troops at Kruty (1918). In yet another appeal to Ukrainian youth, these 'young scions of the Cossack tribe' were called to commemorate the thirtieth anniversary of the Ukrainian people's war against the Bolsheviks (a reference to the first Soviet invasion of Ukraine in 1918). Issued by the OUN Directorate for the Eastern Ukrainian Lands, this leaflet hailed the freedom-loving traditions of Shevchenko and the fighters at Kruty.[51]

The Ukrainian authorities treated these non-conformist anonymous letters and the nationalist 'counter-discourse' on the past with the utmost sobriety. Copies of all captured leaflets and letters were examined by the same senior ideologues who supervised the work of the Academy of Sciences and who demanded that the official historians rebuff nationalistic interpretations. Opposition to party pronouncements on history demonstrated that the official interpretation was not the only version of national memory existing in post-war Ukrainian society. The nationalist variant was available as well, even if it existed in the shadow of the official line, which itself was shaped by a complicated interaction between the party apparatus and the intelligentsia.

Chapter Five

Writing a 'Stalinist History of Ukraine'

At the Kremlin reception for victorious Soviet military commanders on 24 May 1945, Stalin raised his glass and made the following announcement:

> I would like to propose a toast to our Soviet people, and, first of all, to the health of the Russian people. (Loud, continuous applause, shouts of 'hurrah.')
>
> I drink first of all to the health of the Russian people because they are the leading nation of all the nations of the Soviet Union.
>
> I propose a toast to the health of the Russian people because in this war, they earned general recognition as the Soviet Union's guiding force among all the peoples of our country.
>
> I propose a toast to the health of the Russian people not just because they are the leading people, but also because they have a clear mind, a firm character, and patience.[1]

Stalin's toast, which the Ukrainian artist Mykhailo Khmelko portrayed in his monumental painting *To the Great Russian People!* (1947; 3m × 5,15m; Stalin Prize, Second Class, for 1947), inaugurated a celebration of Russian national greatness that knew no bounds. Russian chauvinism and messianism had been an increasing presence in the official discourse since the mid-1930s, but they mushroomed after May 1945. The Soviet media waxed rhapsodic about the Russians' having always been the greatest, wisest, bravest, and most virtuous of all nations.[2]

Developments in Ukraine reflected the general Soviet ideological transfiguration. *Radianska Ukraina* greeted the news of Stalin's toast in a servile editorial, 'Eternal Glory to You, the Great Russian People!' In the years that followed, similar articles appeared regularly in the Ukrainian press.[3] The republic's publishing houses duly translated and released two editions of the new canonical survey of

Russian historical achievements, Anna Pankratova's *The Great Russian People*.[4] Generally, the obligatory paeans to Russian glory occupied a prominent place in the Ukrainian public discourse of the first post-war decade, not least in the works of Ukrainian historians. In history, the notion of Russian superiority modified the 'friendship of peoples' paradigm into one of 'guidance relationships' between the dominant nation and its 'younger brothers.' Stalinist ideologues, historians, and writers presented the Russian Empire's foreign and domestic policies in a positive light as the predecessor of the mighty Russian-dominated, multinational Soviet state.

Although the ideological campaign against 'nationalism' in Ukrainian historiography died out after Kaganovich returned to Moscow in December 1947, his pronouncements were not rescinded. The Sixteenth Congress of the Communist Party of Ukraine praised the party's successes in fighting 'symptoms of nationalism' in the humanities. In his report to the congress, Khrushchev stressed:

> The KP(b)U Central Committee is paying special attention to the struggle against manifestations of bourgeois nationalism, the most harmful and tenacious capitalist remnant in the consciousness of some of our people. It is known that nationalist errors and distortions appeared in the works of some Ukrainian scholars, particularly historians and literary scholars. The VKP(b) and KP(b)U Central Committees uncovered and strongly condemned these mistakes. Measures have been taken to strengthen the Ukrainian SSR Academy of Sciences' Institute of Ukrainian History and the Institute of the History of Ukrainian Literature. Now the researchers at the Institute of Ukrainian History are working diligently to produce a *Short Course on the History of Ukraine*.[5]

Thus, the official denunciations of 1947 remained in force, and Khrushchev continued to use the same anti-nationalist rhetoric as Kaganovich, yet the republic's leaders were clearly embarking on a new course in emphasizing that the past problems had been eliminated and that the intellectuals were now engaged in useful, error-free work.

The Quest for a New Memory

The party demand that scholars produce a new Ukrainian history text should be seen in the wider context of the extraordinary proliferation of historical-synthesis projects in the post-war Soviet Union. Defying the hardships of the reconstruction period, the state financed dozens of historical surveys, from a multi-volume history of the USSR from ancient times to the present day to one-volume histories of minor Soviet nationalities such as the Buriats and Ossetians. In addition, Soviet historians started working on a multi-volume survey of world history and several textbooks on the history of the USSR's new Eastern European satellites.[6]

The official quest for a new historical synthesis reflected the USSR's new self-identification as the successor of the Russian Empire and as one of the world's great powers rather than simply the first workers' state. The great Russian people had grown in stature, practically superseding the working class as a historical agent. Accordingly, non-Russians needed to revise their historical narratives to confirm their subaltern status as the Russians' 'younger brothers.' Eastern European history had to be entirely rewritten from the point of view of both the class struggle and the beneficence of ties with tsarist Russia.

Yet the post-war drive for this new historical synthesis produced miserable results. In 1950 the Soviet Academy of Sciences reported to the VKP(b) Central Committee that seven of the ten projected volumes of the world history survey and ten of the sixteen projected volumes of the *History of the USSR* would be ready by 1954. In fact, both targets were reached only in the 1960s. By 1953 not a single volume of the *History of the USSR* had been sent to the printers.[7] Moscow denounced several non-Russian histories that had been published for 'nationalist' mistakes. Many other projects bogged down in a lengthy review-and-discussion process aimed at ensuring that they were ideologically irreproachable, but because the party line itself kept mutating and because Moscow could not issue authoritative statements on all of the problems and personalities in non-Russian histories, ideologically sound interpretation was often left to local ideologues and historians. For them, the hasty publication of a historical survey entailed the danger of being denounced as 'nationalists,' while the endless revision process ensured safety.

The fate of the Kazakh historical survey reinforced non-Russian ideologues' reluctance to approve their own national textbooks. After the official critique of the first edition in 1943–4, Pankratova and her Kazakh colleagues promptly revised the text, and a second edition of the *History of the Kazakh SSR* appeared in 1949. The authors softened their interpretation of Kazakhstan's conquest by the tsarist army to that of a progressive event connecting the Kazakh people to the forward-looking Russian economy and culture. The Moscow reviewers nevertheless noted that the text still considered the anti-tsarist rebellion led by Kenesary 'liberational.'[8] The book enjoyed moderate success for more than a year until *Pravda* dismissed Ermukhan Bekmakhanov's monograph on Kazakhstan in the 1820s to the 1840s for idealizing the 'reactionary and anti-Russian' Kenesary uprising. The Kazakh party leadership condemned such 'nationalism' in history, and the local scholars were forced to prepare a third edition of the Kazakh history's first volume. The new edition's prospectus maintained that the progressive or reactionary character of all events in Kazakh history would be determined by their relation to Russia.[9]

Moscow taught those who had not yet figured out the direction of change in Soviet historical memory several more public lessons during the early 1950s. The first volume of the *History of the Armenian People* appeared in 1951, but in February 1953 it was discovered that the book 'idealized' local feudal rulers and incorrectly described the country's incorporation into Russia. The Central Committee's experts found exactly the same errors in the *History of Georgia*, which had received the Stalin Prize in 1946, as well as in the two-volume *History of the Peoples of Uzbekistan* (1947–50). The Georgian survey's main sin lay in presenting national history as the 'struggle of a united and monolithic Georgian people against foreign aggressors, for the preservation and well-being of the independent Georgian state.'[10] Needless to say, Ukrainian ideologues and historians closely watched the developments in other republics.

In January 1948 Ukrainian authors completed the first draft in Russian of what was then called the 'Short Course on the History of Ukraine.' Eighty-five reviewers provided detailed comments on this thirty-two–chapter draft, which was then discussed at a special meeting of the republic's Agitprop. In December 1948 the Institute of Ukrainian History published a limited edition of the revised version. The second draft circulated widely, and by the spring of 1949 the authors had received over 100 reviews from major research and educational institutions in Ukraine and other republics, all of which were generally positive.[11] More important, in December 1948 the Ukrainian Politburo had established a special *troika* consisting of Lytvyn, Manuilsky, and President Mykhailo Hrechukha to review the second draft. On 7 April 1949 the three reported their conclusion to Khrushchev; 'Pending final editing, the course can be printed in a mass edition by September 1949.'[12]

Nevertheless, the book did not go to the printers. Apparently mindful of Kaganovich's recent 'discovery' of nationalism in Ukrainian historiography, the republic's leaders sent the text for another round of extensive reviewing. On 27 December 1947 Kasymenko, director of the Institute of Ukrainian History, reported to a party meeting at the Academy of Sciences that the work had finally been completed. In his words, the Institute had 'received final instructions to send this material to the printers for issue as a mass edition.'[13] Just ten days before this announcement, however, Khrushchev left Ukraine for Moscow, leaving Leonid Melnikov in the capacity of first secretary. Although the text had been translated into Ukrainian and the proofs printed in both languages, the new party boss appeared reluctant to take responsibility for such a potentially compromising publication. Instead, in June the republic's authorities ordered that the *History of the Ukrainian SSR* should be issued in a limited edition for the fourth time: 1,500 copies in Ukrainian and 500 in Russian. By then, the bulky survey had been divided into two volumes, the first covering pre-1917 history and the second devoted to the Soviet period. Given the size of the book, the subtitle 'Short Course' had been dropped.[14]

In June 1950 a set of the two-volume, fourth limited edition landed on the desk of the VKP(b) Central Committee secretary Mikhail Suslov. The chief Soviet ideologue decided to submit it to yet another examination by Moscow scholars, but since the Institute of the USSR History had already reviewed the book several times, Suslov assigned the text to the Institute of Marx, Engels, and Lenin (IMEL). Meanwhile, work in Ukraine stalled. The Moscow specialists on Marxism and party history took five months to study the survey of Ukrainian history. On 30 December 1950 they reported to Suslov that the history of Ukraine and its culture was presented in the book 'in some isolation from Russia.' The reviewers demanded that the book emphasize the influence of progressive Russian culture in Ukraine and objected to the application of the name 'Ukraine' to the Ukrainian lands before the twentieth century.[15]

A puzzling episode followed. Within twelve days, including the New Year holiday, the Ukrainian historians reported to Moscow that they had made all the necessary changes. Suslov received the IMEL's review on 30 December, the authors first saw it on 2 January, and on 11 January the VKP(b) Central Committee functionaries Iu. Zhdanov and A. Mitin related to Suslov that the changes had been made and that volume 1 would soon be published.[16] In all probability, the Ukrainian authors resolved to ignore the principal criticism that they had 'isolated' Ukrainian history from Russian history, and they limited the changes to replacing the word 'Ukraine' with 'Ukrainian lands' and the like.

This time, volume 1 of the *History of the Ukrainian SSR* finally made it to press. The proofs were signed on 8 February, and printing began in April, but it was suddenly halted in May by the republic's authorities. Possibly having learned about the historians' reaction to the IMEL criticisms, the KP(b)U Central Committee created a new commission of nine prominent local historians, philosophers, and literary scholars, none of whom was associated with the Institute of Ukrainian History. The commission examined volume 1 for two months and made numerous critical suggestions, which the authors promptly implemented. By early August 1951 they had produced yet another version of the text, but the commission continued to find fault with the book. After a meeting with the commission members, Nazarenko concluded that the present draft could not be published.[17]

Thus, at a time when the apparatus of the VKP(b) Central Committee in Moscow was reminding them about the need to issue an ideologically sound survey of Ukrainian history,[18] the republic's functionaries further postponed this project. Their decision should be understood in a wider political context. On 2 July *Pravda* unexpectedly published a long editorial, 'Against Ideological Distortions in Literature,' attacking the alleged nationalist deviations in the work of the

Ukrainian poet Volodymyr Sosiura. The article caused a comprehensive campaign of criticism in the republic. For several months, writers, artists, composers, and journalists publicly repented their nationalist mistakes and/or ideological blindness. The campaign reached a high point in November, during a three-day plenary meeting of the KP(b)U Central Committee devoted to unmasking 'nationalism' in literature and the arts.[19]

Nazarenko and the commission members realized that in the late summer and autumn of 1951 the Kremlin and the republic's leadership would expect the Ukrainian ideologues to carry out a search for 'nationalism' in the humanities. Publishing a history textbook under such conditions would have been self-destructive. In this light, the decision to pursue further revisions appears a wise defensive strategy.

At the November 1951 plenary meeting, First Secretary Melnikov criticized the delay in producing a historical survey and claimed that the drafts of volume 1 did not incorporate Stalin's recent discoveries in the field of historical linguistics. Still, compared with Melnikov's tirades against 'nationalism' in literature and the arts, this was benign criticism. The first secretary then switched to a more constructive tone and announced: 'Our people very much need a *History of Ukraine*. Everyone needs it, from old men to young children ... There is no doubt that we can create a good Stalinist textbook on the History of Ukraine.'[20]

Defining the Ancient Past

Creating a 'good Stalinist textbook' required bringing the historical narrative into alignment with recent Soviet ideological transmutations. In the immediate post-war years, partly as a belated reaction to Nazi theories of Slavic inferiority and partly as a creation of an august ancient past for the great Russian people, Soviet ideologues extolled the ancient Slavs. The editorial in the first issue of the new Moscow journal, *Voprosy istorii*, announced in 1945 that the war had prioritized some historical problems, which had until then been seen as unimportant. The journal's first example concerned the origins of the Slavs.[21]

Ukrainians shared the same ancestry and, unlike Russians, still populated the heart of the ancient Eastern Slavic domain. After the war, the republic's archaeologists immediately turned their attention to the Slavic past. In the spring of 1946 Khrushchev requested Stalin's permission to convene the First Ukrainian Archaeological Congress. His letter explained: 'The scholarly agenda of the congress will be subordinated to the further and more profound Marxist-Leninist interpretation of two problems. The first central problem will be the origins of Eastern Slavs and the second will be the study of the relics of ancient civilizations [*kultur*] between the Dnieper and the Danube, relics which clearly testify that an advanced ancient civilization already existed on that territory during the late Stone Age and the Bronze Age.'[22] Moscow issued permission, and the Congress convened in Odessa in August 1946. Predictably, the participants claimed that the Slavs did not settle in Eastern Europe in the fifth or sixth century, as had previously been thought, but were descended from autochthonous agriculturalists. The archaeologists also condemned the Norman theory of the creation of Kievan Rus' and stressed the ancient roots of native Slavic statehood.[23] During the first post-war decade, the Institute of Archaeology of the republic's Academy of Sciences promoted further research along these lines, earning in 1950 the praise of the Academy's Presidium and the KP(b)U Central Committee.[24]

The importance of this topic can been seen in the harsh criticism a draft of chapter 1 of the *History of the Ukrainian SSR* suffered precisely because it 'muddled the question of the Slavs' origins.' The author, Lazar Slavin, a senior archaeologist, wrote that Soviet scholars 'were proving' the native roots of Slavs, while the Politburo commission thought that this had already been proved.[25] As late as 1952 the Ukrainian bureaucrats replaced Slavin with two younger archaeologists, who wrote the chapter anew. The new version stressed that the Slavs were natives of Central and Eastern Europe, but Hrushevsky had been wrong to see the ancestors of the Ukrainians in the ancient Antes: the sources 'undeniably attest to the common origins, as well as the linguistic and cultural unity of all southern and northern Eastern Slavic groups.' By comparing Ukrainian archaeological data with the results of excavations in Pskov and the upper Volga region, the authors sought to confirm the cultural unity of 'proto-Ukrainians' and 'proto-Russians' in the fifth and sixth centuries.[26]

Presenting the ancient sedentary agricultural Trypillian civilization (ca 3500–1400 BCE) as proto-Slavic was perhaps the single biggest temptation facing the authors. Even members of the Politburo commission suggested stressing the fact that Trypillian artefacts had been found both in the Kiev region and in Bukovyna, thus underscoring the ancient 'cultural unity of the population of Ukraine's Eastern and Western provinces.' Some reviewers, like Professor D. Poida of the Dnipropetrovsk Party Academy, insisted openly that the Trypillians were the ancestors of the Slavs. Although the 1953 edition of *History* did indeed point out that the Trypillians had settled mostly in Ukraine, from the Dnieper west to the Carpathian mountains, the text was silent on the settlers' relation to the Slavs. Unlike the 1951 limited edition, however, in the final version it was claimed that the Slavic archaeological relics in Eastern Europe dated as far back as the second millennium BCE. If true, this claim would have made the Slavs at least junior contemporaries of the Trypillians, but the authors did not risk elaborating on the possible connection.[27]

Preparing the chapter on Kievan Rus' presented a different quandary, because the Ukrainian Academy of Sciences did not have senior specialists on this period. This topic had been problematic since the authorities denounced Hrushevsky in the late 1920s and 1930s for claiming Kievan Rus' for Ukrainian history. Serafim Iushkov, the authority on ancient Kievan law, formally remained a member of the Institute of Ukrainian History until 1950, but since 1944 he had been teaching at Moscow University and had not written much for Kievans.[28] The Institute usually assigned chapters on Kievan Rus' to Kost Huslysty, whose own research interests were in the fourteenth to sixteenth centuries. Whereas the Institute's working plan for 1949 still showed Iushkov as working on a book about Kievan Rus', the report for 1946–50 listed no monographs or articles on this topic. Still, in his chapter for the *History*, Huslysty succeeded in portraying this state formation as the 'common cradle' of Russians, Ukrainians, and Belarusians. He even published the chapter summary as a separate booklet, *Kievan Rus' as the Cradle of Three Fraternal Peoples.*[29]

In 1950 Volodymyr Dovzhenok of the Institute of Archaeology published the pioneering book *Military Arts in Kievan Rus'*. He concentrated on the history of the (Ukrainian) Dnieper region, although the last two pages contained a brief account of Aleksandr Nevsky's victories over the German knights in the North during 1240–2. A reviewer for an authoritative Moscow journal criticized Dovzhenok for neglecting the military skills of the Grand Prince Andrei Bogoliubsky of Vladimir-Suzdal. The reviewer felt that the prince's marches on Novgorod and the Dnieper area had been particularly important because the 'Grand Prince engaged in the national defence of the Russian land.'[30] In his narrative, the Ukrainian archaeologist had, of course, intentionally suppressed Prince Andrei's march on Kiev in 1169, when the northeasterners had captured the city, pillaged and burned its churches and monasteries, and killed many of its inhabitants. It is astonishing that the Moscow reviewer wanted this episode not only restored but valorized. Yet Ukrainian historians never extended their praise to the Russians' 'great ancestor' Prince Andrei Bogoliubsky. Even in the much-edited volume 1 of the *History of the Ukrainian SSR* his march was characterized as a 'feudal internicine war,' which resulted in the 'ransacking' of Kiev. At the same time, a caution was issued against interpreting this war as a conflict between Russians and Ukrainians: 'it was a feudal war between princes who belonged to the same Old Rus' national-ity.'[31]

Stalinist ideologues saw as one of Hrushevsky's main sins his suggestion that the true successor of Kievan Rus' was the southwestern Galician-Volhynian Princi-pality rather than the northeastern Vladimir-Suzdal. After the war, Ukrainian functionaries displayed extraordinary sensitivity to any scholarly work on Galicia-Volhynia. In 1951 the censors banned the article 'On Some Questions of the History of Ukraine,' which the historian Fedir Shevchenko had written for the

Bulletin of the Ukrainian SSR Academy of Sciences, because the author proposed that 'the origins of Ukrainian statehood [were] in the principalities of south-western Rus', and especially in the Galician-Volhynian Principality.'[32] It is significant that during the first post-war decade the sole book on the principality was published in the capital by the Moscow historian V. Pashuto. Reviewers justly welcomed it as the 'first serious monograph on the history of the Western Ukrainian lands during the period of feudal fragmentation.'[33]

When Ukrainian historians began working on the survey, the problem of exactly when the three Eastern Slavic nations had emerged from the Kievan 'cradle' and developed into separate ethnic groups remained unresolved. Pressed by the ideological importance of dating the beginning of their people's ethnic difference from the Russians, Ukrainian specialists took the lead in the investigation of this issue. Based on the linguistic data, the republic's scholars proposed that the Russian, Ukrainian, and Belarusian nationalities (*narodnosti*) took shape during the fourteenth and fifteenth centuries. The discussion in *Voprosy istorii* during 1949–51 affirmed this dating, which eventually predominated in the Russian and Belarusian historical surveys as well. In 1952 the Moscow historian Militsa Nechkina acknowledged that, unlike her own textbook, the *History of the Ukrainian SSR* offered an innovative and sophisticated interpretation of the origins of the Russian and Ukrainian nationalities.[34]

Remembering the Empire

The topic of Ukraine's 1654 union with Muscovy dominated debates in Early Modern Ukrainian history. The terminological discussions focusing on Ukraine's incorporation into Russia serve as the best example of the complex interaction between historians and ideologues, as well as of the importance of language in the Stalinist narratives of the past. It is interesting that, when Ukrainian dissidents famously raised the question of 'incorporation' versus 'reunification' during the 1960s, they did not mention (or did not know) that the previous generation of historians had already opposed the term 'reunification' in the early 1950s.[35]

Until approximately 1950 both Soviet official pronouncements and scholarly works usually defined the events of 1654 as Ukraine's 'incorporation' into Russia. In Russian, the term was *prisoedinenie* and, in Ukrainian, *pryiednannia*.[36] Scholarly surveys of Russian and Ukrainian history up to and including the 1951 draft of the *History of the Ukrainian SSR* strictly observed the 'incorporation' idiom, whereas popular works like K. Osipov's biography of Khmelnytsky, which appeared in its second edition in 1948, used a confusing array of terms: *vossoedinenie* (reunification), *soedinenie* (unification), and *poddanstvo* (subjection).[37]

The term 'reunification' did not appear by accident in Osipov's book. The author freely borrowed facts and descriptions for his popular biography from nineteenth-century Russian historiography, especially from Kostomarov and his conservative contemporary Gennadii Karpov. On many occasions, Osipov's language betrays him. A Soviet historian of the 1930s would hardly say that Ukraine had 'surrendered herself into [Russian] subjection' (*ottdalas v poddanstvo*),[38] a fairly standard expression in nineteenth-century Russian history writing. The notion of 'reunification' comes from the same source. Russian imperial historians understood the Pereiaslav Treaty as the return of Russia's age-old possessions and considered Ukrainians simply a 'Little Russian tribe' of the Russian people. Hence, in many of the pre-revolutionary works Osipov consulted, Ukraine's incorporation into the Muscovite tsardom appeared as 'reunification.'[39] The new Soviet notion of 'reunification' thus represented a refurbished imperial concept.

In early 1950 the editors of the *Great Soviet Encyclopedia* solicited a long entry on Khmelnytsky from Petrovsky. Given the ideological importance of the hetman's deeds, they requested that the KP(b)U Central Committee sanction the text, which Ukrainian ideologues sent to the Institute of Ukrainian History and to the chair of history at the republic's Party Academy, Ivan Boiko. In his article, Petrovsky, who was very much in tune with the new ideological currents, twice used the word 'reunification.' The Institute wrote back that 'instead of "Ukraine's reunification with Russia," one should use the term "Ukraine's incorporation into Russia."' Boiko also spotted the innovation: 'Both at the beginning and at the end of his article, the author introduces the term "Ukraine's reunification with Russia." I think using the term "union" (*obedinenie*) or "incorporation" (*prisoedinenie*) here would be more correct. Only two branches of one and the same nation can reunite.'[40]

In early 1951 the Institute of Ukrainian History reported that it was still studying the history of 'incorporation.'[41] But the use of this term in the 1951 limited printing of the *History* unexpectedly prompted critical comments from the Institute of USSR History in Moscow. It is interesting that the Moscow historians took their cue from the *Pravda* article 'On the Opera *Bohdan Khmelnytsky*,' which criticized this recent production of the Kiev opera company for minor faults in the libretto and musical form. Although *Pravda*'s comments did not touch upon the portrayal of Russian-Ukrainian relations in the opera, the second sentence in the article read: 'This opera, as is known, is devoted to the events connected with the Ukrainian people's struggle for liberation from the yoke of the Polish gentry and for Ukraine's reunification with the Russian people.' The Moscow historians' critical comments apparently suggested adopting this term for 'incorporation.' In any case, their Ukrainian colleagues directly linked the criticisms to the *Pravda* article.[42]

In July 1952 the Ukrainian side sent Ivan Boiko, the author of the chapter on the War of Liberation, to Moscow. During a special meeting at the Institute of USSR History, he outlined the arguments against 'reunification.' The Kievans maintained that only two parts of one and the same nation can reunite, whereas by the mid-seventeenth century Ukrainians and Russians were definitely two separate peoples. Boiko went as far as digging up a *Pravda* interview with Stalin from 1918 in which he characterized the Ukrainians as having been the people most oppressed by Russian tsarism. An animated discussion followed. Some Moscow historians, such as E. Kusheva and N. Pavlenko, insisted that one could speak of 'reunification' because the territories of seventeenth-century Muscovy and Cossack Ukraine once were included in Kievan Rus'. In addition, both peoples had descended from a single Old Rus' nationality. A leading specialist on the nineteenth century, academician N. Druzhinin, shared this position. The majority, however, seemed to be in favour of 'incorporation.' L. Ivanov inquired sarcastically whether one should speak of France's 'reunification' with Germany simply because both countries had once been part of Charlemagne's empire. N. Ustiugov supported Ivanov, while the authority on the fifteenth and sixteenth centuries, academician Lev Cherepnin, went as far as announcing that *Pravda*'s formula was 'illiterate' (*negramotno*).[43]

The historians' conference in Moscow closed with an apparent victory for those wanting 'incorporation,' yet Nazarenko and the KP(b)U Central Committee's special commission overruled this conclusion in favour of 'reunification.' A group of Ukrainian historians then challenged the party decision. The material available in the archives preserves only circumstantial evidence about the ensuing conflict. On 28 October 1952 Nazarenko announced to a conference of the *History* authors and commission members: 'Boiko and Holobutsky notified the VKP(b) Central Committee that they do not agree with the formula we have adopted: "The reunification of the Ukrainian people with the Russian people under the Pereislav Treaty."' According to Nazarenko, the Kremlin ideologues did not support the Ukrainian protestors. Still, Boiko took the floor once more to summarize the arguments against 'reunification,' again stressing that the whole affair had started with a largely irrelevant *Pravda* article about an opera. Boiko announced that leading Ukrainian historians such as Fedir Shevchenko and Fedir Los also advocated the notion of 'incorporation,' while Oleksandr Kasymenko, the Institute's director, supported 'reunification.' Then Kasymenko and the commission members argued for 'reunification' on the grounds of the 'historical kinship' between Russians and Ukrainians.[44]

The debate flared up again during the commission's meeting with the authors on 22 November. This time, Ienevych suggested that the word *reunification* had a second meaning, that of the union between two fraternal peoples. An unidentified voice from the audience shouted: 'Ushakov's *Dictionary* [*of the Russian Language*] says that one can only reunite what has been previously separated [from the whole].' Nazarenko immediately intervened: 'There can be a reunification of two nations as well. Let us leave it at that.' Commission member O. Koshyk seconded him: 'This is how the article in *Pravda* put it.'[45] In late November and December of 1952 the commission continued meetings with the authors. At these gatherings, historians read the manuscript aloud paragraph by paragraph, changing 'incorporation' to 'reunification' throughout.[46]

Another conceptual change emanating from Moscow removed from historical narratives a residue of class history in the form of the 'lesser evil' theory. The restoration of Russian imperial concepts during and after the war made the notion of the 'lesser evil' frustratingly outdated. In 1951 Nechkina published a letter to the editor in *Voprosy istorii*, suggesting that this formula should be either dropped or reinterpreted as referring to the tsarist colonial policies rather than to incorporation into Russia in general. Although other historians for most part supported Nechkina, the official *Bolshevik* initially reprimanded *Voprosy istorii* for publishing discussions on the problems that 'have long been resolved in Marxist-Leninist scholarship.' Subsequently, however, the first secretary of the Communist party of Azerbaijan and the party authority on the nationality question, M.D. Bagirov, overturned this criticism in a speech to the Nineteenth Party Congress in October 1952. Bagirov also found fault with *Voprosy istorii*, but he expected the journal to make a clear statement on the 'progressive and fruitful nature of the incorporation of non-Russian peoples into Russia.'[47] After the Nineteenth Congress, the 'lesser evil' theory disappeared from both scholarly and journalistic works.

In the 1951 draft of the *History of the Ukrainian SSR* the 1937 party communiqué was dutifully cited and why Ukraine's incorporation into Russia represented a 'lesser evil' was explained. But even before the outcome of the discussions in Moscow became clear, some Ukrainian reviewers had suggested abandoning this term. Historians from Dnipropetrovsk University, in particular, insisted on revising the notion of the 'lesser evil.' Instead, they wanted the authors to stress the 'great historically positive role of this event' and proposed the term 'reunification' instead of 'incorporation.'[48] In the final version, indeed, there was no mention of the 'lesser evil' theory; instead, the union's beneficial consequences for Ukraine were elaborated on. As a result, the then innovative usage of the 'reunification' concept was justified: 'Both peoples' common origin in the Old Rus' nationality and the unbreakable unity of their subsequent historical development determined the constant and truly popular desire to reunite all the lands that from ancient times bore the name Rus'.'[49]

No post-1654 topic caused serious disagreements between the authors and their ideological supervisors. All variants of the survey routinely denounced as 'traitors' the Cossack hetmans who attempted to break Muscovy's hold over Ukraine. A standard formula explained that this or that hetman had betrayed the interests of the Ukrainian people by allying himself with Poland, Turkey, Sweden, or some other foreign power, but none was accused of trying to create an independent Ukrainian state as such. (A polity of this kind could have been an even 'lesser evil' for the Ukrainian people than the Russian Empire.) However, Hetman Demian Mnohohrishny (who ruled between 1669 and 1672) created a problem. The 1951 *History* held that he had intended to break the faith by establishing contacts not with a foreign power, but with the concurrent independent Ukrainian ruler of the territories west of the Dnieper, Hetman Petro Doroshenko. Because the Central Committee commission found such an explanation unacceptable, the charge against Mnohohrishny was dropped altogether from the 1953 *History*.[50]

The ideologues and historians studied the chapter on Ukraine during Hetman Mazepa's time with such attention that the commission members Kravchenko and Rumiantsev even brought charges of plagiarism against Professor Vadym Diadychenko. Having compared his text with previously denounced works on the topic, the two concluded that Diadychenko's chapter relied heavily on the pre-war writings of a later 'Nazi collaborator and nationalist émigré,' Oleksandr Ohloblyn. In addition to borrowing facts and descriptions, Diadychenko allegedly had 'snuck in Ohloblyn's concept of Ukrainian statehood.' After a prolonged investigation, the authorities shelved the accusation of plagiarism, while Diadychenko added more black paint to his already loathsome portrait of the 'traitor' Hetman Mazepa.[51]

The discussion of the rest of volume 1 revealed no significant interpretive changes or problematic points until the description of the Cyril and Methodius Brotherhood (1845–7), from which both nationalists and Ukrainian socialists would trace their ideological pedigrees. It was claimed in the 1951 version that student youth influenced by Shevchenko organized the society. Although Kostomarov, Kulish, and some other participants professed 'liberal' views, the group's political direction was 'determined primarily by the revolutionary views of Shevchenko and members close to him.' The society demanded the abolition of serfdom and 'raised the issue of creating an Ukrainian state within a federal republic of Slavic peoples.' These progressive demands testified to the 'growth of national-liberation aspirations' in Ukraine in the mid-nineteenth century.[52]

The reviewers noted that such an interpretation contradicted the 1946 party resolution on the journal *Vitchyzna*, which had warned against presenting the society as a revolutionary democratic body with no internal class contradictions between true revolutionaries and bourgeois liberals. Following this line, the Central Committee commission concluded in April 1952 that the text 'did not reveal the political profile of the Cyril and Methodius Brotherhood and the political struggle within it.'[53] Ukrainian functionaries knew well when it was time to protect themselves. Just a few months after the decision, in July 1952 *Bolshevik* attacked *Voprosy istorii* for a wide array of ideological errors that included publishing an article by the Ukrainian historian Leonid Kovalenko: 'One should strongly object to Kovalenko's article presenting the Cyril and Methodius Society as a revolutionary democratic organization and portraying Shevchenko as its head.' Instead, attention should have been paid to the struggle between the group's revolutionary and liberal wings.[54]

In the 1953 *History* the society was presented as an organization created by liberals, albeit later joined by Shevchenko and some other radical members. Now, the official line was that the two groups had clashed over how to implement the agrarian reforms and liberate Ukrainians from tsarist oppression. As well, according to the new account, the liberals were also bourgeois nationalists who treated Ukraine as an egalitarian nation without class antagonisms. 'Reflecting the interests of the emerging Ukrainian bourgeoisie, which was commencing its struggle for the national market,' the liberals advanced the idea of Ukrainian statehood – which was no longer as progressive a concept as it had been in the previous draft). Shevchenko and his fellow revolutionary democrats condemned these nationalistic tendencies, advocating instead a 'united republic of Slavic peoples.'[55]

The rest of the narrative charted two lines of succession in the national history: from the revolutionary democrats to Soviet Ukraine and from bourgeois liberals to present-day nationalists. Occasionally, the question as to which camp this or that figure should belong caused a minor debate, as in the case of Mykhailo Drahomanov,[56] but the historians were usually able to successfully apply the general party guidelines for delineating Soviet and nationalist ideological ancestry. The commission requested only that the bourgeois nationalists of the late-nineteenth-century *hromady* movement be condemned more explicitly in the text or that the 'revolutionary democrats' Ivan Franko, Lesia Ukrainka, and others be portrayed as their staunch opponents.[57] The last four chapters covering the period from 1900 to February 1917 elicited no criticism other than a comment about an abundance of 'verbatim quotations from the *Short Course* [of the party history] without attribution.'[58]

During 1952 the text of volume 1 underwent a final round of extensive reviewing, which resulted in an array of minor comments, but no major criticism.[59] Nevertheless, the Central Committee commission produced a long list of 'insufficiently explained' problems and demanded another round of revisions to be followed by the publication of a limited edition in January 1953 in conjunction with subsequent internal discussion of the text. The commission's principal recommendation was to ensure the presentation of pre-1917 Ukrainian history as an 'organic, integral, and inseparable part of the history of Russia.'[60]

In the end, the republic's ideologues postponed the publication of the *History of the Ukrainian SSR* until the first signs of political liberalization after Stalin's death.

Volume 1 was formally approved for publication on 23 December 1953 and appeared in the bookstores in the spring of 1954,[61] just in time for the lavish celebration of the tercentenary of Ukraine's union with Russia. Thus, paradoxically, a 'Stalinist history of Ukraine' was not published under Stalin.

Narrating the Nation

The monumental 800-page survey of the pre-revolutionary Ukrainian past opened with the statement, 'The Ukrainian people possess a heroic history that is centuries old and inseparably connected with the history of the great Russian people and the other peoples of our Fatherland.' Although due attention was paid to the development of 'productive forces,' the principal narrative line remained a story of statehood and nationhood. The writers extolled Kievan Rus', the common heritage of the three fraternal Eastern Slavic peoples, as the 'biggest and mightiest state in medieval Europe.' The Pereiaslav Treaty reunited 'two great Slavic peoples.' In a claim shared with many other imperial histories, the authors stressed that by joining Russia, the Ukrainians had not endangered their national identity; on the contrary, this act 'furthered the development of the Ukrainian nationality and its transformation into a nation.'[62]

Other jubilee publications of 1953–4 similarly suggested that the Ukrainians had reached full nationhood only because their ancestors had once joined the Russian Empire. Thus, Ivan Boiko's pamphlet *The Tercentenary of Ukraine's Reunification with Russia*, which had an impressive print run of 300,000 copies in Ukrainian and 230,000 in Russian, praised the 'wonderful fruits' of Russian-Ukrainian friendship such as Ukrainian statehood (in the form of the Ukrainian SSR) and the reunification of all Ukrainian lands in one polity.[63] The story of the empire thus remained a sum of the national narratives of the past. Although Ukraine's historical trajectory mouthed into the Russian Empire, the development of the Ukrainian nation remained the essence of its historical process. The republic's pedagogical journal, *Radianska shkola*, instructed schoolteachers to update the interpretations found in the standard textbook as follows:

> The textbook on USSR History for grade 8, edited by Professor A.M. Pankratova, presents the Ukrainian People's War of Liberation that began in the spring of 1648 under the leadership of the prominent statesman and military leader, the intelligent and far-sighted politician Bohdan Khmelnytsky, as a war against 'landlords' oppression and Polish domination.' In reality, the Ukrainian peasantry, which represented the main force in the liberation movement, fought not only against feudal oppression in all its forms and manifestations, but also for national independence (*za natsionalnu nezalezhnist*). The teacher should stress that, in the course of the War of Liberation, it

was precisely this factor that contributed to the Ukrainian people's increasingly insistent demands for reunification with the Russian people.[64]

Volume 1 of the *History* generally received good press. Both scholarly and political journals published highly positive reviews of the work, as did *Pravda*. At the Eighteenth Congress of the Ukrainian Communist Party in March 1954 Nazarenko praised the book *ex cathedra* as a work demonstrating that the Ukrainians' past had been 'connected inseparably with the history of the Russian people.'[65] However, the first signs of political liberalization after Stalin's death emboldened those Ukrainian intellectuals who saw the *History* as a retreat from the wartime promotion of national memory. One of them, the decorated partisan commander and writer Petro Vershyhora,[66] attacked the *History* in print. In his essay on the partisan movement that appeared in number 4 (1954) of the Moscow literary journal *Oktiabr*, Vershyhora criticized Ukrainian historians for insufficiently glorifying the Cossacks as a 'patriotic and freedom-loving element': 'For example, the evasive *History of Ukraine* (Kiev: The Ukrainian SSR Academy of Sciences Press, 1953) is, in my opinion, a disgraceful attempt to write history by leaving history out, by portraying the people's development without the brightest page of their early life, a page embodying the creativity of the masses and, most of all, of the toiling peasantry, who expressed their patriotism in the Cossack partisan war. This book is an example that should not be followed, a telling example of bureaucratic "double insurance" lacking the principal kernel of a historical study – patriotism.'[67] Vershyhora did not stop there. In April he submitted to *Pravda* a dismissive article on the *History*, accusing the writers of 'watering down everything heroic in the history of the Ukrainian people.' No wonder that Soviet readers continued to be attracted to the works of the old Ukrainian nationalist historians: 'I have personally heard many times both in Ukraine and in Moscow from our honest Soviet people, whose interest in the history of the fraternal commonwealth was ignited by the tercentenary celebrations, that they were reading Hrushevsky, Kulish or, at least, Kostomarov, but not our Soviet historical works.'[68]

Functionaries organized historians to rebuff the patriotic Ukrainian writer. Vershyhora was invited to Moscow, where the VKP(b) Central Committee ideological bureaucrats, Oleksii Rumiantsev and Anatolii Lykholat (both transplanted Ukrainians), denounced his views in the presence of four leading Russian historians (M. Tikhomirov, N. Druzhinin, A. Novoselsky, and A. Sidorov) and three Ukrainian specialists on the Cossacks (I. Boiko, V. Diadychenko, and K. Huslysty). In addition, reviews of the *History* in *Pravda* and *Voprosy istorii* cryptically referred to Vershyhora's 'irresponsible riposte.'[69]

The tercentenary prompted the final parole of Ivan Krypiakevcyh, the only remaining Ukrainian authority on the Khmelnytsky period. In 1953 this former 'nationalist' and 'fascist' published timely works such as *The Ties between Western Ukraine and Russia until the Mid-Seventeenth Century* and 'Bohdan Khmelnytsky as an Advocate of Ukraine's Reunification with Russia.' In the same year, the authorities promoted Krypiakevych to the directorship of the Institute of Social Sciences in Lviv.[70] His monumental biography of Khmelnytsky appeared in a luxurious edition in 1954. Even though the book's editor wrote several ideological insertions, fellow historians in Kiev found many of the ideas in this biography disturbing, undermining the imperial framework's limiting power over the national narrative. Reviewers criticized Krypiakevych's designation of the Cossacks as a 'central progressive force' in early modern Ukraine as an idealization. The author failed to stress that Khmelnytsky had wanted to reunite Ukraine with Russia from the first days of the war in 1648. Worse, he suggested that the Cossacks could have defeated the Poles on their own, but reviewers declared that this could have happened only with Russian assistance. Finally, Krypiakevych failed to provide a detailed critique of nationalistic historical concepts and did not sufficiently elaborate on the Ukrainians' ethnic and historic proximity to the Muscovites.[71]

The never-ending balancing act in historical narratives between the empire and the nation kept historians' productivity low. In addition, the preparation of a 'Stalinist textbook' of Ukrainian history consumed the time and energy of the republic's leading specialists for almost a decade. But by 1950 the project's base institution, the Academy of Sciences' Institute of Ukrainian History, had grown to eight departments and more than one hundred full-time researchers.[72] During the post-war years, historians repeatedly proposed that their research expertise be used on other major projects in Ukrainian history, only to be rebuffed by the party bureaucrats each time. In 1949 the Academy of Sciences petitioned the KP(b)U Central Committee to approve the preparation of a twenty-five-volume collection of sources, 'The History of Ukraine in Documents and Materials.' The project was conceived as a grandiose collaborative effort of the Institutes of Archaeology and Ukrainian History, several leading universities, and the Archival Administration. Scholars planned on producing the first seven volumes during 1949–50, adding six more volumes in each subsequent year until 1953. Although the Academy submitted a prospectus of the edition, the Central Committee simply shelved the matter.[73]

Ukrainian functionaries could have had a variety of reasons for not approving this imposing enterprise. The perceived need to concentrate all efforts on the survey, financial constraints, and an unwillingness to accept responsibility for the ideological supervision of another major project all could have contributed to such an outcome. The authorities similarly turned down – twice – the request for a Ukrainian historical journal. Since 1943 the Institute of Ukrainian History has been publishing an irregular series of *Naukovi zapysky* (Scholarly Transactions), only three volumes appearing by 1950. In 1948 the Institute reported to the KP(b)U Central Committee that it was ready and willing to publish as many as five or six issues annually, perhaps under the title *Pytannia istorii Ukrainy* (Issues in the History of Ukraine). Party functionaries rejected this proposal outright. D. Hnatiuk, head of the Publishing Section of the Central Committee's Press Department, attached the following resolution: 'Into the files [*V arkhiv*]. I recommend creating a more modest title for the transactions.'[74]

The Institute renewed its request in late 1950, but party ideologues again concluded that the 'creation of a journal was completely unjustified' and suggested that the historians submit their papers to Moscow's *Voprosy istorii*. In the end, the Central Committee did not allow Ukrainian historians to start their own journal until 1957, long after the completion of the *History* and the beginning of de-Stalinization.[75]

Still, historians used the tercentenary to secure financing for the publication of a large corpus of historical documents, the three-volume collection *The Reunification of Ukraine with Russia*. Despite its rather narrow title, this monumental publication began with documents from 1620 and provided unprecedented insight into the Cossack epoch. More than half of the documents in the collection (446 out of 747) appeared in print for the first time.[76] In the process of its preparation, Ukrainian historians requested that the Lenin Library manuscript division in Moscow return to the republic 6,000 files from the collection of the historian Mykola Markevych (Nikolai Markevich, 1804–60) containing the seventeenth- and eighteenth-century Ukrainian documents. Nazarenko supported the request, but the Lenin Library secured the backing of the VKP(b) Central Committee and agreed to transfer only the microfilms.[77]

Polish archivists, in contrast, proved eager to establish scholarly contacts with their Ukrainian colleagues. In October 1953 the Poles sent more than 2,500 microfilmed pages of historical documents on the Cossack period to Kiev, many of which were subsequently published in the three-volume collection. On 18 January 1954 (the day of the tercentenary) the Polish side presented the Ukrainian republic with thirty original historical documents. In May a delegation of the Polish Sejm donated another seventy-seven documents pertaining to Ukrainian history, including thirteen of Khmelnytsky's original decrees and one letter by Shevchenko.[78]

Aside from this breakthrough with Cossack documents, the authorities did not encourage major projects in Ukrainian history. Apparently, the Ukrainian ideologues designated the forthcoming two-volume *History of the Ukrainian SSR* as the sole ideologically approved source to which teachers, propagandists, and general readers should turn for the proper interpretation of the Ukrainian past.

That said, the 'Stalinist textbook' of Ukrainian history was not intended for use in schools. The history of Ukraine did not exist as a separate subject, although textbooks on USSR History covered landmarks of the Ukrainian past such as Kievan Rus', the Cossack Wars, and Shevchenko. Significantly, Moscow allowed non-Russian republics whose national histories did not lay concurrent claims on such signposts of Russian patrimony to teach them as separate school disciplines. Thus, in 1950 Armenian schoolchildren were spending 114 hours in grades 8, 9, and 10 studying their national history from a 1942 textbook.[79]

Ukrainian history teachers did discuss the republic's past, but only briefly and only when Ukrainian subjects surfaced in the general course on USSR history. Nonetheless, the Ukrainian publisher Radianska shkola translated the all-Union standard textbooks into Ukrainian and published them in mass editions.[80] Standard texts reflected the evolution of the Soviet concept of Ukrainian history, although in truncated and often confusing form. In 1948 a section of Shestakov's grade 4 textbook was entitled 'Ukraine's Struggle against Polish Domination and Its Incorporation into Russia.' In the 1955 edition, the same section was called 'Ukraine's Struggle for Its Liberation from Oppression by the Polish Gentry and [Its] Reunification with Russia.' The two editions also offered differing explanations for the union. The 1948 version read: 'The end of war was nowhere in sight. The Poles were plundering Ukraine. To escape from this difficult situation, Khmelnytsky in 1654 reached an agreement with the Muscovite tsar Aleksei that Ukraine be accepted under Russian suzerainty.' In the 1955 variant one sentence sufficed: 'Expressing the Ukrainian people's striving for union with the fraternal Russian people, Khmelnytsky approached the Russian government with the proposal that Ukraine be reunited with Russia.'[81]

The Ministry of Education recommended that, when covering Ukrainian topics, history teachers should take their students on tours to local historical monuments and to performances of Kocherha's *Iaroslav the Wise* and Korniichuk's *Bohdan Khmelnytsky*. The ministry also required that teachers find time to rebuff the falsifications of the Ukrainian bourgeois nationalists.[82] It is not clear to what degree the average teacher was able to follow these prescriptions. Clearly lacking the administrative capacity to control everyday school instruction, the authorities seemed to presume that teachers strictly followed the Moscow-approved textbooks and needed little guidance. Since Kaganovich's campaign in 1947, Ukrainian ideologues expressed no concern about possible confusion or nationalist deviations at the school level. Rare ideological audits of history teaching appear to have been uniformly positive; inspectors did not pay special attention to Ukrainian issues, and mistakes noted usually concerned the intricacies of the contemporary international situation.[83]

Meanwhile, teachers did find the ever-changing official line on history confusing. When in 1954 the CPSU Central Committee issued its authoritative *Theses* on the tercentenary, the teacher Kobyfa from Kirovohrad province welcomed them as putting 'an end to idle talk about Ukraine's reunification with Russia.' A certain Fesenko, a middle-rank ideologue from Chernivtsi province, also hoped that the document would 'put an end to the different interpretations of this problem by the instructors in educational institutions.'[84]

Mobilizing cadres from the provincial party committees, the Ukrainian ideologues could organize audits of history instruction at regional universities and pedagogical institutes, but discovering major problems (and taking the responsibility for their occurrence) was not in their best interests. Besides, after the campaigns of 1947 and 1951 historians themselves exercised extreme caution. In late 1951 the KP(b)U Central Committee inspected the work of fifty-eight departments of history at various Ukrainian universities and colleges without discovering any nationalistic errors. But since giving the historians a clean bill of health was ideologically risky, First Secretary Melnikov announced that most departments shared the same shortcomings. The instructors 'denounced bourgeois nationalist theories superficially and without real passion [*bez bolshoi strastnosti*],' occasionally relied on old textbooks or interpretations, and sometimes presented the Ukrainian past 'in isolation from the history of the Russian people.'[85]

Until Stalin's death and beyond, the uneasy symbiosis between Ukrainian functionaries and historians – a peculiar entanglement of control, denunciation, resistance, and collaboration – allowed both parties to survive within the oppressive environment of post-war Stalinism. The casualties of this cohabitation were many: historians accomplished little, ideologues could not completely control the writing and teaching of history, and teachers apparently struggled to instil in students both pride in their nation's past and an appreciation of Russian imperial credentials.

Chapter Six

Defining the National Heritage

In March 1951 Soviet Ukraine mourned the ninetieth anniversary of Taras Shevchenko's death. Innumerable speeches, meetings, newspaper articles, and radio broadcasts glorified the nineteenth-century Ukrainian bard as the nation's founding father, with the expression 'our father' (*nash batko*) often being slipped in among more official designations such as 'revolutionary democrat' and 'the founder of Ukrainian literature.' Shevchenko was the only topic to appear on the first three pages in the newspaper of the Ukrainian Writers' Union, *Literaturna hazeta*. The front-page headline read 'Forever Alive' – an epithet usually exclusively reserved in Soviet public discourse for the founding father of the Soviet State, Lenin.[1]

In his article in *Literaturna hazeta*, Stepan Kryzhanivsky proclaimed Shevchenko 'the pride of the Ukrainian socialist nation (*natsii*)' and thanked the party for teaching Ukrainians to value their sense of 'Soviet national pride.' At a memorial meeting in Kiev, the poet Andrii Malyshko concluded his speech with three slogans: 'Glory to the holy (*svitlyi*) genius, Taras Shevchenko, who lives and fights with us and who struggles with us for the happiness and peace of humankind! Glory to our noble people, who produce powerful talents such as his! Glory to our wise leader, the great friend of the Ukrainian people, our dear and beloved Comrade Stalin!'[2]

Every year in late May party and state officials, together with prominent intellectuals, led a solemn pilgrimage to Shevchenko's tomb on the Dnieper hills in Kaniv, a tradition established by the Ukrainian 'nationalist' intelligentsia in the late nineteenth century. By the early 1950s regular participants in these annual trips included professors and students at Kiev University and the Kiev Pedagogical Institute, scholars, writers, artists, composers, as well as representatives of the Kiev Opera Company and two leading professional choirs. In 1951 the KP(b)U Central Committee's internal memo stated approvingly, 'The annual trips that the capital's intelligentsia and students make to Shevchenko's tomb are highly popular.'[3]

These annual Shevchenko celebrations highlight the ambiguity of Soviet Ukrainian historical memory. Although the official discourse stressed Shevchenko's ties to Russian culture and his social views that allegedly anticipated socialism, the poet remained primarily a great 'ethnic' ancestor of all Ukrainians. Unlike the Russians or Uzbeks, Soviet Ukrainians identified themselves as his posterity, as did the émigré nationalists and the Western Ukrainian insurgents.

High Stalinism's idea of a 'nation' required, among other things, the possession of a great cultural tradition.[4] After 1945 celebration of the non-Russian cultural heritage increasingly came to include praise for Russian guidance, yet memorialization of their separate national cultures was prioritized in the republics' elaborate rituals of remembrance. Incorporating the Russian Empire or the 'friendship of peoples' within this empire into the local cults of national heritage proved difficult, warranting the extraordinary attention and vigilance of Stalinist ideologues.

The Ukrainian Classics

The Soviet notion of the Ukrainian 'national classics' referred primarily to the nineteenth century, when the indigenous intelligentsia began developing modern Ukrainian high culture based on the peasant vernacular and folk traditions. To all intents and purposes, Soviet ideologues and intellectuals co-opted the pantheon of national classics established by the Ukrainian pre-revolutionary intelligentsia. Shevchenko topped this pantheon's structure as the 'nation's father,' while Franko implicitly occupied the role of a somewhat junior father figure specifically for Western Ukrainians. To be sure, Soviet representations of these and other classical writers emphasized their political radicalism and connections to Russian culture.

During the post-war decade, figures who had been valorized during the war, such as Kulish or the poet and educator Borys Hrinchenko, came to be suspected of 'nationalism,' and the ideological censors gradually dropped them from the canon of Ukrainian classics. Newspapers no longer claimed Gogol as a 'great son of Ukraine,' but rather hailed him as a 'great Russian writer' with the 'closest of ties to Ukraine.' Ivan Kotliarevsky, the author of the first literary work in modern Ukrainian, preserved his traditional place of honour, although his biographers now highlighted Kotliarevsky's military service in the volunteer corps during the Russian Empire's war with Napoleon.[5]

Most important, however, was the national cult of Shevchenko. Even at the height of the *Zhdanovshchina*, the annual commemorative rallies featured practically unreserved glorification of the 'great father,' whose 'image lives and will always remain in the hearts of the Ukrainian people.'[6] At the same time, the republic's ideologues asserted that Soviet Ukraine embodied Shevchenko's dream of a 'new and free family' and denied the émigré nationalists' claim to his spiritual inheritance. Post-war Soviet statements on Shevchenko presented the 'great son of the Ukrainian people' as a 'revolutionary democrat,' who had headed the radical wing of the Cyril and Methodius Brotherhood. As well, the bard had allegedly maintained close contacts with Russian radicals, admired Russian culture, and despised contemporary Ukrainian 'bourgeois nationalists.'[7]

The official discourse also increasingly cast 'junior' classical writers, such as Franko or Lesia Ukrainka, as revolutionaries and allies of progressive Russian culture. Depending on the current political atmosphere, the press presented Franko as a fighter against either 'bourgeois nationalism' or 'rootless cosmopolitanism,' and occasionally against both these opposite trends simultaneously.[8] The pre-war and wartime patriotic interpretation of the Ukrainian classics now appeared heretical. The KP(b)U Central Committee banned V. Diachenko's book *Mykola Lysenko* because it highlighted the classical composer's role in the Ukrainian national movement, speaking 'too much about Ukrainian culture and too little about the friendship [of peoples].' As it turned out, the author was killed in action during the war and his book had been submitted to the publisher in 1941, when its Ukrainian focus was not considered unorthodox.[9]

The republic's ideologues proceeded carefully in their construction of cults devoted to several more 'junior' classical writers who had lived during the late ninetieth and early twentieth centuries. On 6 May 1949 Khrushchev wrote to Stalin asking for permission to celebrate the centenary of the writer Panas Myrny (1849–1920): 'In his novels *Do Oxen Bellow When the Cribs Are Full?*, *Fallen Woman*, and others, he vividly described the process of class differentiation among the peasants, the exploitation of the poor by the landlords and kulaks, and the growth of the revolutionary movement in the countryside. In his creative work, Panas Myrny demonstrated close links to progressive nineteenth-century Russian writers.'[10] The central Agitprop replied that the Ukrainian authorities did not actually need the Kremlin's permission to celebrate the anniversary in the republic, but Moscow approved the proposal in any case.[11] Within months, Myrny was extolled in the Ukrainian press as 'our national pride,' a 'realist' writer and democrat who, sadly, 'did not rise to Social Democracy.' The government sanctioned the publication of his works, the naming of a street in Kiev after him, and the construction of a monument to him in Poltava.[12]

The populist poet Pavlo Hrabovsky, who had been involved in the Russian *narodniki* revolutionary movement and had died in Siberian exile in 1902, appears to have been a more promising candidate for the role of classical writer linking the national tradition with both Russian culture and the Russian revolutionary heritage. On the 50th anniversary of his death, a KP(b)U Central Committee internal memo proposed that the poet be designated a thinker who had 'accepted Marxism and become its propagandist.' But a senior bureaucrat edited out this untenable claim, and the official pronouncements honoured Hrabovsky as simply a revolutionary poet.[13]

As the republic's ideologues were weighing various writers' revolutionary credentials, Ukrainian intellectuals pushed for the canonization of the famous nineteenth-century blind peasant bard, Ostap Veresai (1803–90). In 1950 the Institute of Ukrainian Art and Folklore, the Writers' Union, and the Composers' Union proposed that the 60th anniversary of his death be commemorated. Veresai, however, had the misfortune of having been invited to perform before the tsar and of being admired by the 'nationalists.' Accordingly, party functionaries advised against this 'untimely' celebration. In 1952 the KP(b)U Central Committee agreed to celebrate the 150th anniversary of his birth in 1953, albeit 'on a more modest scale than the authors had proposed,' without an official festival or the erection of a monument.[14]

Although they often disagreed in their appraisals of specific cultural figures, Ukrainian bureaucrats and intellectuals collaborated in a peculiar 'codification' of the national classics during the post-war decade that was made necessary in the historical memory of High Stalinism by the advent first of the nation and then of the empire. Initially, the Ukrainian elites attempted to collect the surviving manuscripts of all prominent nineteenth-century literary figures in one Kiev depository. In 1949 Korniichuk submitted a proposal to Khrushchev that the heritage of several of the most eminent writers be declared state property. Private persons possessing manuscripts by Kotliarevsky, Shevchenko, Franko, Lesia Ukrainka, and Kotsiubynsky then would have been required to surrender these documents to state organizations. Incredibly, the Politburo rejected this idea as 'infringing on the right to personal property guaranteed in the Constitution.'[15] Nevertheless, the KP(b)U Central Committee supported the Institute of Ukrainian Literature in its efforts to retrieve valuable manuscripts from Russian depositories. As a result of Nazarenko's letter to Suslov, the Theatrical Library in Leningrad turned over the originals of many Ukrainian classical plays from the archives of the Kiev Censorship Committee.[16]

The republic's authorities also supported the plan to concentrate all manuscripts of Ukrainian classical writers in the Manuscript Section of the Institute of Ukrainian Literature. By 1950 this depository held 'practically all' the surviving writings of Shevchenko, Franko, and Myrny, as well as the majority of the other classics manuscripts. With help from the party and the government, the Institute sponsored major efforts in 1950 and 1953 to purchase or otherwise obtain remaining originals from Russian archives and personal collections.[17] The Institute's depository enriched itself at the expense of other Ukrainian museums and research institutions as well. In 1950 the entire archives of Ivan Franko were moved from

Lviv to Kiev, where a twenty-volume collection of the writer's works was then in preparation. When, three years later, Lviv enquired about the fate of the archives, the Central Committee apparatus advised First Secretary Oleksii Kyrychenko that Franko's manuscripts should remain in the capital.[18]

The second stage in the codification process concerned editing and publishing the national classics in new and definitive Soviet editions. During the late 1940s the authorities initiated several grand projects that included no fewer than two 'complete' editions of Shevchenko's oeuvre. The first version of the poet's *Complete Works* appeared in 1949 in three large, luxurious volumes with an impressive print run of 100,000 and an incredible price of merely 50 rubles, but it included only 'selected letters' and a portion of Shevchenko's artwork. By the end of 1951 the Institute of Ukrainian Literature had prepared five of an envisaged ten volumes of another, more academic edition under the same name. The project's researchers sought to undo the editorial changes introduced by the poet's 'bourgeois-national-ist' mentors and, in particular, substituted the original draft of Shevchenko's autobiography for the traditional version edited by Kulish. The Institute also prepared new ideologically sound commentary for the edition. The first six volumes went to press during the early 1950s, but the colour reproduction of Shevchenko's artwork in the last four volumes required such sophisticated poly-graphic technology that it had to be completed in Moscow.[19]

In May 1950 the Institute also prepared the twenty-volume *Works* of Ivan Franko for publication, with the intention of having the entire series published during 1950–1. Although newspaper coverage did not report any omissions, the editors excluded several of Franko's political articles and poems that espoused what might be perceived as his 'nationalistic' views. In any case, in 1954 publication of both the ten-volume Shevchenko collection and the twenty-volume Franko set remained incomplete.[20]

Financial and human resources in post-war Ukraine could not fully support this drive to codify and canonize the national classics by subsidizing luxurious multi-volume editions of all prominent cultural figures. In 1945 the authorities an-nounced a plan to publish a thirty-one-volume complete works of the 'founder of Ukrainian national music,' Mykola Lysenko. By 1950 this project had shrunk to twenty volumes, although their publication was nowhere in sight. When celebrat-ing the 75th anniversary of Lesia Ukrainka's birth in 1946, the authorities decreed the publication of her complete works in fifteen volumes, but when commemorat-ing the eightieth anniversary five years later, the republic's bureaucrats tacitly suppressed the old plan and promised instead to publish a three-volume collection of her work. In contrast to this last decision, the Institute of Ukrainian Literature reported in 1954 that it was preparing a five-volume edition of her oeuvre. As of August 1954 the publication of the works of Panas Myrny in five volumes,

Mykhailo Kotsiubynsky in five, Marko Vovchok in six, Vasyl Stefanyk in three, and Pavlo Hrabovsky in two volumes remained unfinished.[21]

During 1948–9, however, the authorities succeeded in publishing in one-volume mass editions the selected works of the majority of the Ukrainian classical writers. These selections appeared in two popular series, 'The Ukrainian Classical Novel' and 'Kolkhoz Library.' Although the state kept book prices artificially low, the population could not afford to collect the 'national classics' during the late 1940s. In 1949 the bookstores of Drohobych province in Western Ukraine received 990 copies of Franko's one-volume works and sold 175 copies, or 17.68 per cent. Kotliarevsky's works sold slightly better (20 per cent) and Kotsiubynsky's much worse (9.74 per cent), but these figures actually represented success compared with the sales of Soviet literary works and political literature. Aleksandr Fadeev's *The Rout*, for example, was able to manage only 3.76 per cent and Dmitrii Furmanov's *Chapaev* 4.21 per cent. Amazingly, none of the 400 subscribers to Lenin's multi-volume *Collected Works* in Ukrainian in the city of Drohobych picked up volumes 1 and 2, and only 9 out of 350 cared to collect the 7 available volumes of Stalin's *Works*.[22] In impoverished post-war Drohobych, Ukrainian classics appear to have been more popular than the writings of the Soviet leaders.

Literary scholars carefully edited out ideologically problematic passages from the classical works before sending them to print. As the Institute of Ukrainian Literature reported to First Secretary Kyrychenko in 1954, 'Literary works and other material by the Ukrainian classical writers (some letters, notes, etc.) are not included in their collected works if these materials are not of socio-political or literary-historical importance, or if they might prompt in the present-day reader a reaction incompatible with the Soviet policy of mass education. By the way, the amount of such material in the Ukrainian classical heritage is insignificant.'[23]

Yet the party apparatus did not rely on the scholars' 'internal censors.' In 1951 the Central Committee's experts halted the publication of volume 4 of Kotsiubynsky's *Works* because some of his letters 'contained certain uncharacteristically erroneous statements.' The functionaries demanded that the letters in which Kotsiubynsky acknowledged the influence of Ibsen and Maeterlink and referred to his literary school as 'European' be excluded, as well as his correspondence with the 'nationalists' Mykola Shrah, Borys Hrinchenko, and Mykhailo Komarov, in which the writer had approved of their activities, mentioned Hrushevsky, and made problematic comments about Russians.[24] In a communication to Nazarenko, Oleksandr Biletsky, the director of the Institute of Ukrainian Literature, strongly defended the original selection of letters, but to no avail. The debate between the Institute, the State Publishing House (Derzhlitvydav), and the Central Committee lasted more than ten months, delaying the completion of Kotsiubynsky's five-volume *Works* for years.[25] The censors likewise banned the publication of Myrny's letters to the publishing house Vik simply because they were addressed to Serhii Iefremov, its 'nationalist' director. The Institute proposed dropping Iefremov's name and including the valuable letters in Myrny's *Works*, but the Central Committee apparatus shelved the matter. Eventually, Myrny's *Works* were published without his letters to Iefremov.[26]

In the House of History

In early 1950 Ukrainian authorities turned their attention to the sites where ordinary citizens encountered the past: the republic's museums. The government decreed a total audit of all existing museums and an ideological revision of their expositions, which were henceforth to be approved by special commissions. The edict expected historical museums to 'display the heroic history of the Ukrainian people in connection with the history of the great Russian people and other fraternal peoples of the USSR.' It instructed Western Ukrainian museums to 'stress the common origins and historical unity of the Russian, Ukrainian, and Belarusian peoples' and required that all historical museums open separate sections devoted to the Soviet period. The document specifically demanded the construction of a museum in Poltava commemorating the Russian victory over the Swedish army and the 'traitor' Hetman Mazepa in 1709. [27]

In June Iakiv Sirchenko, the head of the Committee on Cultural and Educational Institutions, reported to Nazarenko on the measures that the museums had taken in response to the decree. Although the minister prepared this memo to show how the decree had changed the work of the museums, his report unwittingly portrayed the field in a state of total disarray. Museums reported on whatever they had accomplished recently rather than on how they had implemented the official directive. The Dnipropetrovsk Historical Museum described the development of its section on the Zaporozhian Host 'and its importance for the Ukrainian people's struggle for liberation.' The Lviv Historical Museum boasted of its new archaeological section, which 'proved that the Slavs were autochthonous settlers of Western Ukrainian lands.' Although the Dnipropetrovsk museum planned on creating a separate Soviet history section, its Lviv counterpart did not even have a display on the eighteenth and nineteenth centuries. Moreover, the KP(b)U Central Committee inspectors found that the materials on the earlier times neither uncovered the reactionary role of the Uniate Church nor highlighted the region's historical ties with Russia. The republic's ideologues focused their attention on the shortcomings of museum work in Western Ukraine, although museums in the East also were not reporting impressive achievements. The only breakthrough seemed to be the accelerated construction of the Museum of the Battle at Poltava.[28]

What is more, the 1950 decree and subsequent reports neglected to mention a disturbing fact looming large in archival correspondence. In mid-1950 the Central Committee apparatus presented to First Secretary Melnikov statistical data on museum attendance showing that the Kievan Caves Monastery was the most popular historical museum in Ukraine. In 1949 it registered 110,700 visitors, compared with 73,100 at the Shevchenko Museum in Kiev and 70,200 at the new Museum of the Defence of Odessa. During the first ten months of 1950 the Caves Monastery reported 137,000 visitors, compared with 80,000 at the Shevchenko Museum and 49,835 at the State Historical Museum in Kiev, which ranked third that year.[29]

The Kievan Caves Monastery was more than simply a cluster of museums or a 'historical-cultural preserve.' Occupying a picturesque site in a park high up in the Dnieper hills, the golden-domed churches of this eleventh-century monastery represented a vivid material link to Kievan Rus', whose first known chronicler, artist, and doctor were monks in the Kievan Caves. The monastery's many other monuments attested to the vitality of Ukrainian early modern culture, particularly the development of printing and higher learning. For centuries, the Kievan Caves Monastery, with its relics and tombs of the holy hermits, had served as one of the most popular places of pilgrimage in the Russian Empire. Soviet authorities used its buildings to house the museums of Historical Treasures (primarily church antiquities provided with materialistic interpretations), of the Book and Book Printing, of the Theatre, of the Ukrainian Decorative Folk Arts, and others.

Visitors, however, were attracted primarily to the historical site itself. Some complained that none of the museums featured a coherent display on the history of the Kievan Caves Monastery; others regretted the absence of postcards with views of the monastery's golden domes.[30] To complicate matters further, the wartime rapprochement between the Soviet state and the Orthodox Church had enabled a small community of monks to return to the Kievan Caves. Purely religious pilgrimages resumed as well, to the consternation of Ukrainian ideologues. In one curious episode, in 1952 a rumour spreading among pilgrims put the KP(b)U Central Committee on alert. The monks allegedly were telling visitors that the hermit Archbishop Antonii, who was buried at the entrance to the Near Caves, had been Comrade Stalin's teacher at the Gori Church Seminary and until the end of his life had corresponded with the Soviet leader.[31] Public interest in the Kievan Caves forced Ukrainian functionaries to pay special attention to this museum complex, which was, ideologically, not high on their list of priorities. The official correspondence of the time shows considerable concern about the maintenance and renovation of the Kievan Caves Historical-Cultural Preserve.[32]

Ukrainian authorities realized that, as a historical site, the Kievan Caves Monastery embodied Kiev's past religious glory and that visitors were motivated by this 'holy city's' traditional place in Ukrainian and Russian historical memory. Accordingly, they instructed museum guides to cast the monastery's buildings and treasures as 'history of Eastern Slavic material culture.'[33] Periodic cleansings of museum holdings were aimed primarily at church history and religious art. Thus, a 1953 report on writing off the 'decrepit and less valuable' engravings lists the eighteenth-century portraits of bishops and Prince Volodymyr the Saint as well as a depiction of Christ's interment and other religious works.[34]

Triggered by *Pravda*'s editorial 'Against Ideological Distortions in Literature' in July 1951, the ideological purge of Ukrainian culture did not affect the museums until the late autumn. On 13 September *Pravda*'s Lviv correspondent M. Odinets initiated the critique with his article 'What Do Lviv's Museums Popularize?' The authoritative newspaper's envoy announced that the Lviv Historical Museum had indulged in undue glorification of princes, lords, sultans, Cossack colonels, and bishops. Most disturbing, the display on Kievan Rus' featured an unidentified twelfth-century princely skull on a stand with a glass case. In general, the exposition allegedly downplayed major themes such as class struggle and the Ukrainian people's efforts to reunite with their Russian brethren. The Lviv State Museum of Ukrainian Art emphasized the old Ukrainian artistic tradition over the achievements of the Soviet period. The Lviv Art Gallery featured an impressive collection of Polish, German, Austrian, Italian, and Dutch paintings 'in splendid frames,' but a mere thirty-two works out of five hundred represented the Russian nineteenth-century classics. Worse, the gallery had no more than a dozen Soviet paintings.[35]

The *Pravda* article resulted in heightened attention being paid to Ukrainian museums in the latter phase of the ideological purge during October and November 1951. On 15 November the KP(b)U Central Committee decreed that museums improve their portrayal of the friendship of peoples, class struggle, and Soviet achievements. Kiev party authorities reacted by firing several employees at the State Historical Museum who had remained in the city under Nazi occupation, had been POWs, or had relatives in the Gulag. The Kherson provincial committee requested that the local historical museum create a display on the ancient Slavs, add more materials on the union with Russia, and drastically improve the display on Soviet history. Vinnytsia authorities ordered that their museums improve their depiction of historical ties with Russia, as well as the Soviet present. In Drohobych and Chernivtsi, local functionaries also focused on the portrayal of Russian-Ukrainian friendship and Soviet achievements.[36]

It is not surprising that Ukrainian ideologues paid special attention to the errors of the Lviv museums. At the November 1951 plenary meeting of the Central Committee, Sirchenko stated that 'it would not be enough to merely put away the princely skull and the lords' portraits,' and that the Lviv Historical Museum needed a radical review of its entire exposition.[37] The museum did not close its doors, receiving more than 55,000 visitors during 1951. At the same time, its staff proceeded to create a new exhibition on prehistoric times, to dismantle a display on Greek and Scythian cities along the Black Sea coast, and to prepare a new exhibition on Kievan Rus'. Given the *Pravda* critique, the museum submitted the new plan of its Kievan Rus' section to the KP(b)U Central Committee for approval. The museum's staff also revised the display on the early modern period to highlight cultural ties with Muscovy during the sixteenth and seventeenth centuries and started working on exhibitions devoted to the periods of Capitalism and Socialism. However, these displays were not ready until late in 1954.[38]

Before historians at the Lviv Historical Museums began preparing new displays, the local functionaries had 'removed documents and exhibits distorting the history of the Ukrainian people, as well as reviewed the whole exposition and cleared rubbish (*khlam*) from it.'[39] During 1952 the authorities continued a similar purge of expositions in other Ukrainian museums under the guise of 'removing exhibits without historical value.' These included artefacts that did not fit into the Soviet version of Ukrainian historical memory. For instance, the regional historical museum in Poltava destroyed the engravings of Hetman Mazepa, photos of Ukrainian icons, and portraits of nineteenth-century 'nationalists' such as Kulish and Pavlo Chubynsky. In Lviv, Lytvyn, the former Central Committee secretary for ideology and now the first secretary of the provincial party committee, personally supervised the destruction of the 'nationalistic and anti-Soviet' holdings of the State Museum of Ukrainian Art. Portraits of the Habsburg emperors, bishops of the Uniate Church, and the Ukrainian Sich Sharpshooters were burned and the sculptures smashed with a hammer.[40]

In a case typical for the Western provinces, in February 1952 Rivne party bureaucrats reviewed the exposition of the local historical museum. They criticized the pre-Soviet painting *Pope Innocent III in 1206 Asks Prince Roman of Halych to Accept Catholicism* as reflecting the influence of Polish bourgeois historical concepts, complete with 'diminishing Russia's historic role.' The museum did not sufficiently highlight the emergence of Moscow, paid too much attention to the 1569 union between Poland and Lithuania, and did not show Shevchenko's ties to Russian revolutionary democrats. Following the audit, museum workers set about correcting the exposition.[41]

By March 1952 major historical museums in Kiev, Kharkiv, and Chernivtsi reported the completion of their revisions, while others were still restructuring their displays. In July the KP(b)U Central Committee reiterated the same directives in another decree on museums and in 1953 ordered one more survey of the museums' compliance.[42]

At least in some cases, the party's ideological regimentation of Ukrainian museums led to ambiguous results. Before the campaigns of the early 1950s the

State Museum of Ukrainian Art in Kiev had no exhibition on Kievan Rus'; the exposition began with sixteenth-century Ukrainian folk art and icons. The State Museum of Russian Art in Kiev, however, boasted a collection of ancient Kievan icons, including the famous thirteenth-century image of Saints Borys and Hlib.[43] In early 1951 the Museum of Ukrainian Art closed its doors for renovations and exposition restructuring aimed at demonstrating the 'beneficial influence' of Russian art. In practice, this reorganization resulted in an imposing display of ancient Kievan art as part of the Ukrainian cultural heritage. The authorities transferred numerous ceramic bowls and jewellery to the museum from the Archaeological Museum as well as bas-relief carvings of Samson and Delilah from the Kievan Caves Monastery. While reviewing the new exposition in 1952, the government commission's members recommended 'collecting more Kievan Rus' art.' The press also suggested building up the Kievan Rus' section.[44]

The artist Mykhailo Derehus, who was known for his work on the Cossack epoch and who had just assumed the museum's directorship, proposed that the portrait of the Russian imperial bureaucrat Prince Dolgorukii, painted in the characteristic Cossack style of the early eighteenth century, be removed from the exhibition because it was 'not of significant interest.' The commission members supported Derehus's suggestion to display a 'unique' portrait of the Cossack nobleman Myklashevsky in its stead. First Secretary Melnikov himself demanded the inclusion of more 'Ukrainian classical painting.'[45] As a result of such restructuring, the new exposition claimed the art of Kievan Rus' for Ukrainian historical memory and boosted national pride by presenting a comprehensive display of Ukrainian artistic accomplishments during the Cossack period and the age of national revival.

The republic's authorities never seemed satisfied with the role of memorial museums devoted to the Ukrainian classical writers. On the one hand, the Stalinist notion of nationhood included the commemoration of the creators of national culture. On the other, during the post-war decade Ukrainian ideologues felt the need to modify the solemnization of the Ukrainian heritage by stressing both historical Russian guidance and the resulting Soviet present. In 1952 the Committee on Cultural and Educational Institutions reported to the Ukrainian party leadership that the ongoing restructuring of expositions in literary memorial museums was 'directed at portraying more profoundly the ideological content of a writer's works, a writer's role in the development of progressive Ukrainian literature, [a writer's] struggle for the social and national liberation of the Ukrainian people, working for the friendship with the great Russian people and against the enemies of the Ukrainian people, the Ukrainian bourgeois nationalists.'[46] The question remained whether this interpretation would sufficiently modify the primary symbolic role of classical writers as the great builders of the national culture.

Kotliarevsky, who was the first to write literary works in the peasant vernacular, could not be cast as a 'revolutionary' of any kind, but in 1950 the authorities opened a museum in his Poltava house. Second Secretary Kyrychenko deemed it appropriate to pay homage to the museum during his visit to the city in January 1953.[47] Shevchenko, Franko, and Lesia Ukrainka could, with varying degrees of success, be presented as revolutionaries and friends of Russia, but many of their mentors and comrades-in-arms were 'nationalists.' Although plans existed to open a Lesia Ukrainka Museum in Kiev, the government's lack of financing did not allow for this during the post-war decade. The Franko Museum in Lviv had been in operation since 1946, and during the museum audit of early 1950 it successfully revised its exposition 'in the spirit of Soviet literary scholarship.' In contrast, the local ideologues deemed the display in a small memorial museum in Franko's native village 'unacceptable.' After extensive renovations and restructuring of the exposition, the museum reopened its doors in 1951.[48]

In addition to the museums in Shevchenko's native village, the poet's tomb in Kaniv, and his house in Kiev, the State Shevchenko Museum was solemnly opened in the capital in April 1949. As noted earlier, it soon became the second most attended historical museum in the republic after the Kievan Caves Monastery. Between 1949 and 1954 more than 542,000 people visited the museum.[49] Ukrainian ideologues, meanwhile, were constantly concerned that Shevchenko be properly represented in the museum's exposition. In 1953 the Central Committee apparatus did not allow the museum to commission a painting entitled *T.H. Shevchenko among the Members of the Cyril and Methodius Brotherhood* because such a canvas would inevitably have portrayed the 'nationalists' Kulish and Kostomarov as the great poet's comrades-in-arms.[50] After all the ideological audits of the early 1950s, the KP(b)U Central Committee concluded in 1954 that the museum's presentation of Shevchenko as revolutionary and its depiction of his ties with Russia were not 'sufficient.'[51]

Mindful of the forthcoming tercentenary of the 1654 union with Russia, Ukrainian functionaries and museum workers became obsessed with exhibitions on the Early Modern period. During 1952–3, the republic's museums acquired and put on display hundreds of exhibits pertaining to the Cossack period. The new expositions ostensibly highlighted the friendship of peoples and the Ukrainians' desire to unite with their Russian brethren, but they also restored the Cossack glory, somewhat suppressed after the campaigns of 1947 and 1951, to its previous place in official national memory. The Kiev Historical Museum bought three original decrees by Khmelnytsky. The Chernihiv museum displayed its rich collection of Cossack artefacts, including Khmelnytsky's sabre, numerous historical documents, and authentic Cossack clothing and arms. The government upgraded the status of the Pereiaslav-Khmelnytsky regional museum to republican and provided it with spare Cossack arms from the Moscow Historical Museum as well as with enough money to purchase Derehus's monumental painting *The Pereiaslav Council*. The Kharkiv museum acquired Cossack arms, portraits of the Cossack leaders, and numerous historical paintings. The Kharkivites could afford the originals of seven canvases, including Soviet works and pre-revolutionary paintings, such as Feodosii Krasytsky's *A Guest from the Zaporozhian Host* (1901; variants 1910 and 1916), a work previously cited as an example of the nationalistic 'romantic idealization' of the Ukrainian past.[52]

Sites of Remembrance

The Soviet authorities' management of historical monuments and memorials during the post-war decade reveals both a desire for total ideological control over historical sites and a lack of financial and administrative means for such supervision. They pushed for a comprehensive cataloging of historical monuments, resulting in the still-incomplete Ukrainian inventory, which in 1953 included 43,206 historical and 4,002 archaeological monuments. Although the overwhelming majority of 'historical monuments' were wartime graves of Soviet soldiers, the effort was impressive nonetheless.[53]

Unfortunately, the preservation of monuments did not move far beyond the creation of a database for them. The Zbarazh fortress (1631), a relic of the Cossack wars and a registered historical site, illustrates well the plight of historical monuments located far from the capital. Soldiers from a Soviet Army unit that was stationed in the fortress were dismantling it and using the bricks for their construction needs. Acting on a message from local intellectuals, the deputy premier in charge of culture, the poet Mykola Bazhan, was able to put a halt to the destruction but not to restore the damage or relocate the military detachment.[54]

The Ukrainian authorities struggled to maintain at least the most famous historical monuments in the largest cities. Even minor maintenance work on historical sites in Kiev forced Bazhan to search for unorthodox financing solutions. In 1947 he was able to allocate modest funds for strengthening the walls of St Cyril's Church and financing excavations on the territory of the eleventh-century St Sophia Cathedral, but he failed to persuade the city council to finance maintenance work in the tenth-century Zvirynets caves. The city provided 47,000 rubles to strengthen the ruins of the eleventh-century Golden Gate 'with the aim of preventing their further deterioration,' but this sum covered only the purchase of the bricks, cement, and sheet iron, while the actual work had to be postponed until 1949. In 1948 the Commission on the Preservation of the Monuments of Culture and Antiquity, which Bazhan also headed, approved the lease of the capital's major landmark, the eighteenth-century St Andrew's Church, to the Russian Orthodox Church because the lessee had promised to undertake much-needed renovations.[55]

By 1951 another Kievan symbol, the monument to Prince Volodymyr the Saint (1853), also needed urgent renovations. The bronze statue standing with a cross high on the Dnieper hills was covered with rust, the bas-relief carvings on its pedestal were damaged, and the monument itself was leaning forward after a landslide. The city authorities fully cooperated with Bazhan's Commission, but the Kiev Administration of Architecture declined to finance renovations because the statue was not listed in any catalogue of architectural monuments. Instead, it was found on a list of historical monuments, which typically included authentic old buildings and a handful of later monuments commemorating momentous historical events.[56] Since the statue's point of reference was the baptism of Kievan Rus', its place on the Ukrainian Soviet register of historical monuments was significant in itself.

For the moment, it created only more bureaucratic confusion. Fortunately, the list of all-Union architectural treasures included a statue of St Volodymyr by the famous sculptor Petr Klodt, and in 1953 the Ukrainian functionaries cleared the question of renovations with the USSR Ministry of Culture. The Kiev provincial Soviet, which technically had no authority over the capital city and no responsibility for its architecture but happened to have some spare money in its budget, was to finance the work. As an amusing sidelight, in his letter to Moscow V. Iatsenko of the Ukrainian Ministry of Culture confused Prince Volodymyr I the Saint ('Vladimir' in Russian; also known as the Great or the Baptiser, ca. 956–1015) with Volodymyr II Monomakh (1053–1125). Within two weeks, the ministry discovered the mistake and sent a note correcting the error. In order to prevent further confusion, yet to avoid using the religious epithet 'Saint,' the Moscow bureaucrats described the ancient prince as they would a Soviet citizen by putting his patronymic on the cover of the file: Vladimir Sviatoslavovich.[57]

The incident of the monument to St Volodymyr raises the question of whether ideological control over the registering of memorial sites even existed. After all, the 1953 inventory of Kiev's historical monuments and memorials included entry no. 21, 'a memorial building at 22 Zhadanivsky St, where the historian Antonovych lived and died in 1908,' although the official press had long denounced Antonovych as a 'staunch bourgeois nationalist,' racist, and teacher of Hrushevsky. The register also included Antonovych's tomb, as well as those of other outcast Ukrainian nation-builders such as Pavlo Zhytetsky, Oleksandr Konysky, Borys Hrinchenko, and the millionaire art collector Mykola Khanenko.[58]

Several surviving documents suggest that the public petitioned the authorities to care for historical monuments. Scholars have identified public concern for the preservation of Russian historical monuments as an early manifestation of popular

Russian nationalism in the Soviet Union during the 1960s.[59] Similar Ukrainian evidence dating from the late 1940s and early 1950s is too scarce to permit this kind of conclusion, but it is interesting to note which past the population 'remembered' and wanted commemorated.

On 31 August 1950 a group of farmers from the state farm 'Red Miner' in the Dnipropetrovsk province, S. Shevchenko, V. Stepanenko, H. Kolisnychenko, I. Shulha, and I. Bondar, sent a letter to the chairman of the Ukrainian SSR Council of Ministers, Demian Korotchenko. The villagers were concerned about a neglected tomb on the steppe that they attributed to the eighteenth-century Cossack rebel Sava Chaly, the main character of Taras Shevchenko's popular historical drama *Sava Chaly*. They wrote: 'We love our glorious ancestors, we love our history and our people, and we are asking you, Demian Sergeevich, to share our anger at the destruction of monuments of our historical past and listen to us.' The five farmers asked the government to restore the tomb and the cross, as well as to erect a monument to Khmelnytsky in their district.[60] While the subsequent investigation revealed that the cross could not have marked Sava Chaly's tomb (the Cossack chieftain died in 1741 and the year carved on the cross was 1783), the provincial authorities nevertheless reported their intention to unveil a memorial stone with a dedication to the Ukrainian Cossacks by the time of the tercentenary celebrations.[61]

Ukrainian intellectuals sometimes created ad hoc voluntary committees to examine the state of specific historical monuments as well. In May 1948 the actor Amvrosii Buchma, the writer Petro Panch, and the historian Olena Apanovych designated themselves a 'public commission' (*hromadska komisiia*) and prepared a report on the decay of the eleventh-century Vydubychi Monastery in Kiev. Bazhan was sympathetic to their cause but was unable to arrange for any immediate restoration work.[62]

In 1952 the KP(b)U Central Committee's inspector V. Stetsenko reported to First Secretary Melnikov that the construction of a hydroelectric dam near Nikopol would submerge an eighteenth-century Cossack hut and the tomb of the seventeenth-century Zaporozhian chieftain Ivan Sirko. Sirko, the inspector wisely argued, was a 'progressive person who continued Bohdan Khmelnytsky's policy on reunion with the great Russian people.' More important, Sirko wrote a famous mocking reply to the sultan that provided the subject matter for the most popular historical painting portraying the Cossacks, Ilia Repin's *The Zaporozhian Cossacks Write a Letter to the Sultan* (1880–91). Stetsenko did not indicate who had alerted him, but it is probable that local Ukrainian intellectuals had brought the endangered historical sites to his attention. As a result, the province's authorities assured Kiev that they would move both the tomb and the hut to another location nearby. By 1953 they also planned on erecting a small monument to Sirko, which was unveiled in 1955.[63]

As these examples illustrate, neither the general public, nor the party bureaucrats understood concern about Ukrainian historical monuments as 'nationalist deviation.' Rather, historic preservation became an aspect of the official policy of memory that Ukrainian intellectuals and common people could exploit to express their identities.

During the post-war decade, even the authorities distanced themselves from their pre-war predecessors, who had unceremoniously destroyed ancient churches to create space for new squares suitable for parades. In 1952 the Ukrainian Academy of Architecture transferred the surviving mosaics and frescoes from St Michael's Golden-Domed Church (1113) to St Sophia Cathedral Historical Preserve for public exhibition. St Michael's Church was destroyed during Kiev's 'reconstruction' in the mid-1930s, and the authorities expected some visitors to ask difficult questions about this event. The apparatus of the KP(b)U Central Committee provided the following standard explanation that museum guides were to repeat: 'In 1935 the monument was barbarously demolished by the enemies of the people, the monsters of the Bukharin-Trotsky gang, and the lackeys of the foreign bourgeois intelligence services, who intended to destroy the party and the Soviet state, as well as to annihilate our people's achievements.'[64]

Worth noting is that Ukrainian functionaries also did not press for a purge of pre-Soviet monuments and memorials in Western Ukraine. The KP(b)U Central Committee first raised this question in 1947 by way of a request for the opinion of the republic's Committee on Cultural and Educational Institutions. The latter dispatched the historian Mykola Petrovsky to Lviv for research and, based on his report, submitted the following cautious suggestion: 'to remove monuments built to commemorate reactionary Austrian and Polish political, military, and civic figures in Lviv and Lviv province, as well as memorial plaques honouring certain events and the activities of some persons who played a mostly reactionary role in the history of Poland and [whose actions] were directed against the interests of the Ukrainian people.'[65] Petrovsky proposed that 'the people of the Polish Democratic Republic' would consider only the following monuments interesting and valuable: the statues of King Jan III Sobieski and the seventeenth-century military leader Stanisław Jabłonowski, both of whom represented Polish military glory, and the statues of the prominent writers Kornel Ujejski and Aleksander Fredro. (In 1946 Khrushchev had already expressed his desire to retain in Lviv a monument to the greatest Polish national poet, Adam Mickiewicz, 'a writer popular among the Ukrainian people and loved by them.')[66] The Ukrainian leaders resolved to shelve the question until a later date.

Returning to the issue only in 1949, the KP(b)U Central Committee finally approved a detailed list of undesirable monuments. Statues of Jan Sobieski, Stanisław Jabłonowski, Kornel Ujejski, Aleksander Fredro, and nineteenth-century Polish politicians in Austro-Hungarian Galicia, Agenor Gołuchowski and Franciszek Smolka, disappeared from the streets. The authorities also removed memorial plaques honouring Polish kings and politicians, the Polish constitution of 3 May 1791, and the Poles who had defended Lviv against the Red Army (1920), as well as a plaque commemorating 'the Ukrainian bourgeois-nationalist historian Hrushevsky.' The Polish government subsequently reclaimed the statues of Sobieski, Ujejski, and Fredro. Khrushchev favoured the transfer but deemed it necessary to receive Stalin's personal approval in this matter.[67]

The list of proposed new memorial plaques demonstrates a mix of Ukrainian, Russian, and Soviet historical mythologies characteristic of High Stalinism. Ukrainian ideologues intended to honour Khmelnytsky, the Cossack colonel Maksym Kryvonis, the *haidamaka* anti-Polish rebellion of 1768, various Ukrainian classical writers and composers (Ivan Franko, Vasyl Stefanyk, Mykhailo Kotsiubynsky, Filaret Kolessa), and the 1939 reunification. At the same time, the authorities did not forget visitors to Lviv such as the sixteenth-century printer Ivan Fedorov, 'the Muscovite'; Tsar Peter I; and the Russian heroes of the First World War, General Aleksei Brusilov and the pilot Petr Nesterov. Finally, interwar workers' rallies, three Galician communist writers killed by a German bomb on the first day of the war, and the civic victims of the Nazi occupation were also to be commemorated.[68]

Ideological bureaucrats characteristically limited their immediate plans for implanting Ukrainian Soviet historical memory in Lviv to mounting cheap memorial plaques rather than expensive statues. The republic's share of the all-Union culture budget could support the building of approximately two major monuments annually. As late as 1953, the KP(b)U Central Committee apparatus made the following calculation: 'The Ukrainian SSR has been allotted 2,350,000 rubles for the construction of monuments during 1953. Of these, 1,111,000 rubles have been earmarked for a monument to Shchors in Kiev and 1,239,000 for a monument to Bohdan Khmelnytsky in Pereiaslav-Khmelnytsky; financing a monument to Shevchenko in Stalino [Donetsk] is thus not possible.'[69]

Operating under such financial constraints, the Ukrainian leadership carefully considered the ideological implications of every new monument. In 1950, after consulting with local intellectuals and architects, Lviv party authorities finally selected the best place for an envisaged monument to Ivan Franko: a square in front of the main building of the Franko Lviv State University (formerly the seat of the Galician legislature). However, a note in the file reads: 'Reported to the Secretariat [of the KP(b)U Central Committee]. Received the directive to postpone the final decision until the completion of the monument to Lenin [in Lviv].'[70] The story of Lenin's monument in Lviv is a testimony to Soviet bureaucratic inefficiency even in matters of ideological priority. The all-Union government originally decreed its construction in 1941. On 20 March 1945 the Ukrainian government ruled that the construction should be completed by 1948. The official commission approved the design of the modest half-length bronze statue in 1947, but the monument was not unveiled until 20 January 1952.[71] In 1956 a mass rally marked the unveiling of a much more imposing monument to Franko.

The 'Lenin in Lviv' decision became a policy-setting precedent. In the following years, the Central Committee apparatus would routinely turn down local proposals to erect monuments to Ukrainian classical writers if the city in question did not have a monument to Lenin. In 1951 party authorities in Odessa and Dnipropetrovsk petitioned Kiev for permission to construct monuments to Shevchenko. Although the bronze statues of the poet were ready, the Central Committee postponed the decision on the same grounds.[72] This practice highlights a curious symbolic hierarchy of monuments in Soviet Ukraine: Lenin came first, followed closely by Shevchenko in the East and Franko in the West. Stalin and the Unknown Soldier were losing the race to the Ukrainian fathers of the nation.[73]

Bureaucrats in the provinces apparently felt that having a monument to Shevchenko, as Kiev and Kharkiv had, would raise the prestige of their capital cities. Also, it would provide a site for the annual Shevchenko celebrations and other Ukrainian holidays during which officialdom could brief the population on its ever-changing understanding of 'Ukrainianness.' Thus, although the republic's budget had no money to build a Shevchenko monument in Stalino, local authorities came up with the financing for a pedestal. Then they petitioned the Ministry of Culture for a spare statue of the poet that had been created as a gift to Ukrainian Canadians but for some reason remained in Kiev. As a result, in 1954 Stalino bureaucrats were able to unveil their own Shevchenko monument.[74]

The tombs of national classical writers, except Shevchenko, were located in places not suitable for mass rallies. During the early 1950s some of them were in great need of renovations, and functionaries felt public pressure to take care of certain grave sites. Kotsiubynsky's neglected tomb in Chernihiv became a public issue in 1950, when *Radianska Ukraina* received several letters demanding immediate action, from the Kievan historian Professor Holobutsky, V.I. Murashko (the chief curator of the Chernihiv Historical Museum), and numerous tourists. Nazarenko was prompted to report the matter to the Central Committee Secretariat. However, no renovations were made at the time. In August 1951 Mykhailyna Kotsiubynska, the writer's granddaughter and a student at Kiev University, submitted a poem to *Literaturna hazeta* bemoaning the decay of the tomb. Nazarenko again requested that the Council of Ministers take the appropriate measures.[75] As well as providing a new tombstone, the Ministry of Culture subsequently approved renovations for the Kotsiubynsky memorial museum and the construction of a small monument on the writer's grave.[76]

The drive to honour the Ukrainian classical writers coincided with the beginning of another commemorative campaign to mark the upcoming tercentenary. As early as 1952 the Committee on Cultural and Educational Institutions proposed to 'survey and restore the monuments of the War of Liberation, as well as to place memorial plaques and monuments on the sites of victories.'[77] In 1953 the KP(b)U Central Committee came up with two additional and much more monumental projects while drafting a letter to Moscow: a statue of Khmelnytsky in Pereialslav-Khmelnytsky and a Triumphal Arch in Kiev. Having second thoughts, the Ukrainian ideologues substituted a monument to the reunification for the envisaged statue of the hetman,[78] lest anyone in Moscow doubt what was being commemorated: Ukraine's nationhood as such or nationhood together with Ukraine's incorporation into the empire.

Local authorities, intellectuals, and even individual enthusiasts from among the general public zealously responded to Kiev's call for proposals. In April 1953 Volhyn province sent the first local feedback, requesting the construction of a monument to Khmelnytsky and an obelisk to fallen Cossacks at the site of the Battle at Berestechko. The Institute of Architecture proposed the restoration of the church in Subotiv, where Khmelnytsky was buried, and the installation of a luxurious symbolic sarcophagus.[79] Other provinces and institutions followed suit. In November 1953 the Institute of History submitted a list of twenty-five sites of battles and other important events during the War of Liberation where obelisks could be constructed or memorial plaques placed. Later the same month, the writer Ivan Le supported this idea at a writers' conference in Kiev. Zaporizhzhia province wanted to build an obelisk to the Zaporozhian Host on its famous seat, the Dnieper island of Khortytsia. Dnipropetrovsk province requested four obelisks and a monument for Ivan Sirko's grave. Lviv authorities planned to install four memorial plaques in the city and enlisted Krypiakevych to prepare their texts. A certain Hrushchynsky, a railway employee from Zhmerynka, proposed that Vinnytsia erect a monument to Colonel Bohun 'for his services to the Ukrainian people' and provided a sketch of the statue he himself had drawn. Moreover, as head of the material management section of the Zhmerynka station, he was able to assure the party ideologues that a proper pedestal was already available.[80]

Some local functionaries did not wait for authorization from Kiev. The Kirovohrad provincial Soviet financed the production of a pedestal for a Khmelnytsky statue, which the Ministry of Culture did not approve. Consequently, Kiev refused to reimburse Kirovohrad the 40,000 rubles it had spent on the pedestal. Citing a lack of finances, republic-level bureaucrats denied requests for a Khmelnytsky monument in Korsun-Shevchenkivsky and Krolevets. Uman authorities had supported their plea for a similar monument by referring to materials from their local museum, *The*

Great Soviet Encyclopedia, and even Rybak's novel *The Pereiaslav Council.* They correctly pointed out that Khmelnytsky had visited their city, but the Central Committee denied their request nevertheless.[81]

The number of petitions and the ideologues' reactions to them suggest that local functionaries were eager to distinguish themselves as promoters of the newly rehabilitated cult of the Cossacks, whereas Kiev, being wary of potential accusations of abetting nationalism, attempted to check their enthusiasm. The local requests usually concerned the commemoration of the War of Liberation, the great national hero Khmelnytsky, and his colonels. The republic's leaders were apparently apprehensive of these proposals, since they did not focus on historic reunification as such. In at least two cases, the KP(b)U Central Committee turned down proposals for Khmelnytsky monuments when sculptures were already available: in Stanyslaviv (since 1956 Ivano-Frankivsk) and Cherkasy.[82] In one exceptional case, however, workers at the Konotip branch of the Moscow-Kiev railway volunteered – and gained permission – to build a monument to Khmelnytsky at the Khutir Mykhailivsky station at the Russian-Ukrainian border, thus marking the first mile of Ukrainian territory with a statue of the nation's founding father.[83]

In April 1954, with just a month remaining until the celebrations, the Ukrainian government finally produced a list of approved memorials. The authorities decided to erect a majestic monument to the Reunification in Pereiaslav, while they also planned a modest monument to Khmelnytsky for Zamkova Hill in Chyhyryn. (The former was not unveiled until 1961, and the latter was never built.) The Kiev functionaries accepted the plan to renovate St Elias's Church in Subotiv and to install a labradorite tombstone dedicated to the 'great son of the Ukrainian people,' Hetman Khmelnytsky. They also approved six obelisks for the battlefields of the War of Liberation and a number of memorial plaques for historical buildings.[84] But as soon as the celebrations were over, the republic's authorities quietly abandoned one of the principal memorial projects, the Triumphal Arch in Kiev. Although the party bosses had duly dedicated a spot for it in May 1954, after considering 257 drafts and 61 proposals, the competition jury eventually decided not to award a first prize or recommend any project for implementation.[85]

Before the budget for the restoration of historical monuments could be finalized, the Ukrainian party leadership had to investigate the question of where Khmelnytsky was born. V. Horbenko, an attentive district-level functionary in Kirovohrad province, noticed that the Central Committee resolution of 6 November 1943 spoke of Chyhyryn as the hetman's bithplace, while the 1943 decree on renaming Pereiaslav as Pereiaslav-Khmelnytsky held that the hetman had been born in that city, as did *The Great Soviet Encyclopedia.* The Institute of History reported that dissenting sources did not allow for a definite conclusion, but

Chyhyryn or a nearby village, Subotiv, seemed a likely place. The secretaries of the KP(b)U Central Committee considered the matter twice: on 1 December 1953, when the party leadership requested scholarly expertise, and in early 1954, when the party bosses, according to the minutes, 'concluded that the most probable birthplace of Bohdan Khmelnytsky was Chyhyryn or Subotiv.'[86]

Aside from 'establishing' the birthplace of the nation's founder, the resolution had immediate practical significance. Together with Kiev and Pereiaslav, Chyhyryn and Subotiv received considerable sums for the restoration of historical monuments and street improvements.[87] In Kiev, work included the restoration of the Khmelnytsky monument (1886) and extensive renovations to the nearby St Sophia Cathedral. In Pereiaslav, the whole city centre was rebuilt to create Khmelnytsky Square, the future site of the Reunification monument. The authorities installed a bronze bas-relief, 'The Pereiaslav Council,' on the Kiev-Kharkiv highway near the turn-off to Pereiaslav and a bust of Khmelnytsky on the Pereiaslav pier on the Trubizh river.[88]

The state also began organizing public excursions to historical sites in Kiev, Pereiaslav, and the battlefields of the Khmelnytsky War. The press recommended that teachers take their classes on these trips.[89] The Central Committee proposed that excursions to Kiev start at the Lenin statue, move to the Shevchenko monument, and then proceed to memorial sites such as the Golden Gate, St Sophia Cathedral, Tithe Church, the monument to St Volodymyr, the statue of Khmelnytsky, Askold's Tomb, the Caves Monastery, the Vydubychi Monastery, the Shevchenko Museum, and finally to monuments and buildings from the Soviet era.[90] With schoolchildren throughout Ukraine going on similar tours, the government unwittingly prepared the ground for a popular movement to study and preserve historical monuments, a movement whose nationalist proclivities would begin worrying Ukrainian ideologues during the 1960s and 1970s.[91]

Stalinist ideologues were not able to invent a specifically Soviet Ukrainian cultural and historical tradition that was completely separate from the Ukrainian heritage treasured by nationalists. As they nurtured the official cult of national patrimony, Ukrainian party bureaucrats remained ever suspicious of the danger that it would generate an exclusive national memory. In this light, the intelligentsia's lobbying to honour pre-revolutionary cultural figures, the local functionaries' enthusiasm for glorifying Khmelnytsky, and the public's interest in the preservation of historical monuments could equally well be interpreted as either the success or the failure of the official politics of memory. Either way, the Stalinist idea of national patrimony remained inherently ambiguous.

Chapter Seven

Empire and Nation in the Artistic Imagination

In June 1951 hundreds of Ukrainian writers, actors, musicians, and artists arrived in Moscow for a *dekada* (ten-day festival) of Ukrainian art. This grandiose exhibition of Soviet Ukraine's cultural achievements appeared to be a huge success and was crowned by the decoration of 669 Ukrainians with various orders, medals, and honorary artistic titles. *Pravda* provided extensive, enthusiastic coverage of the festival, expressing only minor criticism regarding the opera *Bohdan Khmelnytsky*, which, according to the newspaper, did not contain a single battle scene and did not portray the Polish gentry as the enemy.[1]

The ambassadors of Ukrainian culture left Moscow in high spirits, sending telegraphed expressions of gratitude to Stalin, the party, and the government. On 2 July, however, *Pravda* unexpectedly fired a devastating ideological salvo at the Ukrainians in the form of the editorial 'Against Ideological Distortions in Literature.' Unsigned but engineered by Stalin himself, this long article was ostensibly devoted to just one 'distortion,' Volodymyr Sosiura's short poem 'Love Ukraine' (1944), which had appeared in Russian translation in the fifth issue of the Leningrad journal *Zvezda* in 1951. The poem opened thus:

> Love your Ukraine, love as you would the sun,
> The wind, the grasses and the streams together ...
> Love her in happy hours, when joys are won,
> And love her in her time of stormy weather.[2]

In the remaining seven stanzas, Sosiura belaboured the concept of patriotic love of Ukraine as the highest virtue. *Pravda* accused the poem, written during the patriotic fervour of 1944, of glorifying 'a primordial Ukraine, Ukraine in general,' rather than Soviet Ukraine. In an aside, cryptic reference was made to other serious shortcomings in the work of the KP(b)U Central Committee.[3]

Within days of *Pravda*'s publication, Ukrainian authorities launched a campaign of ideological purification in the republic, complete with condemnations of 'nationalist deviations' in all areas and genres of creative activity.[4] Similar campaigns took place in other republics, and, in contrast to the nine celebrations of non-Russian art – Kazakh, Georgian, Uzbek, Azerbaijani, Kirghiz, Armenian, Belarusian, Buriat, and Tajik – that had followed the 1936 Ukrainian *dekada* in Moscow between 1936 and 1941, no festivals ensued immediately after the ill-fated Ukrainian *dekada* of 1951. (They would resume only after 1953.) In a separate, albeit closely linked, campaign, the Kremlin discovered the 'poison of nationalism' in Azerbaijani, Turkmen, Uzbek, and Kirghiz traditional epic poems. Given also the harshness of the 'anti-Zionist' purge that took place during 1952 and early 1953, scholars speak of apparent preparations for a general crackdown on nationalities during Stalin's last years.[5] Whether or not this was the case, the 1951 attack on Ukrainian 'primordialism' pushed the celebration of non-Russian patrimonies further towards the periphery of Soviet cultural life, a trend reinforced by the increasingly Russocentric character of mainstream Soviet culture.

While the *Pravda* editorial dealt only with a single poem's failure to stress love for Soviet Ukraine, the Ukrainian leaders discerned a larger ideological significance between the lines. The republic's ideologues interpreted the critique's emphasis according to what they perceived as the main threat to the Stalinist imperial project in Ukraine, a 'harmful obsession' with the national past and concomitant insufficiency in the portrayal of historical ties with Russia. On 2 August First Secretary Melnikov reported to Stalin's deputy for party affairs, Georgii Malenkov, that the Ukrainian intelligentsia, 'in their creative and scholarly work, often idealize the past.' He assured Moscow that his subordinates would instruct local intellectuals to portray Ukraine as an 'inseparable part of our great fatherland.' Writing to Stalin on 14 August, Melnikov expressed his regret that the Ukrainian leaders had overlooked 'attempts to portray the historical process in Ukraine as separate from the history of the peoples of the USSR.'[6] Generally, the ideological gatherings held in the republic concentrated more on condemning what they considered to be an inappropriate infatuation with the national past than on bemoaning insufficient celebration of the Soviet present.

Writers' Licence

As a result of the Dovzhenko affair of 1944 and two campaigns against the 'idealization' of the Ukrainian past (1946–7), ideological control over the historical genre in the republic was already tight. The republic's bureaucrats, censors, and critics subjected each new work to such scrutiny that Ukrainian writers often found it easier to publish in Moscow.

In 1945 the central publisher Sovetskii pisatel released a Russian translation of *St. Petersburg Autumn* by Oleksandr Ilchenko, a revised version of the author's 1939 novel, *The Heart Is Waiting*, which depicted Shevchenko's life in the imperial capital during 1858–9. The 1945 version emphasized the poet's contacts with Russian 'revolutionary democrats' and featured new scenes describing Shevchenko's cordial meetings with their leading figure, Nikolai Chernyshevsky. (In *The Heart Is Waiting*, Shevchenko and Chernyshevsky meet only briefly and purely by accident in a streetcar. There is no documentary or memoir evidence that the two ever met.) Over the next two years, the Russian translation of the book was reprinted twice. The novel fit the post-war politics of memory so well that in August 1947 the KP(b)U Central Committee decided to investigate why the original Ukrainian text had never been published in the republic. As it happened, Ilchenko did not submit the original text for publication until after the Moscow publisher had released the Russian translation in November 1946 and it had been favourably reviewed in the press. Only then did Ilchenko give the Ukrainian version to Derzhlitvydav. But with the campaign against the historical genre at its peak, this Ukrainian publisher did not hurry to print the novel, the success of the Russian edition notwithstanding. The Central Committee ordered that *St. Petersburg Autumn*, which 'correctly presented [Shevchenko's] friendship with prominent progressive Russian figures as well as his differences with Kulish,' be published as soon as possible.[7]

The Ukrainian edition of *St. Petersburg Autumn* appeared in late 1947. Because of Shevchenko's importance as a national symbol, Ukrainian ideologues continued to reshape his biography in the following years to highlight the poet's ties to Russian culture. In 1951 Ilchenko completed another, even more pro-Russian, version of the novel, which then underwent extensive review in the apparatus of the Central Committee. The text was released in 1952 as an 'updated edition.'[8]

After Kaganovich's departure for Moscow, Ukrainian writers began pushing for the rehabilitation of the historical genre. At the writers' congress in 1948 Petro Panch called upon his colleagues to depict the Revolution, the Civil War, the Great Patriotic War and, 'to some degree,' Ukraine's pre-revolutionary past. He went on to explain: 'Let me stress this: to some degree, our history [must be portrayed] as well. I think such topics as the Ukrainian people's War of Liberation, their reunification with the Russian people, and the patriotism [that has been] born in the common struggle of the Russians and Ukrainians against foreign encroachment on our lands should receive much wider coverage in Ukrainian literature.'[9] Kocherha supported this appeal by recalling the success in 1946, against great odds, of his *Iaroslav the Wise*.[10] Ideological bureaucrats did not rebuff the writers' call, thus opening the door for the revival of the historical genre.

Natan Rybak broke new ground with his epic novel, *The Pereiaslav Council*.

Although one could hardly find a more timely historical topic than Ukraine's union with Russia, the press welcomed the novel rather reservedly. In August 1947 *Literaturna hazeta* reacted with approval, albeit without enthusiasm, to the publication of select chapters of the novel in a journal. When a book edition appeared in late 1948 in a relatively modest print run of 20,000 copies, the same newspaper noted the publication but did not run a book review for several months.[11]

The novel presents an epic picture of the Khmelnytsky Uprising, ending with the Pereiaslav Council of 1654. Although Rybak combined several narrative lines featuring main characters from various social strata, all developing the theme of Russian-Ukrainian friendship, his main emphasis was clearly the deeds of the Cossack leader. Like many other positive historical characters in Stalinist literature, Rybak's Khmelnytsky appears as an ideal ruler imbued with traits similar to those of Stalin. The hetman is an omnipresent and omnipotent father of the people who governs his state with an iron hand:

> Only a short time had passed, but he had accomplished much, and he had the right to credit himself with having done so. The entire country was now divided into regiments and colonels elected in each regiment. He had often had to suggest who should be elected, but these suggestions had been necessary. He had had to dismiss those independent in thought [*iaki myslyly svoieumno*] and slow in action, he had had to threaten some and exile others to the Crimea, ordering them to stay there until he recalled them. Yet others he had removed in such a way that nobody knew what happened to them, and if anyone happened to mention them in conversation, Lavryn Kapusta [the head of the secret police] could only shrug his shoulders non-committally.[12]

Rybak's Khmelnytsky is not a feudal lord; like the Stalin of post-war propaganda, he stands above all social strata, wisely guiding the Ukrainian nation in its entirety towards reunion with Muscovy, while at the same time expressing care and concern for the common people in periodic cleansings of the upper classes.

More important, Rybak struck a fine balance between national history and class history by representing reunification as beneficial to both the Ukrainian nation as a whole and the Ukrainian toiling masses in particular. When his vision so dictated, he did not hesitate to radically rewrite events. The critics hailed Rybak's treatment of the controversial Colonel Bohun, who had neither attended the Pereiaslav Council nor taken an oath to the tsar. In his *Fighters for Freedom*, the pre-revolutionary nationalist novelist Adrian Kashchenko had portrayed Bohun as an opponent of the union with Russia. In *Bohun*, the early Soviet Ukrainian writer Oleksandr Sokolovsky had depicted the colonel as a true representative of the toiling masses and the enemy of the feudal lord Khmelnytsky. In *Bohdan*

Khmelnytsky, Korniichuk had chosen not to mention Bohun at all in his description of the Pereiaslav Council and the subsequent events. Rybak was the first writer to claim that Bohun had, in fact, always supported Khmelnytsky and had even taken an oath to the tsar.[13]

The first indication of the novel's official acceptance came from Liubomyr Dmyterko, the secretary of the Writer's Union, in his report to the writers' congress in December 1949. After praising new novels on Soviet topics, he added: 'Together with the works on contemporary subjects – and I repeat, there are dozens of them – Natan Rybak's weighty historical novel, *The Pereiaslav Council*, stands at the vanguard of Soviet Ukrainian prose.' Dmyterko went on to approve of the topic and the style, as well as to read aloud extensively from the book's description of the Pereiaslav Council. The novel earned its author a Stalin Prize, Second Class.[14]

In marking new limits for what was permissible and warranted official approval, the plots of two historical plays, both completed in 1949, highlight the new politics of memory. Leonid Smilainsky's drama *Sahaidachny* attempted to recast this Cossack leader as an early promoter of union with Russia. However, it was no mean task. Although Sahaidachny had sent a friendly embassy to the tsar in 1619 or 1620, he had also participated in the Polish army's march on Moscow in the previous year. The KP(b)U Central Committee's expert felt that even passing references to the war with Russia were inappropriate and that the entire last scene, in which Sahaidachny dies with the words 'Bells, bells' on his lips, was ambiguous: 'Is he referring to the bells greeting the Cossack envoy in Moscow or to the bells sounding the alarm when Sahaidachny together with the Polish prince invaded Russian territory?'[15]

Although Smilansky revised the drama, renaming it *Rus' is Rus'* and adding an epigraph from the 1943 manifesto that listed Sahaidachny among progressive historical figures, the Ukrainian Agitprop withheld its approval.[16] The imperial project of memory required that all mention of the military clash between the Cossacks and the Muscovites some thirty-five years before their 'reunification' be suppressed. Accordingly, there was no longer a place for Hetman Sahaidachny on the list of Soviet Ukrainians' 'great ancestors.'

In contrast, Liubomyr Dmyterko's *Together Forever* passed the censors with flying colours. The play depicts events in Ukraine after Bohdan Khmelnytsky's death (1657), when Hetman Ivan Vyhovsky attempted to break with Muscovy. Dmyterko discredits Vyhovsky and his followers, who are cast as lacking mass support and who are opposed in the play by the pro-Russian Cossack leaders, including Ivan Sirko, Martyn Pushkar, and Khmelnytsky's widow, Hanna. First published in June 1949, the play immediately earned good reviews, and the Sumy

Drama Company staged it as early as November 1949. When Kharkiv's Shevchenko Theatre, Ukraine's leading drama company during the post-war decade, first performed *Together Forever* in February 1950, the press hailed the premiere as a success of national significance.[17] In contrast to Korniichuk's *Bohdan Khmelnytsky*, however, Dmyterko's play had a considerably shorter theatrical run. Staged by practically all Ukrainian companies in 1950, by 1952 it was no longer being produced in Kiev, Kharkiv, or Lviv. Contemporary theatre critics attributed the quick decline of interest in the play to its low artistic quality, namely, its lack of developed and vivid positive characters.[18]

Meanwhile, although they were less attuned to the most recent ideological winds, Kocherha's *Iaroslav the Wise* and Korniichuk's *Bohdan Khmelnytsky* remained the mainstays of Ukrainian repertoire. Three and a half years after its premiere, in June 1950 the Kharkiv company took *Iaroslav* to Kiev on a highly successful tour. Korniichuk's play survived, overcoming one hurdle after another. After the war, the influential playwright revised *Bohdan* to eliminate the work's anti-Polish animus by changing 'the Poles' to 'the gentry' throughout. In 1951, when *Pravda* criticized Korniichuk's libretto of the opera *Bohdan Khmelnytsky*, some companies suspended productions of the play, but they promptly renewed its staging after the success of the opera's second redaction in 1953.[19] Aside from the different artistic qualities of the three plays, their celebration of the great ancestors might be the key to the popularity of the optimistic *Bohdan* and *Yaroslav*, just as its blackening of separatist historical figures might explain the audiences' tepid enthusiasm for the more negative *Together*.

In early 1952 Ukrainian functionaries and writers already were thinking about the preparation of new literary works to celebrate the tercentenary. A conference at a major publishing house, Radianskyi pysmennyk, called upon litterateurs to compose new paeans to the 'age-old friendship' with Russia. The Writers' Union proposed that the leading poets be mobilized to create a monumental collective ode to said friendship.[20]

Too much should not be attributed to such 'planning,' since the two major historical novels published in 1953–4 had been in process long before the authorities issued an appeal for them. The topicality of Pereiaslav enabled two authors to revive Cossack glory as a major component of the Ukrainian national memory. Petro Panch revised his 1946 novel, *The Zaporozhians*, adding two more parts and publishing the resulting bulky volume under the title *Ukraine Was Humming*. Only later did Ukrainian ideologues notice that Panch 'had not properly eliminated' the mistakes for which the party had denounced *The Zaporozhians* in 1947. The publication of volume 2 of Rybak's *The Pereiaslav Council* was the major event in Ukrainian literary life in 1953. Contemporary critics agreed that the sequel was artistically superior to the original, even though Rybak had further developed elements of adventure, intrigue, and espionage not considered proper in a serious historical novel.[21]

The tercentenary celebrations marked the culmination of the historical genre's rehabilitation. As the best novel embodying the new official memory, *The Pereiaslav Council* was elevated to the near-sacred status of a work that authorities exhorted the populace to 'study' (not unlike the *Communist Manifesto* or the *Short Course* of the party history). Between January and May 1954 all Ukrainian provinces reported the organization of public readings, readers' conferences, study workshops, and amateur dramatizations of the novel. In Stanyslaviv province alone, more than a hundred readers' conferences took place. The village of Vovkovyi in Rivne province, where a readers' conference with 190 participants was preceded by a lecture, 'The Pereiaslav Council and Its Historical Importance,' and followed by the screening of *Bohdan Khmelnytsky*, could serve as a typical example.[22]

The *Pereiaslav Council* went through several mass editions during 1953–4, including a luxurious Ukrainian two-volume set with colour illustrations by A. Riznychenko. Three Moscow publishers planned to issue a Russian translation of the novel in 1954, causing the KPSS Central Committee to intervene and decide that the jubilee edition would be printed by Goslitizdat. As if all this propaganda were not enough, Ukrainian radio broadcast readings of the novel, chapter by chapter, and dramatized selected fragments in a kind of historical soap opera.[23]

Following in Rybak's footsteps, many other writers speedily produced novels about the Ukrainian, mostly Cossack, past that emphasized Russian help and the Ukrainians' age-old desire to unite with their Russian brethren. These works included Ivan Le's *Sworn Brothers* and the second variant of *Nalyvaiko*, Iakiv Kachura's *Ivan Bohun*, Vasyl Kucher's *Ustym Karmaliuk*, and Iurii Mushketyk's *Semen Palii*.[24] Dmyterko produced a new version of *Together Forever*, which many theatres staged in time for the tercentenary celebrations. Other companies chose to renew Korniichuk's *Bohdan Khmelnytsky*, which was also included, together with Rybak's novel, in the school curriculum for senior grades.[25]

Significantly, intellectuals again began including Kievan Rus' into their notion of Ukrainian national memory. In January 1954 the Zankovetska Drama Company (Lviv) for the first time in Soviet theatre history staged Ivan Franko's mystic drama *The Dream of Prince Sviatoslav* (1895), substituting the 'voice of the common people' for that of the ghost in the original. As early as 1945 some Ukrainian intellectuals had proposed the production of this patriotic play, but the *Zhdanovshchina* had curtailed their plans. Now, however, the Lviv intelligentsia managed to bring off a production of this pre-Soviet Ukrainian interpretation of the Kievan heritage. Following Lviv's lead, many other companies produced the play.[26] During this time, the writer Semen Skliarenko began working on the first post-war Ukrainian novel about Kievan Rus'. According to his 1953 report to the Writers' Union, Skliarenko was composing the novel 'The Great Rus'' – the first stage of a project that would eventually result in two best-selling historical novels in the Thaw period, *Sviatoslav* (1957) and *Volodymyr* (1963).[27]

The Ukrainian writers had so successfully recovered from the official purge of the historical genre in 1946–7 that in May 1954 Moscow's Institute of World Literature convened a special conference on the Ukrainian historical novel. At the Third Congress of the Ukrainian Writers' Union in October 1954 nobody felt it necessary to defend the historical genre. Mykola Bazhan, head of the organization, praised the recent works of Rybak, Panch, Le, and others as Soviet Ukrainian prose's most notable accomplishments, declaring, 'The important role of contemporary subjects for the successful development of Socialist Realism in literature does not at all diminish the significance of historical subjects.'[28]

Despite the party's ideological supervision, writers were still able to mount a subtle but effective defence of the historical genre. Regimenting the public's perception of their books was beyond even the Communist Party's capabilities.

The numerous letters from readers, which can be found in Natan Rybak's personal archive, allow an insight into how the post-war public perceived his novel. Reactions varied from a sentiment expressed in an anonymous note, which claimed that reading the epic narrative of the Cossacks' heroic deeds and resulting incorporation into Russia 'left a sense of both elevated pride and burning bitterness in the heart,' to lengthy tirades that seemed to confirm the novel's desired educational impact. Petro Zhytnyk, from the village of Mykolaivka of Nekhvoroshcha district in Poltava province, wrote to Rybak on 27 February 1952:

> The history of Ukraine and, in particular, the life and activities of the great statesman Bohdan Khmelnytsky have been of interest to me since childhood. Under the influence of Kulish's *Black Council*, I had formed wrong conceptions about Ukrainian history and Hetman Khmelnytsky's role, and I was not able to free myself from those ideas for a long time. Much later, in 1943, having read O. Korniichuk's play *Bohdan Khmelnytsky*, watched the film of the same name, and having read your novel *The Pereiaslav Council* for the first time in 1949, I finally understood with profundity the age of Bohdan Khmelnytsky, his services in liberating Ukraine from foreign oppression and uniting it with Russia. These wonderful works allowed me, a common citizen, to see the great truth![29]

Ideologically correct as it is, the letter reveals that this reader was not interested in the notions of the friendship of peoples, class struggle, and the fraternal aid of the Russian elder brother so dear to Soviet ideologues' hearts and sown so abundantly throughout the novel. Instead, Zhytnyk understood the great hero

Khmelnytsky as a historical agent who had liberated Ukraine and brought it to its beneficial union with Muscovy.

Other Ukrainian readers also perceived *The Pereiaslav Council* as simply a work glorifying their nation's heroic past, as if the 'friendship of peoples' paradigm never existed. Ivan Burlaka, from the village of Èrazmivka in Oleksandrivka district in Kirovohrad province, wrote to Rybak in December 1950: 'Khmelnytsky, the Cossack leader and the liberator of all Ukrainian people, is shown so forcefully. It is a truly patriotic book that explains the state-building aims and humane ideals of the heroic Ukrainian people's national liberational movement.'[30]

Most striking is the number of letters Rybak received from ethnic Ukrainians living in other Soviet republics. All his correspondents from Kuban, Sverdlovsk province, and Georgia wrote of their Ukrainian or even Cossack roots with pride and complained about the difficulties in obtaining Ukrainian historical novels in Russia. Dmytro Krykun in Kuban informed the writer that the local bookstore had sold out its allotment of *The Pereiaslav Council* in a week. Krykun considered himself lucky to have procured a book in a second-hand shop; although only volume 1 was available, at least it was in Ukrainian.[31]

Having read the first volume in Russian translation, Colonel Hryhorii Bludenko, who was stationed in Bukhta Olga in the Primore region in the Russian Far East, wrote to Rybak in May 1951: 'I am sure that your *Pereiaslav Council* reads much better in Ukrainian. I am serving here on the Pacific Ocean among many other Ukrainians who do not want to ever forget their people, their language, and their glorious ancestors, such as Bohdan Khmelnytsky.'[32]

The readers could apparently interpret selectively even the most ideologically correct historical novel, overlooking its descriptions of class struggle and friendship with Russia and reading it instead as a fascinating account of their ancestors' glorious past. Imbibing a Ukrainian historical novel did not always mean swallowing wholesale a text ideologically sweetened with the right measures of class and national history, both modified by the doctrine of Russian guidance. For many, reading such a work was a heady act of discovering or reaffirming their national identity.

Filmmakers and Artists Imagine the Past

The ideology of High Stalinism, that history was a series of events initiated and controlled by great men, caused the genre of film biography to proliferate during the post-war decade. Between 1946 and 1953 the Soviet film industry produced seventeen full-length movies about great military leaders, scientists, composers, and writers.[33] It is significant that not all of these great men were Russians; the list of seventeen films included *Rainis* (dir. Iu. Raizman, Riga, 1949), *Taras Shevchenko* (dir. I. Savchenko, Kiev, 1951), and *Dzhambul* (dir. Ie. Dzigan, Alma-Ata, 1952), in which Stalinist ideologues sought to provide officially sanctioned fictionalized 'biographies' of three revered figures in Latvian, Ukrainian, and Kazakh letters, respectively. Unlike pre-war films, such as *Bohdan Khmelnytsky*, these post-war projects were designed to reflect the new official memory and highlight the Russian elder brother's historical patronage.

By the late 1940s a canonical film biography of Ukraine's 'father of the nation' was long overdue. A previous version, the 1926 *Taras Shevchenko* (dir. P. Chardynin, Odessa Film Studios) had been produced at the height of the Ukrainization campaign and reflected the contemporary nationalizing and anti-colonialist ethos. In 1937, the authorities had denounced the film as counter-revolutionary, fascist, and nationalistic.[34] A new biography of Shevchenko was the first major project that the Kiev Film Studios contemplated after the war.

Ilchenko wrote a provisional screenplay, basing it on his novel *St. Petersburg Autumn*, and the director I. Annensky began filming *Taras Shevchenko* in the summer of 1947. As the crusade against nationalism in the humanities unfolded, however, Ukrainian ideologues rejected biographical vignettes of the poet's life in St Petersburg in favour of a wider panorama of nineteenth-century Ukraine showcasing social oppression, peasant rebellions, and the Russian revolutionaries' tutelage.[35] The authorities then appointed Savchenko to take charge of the film as its director and scriptwriter. He promptly produced a new script portraying Shevchenko as more of a social activist and student of the Russian revolutionaries, and in early 1949 the KP(b)U Central Committee authorized Savchenko to begin filming.[36]

By June 1950, when the Central Committee had organized a discussion of the film's first cut, the campaign against 'nationalism' in the arts had long since petered out. While some participants followed the earlier party directives in demanding further emphasis on class struggle and vilification of contemporary 'bourgeois nationalists,' others dared to oppose it. When the literary historian Novikov branded Kostomarov a 'scholar in quotation marks,' Korniichuk intervened to defend the nineteenth-century historian who had 'understood many things correctly.' Anatol Petrytsky, Ukraine's leading theatre set designer, took the floor to ridicule the never-ending calls for the inclusion of additional ideological statements: 'Even Repin complained that audiences often expected more from his paintings than these works could possibly have contained. For instance, say the artist is painting a canvas depicting the Zaporozhian Cossacks. He captures only the single moment when they are writing the letter to the Turkish Sultan. But no, that is not enough. Some begin demanding that he also portray the emergence of the Zaporozhian Host, what happened to it, how Catherine was involved, and so on. (Laughter, applause.) They even want to see the Zaporozhians beyond the

Danube. (More laughter.)'[37] The poet Maksym Rylsky, the artist Oleksandr Pashchenko, and the writer Wanda Wasilewska all praised the director's cut. Then, Nazarenko and the Central Committee expert Oleksii Rumiantsev returned to the earlier criticisms. (During the meeting, Savchenko suffered a mild heart attack and had to rest on a couch in an adjoining room.) Although the discussion ended inconclusively, Nazarenko ordered the conformist literary critic Illia Stebun and the head of Agitprop, Davyd Kopytsia, to write critical reviews of the film. Both commentators requested that the portrayal of Shevchenko's ties to the Russian 'revolutionary democrats' be improved. As well, Stebun suggested including Shevchenko's positive remark about Khmelnytsky and a condemnation of Mazepa.[38]

Armed with these reviews, the Ukrainian Politburo established a commission to supervise the film's editing that included President Hrechukha, Central Committee secretaries Nazarenko and Ivan Senin, Minister of Culture Lytvyn, and Kopytsia. On 1 July 1950 members of the Politburo watched the film and proposed further improvements. In particular, Second Secretary Kyrychenko requested the depiction of the poet's 'warm meeting with the Russian revolutionary democrats after his return from exile.' First Secretary Melnikov acknowledged, 'Our people and our intelligentsia are so permeated with the deepest love for Shevchenko that they would have accepted enthusiastically even an imperfect film about him.'[39] Yet the commission proceeded to attempt to bring the screenplay to perfection. Nazarenko suggested downplaying the role of the Polish revolutionary Zygmunt Sierakowski, since otherwise the 'Ukrainian-Polish connection would appear more prominent than the Ukrainian-Russian one, which was in reality decisive both in Shevchenko's life and in history.' The ideologues proposed a number of other minor improvements with which Savchenko disagreed strongly.[40]

The director was hoping for support from Moscow. Although in mid-July the Kievan bureaucrats were still reporting on their 'work' on the film to their direct superiors on the VKP(b) Central Committee, the initiative now passed to Ivan Bolshakov, the minister of cinema and Stalin's confidant, who organized a new discussion of *Taras Shevchenko* in Moscow. Many comments paralleled those made in Kiev, but the participants were generally approving and their criticisms constructive.[41]

Although Moscow had assumed responsibility for the film, Ukrainian ideologues did not relent. Perceiving the interpretation of the Ukrainian past as the prerogative of the republic's functionaries, Nazarenko bombarded Bolshakov with telegrams during October and November 1950. He repeatedly suggested adding an episode about the 'progressive Russian people buying Shevchenko out of serfdom,' enquired whether the beautiful Ukrainian landscapes were represented properly in the new version, and requested a new musical score. Bolshakov ignored these appeals from Ukraine. Accordingly, in October Ukrainian bureaucrats sent

Oleksandr Levada, the chief editor of the republic's Ministry of Cinema, to Moscow. He attempted to visit Bolshakov during regular office hours but was referred to the minister's deputy, who told the Ukrainian envoy that the 'question is settled; the plan for revisions has been cleared by the Central Committee and by Comrade Suslov personally.' Levada then sneaked into the Central Committee's Department of Propaganda, where a functionary named Groshev 'guardedly advised [him] that revising the plan for the film's alterations would be difficult,' since the party leadership had already approved Bolshakov's plan.[42]

Aside from feeling excluded, Ukrainian ideologues had little reason to complain. The Moscow-approved new scenes included Shevchenko's fiery speech inciting the peasants to rebel, the Russian revolutionaries' discussion of how to bring Shevchenko back from exile, and the Ukrainian poet's cordial meeting with Chernyshevsky. (None of these episodes had any basis in reality.) As well, Chernyshevsky referred to Kulish in passing as 'that pig good only for lard,' and Sierakowski no longer participated in the movie's closing scene.[43] Filming of the additional episodes began in December 1950, but it is not clear whether Savchenko ever agreed to implement the revisions: on 14 December the forty-five-year-old director died of a heart attack. Korniichuk prepared the final version of the screenplay, while several of Savchenko's students at the Institute of Cinema took over the filming of the new scenes.

In July 1950 I. Mazepa, the new Ukrainian minister of cinema, related to First Secretary Melnikov: 'I hereby report that, according to the information from the USSR Minister of Cinema, Comrade Bolshakov, a private government screening of the full-length colour film *Taras Shevchenko* took place in Moscow after the completion of revisions and the film was approved without further revisions.'[44] Stalin and his inner circle, which now included Khrushchev, did not even bother to ask the republic's leaders what they thought of this latest representation of Ukraine's national icon. Soon after the film was released, Ukrainian ideologues made one last, weak attempt to reclaim their right to interpret Shevchenko. When the writer Marietta Shaginian asserted in her *Izvestiia* review of the film that the Cyril and Methodius Brotherhood had been a nationalist group, which Shevchenko had joined by accident and which had taken advantage of his talent, Nazarenko initially ordered the preparation of a refutation and a letter of protest to Suslov, but the matter was eventually dropped.[45]

The authorities staged the simultaneous release of *Taras Shevchenko* in Ukrainian and Russian in December 1951 as a major event in Ukraine's cultural life. The largest theatres displayed exhibitions on the poet's life, inviting scholars to give lectures about Shevchenko before the screening. The newspapers hailed the film as a great success, a 'work of enormous impact' that created a 'majestic image of the immortal poet-fighter.' In March 1952 the film won the Stalin Prize, First Class –

the first post-war work by the Kiev Film Studios to earn this most prestigious Soviet accolade.[46]

A grandiose undertaking on a scale comparable to that of the *History of the Ukrainian SSR*, *Taras Shevchenko* drained the republic's financial and human resources, making the simultaneous production of another historical film impossible. Thus, the triumph of Stalinist ideology in the much-edited *Taras* precipitated Soviet Ukraine's failure to produce a new, ideologically correct historical film in time for the tercentenary of Pereiaslav. The republic's ideologues realized that the changes in the official politics of memory over the last decade generated the need for a vision of the Khmelnytsky Uprising very different from that offered in the 1941 *Bohdan Khmelnytsky*. Yet the revisions to *Taras Shevchenko* prevented them from addressing this problem. In 1951 the Kiev Film Studios considered beginning work on the film *The Pereiaslav Council*, possibly based on Rybak's novel, but the apparatus of the KP(b)U Central Committee did not even discuss this idea until mid-1952, when it was shelved for lack of financing.[47]

In March 1953, with the jubilee looming large, the desperate Ukrainian bureaucrats began exploring a cheaper option: remaking the old *Bohdan Khmelnytsky* in colour, with some revisions. Korniichuk suggesting the following changes: showing the tsar receiving the hetman's ambassadors, portraying the Pereiaslav Council, and refilming the Battle at Batih after adding the Russian Don Cossacks to the scene. An ideologically acceptable script was ready by mid-1954, in which Korniichuk emphasized Russia's role throughout and inserted scenes showing that from the very beginning of the war, Ukrainians had dreamt of uniting with Muscovy. As a final coup, he completely rewrote Khmelnytsky's speech at the Pereiaslav Council, making the hetman say that union with Russia was something 'our grandfathers and great-grandfathers had wished' and having him express the Ukrainians' desire to be 'forever united with their [Russian] brethren in one state, great Russia.'[48]

For all these achievements in historical fiction, the actual filming still had not started one month before the May 1954 celebrations. In desperation, the republic's Ministry of Cinema petitioned the KP(b)U Central Committee to allow a quick, low-cost filming of Dmyterko's play *Together Forever*, otherwise Ukrainian cinema would have nothing to present. The Kievan bureaucrats, however, decided against simultaneously undertaking two similar projects.[49]

Filming of the new *Bohdan Khmelnytsky*, now provisionally called *The Great Brotherhood*, did not start until August 1954, well after the tercentenary celebrations. Korniichuk secured the Russian director Vladimir Petrov, who had pro-[duced the celebrated historical movie, *Peter the First* (Leningrad Film Studios, Parts I and II, 1937–8), for the project. Petrov made a majestic and expensive film, parts of which were shot in the Kremlin and which took almost two years to complete. The Soviet film industry released the movie as *Three Centuries Ago* in the autumn of 1956, when the country's political and cultural life was no longer the same as it had been under Stalin.[50]

For the purposes of the everyday politics of memory, this delay meant a fiasco that was not immediately obvious and that went unnoticed by the public. Already in 1953 Nazarenko had reported to Pospelov, the new secretary of the VKP(b) Central Committee in charge of propaganda and culture, that the republic needed more copies of the 1941 *Bohdan Khmelnytsky*. The movie was still very much in demand, and the Ukrainian film circulation division had only 54 copies left (24 of them had 'worn out'). The Ukrainian ideologue placed an order for 250 new copies.[51] To mark the tercentenary, during the spring and summer of 1954, all 4,009 of the republic's cinemas and all 3,823 mobile film projectors showed a series of 30 Soviet films, opening with *Bohdan Khmelnytsky* and *Taras Shevchenko*. For this purpose, the authorities ordered an additional 200 copies of the former and 347 of the latter. *Radianska osvita* advised teachers to take their classes to see *Bohdan* and *Taras* as a part of the history curriculum.[52] The post-war generation of Ukrainians thus became exposed to *Bohdan*'s 1941 patriotic vision of the Cossack past.

In contrast to the film industry, the development of the historical genre in art was not dependent on large investments from the state, nor was it possible for party ideologues to supervise the drafting of every historical painting or sculpture. As a result, the trajectory of changing artistic representations of the past was considerably more complicated.

Ukrainian artists were the first among the republic's cultural elite to recover after the ideological purges of 1946–7. As explained in chapter 4, Hryhorii Melikhov's award-winning canvas *Young Taras Shevchenko Visiting the Artist K.P. Briullov* (1947) perfectly illustrated the new official vision of Ukrainians as having always been guided by the Russian 'elder brother.' Other artists emulated Melikhov and portrayed Russian historical figures tutoring their Ukrainian contemporaries or, at least, visiting Ukraine. Notable among works on this topic were the following paintings: M. Dobronravov's *Peter the First in Lviv* (1947), H. Svitlytsky's *The Composer P.I. Tchaikovsky in Ukraine* (1947), K. Trokhymenko's *Gorky Reading Shevchenko to the Peasants* (1949), M. Khaertinov's *After the Battle at Poltava* (1950), V. Puteiko's *Maxim Gorky and Mykhailo Kotsiubynsky on the Island of Capri* (1951), P. Parkhet's *The Assault on Khadzhibei* (1953), V. Zabashta's *P.I. Tchaikovsky and M.V. Lysenko* (1953), and F. Shostak's *The Printer Ivan Fedorov in Lviv* (1954). Graphic artists and sculptors also produced numerous works on the topic of Russian-Ukrainian friendship, such as O. Kulchytska's lithograph *Ivan Fedorov among the Townspeople of Lviv* (1949), M. Vronsky's sculpture *T.H. Shevchenko and N.G. Chernyshevsky* (1954), and S. Besedin's drawings *Pushkin in Ukraine, T.H. Shevchenko among Progressive Russian Cultural Figures*, and *P.I. Tchaikovsky Visiting M.V. Lysenko* (all 1954).[53]

While stressing Ukraine's historical connection to Russia, artists shied away from portrayals of their nation's 'separate' heroic past. Until 1954, when S. Adamovych displayed his canvas *Danylo of Halych* at the Tercentenary Exhibition, no painter dared to work on the history of the Galician-Volhynian Principality. Adamovych himself came under harsh criticism. Depicting the prince on the battlefield after his victory over the Teutonic knights, his painting did not develop the theme of Russian-Ukrainian friendship and was soon dismissed in the press as 'pointless' (*bezzmistovne*).[54] The rehabilitation of Cossack glory as a legitimate topic also proved difficult. After the critics condemned Mykhailo Derehus's series on the Khmelnytsky Uprising (1946), the artist concentrated on illustrating historical novels, including Gogol's *Taras Bulba* and Rybak's *The Pereiaslav Council*. During the *dekada* of Ukrainian art in Moscow in June 1951 Derehus finally brought his Cossack heroes back into the mainstream of official art with his large painting *The Pereiaslav Council* (on which he was assisted by S. Repin and V. Savenkov).[55] Although mildly criticized for its lack of action and dramatic tension, the work's timely subject probably protected Derehus during the ensuing purge of 'nationalist errors' in Ukrainian culture.

Later in 1951 young Mykhailo Khmelko, who had already earned two Stalin Prizes for paintings on Soviet topics, presented his monumental canvas *Forever with Moscow, Forever with the Russian People*. This large, magnificent painting portrayed Khmelnytsky and the Russian ambassador addressing a cheering crowd in front of the cathedral in Pereiaslav. Khmelko put the Cossack colonels, Muscovite boyars, and bishops in the foreground, including every detail of their decorative garments and gonfalons.[56] However, the republic's artistic community, apparently upset with the success of Khmelko's decorative monumentalism during a time when lyrical and genre works on Ukrainian subjects were dismissed as untopical, used the language of class to attack the authorities' favourite. When the painting was first exhibited in Moscow, Ukrainian critics accused Khmelko of indulging in 'excessive theatrical splendor.' Soon Lidiia Popova published a more damaging objection, namely, that the artist had ignored the 'representatives of the common people.' During the artists' conference in 1952, Serhii Hryhoriev lectured Khmelko that a historical painting 'should depict not a farce or parade, but the drama of history.'[57]

In January 1953 the newspaper of the Artists' Union, *Radianske mystetstvo*, went as far as publishing ironic verses critical of Khmelko:

Rubies, steel, enamel, and cut glass;
Satin, brocade, and a sledge with fretwork.
This is all good, but one thing is unfortunate,
That the people are in the background.[58]

The critic Valentyna Kuryltseva concluded that Khmelko had not studied history thoroughly enough.[59] For lack of another magnificent depiction of the act of union, in 1953 the authorities adopted the unsophisticated *Pereiaslav Council* by Derehus, Repin, and Savenkov as the principal official image of reunification, later to be reproduced on stamps, tapestries, and vases in massive numbers.[60]

Nevertheless, the critics' sympathies went to three new, artistically superior works by young Ukrainian artists. Oleksandr Khmelnytsky's dynamic *Together Forever* (1953) portrayed the robust and almost unruly Ukrainian and Russian masses rejoicing outside the cathedral in Pereiaslav, V. Zadorozhnyi's unusual *Bohdan Khmelnytsky Leaves His Son Tymish as a Hostage with the Crimean Khan* (1954) depicted the human side of the hetman, and Mykhailo Kryvenko's lyrical *When the Cossack Went to War* (1954) illustrated a folksong about a girl bidding farewell to a young Cossack.[61] The gradual rehabilitation of the Cossacks as part of Ukrainian historical memory led Derehus to rework one of his illustrations to *Taras Bulba*, the result being the painting *Taras at the Head of the Army* (1952). The graphic artist Oleksandr Danchenko produced a remarkable and highly acclaimed series of etchings with a title reminiscent of Derehus's 1946 series, 'The Ukrainian People's War of Liberation (1648–1654).' The centrepiece of the series, *The Feat of Three Hundred at Berestechko*, glorified the heroism of the nation's great ancestors with an enthusiasm unseen since the war years.[62]

In early 1954 the industrious Khmelko presented a new variant of his *Forever with Moscow* and, taking advantage of his position as the party-appointed chairman of the Artists' Union, used the tercentenary celebrations to manoeuvre his monumental painting back into the official canon. The changes were purely cosmetic: dressing some personages in dark clothes instead of gold-embroidered garments, making the colours less bright, and adding an old peasant bard in rags in the foreground. Although the revised painting was not praised as the definitive account of the council or nominated for any prizes, the authorities ensured that it was widely exhibited during the celebrations. In addition, Khmelko secured publication of the work on postcards, with a print run of 50,000.[63] At the insistence of Central Committee functionaries, a colour reproduction of the painting was included in the *History of the Ukrainian SSR*, over the objections of the distinguished artist Vasyl Kasiian, who punned that this canvas 'had not received an appraisal warranting it a place in history [nor in the *History*].'[64]

Together with other contemporary historical paintings, Khmelko's work was also displayed at a jubilee exhibition in the State Museum of Ukrainian Art in Kiev. The archives preserve the book of visitors' comments from this exhibition, and, although some entries have been blackened with ink, the remaining remarks shed an interesting light on the popular reception of the historical genre. Hidden among numerous ideologically correct notes (many of them signed by officially organized groups of visitors, including schoolchildren and soldiers), one finds the unorthodox opinions of individual spectators. In particular, many visitors were disappointed with Khmelko, whose work, in the words of one, 'looked better on postcards.' Another anonymous observer noted: 'The more I look at Khmelko, the more I like Velazquez.' The visitors Koptilov and Koptilova suggested: 'Many paintings depicting Bohdan Khmelnytsky would have benefited if he had been dressed more modestly.' Another spectator, with an illegible signature, found Ie. Bilostotsky's bust of the hetman scandalous because the facial features were not those of a great national hero: 'Why, then, all these radio programs? A stupid expression and a weak-willed lower lip. The spirit of history is totally absent.' Several visitors singled out Kryvenko's lyrical painting, *When the Cossack Went to War*, as a work into which the author had 'put his heart.'[65]

Even more important than some visitors' independent readings of historical images was the fact that this mammoth exhibition included frescoes from Kievan Rus', icons from the sixteenth to the eighteenth centuries, Cossack portraits, Shevchenko's historical drawings, as well as pre-revolutionary historical paintings that had previously been deemed ideologically harmful: Feodosii Krasytsky's *Guest from the Zaporozhian Host* (1901; variants 1910 and 1916) and O. Murashko's *The Funeral of the Chieftain* (1900). By exhibiting these works together with numerous Soviet paintings on subjects from the Ukrainian past, particularly from the Cossack times, the authorities were de facto making an important acknowledgement. The display recognized the continuity of Ukraine's cultural development through the ages, as well as the succession of artistic traditions in the portrayal of the national past. Embodied in pre-revolutionary historical paintings, Ukrainian national mythology was now implicitly, if selectively, accepted as part of Soviet Ukrainian historical memory.

History at the Opera

The genre of grand historical opera afforded a unique opportunity to combine Stalinism's quest for monumentalism and traditionalism in the arts with the system's regard for national history. Since the late 1930s authorities in both Moscow and Kiev favoured the idea of producing a Ukrainian patriotic historical opera that would provide Soviet Ukrainians with a truly imposing representation of their heroic past, just as the 1939 production of *Ivan Susanin* had done for the

Russians. Several attempts to rework the only Ukrainian classical historical opera, Lysenko's *Taras Bulba* (1890), had not resulted in the kind of spectacle that was both ideologically sound and popular with the public.[66]

In May 1948 the prospect of going to Moscow for the *dekada* forced the Ukrainian functionaries to prioritize the writing of a Soviet Ukrainian historical opera. Significantly, with the post-war cult of the 'Russian elder brother' on the rise, the Ukrainian establishment preferred a new work celebrating union with Russia to yet another revival of the classic *Taras Bulba*, in which Russian help and tutelage were not portrayed. In two months, the resourceful Korniichuk produced a verse libretto of *Bohdan Khmelnytsky* co-authored with his wife, Wanda Wasilewska. The libretto was based on Korniichuk's earlier play but stressed the Ukrainians' desire to unite with the Russians. In July the press reported that the composer Kost Dankevych was already hard at work on the score.[67]

Ukrainian ideologues turned the writing of *Bohdan Khmelnytsky* into an affair of state. As soon as the Odessan Dankevych had completed the score's first draft on 27 January 1950, he telegraphed the news to both Second Secretary Kyrychenko and Nazarenko. As early as 15 February the newspapers announced that the score's first audition at the republic's Committee for the Arts had been a success. By August Dankevych had delivered the final version of the score.[68]

Bohdan turned out to be a grand historical opera, a work that had little in common with the conventions of twentieth-century western musical theatre. Based on national motifs, it imitated the form and dramatic structure of nineteenth-century Russian and Western European operas. *Bohdan* also contained direct musical quotations—Glinka's 'Glory' from *Ivan Susanin* reverberated as the theme of the Muscovite ambassador and sounded again in the finale. The plot developed against the background of the Cossack war with Poland, ending with the decision to ask the tsar for protection (but not the act of union itself). Both Ukrainian newspapers and internal reviews characterized the Kiev premiere of *Bohdan Khmelnytsky* in January 1951 as a triumph.[69]

During the Moscow *dekada* of Ukrainian art in June 1951 the Kiev Opera Company performed *Bohdan* four times at the Bolshoi Theatre with apparent success.[70] *Pravda*, however, expressed reservations regarding this opera, which, as mentioned above, in the newspaper's opinion did not sufficiently portray the Polish gentry as the enemy and did not have a single battle scene.[71] At first, this comment might appear as nothing more than an isolated low-key critique of an otherwise laudable work. Yet in the wake of *Pravda*'s editorial 'Against Ideological Distortions in Literature' (2 July), all problems in Ukrainian culture suddenly acquired an ideological colouring. While the ideological offensive in Ukraine was just beginning, *Pravda* intervened again on 20 July with an equally long editorial, 'On the Opera *Bohdan Khmelnytsky*.' Even then, the flagship of the party press did not call the opera nationalistic, nor did it demand a better portrayal of the Russian 'elder brother.' The editor praised the opera's subject and music, as well as the singers' performances, but also elaborated on several critical lacks: no proper depiction of the enemies, no suffering of the masses, no battles, and no more than one duet.[72]

Bewildered by the insignificance of these accusations, Ukrainian functionaries themselves broadened the critique of *Bohdan*, interpreting the pronouncements from Moscow to mean that the opera was guilty of insufficiently glorifying the historical Russian-Ukrainian friendship.[73] This indictment reflected post-war Ukrainian ideologues' obsession with the issues of historical memory and national identity, a concern reinforced by numerous previous reprimands from the Kremlin and insecurity concerning the ideological appropriation of Western Ukraine.

By January 1952 Korniichuk and Wasilewska had prepared a new libretto, but several exhaustive discussions of the text at the republic's Writers' Union, Academy of Sciences, Committee for the Arts, and Composers' Union took months, each resulting in dozens of minor critical comments and further revisions. The new libretto contained a new act 1, scene 1 portraying the execution of Cossack rebels and the people's suffering under the yoke of the Polish lords. Another addition, act 2, scene 2, showed the Polish gentry hatching their evil plans and Cossacks storming a Polish castle. Finally, the Russian Don Cossack appeared on the scene, and a new act 4 depicted the Pereiaslav Council of 1654 as the apotheosis of the Ukrainians' historical association with the Russian people.[74]

Critical comments on the draft libretto in Ukraine reveal just how unanimously the republic's officials and artistic elite had 'developed' Moscow's vague critique. The apparatus of the KP(b)U Central Committee, in particular, demanded a more elaborate depiction of fraternal assistance from Russia (the librettists decided to show the arrival of a cart with Russian weapons). The ideologues also felt that in the opera, 'the word "Ukraine" was used too often.'[75] Less subtly, other Ukrainian reviewers suggested changing the last words of the final chorus from 'Glory to Bohdan Khmelnytsky!' to 'Glory to the Russian people!' which was duly implemented. Nevertheless, the Ukrainian Composers' Union still demanded 'a more powerful representation [of the Ukrainians'] striving to unite with the great Russian people.'[76] As a result, work on *Bohdan Khmelnytsky* dragged on. Like the *History of the Ukrainian SSR*, this impressive monument to Stalinist historical memory remained unfinished at the time of Stalin's death in March 1953.

At about the same time, polemics surrounding another Ukrainian opera highlighted the limits of Moscow's control, as well as the compromises inherent in Stalinist cultural production. On 11 October 1950 the jubilee 500th performance of Semen Hulak-Artemovsky's classic, *The Zaporozhian Cossack beyond the Danube* (1863), in Kiev was broadcast throughout the Soviet Union. Although this politically harmless and genuinely entertaining comic opera was sung in Ukrainian, sensitive bureaucratic ears in Moscow detected several ideological heresies.

The opera's plot concerned Cossacks fleeing to Turkish-controlled territory beyond the Danube after Catherine II ordered the destruciton of the Zaporozhian Host in 1775. After some humorous and romantic adventures, which are actually central to the plot, the sultan allows the Cossacks to return home in the finale. To a Moscow official, these elements constituted a 'slanderous story.' Moreover, the 'bourgeois historian' Kostomarov, who wrote the dialogue for Hulak-Artemovsky's opera, had 'distorted historical reality.' In particular, Kostomarov portrayed the Cossacks as mercenaries of the sultan and made the main character, Ivan Karas, boast of bloody Cossack victories over the Arnauts, who unfortunately turned out to be the ancestors of the modern-day fraternal Albanians. The libretto inappropriately represented the sultan as a magnanimous ruler, friendly to the Cossacks, while 'in reality, the Cossacks had been returned to their country thanks to the intervention of the Russian ambassador in Turkey.' It appeared, furthermore, that although Soviet censorship had banned the Russian text of *The Zaporozhian Cossack* libretto in 1948, the Kiev, Kharkiv, Lviv, and Odessa opera companies were continuing to use a slightly edited version of an old Ukrainian text, presumably owing to a bureaucratic error.[77]

Meanwhile, in October 1951 the Stanislavsky and Nemirovich-Danchenko Musical Theatre in Moscow premiered *The Zaporozhian Cossack* 'in a new Russian translation by G. Shipov' that had been reviewed and approved by the apparatus of the VKP(b) Central Committee. The newspapers advertised the new version as 'prepared on the basis of historical documents.'[78] A closer look at the new Russian libretto, approved by the censors for publication and staging throughout the USSR three months after the premiere, reveals heavy-handed editing and rewriting. Ukrainian bureaucrats and intellectuals revered *The Zaporozhian Cossack* as their first national opera; Rylsky described in 1949 the 'lofty patriotism that permeates this opera from the first note to the last.' Shipov, however, redefined the work 'popular musical comedy.' He introduced a negative Cossack character, the clerk Prokop, as if to offset the new positive role – the Russian ambassador who sings the aria 'The hour of liberation approaches.' Throughout the libretto, Shipov skilfully cast aspersions on the Turks and made the Cossacks complain of their life in the Ottoman Empire. To improve Hulak-Artemovsky's work, he also included several of the most popular Ukrainian folk songs as additional arias.[79]

The 'musical comedy' ran in Moscow with considerable success for two and a half years until Nazarenko attended a performance during one of his visits to the capital in April 1953. The theatre-loving Ukrainian ideologue indignantly stormed out of the house and immediately submitted a report to the party's Central Committee. The production, he wrote, had 'little in common with the authentic version presented in Ukrainian theatres.' Applying the rhetoric of 'heritage authenticity' to this Ukrainian operatic classic, Nazarenko demanded nothing less than the banning of the new Russian libretto. However, the Moscow functionaries justified the company's right to 'adjust' (*podvodit*) classical operas by referring to the precedent of Russian works: *Ivan Susanin*, *Boris Godunov*, and *Khovanshchina* at the Bolshoi. At the same time, the Central Committee's bureaucrats also saw the staging of two different versions of *The Zaporozhian Cossack* – one in Ukrainian in Ukraine and another in Russian in Russia – as inappropriate. They suggested that a joint commission be appointed to work out a standard synopsis and libretto.[80] The archives, however, preserve no trace of such a commission. Ten months later, the artistic director of the Kiev Opera referred at the local meeting to certain 'discussions about a macaronic approach to the classics' provoked by the Moscow production of *The Zaporozhian Cossack*, but that is all.[81]

Nazarenko's motivation bears closer scrutiny. He must surely have been aware of the various adjustments Ukrainian companies had made to the opera's libretto and score. In the mid-1930s, during Nazarenko's tenure as secretary for propaganda of the Kharkiv provincial party committee, the local company had Ivan Karas curse Catherine II and Prince Potemkin for ordering the destruction of the Zaporozhian Host. During the 1936 Ukrainian *dekada* in Moscow, the Kievans' Karas also condemned Potemkin, that 'oppressor of the Zaporozhian Host,' although apparently not the tsarina. This cue was, of course, absent from the original libretto and soon disappeared from the text with the rehabilitation of the Russian imperial tradition in the late 1930s.[82] Even the post-war Ukrainian 'authentic version' was subject to minor ideological editing from time to time, of which Nazarenko must also have been aware. In other words, the secretary was defending not so much the 'authenticity' of the Ukrainian cultural heritage as the exclusive right of local ideologues, poets, and musicians to edit 'their' classics.

Remarkably, the clash between Moscow and Kiev over *The Zaporozhian Cossack* ended in an implicit compromise. The Stanislavsky and Nemirovich-Danchenko Theatre staged the 'new' version of the opera, in which the Russian ambassador liberates the Cossacks, while the Ukrainian companies held to the traditional plot, with the sultan performing this feat. Rylsky, who was also the Kiev Opera's literary consultant, made only two changes to the libretto, eliminating mention of the Arnauts and making one episodic character hint that the Cossacks had received letters from Muscovy.[83]

Given these alterations, the script Rylsky had to produce in 1951 for the Kiev Film Studios' film version of *The Zaporozhian Cossack*, which would be seen in every corner of the Soviet Union, was necessarily much different. Although the Russian ambassador did not put in an appearance, the overture was accompanied by the following explanatory text: 'Realizing that Russia would support the

Cossacks' demands and that the Zaporozhians were preparing an armed mutiny, the Turkish Sultan was forced to allow them to return to their homeland.' In this script, Ivan Karas marks his first appearance with the announcement, 'we and the Muscovites are of the same faith and blood, so perhaps we will attain a better life together.' (Ironically, just before making this important ideological pronouncement, Karas complains about having a terrible hangover and downs a shot of hard liquor.) Furthermore, even the sultan acknowledges that 'It is not easy to rule over [the Cossacks]. They have a mighty defender.' The Kiev Film Studios released the film in the summer of 1953, thus giving birth to a third version of the popular opera, a strange hybrid of the Kiev and Moscow productions.[84]

Mindful of the imminent tercentenary celebrations planned for early 1954, Ukrainian authorities meanwhile were coordinating feverish efforts to stage a new version of Dankevych's *Bohdan Khmelnytsky*. On 27 September 1953 the Kiev opera company opened its new season with this *Bohdan*, more pro-Russian than ever. A flood of lengthy reviews promptly announced that it was a 'great achievement' of the Soviet Ukrainian musical theatre.[85] The subsequent lavish celebration of the 300th anniversary of the Pereiaslav Treaty cemented the opera's place in the canon of Soviet Ukrainian culture. The Kharkiv, Odessa, and Stalino (Donetsk) opera companies staged *Bohdan* – reportedly with phenomenal success – in the spring of 1954. In May the Kiev Opera went to Moscow for the *dekada*, where they presented *Bohdan* to great acclaim.[86] Soviet television broadcast *Bohdan* live from the Bolshoi on 10 May. In his introductory comments, Dankevych claimed that the Kievans had come to the Bolshoi to express 'their feelings of brotherly love and boundless gratitude' to the Russian people. The opera was also repeatedly broadcast in full on all-Union and Ukrainian radio and released on gramophone records. The festive tercentenary concert in Kiev included no fewer than three arias from Dankevych's work. The composer himself became a People's Artist of the Soviet Union.[87]

The lack of reliable sources makes it difficult to reconstruct historical opera's influence on contemporary national memory. Tens of thousands of Soviet Ukrainians attended performances of *Bohdan Khmelnytsky*, and millions heard the opera on radio. Yet no one carried out an independent poll of the listeners in 1954 to determine just how they 'read' this cultural product. In January 1954 the Paris correspondent of the Ukrainian émigré newspaper, *Novyi shliakh* (New Path, Toronto), allegedly was told by visitors from Soviet Ukraine: 'One must buy tickets to the Kiev Opera three or four weeks in advance to attend *Bohdan Khmelnytsky*. The public enthusiastically applauds the excellent Ukrainian settings and costumes; Ukrainians serving in the military greet the Cossack banners loudly. And the whole house listens as if in a trance to Bohdan's boring aria on the need to 'reunite' [with Russia].'[88] Although some Canadian informants deemed this passage important enough to report to the Soviet All-Slavic Committee, which oversaw contacts with foreign Slavs,[89] no other source corroborates the émigré newspaper's information. Reading both the Soviet archival documents and the press of the time, one might just as easily conclude that *Bohdan* was popular precisely because it embodied the idea of a union of Russians and Ukrainians.

The archives, however, shed interesting new light on the extent of the opera's popularity. The attendance records of the Kiev Opera for 1954 show that *Bohdan* was the public's absolute favourite: the company performed it 36 times that season with a total of 52,768 tickets sold, that is, to an average audience of 1,466 people. In the same season, the company performed the 'official' Russian patriotic opera *Ivan Susanin* 8 times for a total of 6,950 listeners (an average of 869 at each performance), *Boris Godunov* 7 times for a total audience of 7,183 (an average of 1,026), and *Carmen* 9 times for a total audience of 9,894 (an average of 1,099).[90] A general statistical survey of all Soviet opera companies in 1954 reveals that 7 theatres – Kiev and 6 other smaller provincial houses, all of them in Ukraine – staged 129 performances of *Bohdan* for a total of 136,123 spectators, an average of 1,055. No Russian classical opera enjoyed such an average attendance Union wide that year. *Ivan Susanin*, staged by all the largest opera houses, came close, with 15 theatres, 126 performances, and 128,276 patrons (1,018). *Eugene Onegin*, *The Queen of Spades*, and other classics lagged far behind. The opera most often performed on a Soviet subject, Iulii Meitus's *The Young Guard*, incidentally also a work by a Ukrainian composer, scored 9 – 87 – 49,980 (574).[91]

These statistics are convincing: *Bohdan* enjoyed unprecedented popularity in Ukraine. How many listeners craved a Ukrainian patriotic opera and how many the authorities 'organized' to listen to a new and topical musical work about Russian-Ukrainian friendship are open to discussion. But for all practical purposes, *Bohdan* did become *the* Ukrainian national historical opera in the 1950s. Whatever its intended propaganda message, the operatic synthesis of the representation of the nation's past with grand spectacle and theatrical ritual filled an important niche among the cultural pillars of Ukrainian national memory. While *Bohdan*'s content duly glorified the 'elder brother,' the opera also exalted the heroic Cossack past and the homeland's liberation from foreign oppression. Thus, *Bohdan Khmelnytsky* offered Ukrainian listeners the experience of identifying with their glorious ancestors.

In an angry and touching letter to Khrushchev, the singer Mykhailo Hryshko, unhappy with critics' comments about his 'static' portrayal of Bohdan, expressed this sense of belonging to a historical community. Hryshko had read the scholarly books, chronicles, and historical novels on the subject, sometimes almost feeling as if he were meeting Khmelnytsky's colonels on the street. The singer thought of himself as 'a son of [his] people, in whose veins runs the blood of ancestors who passed into eternity and dreamt of seeing their Fatherland free and independent.'[92] Similarly, the students of a small-town school wrote to Korniichuk in 1954 that his play *Bohdan Khmelnytsky* 'teaches us to love and be proud of our people, who defended their independence in arduous struggle.'[93] It was precisely the possibility of such a selective reading of non-Russian representations of the national past that undermined the principal message encoded in the official memory, that of the Russian-dominated 'friendship.'

Epilogue

Having completed an ideological purification campaign in late 1951, the Ukrainian leadership was satisfied with its efforts. From November 1951 to May 1952 no ideological decrees or major public statements indicated the party's concern with any 'nationalist deviations' in culture and scholarship. Soon, however, the republic's bosses discovered that Stalin himself remained suspicious of Ukraine's ideological situation. In May 1952 First Secretary Melnikov disclosed to the members of the KP(b)U Central Committee: 'On 14 April Comrade Korotchenko and I were received by Comrade Stalin. In a conversation that lasted approximately four hours, Iosif Vissarionovich showed great interest in the state of Ukrainian industry, agriculture, and culture.' The Ukrainian party leader went on to report on Stalin's approval of Ukraine's post-war reconstruction, but he saved the bad news for the end: 'Comrade Stalin was keenly interested in the state of ideological work in Ukraine and expressed the opinion that things were not going particularly satisfactorily in this field [*cho zdes delo u nas obstoit neblagopoluchno*].'[1]

Melnikov did not specify whether Stalin had elaborated on the problems motivating his concern. Yet one is tempted to surmise that the omniscient 'father of peoples' realized that his viceroys had failed to fashion a Soviet Ukrainian historical memory completely separate from the non-Soviet Ukrainian national memory. Perhaps Stalin bemoaned the limits of the state's ideological control over the production of historical works and the influential role of local bureaucrats and intellectuals in shaping the sense of nationhood in his many nations. Perhaps he was also frustrated by the Ukrainian public's apparent ability to 'read' the much-edited cultural products selectively, interpreting them as heroic narratives of their national past. Like Russians, who by the end of Stalin's period, were increasingly able 'to articulate what it meant to be members of a Russian national community,'[2] Soviet Ukrainians preserved their sense of ethnic identity forged during the Ukrainization drive.

Although they maintained the 'friendship of peoples' ideology until the USSR's very last days, Stalin's successors never fully reconciled the Soviet peoples' multiple national histories. As argued in the preceding chapters, the Kremlin was eager to prescribe the meaning of patriotism and historical memory in Ukraine. Nonetheless, these notions were opened to interpretation by local intellectuals and the public, resulting in Moscow's several campaigns against 'Ukrainian nationalism.' The Stalinist project of unified memory was also undermined by the fact that no matter how much representations of the past celebrated the historical unity of Soviet peoples, they never denied the non-Russians' ethnic difference. Ultimately, the ambiguities of the Stalinist politics of memory explain the failure to mould the multinational Soviet Union into a single, coherent community.

The Last Stalinist Festival

Stalin died on 5 March 1953, but the Stalinist models of remembrance were still in force in the spring of 1954, when the Soviet authorities celebrated the tercentenary of the Pereiaslav Treaty with unprecedented pomp. However, Stalin's death and the subsequent political reshuffling in the Kremlin did worsen the usual Soviet bureaucratic inefficiency. In December 1953 the top leaders suddenly realized that none of the official announcements specified the exact date for the festivities. Since the treaty's 300th anniversary was to fall on 18 January, local officials in Ukraine and Russia were becoming concerned about the lack of preparation time for the commemorative events. Moreover, the middle of winter did not seem an appropriate moment for festivals and parades. On 14 December Pospelov and the new Ukrainian first secretary, Oleksii Kyrychenko, finally reported the problem to Khrushchev. The resulting official announcement in the press explained that the authorities 'accepted the proposal of party, Soviet, and civic organizations' to move the festivities from January to May 1954.[3]

In preparation for the celebration, Ukrainian party bureaucrats speedily finalized proposals for several monuments and ideological pronouncements to mark the tercentenary.[4] While none of the architectural projects was completed by May 1954 – nor, indeed, during the 1950s – ideologues in Kiev and Moscow managed to produce on time a number of slogans, open letters, and the *Theses on the Tercentenary of Ukraine's Reunification with Russia*.

The initiative to produce the last document, which became the definitive Soviet pronouncement on Russia's historical relations with non-Russians, belonged to Ukrainian ideologues. Although formally issued by the KPSS Central Committee in Moscow, Ukrainian historians played a major role in the preparation of the *Theses*. The Central Committee's Department of Learning and Culture appointed its officials F.D. Khrustov, I.A. Khliabich, and A.V. Lykholat (Likholat) to coordinate the project, but in practice, the organizer's role passed to Lykholat, a Ukrainian historian specializing in the revolution and civil war period.[5]

The Central Committee resolution of 21 September 1953 obliged its apparatus to produce the *Theses* by the New Year. In order to accomplish this task, Lykholat enlisted the services of the leading historians in Kiev (Boiko, Holobutsky, Huslysty, Kasymenko, Shevchenko) and Moscow (Bazilevich, Cherepnin, Pankratova, Picheta, Sidorov, Tikhomirov) to prepare draft materials. He then compiled the final version of the text in consultation with Pospelov and Oleksii (Aleksei) Rumiantsev, the head of the Department of Learning and Culture and himself a transplanted Ukrainian economist. Lykholat also consulted with Nazarenko, Korniichuk, and Rumiantsev's Ukrainian counterpart, S.V. Chervonenko.[6] On 5 January 1954 the final draft was submitted to Khrushchev, but neither his copy, nor the copy sent to the Ukrainian Politburo has significant marginal notes. The Lykholat draft appeared practically unchanged as the Central Committee's authoritative pronouncement.[7]

The *Theses* did not impose on Ukrainian ideologues and intellectuals an alien interpretive model; rather, this document affirmed the strategies of memory that the Ukrainian elites had been developing for at least a decade. Nations, rather than classes, were presented as subjects of history, and the mighty Russian-dominated Soviet Union, rather than the victory of socialism, was given as history's teleological outcome.[8] By celebrating Ukraine's 'fraternal union' with Muscovy, Stalinist ideologues were establishing historical continuity between the Russian Empire and the Soviet Union. But hailing the Ukrainians' membership in the empire was possible only by proving that it was beneficial for the development of the Ukrainian nation. Conversely, Ukrainian national memory could be promoted only within the imperial framework of Russian guidance. The *Theses* and other official pronouncements of the time thus had an inherently double-edged nature: they both restored the Ukrainian nation as a historical agent and prescribed its historical trajectory as leading to the protection of the Russian elder brother.

The *Theses* asserted, accordingly, that reunification had not resulted in the loss of Ukrainian ethnic identity or historical agency. On the contrary, it resulted in the Russian people's becoming the Ukrainians' 'great ally, faithful friend, and defender in the struggle for social and national liberation.' In this scheme of things, the Bolshevik Revolution appeared to have been an important landmark in the ethnic history of the Ukrainians. With help from their Russian brethren, they 'achieved their age-old dream of establishing a truly free and sovereign national state occupying a prominent place in the family of Soviet republics.' Moreover, their membership in the Soviet Union allowed Ukrainians to unite all their ethnic lands in one polity, the Ukrainian SSR, which became 'one of the largest states in Europe,' with economic powers surpassing those of France or Italy.[9]

The *Theses* was published in major Russian and Ukrainian newspapers on 12 January 1954 and reprinted in practically all Soviet newspapers, magazines, and journals immediately after. As if this wide distribution were not enough, it also appeared as a separate booklet in Russian in 1 million copies and in Ukrainian in 400,000 copies. On 13 and 14 January party activists in most enterprises, collective farms, schools, and offices throughout Ukraine organized public readings of the *Theses*.[10]

Meanwhile, the authorities concerned themselves with the production of various memorabilia, including a souvenir medal depicting two men, a Russian and a Ukrainian, holding the Soviet coat of arms against the background of the Kremlin wall. The ideal Russian was taller than his Ukrainian younger brother, on whose shoulder he patronizingly rested his left hand. The Russian also represented Soviet modernity by wearing a formal suit with a tie, while the Ukrainian wore an 'ethnographic' embroidered shirt. (The cover of the May 1954 issue of the magazine *Ukraina* features a similar composition depicting the two surrounded by the crowd of happy representatives of other Soviet nations.) The medal's reverse side depicted the Pereiaslav Council. The medal was intended for the Ukrainian establishment and distinguished guests. For the general public, the authorities ordered 2 million copies of a simpler badge picturing the Kremlin tower, the flags of Soviet Russia and Soviet Ukraine, and the number '300.' Special-edition stamps were also released featuring Derehus's painting *The Pereiaslav Council*, the Order of Bohdan Khmelnytsky, and the hetman's statue in Kiev.[11]

To ensure that ordinary citizens remembered the reunification, Ukrainian ideologues ordered a long list of products to be sold in festive wrappings featuring the monument to Khmelnytsky in Kiev, the Kremlin, and the words '300 years.' The list included unexpected items such as women's bras and silk nightdresses (200,000); stockings (250,000); men's socks (200,000); cigarettes of the 'Zaporozhians' brand (2,000,000 packages); wine glasses with the inscription 'Reunification'; and a special beer, 'Pereiaslavske' (27,000 decalitres). Ukrainian brewers developed this strong beer especially for the jubilee by using 'historical' ingredients such as honey and rice.[12]

The anniversary date itself, 18 January 1954, was not marked by any special events. On the 17th, however, the authorities announced the renaming of the Ukrainian city of Proskuriv as Khmelnytsky and Kamianets-Podilsky province as Khmelnytsky province. Maroseika Street in Moscow became Khmelnytsky Street. On 19 February the Russian Federation presented the Ukrainian Republic with a precious festive gift: the Crimea province. Although the Crimea was historically Tatar and ethnically Russian, Mykola Bazhan claimed at the USSR Supreme Soviet Presidium meeting, at which the transfer was formalized, that 'close economic and cultural ties between Ukraine and Crimea had emerged in ancient times.' In April festive sessions of the Ukrainian and All-Union Academies of Sciences took place in Kiev and Moscow, featuring numerous speeches about the historical Russian-Ukrainian friendship. On 24 April a major Ukrainian concert was held in Moscow, followed from 6 to 16 May by the *dekady* of Ukrainian culture in Moscow and Russian art in Kiev.[13]

The celebrations reached their apogee in late May 1954. On 22 May a festive session of the Ukrainian Supreme Soviet opened in Kiev, with delegations from all other Soviet republics and the Polish Sejm in attendance. First Secretary Kyrychenko gave a lengthy speech elaborating on the *Theses*. Hundreds of organizations – from the Mongolian parliament to obscure collective farms – telegraphed their congratulations to the Ukrainian people.[14] On 23 May military and civilian parades were held in Kiev, Kharkiv, Lviv, Sevastopol, Odessa, and Pereiaslav-Khmelnytsky, followed by twenty-gun military salutes in the evening. In Kiev some 500,000 people marched down Khreshchatyk Street, many wearing Ukrainian ethnic costumes. The column of the Molotov District paraded a huge picture, *The Pereiaslav Council*, mounted on a truck. Centrally located Khmelnytsky Square (formerly St Sophia Square) was decorated with a gigantic copy of Khmelko's *Forever with Moscow*.[15]

To mark the anniversary, Russia and Ukraine exchanged symbolic gifts, including historical paintings, decorated boxes, vases, statues, carpets, and albums. Among the Ukrainian gifts were Khmelko's *Forever with Moscow*, a tapestry version of Derehus's *The Pereiaslav Council*, numerous boxes and vases with portraits of Khmelnytsky, and an imitation of the Cossack colonel's mace. (In addition, the Ukrainian authorities presented eighteen Soviet marshals and generals with copies of the mace.) The list, however, also included such manifestly modern items as a TV set, a tape recorder, and a camera. Russia responded with pseudo-antique caps, heavily decorated boxes, sculptures, and carpets, as well as some modern items. Other republics also presented gifts to both Russia and Ukraine. After the celebration, the State Historical Museums in Moscow and Kiev held exhibitions of the gifts, which displayed this bewildering mix of historical pageantry and Soviet modernity, itself allegedly a result of the seventeenth-century union.[16]

In the last days of May the celebrations moved to Moscow. The Russian Republic's Supreme Soviet opened its jubilee session on 29 May, and military and civilian parades took place in Red Square the next day.[17] The Moscow festivities added a new symbolic dimension to the tercentanary: it was the first time that the Soviet Union officially celebrated the anniversary of a tsarist territorial acquisition as a national holiday. A commemoration of the friendship of peoples and Russian guidance extending back into the past, the tercentenary established the paradigm of memory potentially applicable to other peoples of the USSR, as well as to the Soviet satellites abroad. The press reported on festive meetings, concerts, and lectures in Bulgaria, Czechoslovakia, Eastern Germany, Hungary, Poland, and Romania.[18] In August 1954 Kabarda party authorities were eager to celebrate the 400th anniversary of their land's 'voluntary incorporation into Russia' in 1955. Since the tsarist conquest of Kabarda had taken place in 1557, the Central Committee's experts proposed postponing the festivities until 1957. In 1955 bureaucrats in the Altai Mountains region also designated their land's conquest as 'voluntary incorporation,' while Belarusian scholars claimed that Belarus's 'reunification' with Russia during the late 18th century reflected 'the age-old strivings of the Belarusian people.'[19] More difficult was the case of Astrakhan province, whose leaders asked the Kremlin in March 1955 to approve a lavish celebration of 400 years since the Astrakhan Khanate's incorporation into Russia (1956). Since history textbooks considered the conquest of Kazan and Astrakhan under Ivan IV one of Russia's most famous early military triumphs, the ideological bureaucrats were reluctant to 'rewrite' this event in official memory and did not issue their approval.[20]

Although the tercentenary festivities ostensibly commemorated Russian-Ukrainian friendship, some Ukrainian reactions to the *Theses* demonstrated that local intellectuals were using this official document as a tool to promote their national memory. A senior researcher at the Institute of Ukrainian Literature, a certain Savchenko, stated that the *Theses* did not 'sufficiently elucidate the role of progressive Ukrainian cultural figures' and did not even mention classical writers such as Skovoroda, Franko, Hrabovsky, Kotsiubynsky, and Lesia Ukrainka. At the Institute of History, the researcher Oleksii Voina subtly questioned the binary opposition of 'elder brother' and 'younger brother' by restoring a third historical actor, Poland. According to him, the document did not stress the historical 'cooperation among the Russian, Ukrainian, and Polish peoples.' At Drohobych Pedagogical Institute, a group of students were disappointed that the *Theses* did not restore the controversial Hetman Sahaidachny to Ukrainian historical memory: 'The Institute's students comrades Dyky, Puchkovsky, Kochmar, and others, while approving the *Theses*, expressed the wish to see the role of Hetman Sahaidachny – a native of Sambir district of Drohobych province – during the Ukrainian people's struggle for their liberation clarified.'[21]

A massive propaganda campaign before and during the tercentenary celebrations stimulated the Ukrainian public's interest in their national past. Typical questions asked after the reading of the *Theses* and the Learning Society historical lectures included: 'When did Ukraine organize itself as a nation (*natsiia*)?' 'How many times did Khmelnytstky send his ambassadors to Moscow?' 'What other issues, aside from reunification, were considered at the Pereiaslav Council?' 'Why do we speak of "reunification," rather than "incorporation"?' and 'Why did Shevchenko call Bohdan Khmelnytsky an "unwise son" [of Ukraine] and speak of him negatively in certain poems?'[22] As these questions seemed to indicate familiarity with non-Soviet narratives of the Ukrainian past and a critical attitude to the official explanations, none of them was relayed to Moscow. Ukrainian functionaries were careful in editing their reports on popular reactions to the *Theses*. The selective feedback they forwarded to the Kremlin created the impression that 100 per cent of the republic's population, including Western Ukrainians, had completely internalized the latest version of Stalinist historical memory.[23]

After Stalin

In Ukraine, the beginnings of de-Stalinization were marked by scholars' attempts to undermine the Stalinist concept of the Ukrainian past. During a historians' conference in the summer of 1956 Huslysty criticized the recent glossing over of the tsarist colonial practices and proposed that the contribution of 'bourgeois' historians be re-examined. Boiko suggested that Drahomanov's legacy be studied, Los termed the nineteenth-century Ukrainian national movement 'progressive,' and two other scholars demanded that a Ukrainian historical journal be established. In the same year, the historian M. Lysenko published an article suggesting that recent scholarship had overstressed the historical progressiveness of Ukraine's union with tsarist Russia.[24] Ukrainian literary scholars, meanwhile, proceeded to challenge the Stalinist orthodoxy on Shevchenko. Iieremiia Aizenshtok dismissed the myth of the poet's friendship with Russian radical thinkers as a subjectivist interpretation 'in some instances bordering on fantasy.' Oleksandr Biletsky questioned the practice of labelling Shevchenko a 'revolutionary democrat' and the untenable interpretation of his texts, which aimed at proving the poet's socialist views.[25]

While established scholars criticized only the excesses of Stalinist myth-making, some student youth explored the boundaries between Soviet and 'nationalistic' versions of Ukrainian historical memory. In February 1956 Vasyl Kushnir, the Komsomol organizer in the Faculty of History of Uzhorod University, wrote in his private diary about a conversation with fellow students: 'We discussed the question of whether Ukraine could be independent, and what it would be like now if it had been independent for a long time. I think by now it could have been among the world's most developed states.' In June 1956 he wrote: 'Today we had a discussion about nationalism. Together with a group of comrades, I defended Mazepa and other national heroes.'[26]

During the period 1956 to 1958 the authorities officially revoked the Stalinist denunciation of Sosiura's poem 'Love Ukraine' and Dankevych's opera *Bohdan Khmelnytsky*. Dovzhenko was allowed to publish, and, following his death in 1956, the Ukrainian intelligentsia idolized him as a film director of international stature.

The Ukrainian cultural revival of the 'Thaw' period emphasized national patrimony, the continuity of the Ukrainian cultural tradition, and pride in the national
past. Literature and the arts turned to folkloric and historical themes, and both
establishment intellectuals and young radicals publicly articulated their spiritual
bond to the Ukrainian past. In 1968 a leading prose writer, Oles Honchar,
published the allegorical novel *The Cathedral*, valorizing the Cossack yore and
criticizing the state's destruction of Ukrainian historical monuments, while a
young poet, Vasyl Symonenko, celebrated in his *samizdat* poems the nation's
eternal life and the Cossack blood pulsing in its veins.[27] Reclaiming Shevchenko as
a symbol of the nation, rather than of socialism and Ukraine's ties with Russia,
young intellectuals established their own alternative to the official pilgrimages to
the poet's tomb. On 22 May, from 1966 to 1971, they gathered at Shevchenko's
monument in Kiev to mark the anniversary of the poet's reburial in Ukraine.[28]

Similarly, the return to 'national history' originated within official historiography, and only later did the authorities' reaction channel this interpretation of the
Ukrainian past into dissident self-publishing. In an article apparently written for
publication in 1966, the established historian Mykhailo Braichevsky disputed the
authorized interpretation of 'reunification,' arguing that the Cossack leadership
had regarded the Pereiaslav Treaty as merely a military union, while the tsarist
administration had understood it as an act of incorporation. Never published in
Soviet Ukraine, Braichevsky's *Annexation or Reunification?* circulated widely in
samizdat and was published in the west. The literary critic Ivan Dziuba likewise
wrote *Internationalism or Russification?* (1965–9) with an establishment audience
in mind, attempting a Marxist critique of the Russian and Soviet colonial practices
in Ukraine.[29] The 'sixtiers' took up the restoration of the national narrative not
because they were nationalists by nature but because they had grown up in Stalin's
empire of memory, and that empire had failed to produce a non-national version
of the past. As Ukrainian dissidents were questioning the Soviet myth of the
'friendship of peoples' as diminishing their nation's past, Russian patriotic intellectuals were also beginning to attack it for not doing justice to Russia's historical
greatness.[30] Cracks in the Stalinist community of memory were becoming visible.

Although the republic's authorities periodically suppressed 'nationalist deviations' in scholarship and culture, their own politics of memory remained deeply
ambiguous. In fact, in Ukraine in the 1960s there probably existed a '*de facto*
community of interest between political elites interested in decisional autonomy
and cultural elites interested in expanded cultural expression.'[31] The crackdown
on Ukrainian dissidents during 1971–3 was followed by Petro Shelest's removal as
the KPU first secretary and the subsequent critique of his book *Our Soviet Ukraine*
as allegedly idealizing the Cossacks, minimizing the importance of reunification
with Russia, and promoting Ukraine's economic self-sufficiency. While the first

secretary unquestionably supported Ukrainian culture, western scholars have interpreted accusations of nationalism as the public excuse, rather than the real reason for Shelest's demotion, which was the result of his opposition to renewed economic centralization, as well as of political reshuffling in Moscow. Nevertheless, Shelest emerges in his memoirs as a sincere believer in Ukrainian national patrimony and the vitality of its national culture.[32]

Shelest's removal was followed by a new campaign against the remnants of 'bourgeois nationalism' in Ukrainian culture and scholarship. After 1973 Soviet ideologues closely supervised the activities of intellectuals to ensure that the national narrative remained safely subordinated to the doctrine of Russian guidance. Yet the suppressed tensions within the official historical memory, which simultaneously celebrated the nation and the empire, remained unresolved. When the party's ideological control over society began disintegrating in the late 1980s, the return to the national version of Ukrainian historical memory became a major political issue. As the sociologist Catherine Wanner has suggested in her recent study of post-Soviet Ukrainian commemoration practices, this 'thirst for historical debate was driven by a long-standing and widespread popular rejection of official Soviet histories.'[33] The rehabilitation of Hrushevsky, glorification of the Cossacks, and re-evaluation of the Pereiaslav Treaty rivalled in public attention issues such as Chernobyl and the Stalinist crimes. The emergence of an independent Ukraine in 1991 led to the implosion of the friendship myth and the reinstatement of the nationalist narrative as the official pedigree of the Ukrainian nation.[34]

What Stalinist ideologues had once condemned as 'nationalism' became the official ideology of the independent Ukrainian state. The present-day Ukrainian establishment has reinstalled in the national pantheon great ancestors such as Mazepa and Hrushevsky and rejected class analysis. Yet it still embraces Stalinist heroes such as Danylo of Halych and Khmelnytsky, as well as the linear narrative of the nation's 'natural' historical development towards the reunification of all the Ukrainian ethnic lands in one polity – a vision that the Stalinist ideologues shared with nationalist theoreticians and taught to Soviet Ukrainians. After all, in its search for a national ideology Stalinism arrived precisely at the starting point of the old 'bourgeois nationalism': the idea that an empire was a sum of its nations.

Notes

Note: For translations of archival sources and citation details, see the Bibliography.

Introduction

1 Examples of this approach include Pipes, *Formation of the Soviet Union*; Carrère d'Encausse, *Great Challenge*; idem, *End of the Soviet Empire*; Conquest, *Nation Killers*; idem, *Stalin*.
2 See, especially, Suny, *Revenge of the Past*; Kaiser, *Geography of Nationalism*; Slezkine, 'The USSR as a Communal Apartment.'
3 See Martin, *Affirmative Action Empire*; Hirsch, 'The Soviet Union as a Work-in-Progress.'
4 The literature on 'nativization' is voluminous. For an up-to-date, comprehensive treatment, see Martin, *Affirmative Action Empire*.
5 See Timasheff, *Great Retreat*; Dunham, *In Stalin's Time*; Fitzpatrick, *Cultural Front*.
6 Slezkine, 'The USSR as a Communal Apartment,' 442–7.
7 Brandenberger, *National Bolshevism*, 2.
8 This argument is made by Sheila Fitzpatrick in 'Ascribing Class,' where, referring to the tsarist social estate system in the last sentence of the article, she suggests 'an intriguing possibility that the shadow of *soslovnost'* hung over the construction of national as well as social identity in the Stalin period.' This vision of 'class' was originally articulated in Fitzpatrick's 1988 article, 'The Bolshevik's Dilemma,' with critical comments by Ronald Grigor Suny and Daniel Orlovsky on pp. 614–23. In his later work, Suny describes the same process, while retaining class analysis as an analytical tool and stressing the role of the masses as a historical agent. During the 1920s and 1930s 'the artificial manipulation of class categories and official restrictions on autonomous class activity undermined identification with and loyalty to

class.' He then concludes that 'with the emergence of an articulated civil society in the Soviet Union in the post-Stalin decades, identification with the nationality was for most non-Russians a far more palpable touchstone than the eroded loyalty to social class' (Suny, *Revenge of the Past*, 120–1).

9 Francine Hirsch has shown that the Soviet authorities always employed colonial (political and cultural, including ethnic classification) technologies in governing their multinational state ('The Soviet Union as a Work-in-Progress' and 'Toward an Empire of Nations'). What interests me here is the difference between the two projects in which these colonial technologies were used, the permeable border between which was located somewhere in the mid-1930s.

10 On ethnicization of the Stalinist social imagination and the invention of 'enemy peoples,' see Weiner, 'Nature, Nurture, and Memory in a Socialist Utopia' and Martin, 'Modernization or Neo-Traditionalism?'

11 See, most recently, Baberowski, 'Stalinismus als imperials Phänomen'; Lieven, 'The Russian Empire and the Soviet Union'; Motyl, 'From Imperial Decay to Imperial Collapse'; Suny, 'Ambiguous Categories'; idem, *Revenge of the Past*; Szporluk, 'The Fall of the Tsarist Empire and the USSR.'

12 For current discussion, see H[offman], 'The Soviet Empire'; Michaels, 'Medical Propaganda and Cultural Revolution'; Northrop, 'Languages of Loyalty'; Hirsch, 'Toward an Empire of Nations'; Slezkine, 'Imperialism as the Highest Stage of Socialism.'

13 Beissinger, *Nationalist Mobilization*; Martin, 'The Soviet Union as Empire.'

14 See Pavlyshyn, 'Post-Colonial Features in Contemporary Ukrainian Culture'; Shkandrij, *Russia and Ukraine.*

15 Stoler and Cooper, 'Between Metropole and Colony,' 11–12; Partha Chatterjee, *Nation and Its Fragments.*

16 See, for example, Iurchuk, *Kulturne zhyttia v Ukraini u povoienni roky*; Zamlynska, 'Ideolohichnyi teror ta represii proty tvorchoi intelihentsii u pershi povoienni roky'; Shevchenko, 'Kultura Ukrainy v umovakh stalinskoho totalitaryzmu.'

17 On the socialist polities' need for 'national ideology' and the role of intellectuals in its production, see Verdery, *National Ideology under Socialism*, where she insightfully points out that such 'national ideology,' in fact, 'disrupted Marxist discourse' (4). More generally on intellectuals and nationalism in eastern Europe, see Kennedy and Suny, 'Introduction,' in Kennedy and Suny, *Intellectuals and the Articulation of the Nation.*

18 Dovzhenko, *Hospody, poshly meni syly*; Sosiura, 'Tretia Rota.'

19 With some reservations, I share the understanding of the Stalinist subject that Igal Halfin and Jochen Hellbeck first formulated in their 1996 review article 'Rethinking the Stalinist Subject.' See also Hellbeck, 'Speaking Out'; Krylova, 'The Tenacious Liberal Subject in Soviet Studies.' My principal objection is that this concept ignores

a significant proportion of Stalinist citizens who came of age under tsarism (or, in the case of Western Ukrainians, in pre-war Poland) and never internalized Soviet ideology – as well as those relatives and peers who might have been influenced by their unorthodox views.

20 See Deutsch, *Nationalism and Social Communication*; Hobsbawm, *Nations and Nationalism since 1780*; Hobsbawm and Ranger, *Invention of Tradition*; Anderson, *Imagined Communities*.
21 Gellner, *Nations and Nationalism* 57.
22 See especially H[artley], 'Nation'; Bhabha, *Nation and Narration*.
23 Appadurai, 'The Past as a Scarce Resource.'
24 Thus, I share Anthony Smith's and Rudy Koshar's criticisms of the 'constructivist' argument. See Smith, *Ethnic Origins of Nations*; idem, 'The Nation'; Koshar, *Germany's Transient Pasts*, 8–10.
25 Duara, *Rescuing History from the Nation*, 8.
26 Ibid., 9.
27 See Gedi and Elam, 'Collective Memory.'
28 Halbwachs, *Collective Memory*; idem, *On Collective Memory*.
29 Halbwachs, *Collective Memory*, 50–87, here 78.
30 Nora, *Les lieux de mémoire*; idem, 'Between History and Memory'; Wood, 'Memory Remains'; Yerushalmi, *Zakhor*.
31 Funkenstein, 'Collective Memory and Historical Consciousness'; Crane, 'Writing the Individual Back into Collective Memory.'
32 I also use the term 'national memory' in reference to historical memory that is centred around the narrative of a nation. There is no assumption that this story is necessarily shared by all or even by the majority of the nation's members.
33 Lowell Tillett was the first to analyse the 'friendship' paradigm in his attentive reading of the then available Russian-language publications. See Tillett, *Great Friendship*.
34 See 'Archival Sources' in the Bibliography for a complete list of these archives and the documents used.
35 See, for example, Kostiuk, *Stalinist Rule in the Ukraine*; Sullivant, *Soviet Politics and the Ukraine*; Lewytzkyj, *Die Sowjetukraine*; Bilinsky, *Second Soviet Republic*; Krawchenko, *Social Change and National Consciousness*; Liber, *Soviet Nationality Policy*; Marples, *Stalinism in Ukraine*.
36 See, in particular, Basarab, *Pereiaslav 1654*; Szporluk, 'National History as a Political Battleground'; idem, 'The Ukraine and Russia'; Velychenko, 'The Origins of the Official Soviet Interpretation of Eastern Slavic History'; idem, *Shaping Identity in Eastern Europe and Russia*.
37 See Kuromiya, *Freedom and Terror in the Donbas*; Weiner, *Making Sense of War*; Martin, *Affirmative Action Empire*; Liber, *Alexander Dovzhenko*.
38 Smolii, *U leshchatakh totalitaryzmu*; Slyvka, *Kulturne zhyttia v Ukraini*.

39 See Shapoval, *Ukraina 20-50-kh rokiv*; idem, *Liudyna i systema*; Kozhukalo, 'Vplyv kultu osoby Stalina na ideologichni protsesy na Ukraini'; Rublov and Cherchenko, *Stalinshchyna i dolia zakhidnoukrainskoi intelihentsii*; Shevchenko, 'Kulturno-ideolohichni protsesy v Ukraini u 40-50-kh rr.'; idem, 'Kultura Ukrainy v umovakh stalinskoho totalitaryzmu'; Zamlynska, 'Ideolohichni represii u haluzi kultury v Ukraini u 1948–1953 rr.'; idem, 'Ideolohichnyi teror ta represii proty tvorchoi intelihentsii.'

1: Soviet National Patriots

1   Marx and Engels, 'Manifesto of the Communist Party,' 488, 473. Following the 1888 translation by Samuel Moore, edited by Engels, *Die Arbeiter haben kein Vaterland* is traditionally rendered in English as 'The working men have no country.' I have slightly modified this sentence so that the subsequent translations of Russian and Ukrainian references to it will be clear.

2   See Barber, *Soviet Historians in Crisis*.

3   Stalin, 'O zadachakh khoziaistvennikov,' 445.

4   For a selection of revealing examples, see Oberländer, *Sowjetpatriotismus und Geschichte*, 56–62.

5   *Pravda*, 16 May 1934, 1. This and all the subsequent translations in this book are the author's unless otherwise indicated.

6   See Brandenberger, *National Bolshevism*, chaps 3 and 5; Petrone, *Life Has Become More Joyous, Comrades*, chap. 5.

7   Iavorsky, *Korotka istoriia Ukrainy*, 13.

8   Idem, *Istoriia Ukrainy u styslomu narysi*, 55 (Khmelnytsky); idem, *Korotka istoriia Ukrainy*, 63 (Mazepa) and 75 (Shevchenko); idem, *Narysy z istorii revoliutsiinoi borotby na Ukraini* 1: 179 (Shevchenko).

9   Mace, *Communism and the Dilemmas*, 253–9.

10 Recently, several Ukrainian scholars have studied the campaign against Hrushevsky, using the newly available archival materials: Pyrih, *Zhyttia Mykhaila Hrushevskoho*, chaps. 4–7; Prystaiko and Shapoval, *Mykhailo Hrushevsky i HPU-NKVD*, 79–105.

11 Kostiuk, *Stalinist Rule in the Ukraine*, 93.

12 *Istoriia Ukrainy*, vol. 1: *Peredkapitalistychna doba*.

13 Petrovsky, *Narysy istorii Ukrainy XVII*, 129; Sokolovsky, *Bohun*; Bertram, '(Re-)Writing History.'

14 K[rut], 'Khmelnitsky, Bogdan Zinovii Mikhailovich,' vol. 59: 816, 818. This striking entry has long attracted scholarly attention. Lowell Tillett quotes it in his *Great Friendship*, 46, as does John Basarab in his *Pereiaslav 1654*, 164–5.

15 TsDAHO, f. 1, op. 70, spr. 757, ark. 96 (monument); Krawchenko, *Social Change*,

141 (museums); Soroka, 'Zinaida Tulub,' in Musiienko, *Z poroha smerti*, 426–9 (Tulub).

16 *Pravda*, 24 October 1937, 6; Stanishevsky, *Ukrainskyi radianskyi muzychnyi teatr*, 160–2.

17 TsDAHO, f. 1, op. 6, spr. 409, ark. 24; Santsevich and Komarenko, *Razvitie istoricheskoi nauki v Akademii nauk Ukrainskoi SSR*, 34.

18 Smolii, *U leshchatakh totalitaryzmu* 1: 65; see also 37, n. 21.

19 Ibid., 1: 49; Koval and Rublov, 'Instytut istorii NAN Ukrainy,' 52–3.

20 Smolii, *U leshchatakh totalitaryzmu* 1: 63–4.

21 Kevin M.F. Platt and David Brandenberger show that the rehabilitation of Ivan the Terrible by Russian intellectuals followed the same model. See 'Terribly Romantic, Terribly Progressive, or Terribly Tragic.'

22 *Pravda*, 22 August 1937, 2.

23 Nechkina, 'K itogam diskussii o periodizatsii sovetskoi istoricheskoi nauki,' 74; idem, 'Vopros o M.N. Pokrovskom v postanovleniiakh partii i pravitelstva,' 241. The expression 'lesser evil' appears in the internal memos of the party apparatus and the Ministry of Education as early as December 1936. See Brandenberger and Dubrovsky, '"The People Need a Tsar,"' 878, 889, nn. 46, 47.

24 Shestakov, *Kratkii kurs istorii SSSR*, 50–2.

25 Although Korniichuk's biographer later maintained that he had started working on the play in 1935 and even had spent some time doing research in archives (Gorbunova, *Dramaturgiia A. Korneichuka*, 133), the writer's personal archive does not support this claim. The first draft of the drama, entitled *Bohdan Khmelnytsky: Heroica. Ukraine in the Seventeenth Century*, survived among other materials from 1938. Neither the play's content nor Korniichuk's notebooks reveals any serious work with historical sources. The secret of the play's success was, rather, the result of a novel interpretation of familiar facts. See TsDAMLM, f. 435, op. 1, spr. 33.

26 Picheta was a Belarusian historian of Serbian background who was denounced during the late 1920s as a 'Belarusian bourgeois nationalist' before being exiled from Minsk to Viatka in the early 1930s as a 'Russian monarchist.' In 1935 he returned to Moscow and successfully continued his academic career there. See Lindner, 'Nationalhistoriker im Stalinismus,' 199–201.

27 The minutes of the discussion are held in the archives of the Malyi Theatre Museum and were not available to me. Quoted in Gorbunova, *Dramaturgiia*, 135, 137; Kobyletsky, *Kryla krecheta*, 133–4.

28 RGASPI, f. 17, op. 120, d. 348, ll. 63–71ob and 76–7. I am grateful to Karen Petrone and David Brandenberger for the reference.

29 *Visti*, 5 March 1939, 1, 4; *Komunist*, 1 April 1939, 3; Kobyletsky, *Kryla*, 149–51.

30 Syrotiuk, *Ukrainska istorychna proza za 40 rokiv*, 254–5, 154 (Panch and Kachura);

Mykhailov, *Konstiantyn Fedorovych Dankevych*, 15 (Dankevych); Stanishevsky, *Ukrainskyi radianskyi*, 177 (Shostakovich).

31 On the pre-war debates at the Institute of Ukrainian History, see TsDAHO, f. 1, op. 70, spr. 753, ark. 121; spr. 121, ark. 12. (These are the later references to a discussion of which no documentary traces survive.) Osipov's book appeared in the prestigious 'Lives of Distinguished People' series at the Komsomol publishing house Molodaia gvardiia: Osipov, *Bogdan Khmelnitsky*.

32 Petrovsky, *Vyzvolna viina ukrainskoho narodu*, 4. A priest's son, Petrovsky (1894–1951) received his education before the revolution, worked briefly with Hrushevsky during the 1920s, and was never admitted to the party. During 1942–7 he served as director of the Institute of Ukrainian History; during 1944–7 he was also chair of Ukrainian history at Kiev University. See NAIIU, op. 1L, spr. 115, and Smolii, *Vcheni Instytutu istorii Ukrainy*, 245–50.

33 Baraboi, Review of *Vyzvolna viina ukrainskoho narodu*.

34 RGALI, f. 1992, op. 1, dd. 75, 76 (correspondence between Savchenko and Korniichuk and variants of script); TsDAMLM, f. 435, op. 1, spr. 2137, ark. 3 (Petrovsky); Zak, Parfenov, and Iakubovich-Iasnyi, *Igor Savchenko*, 252 (Savchenko's quote).

35 TsDAHO, f. 1, op. 70, spr. 66, ark. 6–7 (production records); RGALI, f. 1992, op. 1, d. 78. ll. 8, 15, 16 (discussion minutes).

36 RGALI, f. 1992, op. 1, d. 80 (Savchenko's collection of newspaper clippings), here ll. 1–3; Holynsky, *Heroichna tema u tvorchosti I.A. Savchenka*, 50 (use as war propaganda movie).

37 TsDAMLM, f. 435, op. 1, spr. 1959, ark. 23, 35 (Diadychenko); f. 661, op. 1, spr. 130, ark. 4, 9; TsDAHO, f. 1, op. 30, spr. 1875, ark. 72; spr. 2775, ark. 58, 67.

38 *Visti*, 6 March 1939, 1–3; 8 March 1939, 1–2; 9 March 1939, 1; Shevchenko, *Povne zibrannia tvoriv*.

39 Rudenko, *Naibilshe dyvo – zhyttia*, 51.

40 Bilousov et al., *Istoriia Ukrainy*, 39–40, 52–4 (Danylo), 90–2 (Khmelnytsky), 113 (Mazepa), 146 (Shevchenko), 388–94 (reunification of Ukrainian lands).

41 Yaroslav Bilinsky and Roman Szporluk have long argued that the addition of thoroughly 'nationalistic' Western Ukrainians actually strengthened Ukrainian identity and national consciousness in the Ukrainian SSR. See Bilinsky, 'The Incorporation of Western Ukraine'; Szporluk, 'West Ukraine and West Belorussia.'

42 *Komunist*, 18 September 1939, 1; *Pravda*, 19 September 1939, 1. Timoshenko's proclamation is reproduced in Picheta, *Osnovnye momenty*, 128–9.

43 Bielousov [Bilousov] and Ohloblyn, *Zakhidna Ukraina*; Picheta, *Osnovnye momenty*, 3.

44 On the Russians' official elevation to the 'great people,' see Simon, *Nationalism and the Policy toward the Nationalities in the Soviet Union*, 149–50; Velychenko, *Shaping Identity*, 55.

45 *Komunist*, 15 November 1939, 1; 16 November 1939, 1.

46 Petrovsky, *Voennoe proshloe ukrainskogo naroda*, 78.

47 See *Kulturne zhyttia v Ukraini* 1: 52–136; Rublov and Cherchenko, *Stalinshchyna i dolia zakhidnoukrainskoi intelihentsii*, 184–210; Kondratiuk and Luchakivska, 'Zakhidnoukrainska intelihentsiia u pershi roky radianskoi vlady.' To be sure, Krypiakevych already had a PhD degree from Lviv University (1911).

48 *Pravda*, 23 June 1941, 1 (Molotov); 27 December 1941, 3 (Iaroslavsky); 8 November 1941, 1 (Stalin).

49 *Komunist*, 24 June 1941, 3; 28 June 1941, 1; 4 July 1941, 4; *Literaturna hazeta*, 28 June 1941, 2.

50 *Komunist*, 4 July 1941, 1.

51 *Komunist*, 2 July 1941, 3 (Petrovsky); 28 June 1941, 1 (series).

52 *Komunist*, 7 July 1941, 1.

53 'Do ukrainskoho narodu,' 1: 6. Petro Sahaidachny: a Cossack hetman in the early seventeenth century; Vasyl Bozhenko and Mykola Shchors: Soviet heroes of the Civil War in Ukraine.

54 TsDAHO, f. 1, op. 70, spr. 1154, ark. 15.

55 *Radianska Ukraina*, 2 June 1943, 1 (great Ukrainian people); 8 May 1943, 3 (Rylsky). The first attempt to study the meetings is made in Safonova, 'Antyfashystski mitynhy predstavnykiv ukrainskoho narodu.'

56 TsDAHO, f. 1, op. 70, spr. 48, ark. 6–7. See Huslysty, *Danylo Halytsky*; idem, *Petro Konashevych-Sahaidachny*; Petrovsky, *Bohdan Khmelnytsky*.

57 Voblyi et al. *Narys istorii Ukrainy*, 3 (great Ukrainian people), 42–5 (Danylo), and 67–71 (Khmelnytsky); Iushkov, review of *Narys istorii Ukrainy*.

58 Iushkov et al., *Istoriia Ukrainy*, vol. 1, esp. 38–97 on Kievan Rus' and 183–313 on the Cossacks. The archives of the KP(b)U Central Committee preserved the advanced copy with the publication date '1942' (TsDAHO, f. 1, op. 70, spr. 50). The remaining three volumes were never completed and the authors used their drafts during the preparation of the two-volume *History of Ukrainian SSR* (published in 1954–5).

59 TsDAHO, f. 1, op. 23, spr. 441, ark. 5zv. The Ukrainian composer Kost Dankevych would write the opera *Bohdan Khmelnytsky* during 1948–53.

60 Dmytrenko, *Ukrainskyi radianskyi istorychnyi zhyvopys*, 56–7; *Istoriia ukrainskoho mystetstva*, vol. 6, 46.

61 Bazhan, 'Danylo Halytsky,' *Ukrainska literatura*, 52, 53. In all post-1946 editions, 'Ukraine' is changed to 'Slavic lands' and 'Ukrainian fields' are changed to the 'field at Drohochyn' (Bazhan, 'Danylo Halytsky,' in *Virshi i poemy* 206, 208). Stalin Prize winners for 1945 were announced in *Literaturna hazeta*, 4 July 1946, 1.

62 Kondufor, ed., *Kulturne budivnytstvo v Ukrainskii RSR*, 27, 32, 54, 64 (celebrations);

TsDAHO, f. 1, op. 23, spr. 441, ark. 5zv. (Academy); TsDAVOV, f. 2, op. 7, spr. 345, ark. 85–6 (opera).

63 TsDAHO, f. 1, op. 23, spr. 451, ark. 1–3 (wartime publications); *Radianska Ukraina*, 5 June 1943, 4 (review of *Kobzar*).

64 Leonid Vladych, *Vasyl Kasiian*, 75, 80.

65 TsDAHO, f. 1, op. 23, spr. 2858, ark. 22–3 (typescript copy of newspaper publication). Sviatoslav (ruled 962–72) and Volodymyr (Vladimir, ruled 980–1015): grand princes of Kiev. Ivan Mazepa: the hetman of Ukraine in 1687–708, who in 1708 allied himself with King Charles XII of Sweden against Tsar Peter I. Ivan Franko (1856–1916): the leading Western Ukrainian writer and political thinker of the time. Mikhnovsky, Petliura, and Konovalets: twentieth-century nationalist leaders.

66 See K[rypiakevych], *Mala istoriia Ukrainy*, 47–8. Krypiakevych's publishing activities during the war are discussed in Dashkevych, 'Ivan Krypiakevych – istoryk Ukrainy,' 5–21. On the Ukrainian Publishing House, see *Kulturne zhyttia v Ukraini*, 1: 208–9.

67 *Radianska Ukraina*, 9 July 1943, 4.

68 GARF, f. 6646, op. 1, d. 4, ll. 9–10 (Slavic Committee); *Radianska Ukraina*, 16 May 1943, 2–3 (Tychyna).

69 TsDAHO, f. 1, op. 70, spr. 68, ark. 29zv.

70 See Chakrabarty, 'Postcoloniality and the Artifice of History.'

2: The Unbreakable Union

1 *Kulturne budivnytstvo v Ukrainskii RSR* vol. 2, 17 (Ukrainian competition); RGASPI, f. 17, op. 125, d. 300 (competitions in other republics); TsDAHO, f. 1, op. 23, spr. 1608, ark. 6 and 8 (Tychyna and Bazhan).

2 TsDAHO, f.1, op. 23, spr. 2782, ark. 2 (Aleksandrov); *Literaturna hazeta*, 24 July 1948, 1 (anthem inaugurated).

3 Simon, *Nationalism and Policy*, 189–90.

4 See Hrynevych, 'Utvorennia Narkomatu oborony URSR u 1944 r'; idem, 'Utvorennia Narodnoho komisariatu zakordonnykh sprav Ukrainskoi RSR'; *Radianska Ukraina*, 8 February 1944, 1 (editorial on state-building); ibid., 6 February 1944, 1, 5 March 1944, 1 (ministers appointed).

5 TsDAVOV, f. 4750, op. 1, spr. 3959, ark. 50. As a secretary of the Central Committee, Georgii Malenkov supervised the party's organizational work, but since the party authority on ideology, Andrei Zhdanov, spent most of the war in besieged Leningrad, Malenkov also extended his influence to ideological matters. Aleksandrov, himself Zhdanov's former protégé, worked closely with Malenkov, the rising heir apparent See Hann, *Postwar Soviet Politics*, 19–66.

6 *Radianska Ukraina*, 15 November 1944, 1 (aims of encyclopedia); TsDAVOV, f. 4750, op. 1, spr. 2, ark. 1–2; spr. 13, ark. 13–14 (number of volumes, schedules, and

editorial board); spr. 17; f. 2, op. 7, spr. 2747, ark. 20; spr. 3927, ark. 54–5 (work accomplished by 1947).

7 Dovzhenko, *Hospody*, 191. Compare the decrees on establishing the orders of Suvorov, Kutuzov, and Nevsky in *Pravda*, 30 July 1942, 1. Dovzhenko belonged to a small group of leading Ukrainian writers who were drafted into the army as senior political officers to produce propaganda materials.

8 TsDAHO, f. 1, op. 23, spr. 355, ark. 21–2.

9 Ibid., spr. 463, ark. 11; spr. 355, ark. 20.

10 The sketches of the Kharkiv-based artists are in TsDAHO, f. 1, op. 23, spr. 355, ark. 26–42; the spelling is specified on ark. 12. On an additional competition in Moscow and Pashchenko's success, see Dmytrenko, *Ukrainskyi radianskyi istorychnyi zhyvopys*, 56.

11 Whether he made this suggestion in writing or over the phone is not clear. Stalin's telegrams to Khrushchev, if they survived, are not available, and Stalin's role is deduced from Khrushchev's subsequent enquiries on when to announce the renaming 'that you [Stalin] proposed' (TsDAHO, f. 1, op. 23, spr. 355, ark. 15).

12 Ibid., spr. 328, ark. 15.

13 *Pravda*, 11 October 1943, 1.

14 *Radianska Ukraina*, 12 October 1943, 3.

15 TsDAHO, f. 1, op. 23, spr. 328, ark. 1–7.

16 *Pravda*, 13 October 1943, 1; *Radianska Ukraina*, 13 October 1943, 1.

17 Kolesnikov and Rozhkov, *Ordena i medali SSSR*, 71.

18 *Radianska Ukraina*, 24 September 1943, 3; 25 September 1943, 4; 29 September 1943, 3. The quotation is from the title of Petrovsky's article in the 24 September issue.

19 *Radianska Ukraina*, 31 October 1943, 3; Petrovsky, *Nezlamnyi dukh velykoho ukrainskoho narodu*, 4, 6, 10. The opening statement is on p. 3.

20 *Radianska Ukraina*, 18 November 1943, 1; Dovzhenko, *Hospody*, 195.

21 *Radianska Ukraina*, 10 December 1943, 3–4.

22 TsDAHO, f. 1, op. 70, spr. 91, ark. 44; the list of the planned festivities is on ark. 45–7.

23 See *Radianska Ukraina*, 18 January 1944, 1, and *Radianske mystetstvo*, 18 January 1944, 1–2.

24 *Radianska Ukraina*, 9 July 1944, 2.

25 *Radianska Ukraina*, 17 October 1944, 3; 13 November 1944, 2.

26 Brooks, *Thank You, Comrade Stalin!*

27 The classic account of the developments around the *History of Kazakh SSR* is in Tillett, *Great Friendship*, 70–83. The archives of the VKP(b) Central Committee confirm that the book was nominated for a Stalin Prize, but the reviewer, Aleksei Iakovlev, objected to its glorification of anti-Russian uprisings in Kazakhstan as

heroic anti-colonial struggles. The book's co-editor, Anna Pankratova, complained to Agitprop, but its head, Georgii Aleksandrov, only condemned the work even more vigorously as 'anti-Russian.' See RGASPI, f. 17, op. 125, d. 224, ll. 4, 23–5, and 36–43. For a recent, archive-based analysis of the Stalinist politics of history in Kazakhstan and other Soviet Asian republics, see Blitstein, 'Stalin's Nations,' chap. 2.

28 RGASPI, f. 17, op. 125, d. 190, ll. 26–7. Dovzhenko noted in his diary that the same group of Ukrainian writers headed by Iurii Ianovsky prepared the letter (*Hospody*, 195).

29 The text of Stalin's comments has recently been published as Stalin, 'Ob antilenin-skikh oshibkakh.' The novel's initial negative assessment by Agitprop is in RGASPI, f. 17, op. 125, d. 212, ll. 1–3.

30 TsDAHO, f. 1, op. 70, spr. 68, ark. 26–7 (Petrovsky to Lytvyn); spr. 46, ark. 117 (Lytvyn). Lytvyn's note has been published in Smolii, *U leshchatakh totalitaryzmu*, 1: 116.

31 TsDAHO, f. 1, op. 70, spr. 153, ark. 1–272. Bazhan's review is on ark. 1–3; the underlined sentence is on ark. 8.

32 Petrovsky, 'Vossoedinenie ukrainskogo naroda v edinom ukrainskom sovetskom gosudarstve'; *Radianska Ukraina*, 29 February 1944, 4; 1 March 1944, 3–4; Petrovsky, *Vozziednannia ukrainskoho narodu*; idem, *Vossoedinenie*. The Russian-language pamphlet earned a laudatory review in *Istoricheskii zhurnal*; Grekov, Review of *Vossoedinenie ukrainskogo naroda*.

33 Petrovsky, *Vossoedinenie*, 31, 33.

34 Petrovsky, *Bogdan Khmelnitsky*; the quotations displaying the analogy with Stalin are on pp. 9, 13, 26, 29 ('terrorist act'), 38, 40 ('crushed the oppositional group'), 56–7 ('suppressed any opposition').

35 Pashuto, 'Daniil Galitskii'; Iugov, *Daniil Galitskii*, 55; Grekov, 'Sudby naseleniia galitskikh kniazheskikh.' Iugov would eventually publish an acclaimed historical novel about Aleksandr Nevsky and Danylo of Halych, *The Warriors* (Iugov, *Ratobortsy*).

36 A copy of the review, dated 7 January 1944, is preserved in Korniichuk's personal archives: TsDAMLM, f. 435, op. 1, spr. 508, ark. 1–3.

37 TsDAHO, f. 1, op. 70, spr. 388, ark. 4.

38 *Radianska Ukraina*, 11 January 1944, 4; 8 April 1944, 4.

39 TsDAHO, f. 1, op. 23, spr. 1621, ark. 64–6 (Korniichuk's complaint); *Radianska Ukraina*, 18 August 1945, 2 (Moscow's critics).

40 TsDAHO, f. 1, op. 70, spr. 837 (first draft); TsDAVOV, f. 4669, op. 1, spr. 124, ark. 1–3 (Manuilsky's notes).

41 TsDAHO, f. 1, op. 70, spr. 836, ark. 1–6, 42, 54, 58 (the Varangian theme edited out); 41, 93 (Kiev); 77 ('the people's wisdom').

42 *Literatura i mystetstvo*, 23 November 1944, 3; *Radianska Ukraina*, 14 March 1945, 4; 16 March 1945, 2 (excerpts); 23 March 1945, 3 (positive review); *Radianske*

mystetstvo, 17 September 1946, 1 (premiere); Kyryliuk, *Istoriia ukrainskoi literatury*, vol. 7; 314–16.

43 *Istoriia ukrainskoho mystetstva*, 6: 27–9 (images of Shevchenko and Khmelnytsky), 46 (Shulha and Derehus); Dmytrenko, *Ukrainskyi radianskyi istorychnyi zhyvopys*, 56, 75.

44 *Radianske mystetstvo*, 20 November 1945, 1–2 (review of the exhibition); 13 November 1945, 1 (editorial).

45 *Radianska Ukraina*, 12 October 1943, 3; Petrovsky, 'Prisoedinenie Ukrainy k Rossii,' 52. The text of volume 9, parts 1 and 2, of *History of Ukraine-Rus'* does not support Petrovsky's assertion. See Hrushevsky, *Istoriia Ukrainy-Rusy*, vol. 9, 1: 720, 784; part 2, 1492–1508. Hrushevsky says that, for Khmelnytsky, the Pereiaslav Treaty was simply a military union, 'valuable in given circumstances, one more [agreement] in addition to unions with the Tatars, the Turks, and Moldavia' (2: 149–5).

46 *Radianska Ukraina*, 8 August 1944, 2; 23 August 1944, 4; *Literatura i mystetstvo*, 7 August 1944, 3–4.

47 Ivan Pilhuk, 'Mykola Kostomarov,' *Ukrainska literatura*, no. 4–5 (1945): 122.

48 *Radianska Ukraina*, 4 April 1944, 3.

49 *Kulturne budivnytstvo v Ukrainskii RSR*; *Literatura i mystetstvo*, 25 January 1945, 1 (government decree); *Radianska Ukraina*, 21 March 1945, 3 (the laudatory article quoted). The expression '*u svoii vlasnii khati*' (in our own house) had long been used by Ukrainian patriots as a metaphor for independent statehood.

50 TsDAHO, f. 1, op. 23, spr. 1604, ark. 1–3.

51 TsDAHO, f. 1, op. 70, spr. 387, ark. 18 (Panch); TsDAVOV, f. 2, op. 7, spr. 818, ark. 5, 9 (book trade).

52 *Radianska Ukraina*, 19 February 1943, 2; *Pravda*, 20 February 1943, 2. *Izvestiia* and *Krasnaia zvezda* reprinted the article on 21 February, as subsequently did many other papers and magazines. The original manuscript in Ukrainian and the clippings are in Korniichuk's archives in TsDAMLM, f. 435, op. 1, spr. 496.

53 *Radianska Ukraina*, 6 March 1944, 1 (Ukrainian history); 2 (reunification).

54 The cities that Khrushchev named are currently known by their Polish names: Chełm, Hrubieszów, Zamość, Tomaszów, and Jarosław. For an introduction to the history of the Kholm/Chełm region, see Kubijovyč, 'Kholm Region,' 480–5. Curzon Line was the eastern boundary of Poland proposed by the British foreign secretary, Lord Curzon, after the First World War and presumably marking the eastern border of the ethnically Polish settlement. The Treaty of Riga in 1921 moved the Soviet-Polish border east of the Curzon Line.

55 *Radianska Ukraina*, 30 April 1944, 2. See also Mykola Tkachenko, 'Kholmshchyna, Hrubeshiv, Iaroslav.'

56 See Boiechko, Hanzha, and Zakharchuk, *Kordony Ukrainy*, 80–5.

57 *Radianska Ukraina*, 8 August 1944, 2 (article); TsDAHO, f. 1, op. 23, spr. 937, ark. 58–61 (Khrushchev's correspondence with Stalin); spr. 787, ark. 3–288 (petitions).

58 TsDAHO, f. 1, op. 23, spr. 788, ark. 1–5, 10–12; *Radianska Ukraina*, 23 December 1944, 4.
59 *Radianska Ukraina*, 1 July 1945, 3.
60 *Kulturne budivnytstvo*, 2: 86–7; Turianytsia, 'Rozvytok kultury u Zakarpatti'; Magocsi, *Shaping of a National Identity*, 255–71.
61 TsDAHO, f. 1, op. 23, spr. 1652, ark. 103 (teachers); op. 70, spr. 326, ark. 74–6 (Lintur).
62 TsDAHO, f. 1, op. 23, spr. 703, ark. 23–36; spr. 1060, ark. 1–18 (Khrushchev's letters to Stalin); spr. 780, 889, and 890 (the authorities' concerns during 1944). See also Serhiichuk, *Desiat buremnykh lit*, 10–184.
63 Rublov and Cherchenko, *Stalinshchyna*, 211–41 (the number 44,000 is given on p. 211).
64 Manuilsky, *Ukrainsko-nemetskie natsionalisty*, 5–7, 9.
65 TsDAHO, f. 1, op. 70, spr. 385, ark. 212; spr. 539, ark. 6; op. 23, spr. 1652, ark. 83, 87 (Mazepa); 84 (the Ukrainian Galician Army); spr. 1605 (the affair of Halan's article). The report to Khrushchev on the article's effect was recently published in Slyvka, *Kulturne zhyttia v Ukraini*, 1: 267–76. For a comprehensive analysis of the Soviet anti-Uniate campaign of 1945–6, see Bociurkiw, *Ukrainian Greek Catholic Church*, 102–47.
66 TsDAHO, f. 1, op. 70, spr. 399; op. 23, spr. 860 (lectures); Petrovsky, *Zakhidna Ukraina* 3, 4, 17.
67 TsDAVOV, f. 4669, op. 1, spr. 47, ark. 7.
68 During the late 1940s, Ukraine had two Central Committee secretaries supervising the ideological domain: the secretary for ideology, Kost Lytvyn, and the secretary for propaganda, Ivan Nazaranko. Nazarenko also headed the republic's Agitprop.
69 RGASPI, f. 17, op. 125, d. 340, ll. 19–25; TsDAHO, f. 1, op. 70, spr. 326, ark. 64–73zv.
70 TsDAHO, f. 1, op. 70, spr. 394, ark. 1–5; Smolii, *U leshchatakh totalitaryzmu*, 2: 4–6. Although the report is written in Russian, one should assume that Petrovsky conversed with Krypiakevych and others in Ukrainian. The note on ark. 1 of the archival copy reads, 'Com[rade] Khrushchev read. 27. 02. [1945].'
71 *Radianska Ukraina*, 6 August 1944, 4 (pilgrimage); Mezentseva, *Muzei Ukrainy*, 162–3 (museums); *Radianske mystetstvo*, 4 December 1945, 3 (the play).
72 See Himka, *Galician Villagers*; Armstrong, *Ukrainian Nationalism*.

3: Reinventing Ideological Orthodoxy

1 Dmytro Manuilsky (1883–1959) belonged to a small group of well-educated 'old Bolsheviks' who survived the Great Purge. But even within this handful of people, he was probably the only Lenin appointee still enjoying a position of authority after the

Second World War. Manuilsky studied at St Petersburg University and received a law degree from the Sorbonne (1911). After briefly serving as the Ukrainian Communist Party's general secretary in 1921–2, he moved to Moscow as secretary of the Comintern's Executive Committee. In 1944–50 Manuilsky served as the Ukrainian republic's minister of foreign affairs, deputy premier, and head of the Ukrainian delegation to the United Nations.

2 TsDAVOV, f. 4669, op. 1, spr. 23, ark. 5; emphasis in the original.

3 Ibid., ark. 5, 7.

4 I. Martyniuk, 'Rozvyvaty i kultyvuvaty radianskyi patriotyzm'; idem, 'Do trydtsiatyrichchia Ukrainskoi Radianskoi Sotsialistychnoi Respubliky,' ibid., no. 12 (1947): 1–9; Literaturna hazeta, 15 January 1948, 3 (Iuriev).

5 The most recent, detailed discussion of this episode is in Liber, Alexander Dovzhenko, 196–206.

6 RGASPI, f. 17, op. 125, d. 293, ll. 7, 14, 17.

7 Stalin, 'Ob antileninskih oshibkakh,' 90, 93. Although the meeting was not publicized, the Ukrainian participants were allowed to take notes, and, during the ensuing ideological campaign in the republic, some of them publicly referred to Stalin's critique (TsDAMLM, f. 590, op. 1, spr. 39, ark. 20–2 [Korniichuk]). The archives of the KP(b)U Central Committee preserved an unfinished record of Stalin's speech, probably made by one of the republic's dignitaries (TsDAHO, f. 1, op. 70, spr. 282, ark. 200–3). Dovzhenko's widow and Rylsky (who participated in the meeting) later shared their accounts with family and friends, who subsequently published these stories (Literaturna Ukraina, 4 January 1990, 3; 21 June 1990, 4). Finally, the text of Stalin's comments was discovered and published as 'Ob antileninskikh oshibkakh.'

8 See Koval, 'Sprava Oleksandra Dovzhenka.'

9 TsDAHO, f. 1, op. 23, spr. 4504, ark. 1.

10 Ibid., ark. 39–40. See also the first uncensored publication of the novel in Dovzhenko, Hospody, 451.

11 TsDAHO, f. 1, op. 70, spr. 266, ark. 1

12 Ibid., ark. 10, 12.

13 In his memoirs, Khrushchev credits himself with saving Rylsky from persecutions, although he seems to be talking about an unrelated incident during the late 1930s ('Memuary Nikity Sergeevich Khrushcheva,' 88).

14 RGASPI, f. 17, op. 125, d. 224, ll. 102–46ob. (displeasure with Pankratova's letters and her repentance), 1–10 (Pankratova to Zhdanov), 66–75ob. (Pankratova to Stalin, Zhdanov, Malenkov, and Shcherbakov). See also Brandenberger, National Bolshevism, 125–9.

15 Voprosy istorii has recently published the conference's minutes: 'Stenogramma soveshchaniia po voprosam istorii SSSR v TsK VKP(b) v 1944 godu,' Voprosy istorii, no. 2 (1996): 55–86; no. 3: 82–112; no. 4: 65–93; no. 5: 77–106; no. 7: 70–87;

no. 9: 47–77. An insightful introduction by Iu. N. Amiantov, in no. 2: 47–54, provides a road map to the confusing proceedings. See also Konstantinov, 'Nesostoiavshaiasia rasprava'; Brandenberger, *National Bolshevism*, 129.

16 Aleksandrov, 'O nekotorykh zadachakh obshchestvennykh nauk,' 17.

17 TsDAHO, f. 1, op. 23, spr. 1652, ark. 1; op. 70, spr. 385, ark. 1.

18 Ibid., spr. 1652, ark. 146 (memo), 1–56 (minutes). The memo was recently published in Smolii, *U leshchatakh totalitaryzmu*, 2: 16–22.

19 TsDAHO, f. 1, op. 23, spr. 1652, ark. 73.

20 TsDAHO, f. 1, op. 70, spr. 385, ark. 210 (Diadychenko); op. 23, spr. 1652, ark. 50 (Los).

21 TsDAHO, f. 1, op. 70, spr. 385, ark. 147 (heroic past); spr. 388, ark. 4 (Danylo).

22 Ibid., spr. 387, ark. 1–6 (Kyryliuk); op. 23, spr. 1652, ark. 28–31 (Senchenko); op. 70, spr. 385, ark. 181 (Slavin).

23 TsDAHO, f. 1, op. 23, spr. 1652, ark. 91 (shout), 102–5 (Skrypnyk).

24 TsDAHO, f. 1, op. 70, spr. 387, ark. 59; spr. 388, ark. 130 (Lytvyn); spr. 390, ark 1–2 (draft resolution).

25 Ibid., spr. 564, ark. 4–93 (minutes). For a more detailed discussion of the incident's background, see Rublov and Cherchenko, *Stalinshchyna*, 215–19.

26 TsDAHO, f. 1, op. 70, spr. 564, ark. 52, 57.

27 TsDAHO, f. 1, op. 70, spr. 570, ark. 10–12 (halting the campaign); spr. 571, ark. 14–15 (recommendations). Mykhailo Koval and Oleksandr Rublov incorrectly presume that the initial conference of the department was organized 'according to the Central Committee's instructions' ('Instytut istorii Ukrainy,' 62).

28 Recent Russian works on the *Zhdanovshchina* include Aksenov, 'Poslevoennyi stalinizm'; Dobrenko, 'Sumerki kultury'; Zubkova, *Russia after the War*, chap. 12.

29 Hahn, *Postwar Soviet Politics*, 48. Unfortunately, Hahn does not attempt to follow the course of the *Zhdanovshchina* campaign in Ukraine or any other non-Russian republic.

30 See an excellent recent work on this topic: Burds, *The Early Cold War in Soviet West Ukraine, 1944–1948*.

31 TsDAHO, f. 1, op. 70, spr. 436, ark. 10–13 (the worsening ideological climate), 25–35 (Hrushevsky), 47–60 (escapism into the past).

32 Ibid., 35–9 (Lviv incident), 52–3 (textbook).

33 *Kultura i zhizn*, 20 July 1946, 2.

34 The text of the speech is not available because, before leaving Ukraine for Moscow in 1949, Khrushchev removed most of the politically sensitive documents from his files. The archival copy of the session's minutes contains a note: 'The record of Comrade Khrushchev's speech has been withdrawn into [his] personal archive. 2 December 1949' (TsDAHO, f. 1, op. 1, spr. 729, ark. 3). The content of Khrushchev's report is deduced from references to it made by other participants and from its abridged

publication as an editorial in a Ukrainian party journal: 'Rishuche polipshyty dobir, rozstanovku i vykhovannia kadriv,' 8.

35 TsDAHO, f. 1, op. 1, spr. 729, ark. 6, 7–8.

36 Ibid., ark. 10–11 (Nazarenko) and 141 (Lytvyn). Lytvyn overreached himself in this statement, since Soviet historiography postulated the ethic unity of *Eastern* Slavs, not of all Slavs, until the thirteenth century.

37 Ibid., ark. 138–41.

38 Ibid., ark. 74 (Melnikov and Khrushchev), 214 (Bazhan and Khrushchev). Mykola Rudenko, who in the late 1940s edited the Ukrainian komsomol journal *Dnipro*, later testified that 'Melnikov did not know the Ukrainian language at all, understood nothing about literature, and generally lacked culture' (Rudenko, *Naibilshe dyvo – zhyttia*, 188).

39 TsDAHO, f. 1, op. 70, spr. 514, ark. 25–6.

40 Ibid., ark. 34.

41 *Kulturne budivnytstvo v Ukrainskii RSR*, 266–9.

42 Rublov and Cherchenko, *Stalinshchyna*, 219 (closures and Korduba); TsDAHO, f. 1, op. 70, spr. 540, ark. 90–4 (Krypiakevych).

43 TsDAHO, f. 1, op. 70, spr. 459, ark. 15 (no studies of the revolutionary struggle), 16–17 (Historical Museum), 18 (brigade and pamphlets).

44 *Pravda*, 2 September 1946, 2 (decree); McCagg, *Stalin Embattled*, 251 (interpretation).

45 In fact, in 1947 the most prolific Russian historical playwright, Vladimir Solovev, was awarded a Stalin Prize for his verse drama about Ivan the Terrible, *The Great Sovereign*.

46 *Literaturna hazeta*, 12 October 1946, 2. Emphasis in the title added.

47 TsDAMLM, f. 573, op. 1, spr. 46 (contemporary critical discussion); TsDAHO, f. 1, op. 30, spr. 3653, ark. 165–70 (later comments on the causes of the 1946 fiasco); *Radianske mystetstvo*, 4 December 1946, 3 (dismissive review).

48 Ibid., 8 October 1946, 4.

49 Ibid., 17 September 1946, 4 (Shulha); 22 October 1946, 1 (Svitlytsky and Derehus).

50 TsDAMLM, f. 590, op. 1, spr. 57, ark. 107–8. Significantly, this passage was edited out of the version of his speech published in *Literaturna hazeta*, 18 December 1948, 3.

51 *Radianske mystetstvo*, 17 September 1946, 1 (premiere); *Literaturna hazeta*, 12 December 1946, 4; *Radianske mystetstvo*, 12 March 1947, 2 (reviews); *Literaturna hazeta*, 12 June 1947, 1 (Stalin prize), 4 (credit).

52 Romitsyn, *Ukrainske radianske kinomystetstvo*, 78.

53 TsDAHO, f. 1, op. 30, spr. 2426, ark. 73 (Pashchenko); Pashchenko, *IX ukrainskaia khudozhestvennaia vystavka*, 27, 32, 36; *Radianske mystetstvo*, 12 November 1947, 3 (exhibition); *Literaturna hazeta*, 22 April 1948, 1 (Stalin Prizes for 1947). See also an

interesting analysis of Melikhov's painting in Hrabovych [Grabowicz], 'Sovietska albomna shevchenkiana,' 27–8.

54 TsDAHO, f. 1, op. 30, spr. 2041, ark. 36–8.

55 *Literaturna hazeta*, 30 January 1947, 1 (announcement); TsDAVOV, f. 4763, op. 1, spr. 85, ark. 20–2 (the jury's deliberations); *Radianske mystetstvo*, 11 February 1948, 1 (decision announced). The jury awarded the second prize to Liubomyr Dmyterko's Second World War drama, *General Vatutin*, which the Kharkiv Drama Company subsequently staged.

56 TsDAHO, f. 1, op. 23, spr. 4958, ark. 27–31.

57 Ibid., ark. 34–44.

58 Ibid., ark. 45–7.

59 On carnivalization as a strategy of subverting authoritative social discourses, see Bakhtin, *Rabelais and His World*.

4: The Unfinished Crusade of 1947

1 See Bilinsky, *Second Soviet Republic*, 234–5; Marples, 'Khrushchev, Kaganovich and the 1947 Crisis,' in his *Stalinism in Ukraine in the 1940s*; Shapoval, *Ukraina 20-50-kh rokiv*, 265–7. In addition, Jeffrey Burds has speculated recently that Khrushchev's failure to suppress nationalist guerrillas in Western Ukraine may have been another factor involved in Stalin's decision (*Early Cold War*, 27).

2 The photograph of Kaganovich's copy of the Poliburo decision is reproduced in Kaganovich, *Pamiatnye zapiski*, between pp. 288 and 289. On Belarus and Stalin, see 'Otvet P.K. Ponomarenko na voprosy G.A. Kumaneva,' 148–9.

3 *Khrushchev Remembers*, 242. Kaganovich's account of his second appointment in Ukraine is in his *Pamiatnye zapiski*, 487–94.

4 TsDAHO, f. 1, op. 6, spr. 1036, ark. 17. It is not clear just how Krypiakevych managed to continue his career under the Soviet power after the war. A recent Ukrainian documentary publication suggests that, either before or during the war, he had been a Soviet secret police informant in Western Ukrainian ecclesiastical and intellectual circles and that in the autumn of 1944 the NKVD 're-established' contact with him. See Slyvka, *Kulturne zhyttia v Ukraini*, 1: 217.

5 NAIIU, op. 1, spr. 95, ark. 3 (plan for 1947); spr. 215, ark. 1–13 (report for 1946–50).

6 TsDAHO, f. 1, op. 8, spr. 316, ark. 27.

7 TsDAHO, f. 1, op. 70, spr. 763, ark. 4–6 (Los), 14–27 (Petrovsky), 47 (Kaganovych). Excerpts from the conference minutes (not including Petrovsky's speech) recently have been published in Smolii, *U leshchatakh totalitaryzmu*, 2: 31–72.

8 TsDAHO, f. 1, op. 70, spr. 753, ark. 59–62, 82–3, 99, 166 (Petrovsky), 248–50

(Huslysty), 159–60 (Rubach); 113–15, 139, and 254 (references to wartime patriotism).

9 Ibid., ark. 255 (Huslysty) and 139–52 (Bortnikov).
10 Ibid., ark. 262–3; Smolii, *U leshchatakh totalitaryzmu*, 2: 60.
11 K. Litvin [Lytvyn], 'Ob istorii ukrainskogo naroda,' 52.
12 Ibid., 51; TsDAHO, f. 1, op. 70, spr. 753, ark. 260–2 and Smolii, *U leshchatakh totalitaryzmu*, 2: 59.
13 TsDAHO, f. 1, op. 16, spr. 32, ark. 47–8 and 49zv. Manuilsky's personal archives preserved what seems to be the first working draft of the lost anti-nationalist resolution (TsDAVOV, f. 4669, op. 1, spr. 44, ark. 24–9 and 30–9).
14 Shapoval, *Ukraina 20–50–kh rokiv*, 271–2; idem, *Lazar Kahanovych*, 40; Zamlynska, 'Ideolohichnyi teror,' 79–80. At the Twenty-Second Congress of the Communist Party of the Soviet Union in 1962, then Ukrainian first secretary, Mykola Pidhirny [Podgornyi], gave the following account of the abortive plenary session:

> A great master of intrigue and provocation, [Kaganovich] had entirely groundlessly accused the republic's leading writers and some top-rank party workers of nationalism. On his directive, the press carried annihilating articles on the writers, who were devoted to the party and the people.
>
> But this did not satisfy Kaganovich. He began pushing for a plenary meeting of the Central Committee with the agenda 'The Struggle against Nationalism, the Main Danger within the KP(b)U,' although such a danger did not exist at all. And could not have existed; for, happily for us, the Central Committee of the Communist Party of Ukraine had long been headed by the staunch Leninist Nikita Sergeevich Khrushchev, who educated the communists and the Ukrainian people in the spirit of internationalism [storm of applause], the friendship of peoples, and the selfless devotion to the great ideas of Leninism. [Prolonged storm of applause.] (*XXII sezd Kommunisticheskoi partii Sovetskogo Soiuza*, 1: 280)

15 TsDAHO, f. 1, op. 70, spr. 618, ark. 1 and 34. In May, apparently at Kaganovich's request, the Ukrainian Ministry of State Security submitted a lengthy report to him on 'nationalistic attitudes' among the Ukrainian intelligentsia. See RGASPI, f. 81, op. 3, d. 128, 129. I thank Jeffrey Burds for the reference.
16 TsDAHO, f. 1, op. 8, spr. 328, ark. 6–7.
17 TsDAHO, f. 1, op. 6, spr. 1073, ark. 16–18.
18 Ibid, ark. 23.
19 'Do kintsia likviduvaty burzhuazno-natsionalistychni perekruchennia istorii Ukrainy;' *Radianska Ukraina*, 3 October 1947, 3–4.
20 TsDAHO, f. 1, op. 30, spr. 621, ark. 166–208.
21 TsDAHO, f. 1, op. 70, spr. 760, ark. 168–9. Petrovsky's speech is recorded on ark. 28–36, comments by Stoian and Slutsky on ark. 44–7 and 132–45.

22 Ibid., ark. 76. Huslysty referred to the 1940 *Short Course*, not the new project under way in the mid- to late 1940s.
23 Ibid., ark. 170–1 (Huslysty and Nazarenko); op. 30, spr. 621, ark. 166–74 (report to Kaganovich).
24 TsDAHO, f. 1, op. 70, spr. 744, ark. 52–6; spr. 621, ark. 175–86; spr. 1090, ark. 1–10; spr. 1494, ark. 1–10; spr. 1620, ark. 1–11 (other institutes); Smolii, *U leshchatakh totalitaryzmu*, 2: 104–8 (historians).
25 TsDAHO, f. 1, op. 23, spr. 4525, ark. 11–18; spr. 4526; op. 70, spr. 620, ark. 1–34; spr. 761, ark. 36–41; spr. 1095, ark. 1–11 (provinces); spr. 761, ark. 23–35; Smolii, *U leshchatakh totalitaryzmu*, 2: 93–100 (circular letter); *Radianska osvita*, 10 October 1947, 1–2.
26 TsDAHO, f. 1, op. 23, spr. 4526, ark. 22 (Zaporizhzhia), 37 (Uzhhorod), 46 (Kirovohrad), and 53 (Stalino).
27 Ibid., ark. 25–6.
28 TsDAHO, f. 1, op. 73, spr. 398, ark. 1–22, especially 12 and 19 on Western Ukraine.
29 Ibid., op. 8, spr. 340, ark. 13–14; Smolii, *U leshchatakh totalitaryzmu*, 2: 119–20.
30 TsDAHO, f. 1, op. 70, spr. 762, ark. 1–20; spr. 763, ark. 1–35 (outlines). Kasymenko was appointed director on 25 October 1947 and remained at this post until 1964. He graduated from the Poltava Institute of People's Education in 1926 and before the war taught in Poltava and Zhytomyr. During the war, Kasymenko worked in the apparatus of the KP(b)U Central Committee and, in 1945–7, in the republic's Ministry of Foreign Affairs. See Smolii, *Vcheni Instytutu*, 124–5.
31 As usual, the immediate impulse for the campaign came from a timely denunciation, a letter sent to Kaganovich in August by two literary critics, Ievhen Adelheim and Illia Stebun (TsDAHO, f. 1, op. 23, spr. 4515, ark. 3–12; Shapoval, *Ukraina 20-50-kh rokiv*, 269–70).
32 *Literaturna hazeta*, 3 July 1947, 3; 10 July 1947, 1–2. See also Shevchenko, 'Kulturno-ideolohichni protsesy v Ukraini,' 41.
33 See *Literaturna hazeta*, 17 April 1947, 2; Syrotiuk, *Ukrainska istorychna proza za 40 rokiv*, 257. Compare the original publication: Panch, *Zaporozhtsi*; Ostap Buzhinsky's phrase is on 23.
34 TsDAHO, f. 1, op. 23, spr. 4512, ark. 1–47 (Korniichuk), 171–83 (Bazhan, particularly ark. 177–9 on Rylsky), 260–8 (Panch). The original minutes, with a slightly different pagination, are in TsDAMLM, f. 590, op. 1, spr. 39, 40.
35 TsDAHO, f. 1, op. 23, spr. 4512, ark. 267–8.
36 Ibid., spr. 4511, ark. 1–88. Rybak's statement is on ark. 41–3.
37 *Radianska Ukraina*, 2 October 1947, 2–4 (Ienevych); *Literaturna hazeta*, 11 December 1947, 3 (Rylsky); 9 October 1947, 1, 4; 16 October 1947, 2; 23 October 1947, 1; 4 December 1947, 3; 8 January 1948, 4; 15 January 1948, 3.
38 *Literaturna Ukraina*, 13 November 1947, 2; 20 November 1947, 4; Rublov and

Cherchenko, *Stalinshchyna*, 228–9. Highly unusual in the context of the 1947 ideological campaign, the arrest of Patrus-Karpatsky was probably connected with his wartime past, rather than with his post-war activities as poet and editor. During the war, he remained in Transcarpathia under German and Hungarian occupation, possibly as a Soviet secret agent. Later, he made his way to Moscow and served in the (pro-Soviet) Czechoslovak army as aide-de-camp of the future Czechoslovak president, General Ludvik Svoboda. See Musiienko, 'Andrii Patrus-Karpatsky,' 345–7 and Slyvka, *Kulturne zhyttia v Ukraini*, 1: 484–96.

39 *Literaturna hazeta*, 8 April 1948, 1; 14 April 1949, 1–2 (Honchar and Riabokliach). For a comprehensive survey of the proliferation of contemporary subjects in post-war Ukrainian literature, see Kyryliuk, *Istoriia ukrainskoi literatury* vol. 8. On Rybak, see *Literaturna hazeta*, 6 December 1948, 3 (*The Pereiaslav Council* published); 9 March 1950, 1 (Stalin Prize); Rybak, *Pereiaslavska rada*.

40 The offices of the first secretary and premier remained separated. Khrushchev's client Demian Korotchenko became Ukraine's new chairman of the Council of Ministers.

41 *Literaturna hazeta*, 5 March 1949, 2; Kostiuk, 'Vysoka patriotychna rol radianskoho mystetstva,' 40–1, 43. Also compare *Radianske mystetstvo*, 16 February 1949, 4 and *Literaturna hazeta*, 24 February 1949, 1.

42 *Radianska Ukraina*, 8 October 1947, 2–3. Unfortunately, the first series of anonymous letters is missing from the folder in the archives of the Central Committee, having apparently been forwarded to the Ministry of State Security. As more letters followed, the editor started making copies for his party superiors as well. Symon Petliura: one of the leaders of the Ukrainian Revolution of 1917–20. Dmytro Dontsov: the leading theoretician of Ukrainian nationalism in the early twentieth century. Ievhen Konovalets: the pre-war head of the Organization of Ukrainian Nationalists.

43 TsDAHO, f. 1, op. 23, spr. 4957, ark. 3.

44 Ibid., ark. 4–8.

45 Ibid., ark. 2 (the first letter) and 10–21 (the second letter).

46 TsDAHO, f. 1, op. 23, spr. 4956, ark. 6–7.

47 Ibid., spr. 5072, ark. 13.

48 Ibid., ark. 24–5.

49 Ibid., ark. 26–8, 42.

50 TsDAHO, f. 1, op. 23, spr. 4958, ark. 22.

51 Ibid, spr. 5072, ark. 46–8, 14.

5: Writing a 'Stalinist History of Ukraine'

1 Stalin, 'Vystuplenie I.V. Stalina na prieme v Kremle,' 197. For more analysis of this episode, see Brandenberger, *National Bolshevism*, 130–1, 233–4.

2 On the growth of the Russian leadership doctrine, see Barghoorn, *Soviet Russian*

Nationalism, 26–66. Khmelko first presented his canvas at the Ninth Exhibition of Ukrainian Art in Kiev in November 1947. See *Radianske mystetstvo*, 12 November 1947, 3 (exhibition); *Literaturna hazeta*, 22 April 1948, 1 (Stalin Prize).

3 *Radianska Ukraina*, 26 May 1945, 1. See also *Radianska Ukraina*, 16 September 1945, 2, 4 and *Radianske mystetstvo*, 28 May 1947, 2.

4 Pankratova, *Velykyi rosiiskyi narod*.

5 *XVI zizd Komunistychnoi Partii (bilshovykiv) Ukrainy*, 46. Khrushchev misnamed the Institute of Ukrainian Literature, but the editors apparently did not catch his error.

6 See RGASPI, f. 17, op. 132, d. 339 and op. 133, d. 4, as well as the reviews and chronicle sections in *Voprosy istorii* for 1945–54.

7 RGASPI, f. 17, op. 132, d. 339, ll. 147–59; TsKhSD, f. 5, op. 30, d. 39, ll. 11–21.

8 Kim, Review of *Istoriia Kazakhskoi SSR s drevneishikh vremen do nashikh dnei*.

9 RGASPI, f. 17, op. 133, d. 220, ll. 154–9; Dakhshleiger, 'V Institute istorii'; Tillett, *Great Friendship*, 148–54.

10 RGASPI, f. 17, op. 133, d. 303, ll. 14–19, 135–7 (Armenia), 81–4 (Georgia), and 85–7 (Uzbekistan).

11 TsDAHO, f. 1, op. 70, spr. 714, ark. 9–10; op. 30, spr. 1832, ark. 1–3 (reports to the Central Committee); NAIIU, op. 1, spr. 134 (the Institute's report for 1948); spr. 140 (minutes of the discussion at the Agitprop).

12 TsDAHO, f. 1, op. 30, spr. 985, ark. 66 (*troika*); op. 23, spr. 5664, ark. 6–7 (conclusion). Mykhailo Hrechukha served as the chairman of the Executive Committee of the Ukrainian SSR Supreme Soviet.

13 TsDAHO, f. 1, op. 70, spr. 1787, ark. 197; Smolii, *U leshchatakh totalitaryzmu*, 2: 129.

14 TsDAHO, f. 1, op. 30, spr. 2030, ark. 172 (limited edition). The June 1949 limited edition was entitled *The History of Ukraine*, and the title of the 1950 edition was *The History of the Ukrainian SSR* (NAIIU, op. 1, spr. 215, ark. 4–8).

15 TsDAHO, f. 1, op. 30, spr. 2806, ark. 72 (Suslov's decision); RGASPI, f. 17, op. 132, d. 503, ll. 1–4 (IMEL's review).

16 TsDAHO, f. 1, op. 30, spr. 2360, ark. 8; spr. 2806, ark. 72 (5 January); RGASPI, f. 17, op. 132, d. 503, l. 5 (11 January).

17 TsDAHO, f. 1, op. 30, spr. 2360, ark. 8 (proofs); spr. 2806, ark. 72 (printing halted); ark. 74–109 (commission and its criticisms); 73 (new version ready in August), 37–88a (minutes of the meeting), 85–7 (Nazarenko's conclusion).

18 RGASPI, f. 17, op. 133, d. 311, l. 47.

19 In subsequent chapters this campaign is discussed in greater detail.

20 TsDAHO, f. 1, op. 1, spr. 976, ark. 88; Smolii, *U leshchatakh totalitaryzmu*, 2: 152–5.

21 Untitled editorial, *Voprosy istorii*, no. 1 (1945): 5.

22 TsDAVOV, f. 2, op. 7, spr. 3927, ark. 124–5. I am not suggesting here that

Khrushchev personally composed this particular letter or that Stalin even read it, but the Ukrainian ideologues communicated with the apparatus of the VKP(b) Central Committee by addressing their letters to Stalin and having them signed by the first secretary.

23 Ibid., ark. 123–5; spr. 553, ark. 173–9.

24 TsDAHO, f. 1, op. 30, spr. 2003, ark. 112; Shovkoplias, *Arkheolohichni doslidzhennia na Ukraini*, 17–24.

25 TsDAHO, f. 1, op. 24, spr. 1577, ark. 3, 6; op. 30, spr. 1919, ark. 26–8. Compare O.K. Kasymenko, *Istoriia Ukrainskoi SSR* (1951), vol. 1, 20.

26 Kasymenko, *Istoriia* (1953), 29–33.

27 TsDAHO, f. 1, op. 24, spr. 1577, ark. 1 (commission); op. 30, spr. 2339, ark. 32 (Poida); Kasymenko, *Istoriia* (1953), 20–1 (Trypillians), 29 (Slavs).

28 See Smolii, *Vcheni Instytutu istorii Ukrainy*, 376–7.

29 NAIIU, op. 1, spr. 166, ark. 4 (Iushkov); spr. 215, ark. 1 (report); spr. 216, ark. 7 (pamphlet).

30 See Dovzhenok, *Viiskova sprava v Kyivskii Rusi*; Voronin's review in *Voprosy istorii*.

31 Kasymenko, *Istoriia* (1953), 91–2.

32 TsDAHO, f. 1, op. 24, spr. 784, ark. 25.

33 See Pashuto, *Ocherki po istorii Galitsko-Volynskoi Rusi*; Koroliuk's review in *Voprosy istorii*.

34 TsDAHO, f. 1, op. 70, spr. 823, ark. 16; NAIIU, op. 1, spr. 103; Kasymenko, *Istoriia* (1951), 101–2; 'Ob itogakh diskussii o periodizatsii istorii SSSR,' *Voprosy istorii*, 57; NAIIU, op. 1, spr. 355, ark. 16a–17 (Nechkina).

35 The reference here is to the work of the Ukrainian dissident historian Mykhailo Braichevsky, *Pryiednannia chy vozziednannia? Krytychni zauvahy z pryvodu odniiei kontseptsii*, translated as *Annexation or Reunification: Critical Notes on One Conception*.

36 Ukrainian émigré historians in the west often rendered *pryiednannia* as 'annexation,' but, in the Soviet Ukrainian official discourse of the time, *pryiednannia* meant 'incorporation.'

37 See Kasymenko, *Istoriia* (1951), 163–6; Grekov, Bakhrushin, and Lebedev, *Istoriia SSSR*, 494–502 (*prisoedinenie*). John Basarab has explained the terminological confusion in the second edition of Osipov's book by the hasty ideological editing: 'After a hurried re-editing of Osipov's text, the revised edition substituted "reunion" (*vossoedinenie*) for "union" (*soedinenie*) on the chapter's title page; in the body of the chapter, however, it is unchanged' (*Pereiaslav 1654*, 177). In fact, in both the first (1939) and the second (1948) editions of Osipov's book, the chapter on the Pereiaslav Treaty is entitled 'The Reunification' (*Vossoedinenie*). See Osipov, *Bogdan Khmelnitsky*, 347; 2d ed. 379.

38 Osipov, *Bogdan Khmelnitsky*, 2d ed., 385, 394.

39 See, in particular, Kulish, *Istoriia vossoedineniia Rusi*. For a more detailed treatment of imperial Russian views on Pereiaslav, see Basarab, *Pereiaslav 1654*; Velychenko, *National History as Cultural Process*; Sysyn, 'The Changing Image of the Hetman.'

40 TsDAHO, f. 1, op. 30, spr. 2034, ark. 130 (Instutute), 138 (Boiko).

41 Shevchuk, 'Nauchno-issledovatelskaia rabota Instituta istorii Ukrainy Akademii nauk Ukrainskoi SSR za 1950 god,' 157.

42 *Pravda*, 20 July 1951, 3–4. The *Bohdan Khmelnytsky* affair is examined in chapter seven. I was not able to locate the Moscow historians' original dispatch objecting to the term 'incorporation.' However, Boiko referred to the incident as caused by something 'the Institute of USSR History had sent us' (TsDAHO, f. 1, op. 30, spr. 3597, ark. 19).

43 TsDAHO, f. 1, op. 30, spr. 3597, ark. 22–4 (Boiko), 28 (Kusheva), 30 (Ivanov), 33 (Pavlenko), 38 (Cherepnin reporting the opinion of the absent Druzhinin), 33 (Cherepnin).

44 TsDAHO, f. 1, op. 30, spr. 1922, ark. 1 (Nazarenko), 2–3 (Boiko), 8 (Kasymenko).

45 Ibid., spr. 1924, ark. 2 (Ienevych), 4 (comment from the audience, Nazarenko, and Koshyk).

46 Ibid., spr. 1925; NAIIU, op. 1, spr. 353, 354.

47 See Nechkina, 'K voprosu o formule "naimenshee zlo" (Pismo v redaktsiiu),' and replies in no. 9: 97–118 and no. 11: 83–7; Maksimov, 'O zhurnale "Voprosy istorii,"' 62; *Pravda*, 7 October 1952, 5 (Bagirov); Tillett, *Great Friendship*, 161–7.

48 See Kasymenko, *Istoriia* (1951), 164–5 and TsDAHO, f. 1, op. 30, spr. 2339, ark. 34–5.

49 Kasymenko, *Istoriia* (1953), 258.

50 TsDAHO, f. 1, op. 30, spr. 1924, ark. 185–90; Kasymenko, *Istoriia* (1950), 191; (1953), 287.

51 TsDAHO, f. 1, op. 30, spr. 1920, ark. 1–4; Kasymenko, *Istoriia* (1951), 209–11; (1953), 308–10.

52 Kasymenko, *Istoriia* (1951), 314–15.

53 TsDAHO, f. 1, op. 30, spr. 1925, ark. 127–8; spr. 2339, ark. 118; op. 70, spr. 1173, ark. 14 (reviews); op. 30, spr. 1902, ark. 4 (commission).

54 Maksimov, 'O zhurnale "Voprosy istorii,"' 63–64; the article in question is Kovalenko, 'Istoricheskie vzgliady revoliutsionera-demokrata T.G. Shevchenko.'

55 Kasymenko, *Istoriia* (1953), 429–30.

56 TsDAHO, f. 1, op. 30, spr. 1926, ark. 94–7.

57 Ibid., spr. 1902, ark. 5. Established during the early 1860s, *hromady* were the clandestine cultural organizations of the Ukrainian intelligentsia in the Russian Empire. In the course of time, their agenda came to include social and political issues as well.

58 Ibid., op. 24, spr. 2714, ark. 10–14, here 10.

59 Ibid., op. 30, spr. 1916–19, 1921, 2806, 2811; NAIIU, op. 1, spr. 363 (parts 1 and 2).

60 TsDAHO, f. 1, op. 30, spr. 1902, ark. 7; Smolii, *U leshchatakh totalitaryzmy*, 2: 160.

61 Kasymenko, *Istoriia*. The imprimatur date is on 783. The first Ukrainian edition had a print run of 70,000.

62 Ibid., 5, 84, 258–9.

63 Boiko, *300 rokiv vozziednannia Ukrainy z Rosiieiu*, 1; idem, *300-letie vossoedineniia Ukrainy s Rossiei*, 1. See also Kasymenko, *Vikovichna druzhba rosiiskoho i ukrainskoho narodiv*; Diadychenko, Kasymenko, and Shevchenko, *Vyzvolna viina 1648–1654 rr. i vozziednannia Ukrainy z Rosiieiu*; Myshko, 'Pereiaslavskaia rada 1654 goda'; Golobutsky [Holobutsky], 'Rossiia i Osvoboditelnaia voina ukrainskogo naroda.'

64 Ivanov, 'Istorychne znachennia vozziednannia Ukrainy z Rosiieiu,' 22–3.

65 Zimin, Mochalov, and Novoselsky, 'Tsennyi trud po istorii Ukrainskoi SSR'; Bilan et al., 'Knyha pro slavne mynule ukrainskoho narodu'; *Pravda*, 18 April 1954, reprinted in *Radianska Ukraina*, 20 April 1954, 2–3 (reviews); *XVIII zizd Komunistychnoi partii Ukrainy*, 156 (Nazarenko).

66 Before the war Petro Vershyhora (1905–63) worked as an actor and assistant film director in Ukraine. The fortunes of war brought him into a large partisan detachment, where he unexpectedly rose through the ranks as a popular commander. Major-General and Hero of the Soviet Union at war's end, Vershyhora turned to writing and earned a Stalin Prize for his novel *People of Good Conscience* (1946).

67 Vershyhora, 'Bratia po oruzhiiu,' 118.

68 TsKhSD, f. 5, op. 17, d. 470, ll. 171–84, here 172 and 177.

69 Ibid., l. 169; for the reviews see n. 64, above.

70 TsDAHO, f. 1, op. 30, spr. 3652, ark. 58, 60; Krypiakevych, *Zviazky Zakhidnoi Ukrainy*.

71 Krypiakevych, *Bohdan Khmelnytsky*; Boiko and Huslysty, 'Monohrafiia pro Bohdana Khmelnytskoho.' The Kievan historian Fedir Shevchenko served as the book's editor and added to the text some ideologically sound general statements. See Isaievych, 'Peredmova,' in Krypiakevych, *Bohdan Khmelnytsky*, 2d ed., 8.

72 Santsevich and Komarenko, *Razvitie istoricheskoi nauki*, 62–3; TsDAHO, f. 1, op. 70, spr. 1788, ark. 22. New units included the departments of world history, international relations, and the 'countries of people's democracy' – all established in 1949. Given the widening scope of the Institute's research, the Ukrainian government decreed in March 1953 that the institution's name be changed to the Institute of History (TsDAVOV, f. 2, op. 8, spr. 7730, ark. 2).

73 TsDAHO, f. 1, op. 70, spr. 1788, ark. 38–48.

74 Ibid., spr. 1494, ark. 11. The functionary was apparently displeased with the word *Ukraine* in the title.

75 TsDAHO, f. 1, op. 30, spr. 2003, ark. 128–31 (1950); Koval, 'Flahman ukrainskoi istoriografii,' 12–13.

76 See *Vossoedinenie Ukrainy s Rossiei*, vols. 1–3, and the following reviews: I. Boiko et al., 'Sbornik dokumentov o vossoedinenii Ukrainy s Rossiei,' and Kozachenko, 'Tsennoe sobranie istochnikov po istorii vossoedineniia Ukrainy s Rossiei.' The numbers come from TsDAHO, f. 1, op. 30, spr. 3599, ark. 7.

77 TsKhSD, f. 5, op. 17, d. 427, ll. 173–4; NAIIU, op. 1, spr. 352, ark. 1, 10–41.

78 TsKhSD, f. 5, op. 17, d. 470, ll. 125–8; *Literaturna hazeta*, 3 December 1953, 4 (2,500 pages); NAIIU, op. 1, spr. 478a, ark. 13–20 (January); TsDAHO, f. 1, op. 30, spr. 3629, ark. 1–13 (May).

79 RGASPI, f. 17, op. 132, d. 372, l. 4. In December 1952 the KPSS Central Committee finally discovered that the Armenian textbook contained numerous interpretive differences from the standard Russian textbook on USSR History (ibid., ll. 59–60).

80 See TsDAHO, f. 1, op. 30, spr. 2360, ark. 129, 133–4 (data for 1951). In addition, the numerous Russian schools in Ukraine were using the texts published in Russian in Moscow.

81 Shestakov, *Istoriia SSSR* (1948, 1955), 62–3. The more sophisticated interpretation of Pereiaslav in the textbook for grade 8 also was changed along the same lines. See Pankratova, *Istoriia SSSR*, 5th ed., 184–97, and 14th ed., 189–203.

82 TsDAHO, f. 1, op. 70, spr. 1886, ark. 38–40, 136; *Radianska osvita*, 14 March 1947, 1.

83 See TsDAHO, f. 1, op. 73, spr. 585, ark. 1–57; spr. 592, ark. 2–8; op. 30, spr. 2328, ark. 1–130.

84 TsDAHO, f. 1, op. 46, spr. 6822, ark. 53, 104.

85 Ibid., op. 24, spr. 2677, ark. 3–5.

6: Defining the National Heritage

1 *Literaturna hazeta*, 8 March 1951, 1–2.

2 Ibid., 1 (Kryzhanivsky); 15 March 1951, 1 (Malyshko).

3 TsDAHO, f. 1, op. 30, spr. 2325, ark. 72–5. In 1951 the trip had to be postponed until early July because many participants went to Moscow to participate in the *dekada* (ten-day festival) of Ukrainian culture. On the origins of the ritual pilgrimage, see Yekelchyk, 'Creating a Sacred Place: The Ukrainophiles and Shevchenko's Tomb in Kaniv (1861–ca. 1900).

4 Slezkine, 'The USSR as a Communal Apartment,' 446–7.

5 *Literaturna hazeta*, 28 February 1952, 1 (Gogol); 30 December 1948, 3 (Kotliarevsky).

6 Ibid., 24 June 1948, 1.

7 See Ienevych, 'Velykyi syn ukrainskoho narodu'; idem, 'Amerykanskyi falsyfikator ideinoi spadshchyny Shevchenka'; *Literaturna hazeta*, 8 March 1951, 1–2.

8 Shakhovsky, 'Suspilno-politychni pohliady Lesi Ukrainky'; Klymas, 'Ivan Franko.'

9   TsDAHO, f. 1, op. 30, spr. 2357, ark. 206–9.

10 RGASPI, f. 17, op. 132, d. 232, l. 47.

11 Ibid., l. 49.

12 *Literaturna hazeta*, 12 May 1949, 1 (editorial); 17 May 1951, 2 (monument un-veiled); *Kulturne budivnytstvo*, 2: 196–8; (decree). One could hardly imagine Myrny evolving towards Lenin's version of Social Democracy, since the revolution had caught the writer in the position of head of the State Properties Office in Poltava province, with the title 'His Excellency.'

13 TsDAHO, f. 1, op. 30, spr. 2755, ark. 53–61, here 59; Bezpalchy, 'Suspilno-politychni pohliady P.A. Hrabovskoho;' *Literaturna hazeta*, 11 December 1952, 3.

14 TsDAHO, f. 1, op. 30, spr. 1990, ark. 40–4 (1950); spr. 2756, ark. 69–74 (1952).

15 Ibid., op. 70, spr. 1917, ark. 22–3.

16 RGASPI, f. 17, op. 132, d. 416; TsDAHO, f. 1, op. 24, spr. 8, ark. 1–9.

17 TsDAHO, f. 1, op. 70, spr. 1948, ark. 1–5 (1950); TsDAVOV, f. 2, op. 8, spr. 9504, ark. 233–7 (1953).

18 TsDAHO, f. 1, op. 30, spr. 3308, ark. 68–70.

19 Kondufor, *Kulturne budivnytstvo v Ukrainskii RSR: Cherven 1941–1950*, 423 (1949); TsDAVOV, f. 2, op. 8, spr. 9503, ark. 153; TsDAHO, f. 1, op. 30, spr. 3662, ark. 41, 228–9; *Literaturna hazeta*, 27 December 1951, 4 (ten-volume edition).

20 *Literaturna hazeta*, 11 May 1950, 4; TsDAHO, f. 1, op. 30, spr. 3662, ark. 45 (incomplete).

21 On Lysenko, see *Radianske mystetstvo*, 19 March 1947, 4; and TsDAHO, f. 1, op. 30, spr. 2030, ark. 36–8zv. On Lesia Ukrainka, see *Kulturne budivnytstvo*, 2: 90–1; TsDAHO, f. 1, op. 30, spr. 1990, ark. 168; spr. 3662, ark. 45. On other writers, ibid., spr. 3662, ark. 45, 231–2.

22 TsDAHO, f. 1, op. 70, spr. 1334, ark. 1–2a; spr. 1768, ark. 7, 15–16.

23 Ibid., op. 30, spr. 3662, ark. 46.

24 Ibid., op. 72, spr. 1, ark. 18–19. 91–4 and op. 30, spr. 2357, ark. 112–15.

25 Ibid., op. 72, spr. 1, ark. 95–100 (Biletsky) and op. 30, spr. 3662, ark. 231 (vol. 4 still not published in 1954).

26 Ibid., ark. 191–3.

27 *Kulturne budivnytstvo*, 2: 213–20.

28 TsDAHO, f. 1, op. 30, spr. 2047, ark. 54–63. The Museum of the Battle at Poltava opened in September 1950, but the pre-revolutionary monuments on the battle-field were still in need of repair in 1953 (ibid., ark. 101; spr. 3261, ark. 11–13; TsDAVOV, f. 4762, op. 1, spr. 343, ark. 1–150).

29 TsDAHO, f. 1, op. 30, spr. 2047, ark. 104. The Lenin Museum in Kiev reported 186,836 visitors during 1950, but the authorities were sending students and soldiers there by the tens of thousands for obligatory homage (ibid., spr. 1989, ark. 36).

30 Ibid., spr. 2047, ark. 145.

31 Ibid., spr. 2769, ark. 158.
32 Ibid., spr. 2047, ark. 37–46, 83–5; spr. 3655, ark. 144–52. Not much was accomplished, though, since the renovations of this large complex of historical monuments were extremely costly. In 1950 the authorities estimated that only the most urgent maintenance work would require 12 million rubles (TsDAVOV, f. 2, op. 8, spr. 2040, ark. 243).
33 TsDAHO, f. 1, op. 30, spr. 2047, ark. 145.
34 TsDAVOV, f. 5116, op. 10, spr. 20, ark. 6–12.
35 *Pravda*, 13 September 1951, 3. Odinets was relying on the results of a museum audit organized by the provincial party committee, but his article in *Pravda* made the state of Ukrainian museums a major political issue in the republic.
36 TsDAHO, f. 1, op. 30, spr. 2769, ark. 1 (decree); op. 24, spr. 1090, ark. 42–5 (Kiev), 57–60 (Kherson), 72–5 (Vinnytsia); spr. 1105, ark. 86 (Drohobych), 124 (Chernivtsi).
37 Ibid., op. 1, spr. 972, ark. 234.
38 TsDAVOV, f. 4762, op. 1, spr. 562, ark. 1–12 (1951); spr. 669, ark. 4–6 (1952); TsDAHO, f. 1, op. 30, spr. 3655, ark. 179–90 (1954).
39 TsDAVOV, f. 1, op. 30, spr. 2769, ark. 26. In the process, the Hermitage Museum in Leningrad secured for itself a valuable collection of ancient Assyrian cuneiform writings held in the Lviv Historical Museum (ibid., ark. 11–13).
40 TsDAVOV, f. 5116, op. 10, spr. 20, ark. 13–20 (Poltava); Rublov and Cherchenko, *Stalinshchyna*, 238 (Lviv).
41 TsDAHO, f. 1, op. 30, spr. 2769, ark. 16–19. This file also allows a glimpse into the attendance of smaller regional museums. During 1951 the Rivne museum registered 9,046 visitors, including 3,480 schoolchildren (ibid., ark. 21).
42 Ibid., ark. 23–7 (March 1952); spr. 3261, ark. 87 (July 1952), 74–5 (1953).
43 TsDAVOV, f. 4763, op. 1, spr. 58, ark. 27, 28zv (Ukrainian art), 16 (Russian art).
44 TsDAHO, f. 1, op. 30, spr. 2769, ark. 64, 69, 88; *Radianske mystetstvo*, 14 May 1952, 4.
45 TsDAHO, f. 1, op. 30, spr. 2769, ark. 85, 119.
46 TsDAVOV, f. 4762, op. 1, spr. 669, ark. 6–7.
47 TsDAHO, f. 1, op. 30, spr. 2047, ark. 14–17; *Kulturne budivnytstvo*, 2: 221–2 (opened); TsDAVOV, f. 2, op. 8, spr. 2531, ark. 12 (Kyrychenko).
48 TsDAVOV, f. 2, op. 8, spr. 9503, ark. 139, 148 (Lesia Ukrainka); TsDAHO, f. 1, op. 30, spr. 2047, ark. 56–63; op. 24, spr. 774, ark. 11–12; Mezentseva, *Muzei Ukrainy*, 162 (Franko).
49 *Literaturna hazeta*, 28 April 1949, 2 (opened); TsDAHO, f. 1, op. 30, spr. 3674, ark. 95 (number of visitors).
50 TsDAHO, f. 1, op. 30, spr. 3261, ark. 33.
51 Ibid., spr. 3674, ark. 95–7.

52 Ibid., spr. 3640, ark. 100–3 (museums and the tercentenary), 106 (Derehus's paint-ing); TsDAVOV, f. 5116, op. 10, spr. 16, ark. 19 (Kiev), 20 (Chernihiv and Pereiaslav), 39–46 (Kharkiv); f. 4762, op. 1, spr. 669, ark. 11 (Chernihiv); f. 2, op. 8, spr. 10237, ark. 134 and *Kulturne budivnytstvo*, 2: 219 (Pereiaslav).
53 TsDAVOV, f. 4762, op. 1, spr. 669, ark. 19. The list of monuments shrank dramati-cally during the late 1950s, when the authorities 'consolidated' the wartime burials into a much smaller number of mass graves. See Kot, *Okhorona, vykorystannia*, 119.
54 TsDAVOV, f. 2, op. 7, spr. 9527, ark. 120.
55 Ibid., spr. 5568, ark. 35 (St Cyril's Church); spr. 5553, ark. 98 (St Sophia), 21–9 (Zvirynets caves); spr. 9527, ark. 1–12 (Golden Gate); 45–53, 67 (St Andrew's Church), 123–8 (Zvirynets caves).
56 TsDAVOV, f. 4762, op. 1, spr. 566, ark. 44; RGALI, f. 2329, op. 4, d. 101, l. 2.
57 RGALI, f. 2329, op. 4, d.101, ll. 2–4 and the cover.
58 TsDAVOV, f. 5116, op. 10, spr. 19, ark. 16, 18–20.
59 See Dunlop, *Faces of Contemporary Russian Nationalism*; Brudny, *Reinventing Russia*.
60 TsDAVOV, f. 2, op. 8, spr. 2040, ark. 233–5, here 235.
61 Ibid., ark. 237. The cross could have been erected to mark Potemkin's 1783 conquest of what is now Southern Ukraine and the Crimea.
62 TsDAVOV, f. 4906, op. 1, spr. 35, ark. 42; Kot, *Okhorona, vykorystannia*, 166.
63 TsDAHO, f. 1, op. 30, spr. 2756, ark. 80–2; spr. 2768, ark. 126–8; TsDAVOV, f. 5116, op. 10, spr. 16, ark. 31–3.
64 TsDAHO, f. 1, op. 24, spr. 777, ark. 165. Indeed, the head of the official commis-sion on the reconstruction of Kiev during the mid-1930s, the Ukrainian SSR com-missar of internal affairs, Vsevolod Balytsky, and many commission members during the Great Purge were executed as enemies of the people.
65 TsDAVOV, f. 4762, op. 1, spr. 164, ark. 15.
66 Ibid., ark. 15zv (Petrovsky); TsDAVOV, f. 2, op. 7, spr. 3078, ark. 61–2 (Khrushchev).
67 TsDAHO, f. 1, op. 30, spr. 1370, ark. 1–7 (monuments); op. 23, spr. 6259, ark. 205 (letter to Stalin). A similar purge, albeit on a lesser scale, apparently took place in other Western Ukrainian cities. According to the 1953 audit of monuments there, the only representations of the Polish past were statues and busts of Mickiewicz (TsDAVOV, f. 2, op. 8, spr. 9496, ark. 29–34).
68 TsDAHO, f. 1, op. 30, spr. 1370, ark. 9–12.
69 Ibid., spr. 2756, ark. 158. Mykola Shchors: a Soviet hero of the Civil War in Ukraine, who entered Ukrainian Soviet mythology as the local equivalent of Chapaev.
70 Ibid., spr. 1990, ark. 81–107 (minutes of discussion in Lviv), 108 (Kiev's reaction).
71 RGALI, f. 962, op. 3, d. 1995, ll. 29–62; TsDAHO, f. 1, op. 30, spr. 2757, ark. 1–2; *Literaturna hazeta*, 24 January 1952, 2.
72 TsDAHO, f. 1, op. 30, spr. 1990, ark. 206–7.

73 At the time of Stalin's death in March 1953 major Ukrainian cities such as Kiev, Kharkiv, Lviv, and Stalino [Donetsk] had no monuments of the great leader. In the spring of 1953 the republic's authorities considered erecting such memorials, providing that Moscow picked up the bill, but abandoned the plan later in the year. See ibid., spr. 3598, ark. 2–6; spr. 3597, ark. 73–7.

74 TsDAVOV, f. 2, op. 8, spr. 9486, ark. 29; *Kulturne budivnytstvo*, 2: 280.

75 TsDAHO, f. 1, op. 30, spr. 1990, ark. 154–6 (1950); op. 72, spr. 1, ark. 71–3 (1951).

76 TsDAVOV, f. 2, op. 8, spr. 11406, ark. 194; TsDAHO, f. 1, op. 30, spr. 3655, ark. 108–11; *Kulturne budivnytstvo*, 2: 314–15. The renovations at the museum and the construction of the monument began in 1954.

77 TsDAHO, f. 1, op. 30, spr. 3597, ark. 52.

78 Ibid., spr. 3598, ark. 2–6; spr. 3597, ark. 73–7 (original proposal); op. 24, spr. 3504, ark. 163–7 (revised proposal). The Ukrainian Academy of Architecture originally suggested erecting a monument to Khmelnytsky (ibid., ark. 43–4, 52).

79 TsDAVOV, f. 2, op. 8, spr. 9486, ark. 20–1 (Volhyn), 26–7 (Subotiv). This was not the original wooden church, but a later brick structure under the same name and in the same place. Also, Khmelnytsky's ashes had been missing for almost 300 years.

80 TsDAHO, f. 1, op. 30, spr. 3640, ark. 54–70 (list); TsDAVOV, f. 2, op. 8, spr. 11407, ark. 4–5 (Khortytsia); spr. 11406, ark. 48–9 (Dnipropetrovsk), 228–32 (Hrushchynsky); f. 5116, op. 10, spr. 16, ark. 22–4 (Lviv); *Literaturna hazeta*, 3 December 1953, 3 (Le). In the end, Kiev downgraded the obelisk on Khortytsia to a memorial plaque and the monument to Sirko to a tombstone and a bust on his grave (TsDAVOV, f. 2, op. 8, spr. 9880, ark. 29, 31).

81 TsDAVOV, f. 2, op. 8, spr. 11406, ark. 15–17 (Kirovohrad); TsDAHO, f. 1, op. 30, spr. 3628, ark. 1–2 (Korsun), 91 (Krolevets), 102–12 (Uman).

82 Ibid., ark. 114 (Stanyslaviv); op. 24, spr. 3503, ark. 13–21 (Cherkasy).

83 Ibid., op. 30, spr. 3628, ark. 97.

84 Ibid., spr. 3600, ark. 74–7 (monument, tombstone, obelisks, and memorial plaques), 118 (statue in Chyhyryn); TsDAVOV, f. 2, op. 8, spr. 9880, ark. 29–31 (summary); spr. 11408, ark. 2–5 (tombstone and obelisks).

85 TsDAHO, f. 1, op. 30, spr. 3627, ark. 4–10; *Radianska Ukraina*, 25 May 1954, 1 (dedication); *Radianske mystetstvo*, 14 July 1954, 1 (competition).

86 TsDAHO, f. 1, op. 24, spr. 3504, ark. 173–82; op. 30, spr. 3672, ark. 6–36; NAIIU, op. 1, spr. 407, ark. 1–22.

87 TsDAVOV, f. 2, op. 8, spr. 10237, ark. 38–9, 50–60, 88–90; TsDAHO, f. 1, op. 30, spr. 3600, ark. 36–8.

88 TsDAMLM, f. 119, op. 1, spr. 168, ark. 1zv (monument); TsDAVOV, f. 2, op. 8, spr. 10237, ark. 145–6 (cathedral); Apanovych, *Pereiaslav-Khmelnytsky i ioho istorychni pamiatky*, 112, 120 (Pereiaslav).

89 *Radianska osvita,* 19 December 1953, 1; Naulko, 'Vyvchennia periodu Vyzvolnoi viiny ukrainskoho narodu,' 16–17.

90 TsDAHO, f. 1, op. 30, spr. 3640, ark. 71–9 (Kiev), 80–6 (Pereiaslav, Chyhyryn, and the battlefields).

91 See Savchuk, *Kraieznavchyi rukh v Ukraini,* 11; Danyliuk, *Zberezhemo tuiu slavu.*

7: Empire and Nation in the Artistic Imagination

1 See *Pravda,* 14–27 June 1951.

2 [Volodymyr] Sosiura, 'Love Ukraine,' in *The Ukrainian Poets, 1189–1962,* ed. and trans. C.H. Andrusyshen and Watson Kirkconnell (Toronto, 1963), 423.

3 *Pravda,* 2 July 1951, 2. On Stalin's personal involvement, see Shepilov, 'Vospominaniia,' 43–4.

4 See Bilinsky, *Second Soviet Republic,* 15–17; Baran, *Ukraina 1950–1960–kh rr.* 60–5.

5 Simon, *Nationalism,* 206–9; Hann, *Postwar Soviet Politics,* 149–50.

6 RGASPI, f. 17, op. 133, d. 311, ll. 34–50, here 38–9; a draft in TsDAHO, f. 1, op. 30, spr. 2423, ark. 49–50 (2 August); ibid., op. 24, spr. 785, ark. 61–7 (14 August).

7 TsDAHO, f. 1, op. 8, spr. 330, ark. 13–14. The Moscow edition was reviewed in *Literaturna hazeta,* 5 September 1946, 4. Compare Ilchenko, *Sertse zhde* and idem, *Peterburgskaia osen.*

8 TsDAMLM, f. 590, op. 1, spr. 163, ark. 7; TsDAHO, f. 1, op. 30, spr. 2357, ark. 242; Ilchenko, *Peterburzka osin.*

9 *Literaturna hazeta,* 23 December 1948, 2.

10 TsDAMLM, f. 590, op. 1, spr. 57, ark. 107–8. This passage was not included in the abridged text of his speech that appeared in *Literaturna hazeta.*

11 *Literaturna hazeta,* 7 August 1947, 2; 6 December 1948, 3.

12 Rybak, *Pereiaslavska rada* 45.

13 On different writers' portrayals of Bohun, see Syrotiuk, *Ukrainskyi radianskyi istorychnyi roman,* 295–9. On 295 Syrotiuk announces, '*The Pereiaslav Council* conclusively disproves the statement of some bourgeois historians and novelists about acute contradictions and conflicts between Ivan Bohun and Bohdan Khmelnytsky.'

14 L. Dmyterko, 'Ukrainska radianska literatura, 74–5; *Literaturna hazeta,* 9 March 1950, 1 (award).

15 TsDAHO, f. 1, op. 30, spr. 1416, ark. 8.

16 Ibid., ark. 1–3.

17 *Radianske mystetstvo,* 13 July 1949, 2 (review); 12 November 1949, 3 (Sumy); 1 March 1950, 3 (Kharkiv); *Literaturna hazeta,* 14 July 1949, 2 (review). Dmyterko was a Western Ukrainian who adapted well to Stalinist cultural life and made a career as a literary functionary in Kiev. During a readers' conference on his visit to Western

Ukraine in 1950 Dmyterko received an anonymous note asking, 'What were you sick with when you wrote *Together Forever?*' See TsDAHO, f. 1, op. 30, spr. 2042, ark. 13.

18 *Radianske mystetstvo*, 30 July 1952, 3.

19 Ibid., 5 July 1950, 3; 19 July 1950, 2 (*Iaroslav*); Korniichuk, *Bohdan Khmelnytsky* (1939), 31, 53, 59, 76; idem, *Bohdan Khmelnytsky* (1954), 23, 31, 33, 43; TsDAMLM, f. 435, op. 1, spr. 1577, ark. 1–5 (*Bohdan*).

20 *Literaturna hazeta*, 24 April 1952, 3 (conference); TsDAHO, f. 1, op. 30, spr. 3597, ark. 71 (poem).

21 *Literaturna hazeta*, 24 December 1953, 3 (excerpts from *Ukraine Was Humming*); Petro Panch, *Homonila Ukraina* (Kiev, 1954*); XVIII zizd*, 157 (Nazarenko on the insufficient revisions); TsDAMLM, f. 590, op. 1, spr. 204, ark. 3 and *Literaturna hazeta*, 12 November 1953, 3–4 (Rybak).

22 TsDAHO, f. 1, op. 70, spr. 2247; op. 30, spr. 3681, esp. ark. 113 (Stanyslaviv province) and 124 (Vovkovyi).

23 Rybak, *Pereiaslavska rada* (1953); TsKhSD, f. 5, op. 17, d. 454, l. 1 (Moscow publishers); TsDAHO, f. 1, op. 30, spr. 3631, ark. 4, 8; *Literaturna hazeta*, 6 May 1954, 3 (radio).

24 Conveniently grouped together in a report to Moscow in TsKhSD, f. 5, op. 17, d. 454, l. 11.

25 TsDAHO, f. 1, op. 30, spr. 3632, ark. 22–33; op. 70, spr. 2247, ark. 30 (*Forever Together* and *Bohdan Khmelnytsky*); *Radianska osvita*, 3 October 1953, 1; 9 January 1954, 2; 15 May 1954, 4; 22 May, 2; 14 August, 3 (school curriculum).

26 *Literaturna hazeta*, 13 June 1945, 4 (1945); 22 January 1954, 4 (Lviv); TsDAHO, f. 1, op. 30, spr. 3618, ark. 93 (Lviv); spr. 3632, ark. 26–33 (six other companies).

27 TsDAHO, f. 1, op. 30, spr. 3599, ark. 46.

28 TsKhSD, f. 5, op. 17, d. 402, l. 78; *Literaturna hazeta*, 22 May 1954, 4 (conference); TsDAMLM, f. 590, op. 1, spr. 199, ark. 23–4; *Literaturna hazeta*, 28 October 1954, 2 (congress).

29 TsDAMLM, f. 687, op. 1, spr. 47, ark. 23zv (anonymous note) and 29 (Zhytnyk).

30 Ibid., 11–12.

31 Ibid., 7, 9–9zv, 20–20zv, 21zv, 37–8 (Krykun), 54zv.

32 Ibid., 18.

33 Kenez, *Cinema and Soviet Society*, 239–40.

34 Dubenko, *Taras Shevchenko ta ioho heroi na ekrani*, 31–2.

35 TsDAHO, f. 1, op. 70, spr. 689, ark. 1, 4, 9–10.

36 Ibid., op. 30, spr. 1377; RGALI, f. 1992, op. 1, d. 129.

37 TsDAHO, f. 1, op. 30, spr. 1850, ark. 11 (Korniichuk), 13 (Petrytsky). A copy of the minutes is in RGALI, f. 1992, op. 1, d. 124. Petrytsky was referring to Illia Repin's famous painting *The Zaporozhians Writing a Letter to the Sultan* (1880–91), the destruction of the Zaporozhian Host on the orders of Catherine II in 1774, and

Semen Hulak-Artemovsky's popular comic opera, *The Zaporozhian Cossack beyond the Danube* (1863).

38 TsDAHO, f. 1, op. 30, spr. 1850, ark. 18, 21, 24, 26, 33 (discussion); 36–46 (reviews). A copy is in RGALI, f. 1992, op. 1, d. 125, ll. 1–6, 14–17.

39 TsDAHO, f. 1, op. 30, spr. 1850, ark. 55 (commission); spr. 2056, ark. 11–13 (Kyrychenko) and 20 (Melnikov).

40 Ibid., spr. 1850, ark. 55–88.

41 RGALI, f. 1992, op. 1, d. 124, ll. 44–72; RGASPI, f. 17, op. 132, d. 427, ll. 90–1.

42 TsDAHO, f. 1, op. 30, spr. 2056, ark. 26–31 (Nazarenko to Bolshakov), 32–3 (Levada).

43 RGASPI, f. 17, op. 132, d. 427, ll. 90–1; RGALI, f. 1992, op. 1, d. 116, ll. 1–30; TsDAHO, f. 1, op. 30, spr. 1850, ark. 90–100.

44 TsDAHO, f. 1, op. 24, spr. 777, ark. 101.

45 *Izvestiia*, 20 December 1951; TsDAHO, f. 1, op. 30, spr. 2056, ark. 21–5.

46 *Radianske mystetstvo*, 19 December 1951, 3; 26 December 1951, 2; *Literaturna hazeta*, 27 December 1951, 3; TsDAVOV, f. 2, op. 8, spr. 9496, ark. 131 (the studios' report for 1951–3).

47 TsDAHO, f. 1, op. 30, spr. 2347, ark. 18; spr. 3597, ark. 73.

48 TsDAMLM, f. 435, op. 1, spr. 766, ark. 1; spr. 1846, ark. 22–6; RGALI, f. 2329, op. 12, d. 237, ll. 10, 35–6, 115–16, 124–6; TsDAHO, f. 1, op. 30, spr. 3657, ark. 142.

49 TsDAHO, f. 1, op. 30, spr. 3656, ark. 8. The Kiev Film Studios eventually filmed Dmyterko's play in 1956–7 (ibid., ark. 197).

50 TsDAMLM, f. 435, op. 1, spr. 2137, ark. 13, 15, 23–5, 40–5.

51 TsDAHO, f. 1, op. 30, spr. 3268, ark. 107.

52 Ibid., spr. 2347, ark. 18 (1953); spr. 3633, ark. 2–3, 10–11 (1954); *Radianska osvita*, 19 December 1953, 2.

53 *Istoriia ukrainskoho mystetstva*, 6: 125–6; Dmytrenko, *Ukrainskyi radianskyi zhyvopys*, 80, 88; Iukhymets, *Ukrainske radianske mystetstvo*, 96, 112, 140.

54 *Literaturna hazeta*, 17 June 1954, 4; TsDAMLM, f. 665, op. 1, spr. 167, ark. 4.

55 TsDAMLM, f. 196, op. 1, spr. 26, ark. 19; 'Za novye uspekhi izobrazitelnogo iskusstva Ukrainy,' *Iskusstvo*, no. 4 (1954): 7; *Vystavka izobrazitelnogo iskusstva Ukrainskoi SSR* (1951), 17; Kholodkovskaia, Introduction, *Mikhail Gordeevich Deregus*, 19–22, 30–3.

56 The painting was first displayed at the All-Union Artistic Exhibition in Moscow in December 1951 (*Radianske mystetstvo*, 26 December 1951, 1; 1 January 1952, 3).

57 *Literaturna hazeta*, 31 January 1952, 4 ('excessive splendour'); *Radianske mystetstvo*, 14 December 1952, 2 (Popova); TsDAMLM, f. 581, op. 1, spr. 343, ark. 9 (Hryhoriev).

58 *Radianske mystetstvo*, 14 January 1953, 4.

59 Ibid., 25 March 1953, 3.

60 TsDAHO, f. 1, op. 70, spr. 2247, ark. 93, 140; TsDAMLM, f. 119, op. 1, spr. 168, ark. 1; *Literaturna hazeta*, 7 January 1954, 1.
61 TsDAMLM, f. 581, op. 1, spr. 440, ark. 6–9; *Radianske mystetstvo*, 9 June 1954, 2.
62 Iukhymets, *Ukrainske radianske mystetstvo*, 100; *Istoriia ukrainskoho mystetstva*, 6: 229–30.
63 TsDAHO, f. 1, op. 30, spr. 3599, ark. 78–80; spr. 3634, ark. 11; spr. 3643, ark. 112; *Vystavka izobrazitelnogo iskusstva*, 37–72.
64 NAIIU, op. 1, spr. 550, ark. 21.
65 TsDAMLM, f. 665, op. 1, spr. 169, ark. 16, 30 (Khmelko); 18zv (Khmelnytsky's clothing); 46 zv (Bilostotsky); 2, 7, 19 (Kryvenko).
66 For a more detailed discussion of Ukrainian historical opera under Stalin, see Yekelchyk, '*Diktat* and Dialogue in Stalinist Culture.'
67 RGALI, f. 962, op. 11, d. 558, ll. 17, 21, 48 (decision to produce a historical opera); TsDAMLM, f. 435, op. 1, spr. 297 (first draft of the libretto); *Radianske mystetstvo*, 28 July 1948, 3 (Dankevych).
68 TsDAHO, f. 1, op. 30, spr. 2041, ark. 1; spr. 2051, ark. 1 (telegrams); *Radianske mystetstvo*, 15 February 1950, 3 (first audition); 23 August 1950, 3 (score ready).
69 *Radianske mystetstvo*, 31 January 1951, 1; *Literaturna hazeta*, 8 February 1951, 3; RGALI, f. 962, op. 2, d. 2336, l. 13; op. 3, d. 2306, l. 6.
70 TsDAHO, f. 1, op. 30, spr. 2428, ark. 3–85; *Dekada ukrainskoho mystetstva u Moskvi.*
71 *Pravda*, 16 June 1951, 1.
72 Ibid., 20 July 1951, 3–4.
73 *Literaturna hazeta*, 26 July 1951, 4; TsDAHO, f. 1, op. 30, spr. 2424, ark. 13–14; op. 1, spr. 976, ark. 12, 18–20, 227–9.
74 TsDAMLM, f. 435, op. 1, spr. 304, ark. 1–8; spr. 305; TsDAHO, f. 1, op. 30, spr. 2747; TsDAVOV, f. 4763, op. 1, spr. 357, ark. 2–5, 44.
75 TsDAMLM, f. 435, op. 1, spr. 2012, ark. 5–6, 8.
76 TsDAVOV, f. 4763, op. 1, spr. 357, ark. 95 (concluding words); TsDAMLM, f. 435, op. 1, spr. 1959, ark. 15 (Composers' Union).
77 RGASPI, f. 17, op. 132, d. 419, ll. 219–21.
78 Ibid., ll. 222–52; *Radianske mystetstvo*, 24 October 1951, 4.
79 RGALI, f. 962, op. 11, d. 613, ll. 1–47 (Shipov); TsDAMLM, f. 146, op. 1, spr. 192, ark. 2 (Rylsky).
80 TsKhSD, f. 5, op. 17, d. 445, ll. 35–8.
81 TsDAMLM, f. 573, op. 1, spr. 216, ark. 5.
82 See Yekelchyk, '*Diktat* and Dialogue in Stalinist Culture,' 616–17.
83 TsDAMLM, f. 573, op. 4, spr. 17, ark. 17, 25.
84 Ibid., f. 1106, op. 1, spr. 22, ark. 1a, 9–10, 21 (script); TsDAHO, f. 1, op. 30, spr. 3268, ark. 29 (released).

85 *Radianske mystetstvo*, 30 September 1953, 3; 14 October 1953, 3; *Literaturna hazeta*, 1 October 1953, 3; 29 October 1953, 2.
86 TsKhSD, f. 5, op. 17, d. 402, l. 71; TsDAHO, f. 1, op. 24, spr. 3504, ark. 24; op. 30, spr. 3632, ark. 20–2; TsDAVOV, f. 5116, op. 4, spr. 15, ark. 44; spr. 19, ark. 1–2; spr. 20, ark. 1–7, 25.
87 GARF, f. 6903, op. 26, d. 39, TV program and transcripts for 10 May (no pagination); TsKhSD, f. 5, op. 17, d. 402, ll. 76–7 (all-Union radio); TsDAHO, f. 1, op. 30, spr. 3631, ark. 25 (Ukrainian radio); spr. 3633, ark. 47–54 (gramophone disks); spr. 3632, ark. 180–6 (concert); *Radianske mystetstvo*, 17 November 1954, 4 (Dankevych's accolade).
88 *Novyi shliakh*, 15 January 1954, 4. The reference to Bohdan's 'boring' aria on the need for reunification seems to add some credibility to the story. Indeed, two of the hetman's arias were devoted to this subject.
89 GARF, f. 6646, op. 1, d. 356, ll. 14–18.
90 RGALI, f. 2329, op. 3, d. 168, l. 35ob. A real rarity, Puccini's *Tosca*, surpassed *Bohdan*'s record average attendance: 2,959 people showed up at a mere two performances of *Tosca* in Kiev.
91 Ibid., d. 111, ll. 1–3.
92 TsKhSD, f. 5, op. 17, d. 445, ll. 85–6. As an amusing sidelight, there is every likelihood that Hryshko met the bass Borys Hmyria (Colonel Kryvonis in the opera) regularly on Pasazh Street, where both men lived.
93 TsDAMLM, f. 435, op. 1, spr. 1302, ark. 1–2.

Epilogue

1 TsDAHO, f. 24, op. 1605, ark. 19, 23. Demian Korotchenko at the time served as the chairman of Ukraine's Council of Ministers.
2 Brandenberger, *National Bolshevism*, 247.
3 TsKhSD, f. 5, op. 30, d. 9, ll. 115–16; TsDAHO, f. 1, op. 24, spr. 3504, ark. 186.
4 TsDAHO, f. 1, op. 24, spr. 3504, ark. 121–3, 163–7; op. 30, spr. 3597, ark. 73–7; spr. 3598, ark. 2–6, 19–44; TsKhSD, f. 5, op. 30, d. 9, ll. 51–64; d. 52, ll. 96–9, 127–9.
5 TsDAHO, f. 1, op. 24, spr. 3504, ark. 163–7 (Ukrainian initiative); TsKhSD, f. 5, op. 17, d. 402, l. 26 (Lykholat and others).
6 TsKhSD, f. 5, op. 30, d. 9, l. 55 (resolution). Much of this narrative is based on Lykholat's own recollections checked against the archival materials. From 1961 until his death in 1993 he worked at the Institute of History of the Ukrainian Academy of Sciences, the institution I joined as a junior researcher in 1989. Andrii Vasylovych was fond of sharing his reminiscences with younger colleagues. Forty-five years after

the events, however, his chronology was sometimes unreliable. Stephen Velychenko interviewed Lykholat in 1988 and published a similar account of the preparation of the *Theses*, albeit he asserted that Suslov had ordered Lykholat to prepare this document in mid-1952 and that the final draft had been ready by mid-1953 (Velychenko, *Shaping Identity*, 59). Because of archival materials unavailable to Velychenko at the time, such a dating cannot be supported.

7 TsKhSD, f. 5, op. 30, d. 52, ll. 1–29; TsDAHO, f. 1, op. 30, spr. 3642, ark. 35–70.

8 Yaroslav Bilinsky has rightly observed that, in the *Theses*, 'even the "class" character of history is not stressed; the Ukrainian and the Russian people are essentially depicted as single units and not aggregates of warring classes' (*Second Soviet Republic*, 205).

9 *Tezisy o 300-letii vossoedineniia Ukrainy s Rossiei*, 11, 18, 23, 25.

10 *Pravda*, 12 January 1954, 3; *Radianska Ukraina*, 12 January 1954, 3; 14 January 1954, 1; 15 January 1954, 1; TsDAHO, f. 1, op. 30, spr. 3600, ark. 10.

11 RGALI, f. 2329, op. 4, dd. 245, 252; TsDAVOV, f. 2, op. 8, spr. 98882, ark. 96–101, 205; TsDAHO, f. 1, op. 30, spr. 3605, 3606; 3620 (medal); op. 24, spr. 3504, ark. 37–8; op. 30, spr. 3607, ark. 1–5 (badge); spr. 3621, ark. 6 (stamps).

12 TsDAVOV, f. 2, op. 8, spr. 10237, ark. 65–85; TsDAHO, f. 1, op. 30, spr. 3601, ark. 15–37 (list); *Radianska Ukraina*, 5 February 1954, 2 (beer).

13 *Radianska Ukraina*, 17 January 1954, 1 (renaming); 25 April 1954 (concert); GARF, f. 7523, op. 57, d. 963, ll. 1–3; op. 58, d. 19, ll. 2–21 (Crimea); 'Iubileinye nauchnye sessii, posviashchennye 300–letiiu vossoedineniia Ukrainy s Rossiei' (sessions). On the *dekady*, see *Pravda* and *Radianska Ukraina*, 6–18 May 1954.

14 *Radianska Ukraina*, 22 May 1954, 1; 23 May 1954, 2–4 (session); TsDAHO, f. 1, op. 30, spr. 3608, 3611, 3612; TsDAVOV, f. 2, op. 8, spr. 10238 (addresses). Some congratulations eventually were published in *Radianska Ukraina*, 27 May 1954, 2; 29 May 1954, 2.

15 *Vechirnii Kyiv*, 24 May 1954, 1, 3; 20 May 1954, 3; TsDAHO, f. 1, op. 30, spr. 3600, ark. 58–9; spr. 3636, ark. 6–7.

16 TsDAHO, f. 1, op. 16, spr. 74, ark. 104–11; op. 30, spr. 3622, ark. 1–48 (gifts from Ukraine); spr. 3623, ark. 1–19 (gifts to Ukraine); spr. 3601, ark. 87–90; spr. 3641, ark. 138–9; *Radianske mystetstvo*, 9 June 1954, 1; *Literaturna hazeta*, 1 July 1954, 1 (museums).

17 *Pravda*, 30 May 1954, 1–2; 31 May 1954, 1–2.

18 See *Radianska Ukraina*, January-May 1954.

19 TsKhSD, f. 5, op. 17, d. 427, ll. 189–207 (Kabarda); Tadyev, 'Konferentsiia po voprosam izucheniia istorii Gornogo Altaia' (Altai); Korneichik, 'Ėkonomicheskie predposylki formirovaniia belorusskoi burzhuaznoi natsii,' 98.

20 TsKhSD, f. 5, op. 17, d. 518, ll. 70–5.

21 TsDAHO, f. 1, op. 46, spr. 6822, ark. 40, 105.

22 Ibid., ark. 83; op. 30, spr. 3626, ark. 18–19.

23 See TsKhSD, f. 5, op. 30, d. 52, ll. 101–7.

24 Bilinsky, *Second Soviet Republic*, 206–7.

25 Ibid., 193–4.

26 Iurchuk, *Kulturne zhyttia v Ukraini u povoienni roky*, 61.

27 See Farmer, *Ukrainian Nationalism*, 78–121.

28 Baran, *Ukraina 1950–1960–kh rr.*, 146; Kasianov, *Nezhodni*, 70–2.

29 Braichevsky, *Annexation or Reunification*; Dziuba, *Internationalism or Russification?*

30 See Brudny, *Reinventing Russia*; Kozlov, 'The Historical Turn in Late Soviet Culture.'

31 Farmer, *Ukrainian Nationalism*, 95. This is also Bohdan Krawchenko's argument in his *Social Change and National Consciousness*, chap. 5.

32 Shelest, *Da ne sudimy budete*. On Shelest, see Bilinsky, 'Mykola Skrypnyk and Petro Shelest,' 105–43; Tillett, 'Ukrainian Nationalism.'

33 Wanner, *Burden of Dreams*, 38.

34 In addition to Wanner's book, see Kohut, 'History as a Battleground'; Kuzio, *Ukraine;* Plokhy, 'The Ghosts of Pereiaslav'; Sysyn, 'The Reemergence of the Ukrainian Nation.'

Bibliography

Archival Sources

Note: According to the Russian and Ukrainian archival citation systems, every file (*delo* in Russian, *sprava* in Ukrainian) is identified by the number of its *fond* (collection), the number of *opis* or *opys* (literally the 'inventory' of the *fond*'s files, which also means a 'record group'), and the number of the file itself ('zv' and 'ob' in citations translate as 'overleaf' in Ukrainian and Russian, respectively). A more detailed discussion of the structure of the declassified Soviet archives and the nature of their materials lies beyond the scope of this work. The books by Patricia Kennedy Grimsted provide the best guide to the archives of the former Soviet Union. See, in particular, *A Handbook for Archival Research in the USSR* (Washington, D.C., 1989); *Archives and Manuscript Repositories in the USSR: Ukraine and Moldavia* (Princeton, N.J., 1988); and idem, ed., *Archives of Russia: A Directory and Bibliographic Guide to Holdings in Moscow and St. Petersburg* (Armonk, N.Y., 2000). On the opportunities and challenges that the newly opened archives present for students of Soviet nationality policy, see Terry Martin, 'Interpreting the New Archival Signals: Nationalities Policy and the Nature of the Soviet Bureaucracy,' *Cahiers du Monde russe* 40, no. 1–2 (janvier–juin 1999): 113–24, and Peter A. Blitstein, 'Researching Nationality Policy in the Archives,' ibid.: 125–37.

TsDAHO
Tsentralnyi derzhavnyi arkhiv hromadskykh obiednan Ukrainy (The Ukrainian Central State Archive of Civic Organizations, former Party Archive, Kiev)
f. 1 (Communist Party of Ukraine)
    op. 1 (*opysy* 1 through 9 contain minutes of the Central Committee's plenary meetings and other party forums): spr. 729, 972, 976
    op. 6: spr. 409, 1036, 1073
    op. 8: spr. 316, 328, 330, 340

op. 16 (Minutes of the Politburo's and Secretariat's Meetings, Secret Files): spr. 32, 74

op. 23 (Special Section, Secret Files): spr. 328, 355, 441, 451, 463, 703, 780, 787, 788, 860, 889, 890, 937, 1060, 1604, 1605, 1608, 1621, 1652, 2768, 2782, 2858, 4504, 4511, 4512, 4515, 4525, 4526, 4956, 4957, 4958, 5072, 5664, 6259

op. 24 (Special Section, Secret Files, continued): spr. 8, 774, 777, 784, 785, 1090, 1105, 1577, 1605, 2677, 2714, 3503, 3504

op. 30 (Special Section, General Files): spr. 621, 985, 1370, 1377, 1416, 1832, 1850, 1875, 1902, 1916, 1917, 1918, 1919, 1920, 1921, 1922, 1924, 1925, 1926, 1989, 1990, 2003, 2030, 2041, 2042, 2047, 2051, 2056, 2325, 2328, 2330, 2339, 2347, 2357, 2360, 2423, 2424, 2426, 2428, 2747, 2755, 2756, 2757, 2768, 2769, 2775, 2806, 2811, 3261, 3268, 3308, 3597, 3598, 3599, 3600, 3601, 3605, 3606, 3608, 3611, 3612, 3618, 3619, 3620, 3621, 3622, 3623, 3627, 3628, 3629, 3631, 3632, 3633, 3634, 3636, 3640, 3641, 3642, 3643, 3652, 3653, 3655, 3656, 3662, 3657, 3672, 3674, 3681

op. 46 (Department of the Party's Organizational Work): spr. 6822

op. 70 (Department of Propaganda and Agitation): spr. 46, 48, 50, 66, 68, 91, 121, 153, 266, 282, 326, 385, 387, 388, 390, 394, 399, 436, 459, 514, 539, 540, 564, 570, 571, 618, 620, 621, 689, 714, 744, 753, 754, 757, 760, 761, 762, 763, 764, 823, 836, 837, 1090, 1095, 1173, 1154, 1334, 1494, 1620, 1768, 1787, 1788, 1886, 1917, 1948, 2247

op. 72 (Department of Literature and the Arts): spr. 1

op. 73 (School Department): spr. 398, 585, 592

TsDAVOV

Tsentralnyi derzhavnyi arkhiv vyshchykh orhaniv vlady i upravlinnia Ukrainy (The Ukrainian Central State Archive of the Highest Bodies of Power and Administration)

f. 2 (Council of Ministers)

op. 7: spr. 345, 553, 818, 2747, 3078, 3927, 5553, 5568, 9527

op. 8: spr. 2040, 2531, 7730, 9486, 9496, 9503, 9504, 9880, 10237, 10238, 11406, 11407, 11408, 98882

f. 4669 (D.Z. Manuilsky), op. 1, spr. 23, 44, 47, 124

f. 4750 (Ukrainian Soviet Encyclopedia), op. 1: spr. 2, 13, 17, 3959

f. 4762 (Committee on Cultural and Educational Institutions), op.1, spr. 164, 343, 562, 566, 669

f. 4763 (Committee on the Arts), op. 1, spr. 58, 85, 357

f. 4906, op. 1: spr. 35

f. 5116 (Ministry of Culture)

op. 4: spr. 15, 19, 20

op. 10: spr. 16, 19, 20

TsDAMLM
Tsentralnyi derzhavnyi arkhiv-muzei literatury i mystetstva Ukrainy (The Ukrainian
    Central State Archive and Museum of Literature and the Arts)
f. 119 (M.H. Derehus), op. 1: spr. 168
f. 146 (M.P. Stefanovych), op. 1: spr. 192
f. 196 (V.I. Kasiian), op. 1: spr. 26
f. 435 (O.Ie. Korniichuk), op. 1: spr. 33, 297, 304, 496, 508, 766, 1302, 1577, 1846,
    1959, 2012, 2137
f. 573 (National Opera Company of Ukraine), op. 1: spr. 46, 216; op. 4: spr. 17
f. 581 (Artists' Union of Ukraine), op. 1, spr. 343, 440
f. 590 (Writers' Union of Ukraine), op. 1: spr. 39, 40, 57, 163, 199, 204
f. 661 (Composers' Union of Ukraine), op. 1: spr. 130
f. 665 (Directorate of Artistic Exhibitions), op. 1: spr. 167, 169
f. 687 (N.I. Rybak), op. 1: spr. 47
f. 1106 (I.S. Patorzhynsky), op. 1: spr. 22

NAIIU
Naukovyi arkhiv Instytutu istorii Ukrainy NANU (The Scholarly Archive of the Institute
    of Ukrainian History of the National Academy of Sciences of Ukraine)
    op. 1 (plans, reports, meetings minutes, etc.): spr. 95, 103, 134, 140, 166, 215, 352,
    353, 354, 355, 363 (2 parts), 407, 478a, 550
    op. 1L (personal files): spr. 115

RGASPI
Rossiiskii gosudarstvennyi arkhiv sotsialnoi i politicheskoi istorii (The Russian State
    Archive of Social and Political History, former Party Archive, Moscow)
f. 17 (KPSS Central Committee)
    op. 120 (Departments): d. 348
    op. 125 (Administration of Propaganda and Agitation): dd. 190, 212, 224, 293, 300,
    340
    op. 132 (Department of Propaganda and Agitation, 1948–53): dd. 232, 339, 372,
    416, 419, 427, 503
    op. 133 (Departments of the Central Committee, 1951–5): dd. 4, 220, 303, 311

TsKhSD
Tsentr khraneniia sovremennoi dokumentatsii (The Centre for the Preservation of
    Contemporary Documentation, former in-house current archive of the party's Central
    Committee, Moscow)

f. 5 (KPSS Central Committee)
op. 17 (Departments of Learning, Literature and the Arts, Scholarship and Culture):
dd. 402, 427, 445, 454, 470
op. 30 (General Department): dd. 9, 39, 52

GARF
Gosudarstvennyi arkhiv Rossiiskoi Federatsii (The State Archive of the Russian Federation)
f. 6646 (USSR Slavic Committee), op. 1: dd. 4, 356
f. 6903 (USSR Council of Ministers' Committee on Radio and Television Broadcasting), op. 26: d. 39
f. 7523 (Presidium of the USSR Supreme Council), op. 57: d. 963; op. 58, d. 19
f. 9401 (I.V. Stalin's 'Special Folder'), op. 2, d. 138

RGALI
Rossiiskii gosudarstvennyi arkhiv literatury i iskusstva (The Russian State Archive of Literature and the Arts)
f. 962 (All-Union Committee on the Arts, until 1952), op. 2: d. 2336; op. 3: d. 1995; op. 11: d. 558, 613
f. 1992 (I. A. Savchenko), op. 1: dd. 75, 76, 78, 80, 116, 124, 125, 129
f. 2329 (USSR Ministry of Culture, 1953–), op. 3: d. 111, 168; op. 4: d. 101, 245, 252; op. 12: d. 237

Newspapers

Izvestiia (Moscow)
Komunist (Kiev)
Kultura i zhizn (Moscow)
Literatura i mystetstvo (Kiev)
Literaturna hazeta (Kiev)
Literaturna Ukraina (Kiev)
Novyi shliakh (Toronto)
Pravda (Moscow)
Radianska osvita (Kiev)
Radianska Ukraina (Kiev)
Radianske mystetstvo (Kiev)
Vechirnii Kyiv (Kiev)
Visti (Kiev)

Published Sources

XVI zizd Komunistychnoi partii (bilshovykiv) Ukrainy 25–28 sichnia 1949 r.: Materialy zizdu. Kiev, 1949.

XVIII zizd Komunistychnoi partii Ukrainy 23–26 bereznia 1954 r.: Materialy zizdu. Kiev, 1954.

XXII sezd Kommunisticheskoi partii Sovetskogo Soiuza, 17–31 oktiabria 1961 g.: Stenograficheskii otchet. 2 vols. Moscow, 1962.

Aksenov, Iu.S. 'Poslevoennyi stalinizm: Udar po intelligentsii.' *Kentavr*, no. 1 (1991): 80–9.

Aleksandrov, G. 'O nekotorykh zadachakh obshchestvennykh nauk v sovremennykh usloviiakh.' *Bolshevik*, no. 14 (1945): 12–29.

Anderson, Benedict. *Imagined Communities: Reflections on the Origin and Spread of Nationalism*. Rev. ed. London, 1991.

Apanovych, O.M., ed. *Pereiaslav-Khmelnytskyi i ioho istorychni pamiatky*. Kiev, 1954.

Appadurai, A. 'The Past as a Scarce Resource.' *Man* 16 (1981): 201–19.

Armstrong, John A. *Ukrainian Nationalism*. 3d ed. Englewood, Colo., 1990.

Baberowski, Jörg. 'Stalinismus als imperials Phänomen: Die islamischen Regionen der Sowjetunion, 1920–1941.' In *Stalinismus: Neue Forschungen und Konzepte*, ed. Stefan Plaggenborg. Berlin, 1998.

Bakhtin, M.M. *Rabelais and His World*. Trans. H. Iswolsky. 2d ed. Bloomington, Ind., 1984.

Baraboi, A. Review of *Vyzvolna viina ukrainskoho narodu proty hnitu shliakhetskoi Polshchi i pryiednannia Ukrainy do Rosii (1648–1654)*, by M.N. Petrovsky. *Istorik-marksist*, no. 7 (1940): 137–40.

Baran, Volodymyr. *Ukraina 1950–1960-kh rr.: Evoliutsiia totalitarnoi systemy*. Lviv, 1996.

Barber, John. *Soviet Historians in Crisis, 1928–1932*. New York, 1981.

Barghoorn, Frederick C. *Soviet Russian Nationalism*. New York, 1956.

Basarab, John. *Pereiaslav 1654: A Historiographical Study*. Edmonton, 1982.

Bazhan, Mykola. 'Danylo Halytsky.' *Ukrainska literatura*, no. 3–4 (1942): 47–59.

– 'Danylo Halytsky.' In his *Virshi i poemy*. Kiev, 1949.

– ed. *Istoriia ukrainskoho mystetstva v shesty tomakh*. Vol. 6. Kiev, 1968.

Beissinger, Mark R. *Nationalist Mobilization and the Collapse of the Soviet Union*. New York, 2002.

Bertram, Katrin. '(Re-)Writing History: Oleksandr Sokolovs'kyi and the Soviet Ukrainian Historical Novel.' *Harvard Ukrainian Studies* 21, no. 1–2 (1997): 161–72.

Bezpalchy, V. 'Suspilno-politychni pohliady P.A. Hrabovskoho.' *Bilshovyk Ukrainy*, no. 7 (1952): 51–62.

Bhabha, Homi K., ed. *Nation and Narration*. London, 1990.

Bilan, Iu., A. Butsyk, V. Kozynets, V. Kotov, and O. Koshyk. 'Knyha pro slavne mynule ukrainskoho narodu.' *Komunist Ukrainy*, no. 3 (1954): 70–80.

Bilinsky, Yaroslav. 'The Incorporation of Western Ukraine and Its Impact on Politics and Society in Soviet Ukraine.' In *The Influence of East Europe and the Soviet West on the USSR*, ed. Roman Szporluk. New York, 1975.

– 'Mykola Skrypnyk and Petro Shelest: An Essay on the Persistence and Limits of Ukrainian National Communism.' In *Soviet Nationality Policies and Practices*, ed. Jeremy R. Azrael. New York, 1978.

– *The Second Soviet Republic: The Ukraine after World War II*. New Brunswick, N.J., 1964.

Bilousov, S.M., K.H. Huslysty, O.P. Ohloblyn, M.N. Petrovsky, M.I. Suprunenko, and F.O. Iastrebov, eds. *Istoriia Ukrainy: Korotkyi kurs*. Kiev, 1940.

Bilousov, S.M., and O.P. Ohloblyn. *Zakhidna Ukraina*. Kiev, 1940.

Blitstein, Peter A. 'Researching Nationality Policy in the Archives.' *Cahiers du Monde russe* 40, no. 1–2 (janvier–juin 1999): 125–38.

– 'Stalin's Nations: Soviet Nationality Policy between Planning and Primordialism, 1936–1953.' PhD Dissertation, University of California, Berkeley, 1999.

Bociurkiw, Bohdan R. *The Ukrainian Greek Catholic Church and the Soviet State (1939–1950)*. Edmonton, 1996.

Boiechko, Vasyl, Oksana Hanzha, and Borys Zakharchuk. *Kordony Ukrainy: Istorychna retrospektyva ta suchasnyi stan*. Kiev, 1994.

Boiko, I.D. *300-letie vossoedineniia Ukrainy s Rossiei*. Moscow, 1954.

– *300 rokiv vozziednannia Ukrainy z Rosiieiu*. Kiev, 1953.

Boiko, I., and K. Huslysty. 'Monohrafiia pro Bohdana Khmelnytskoho.' *Komunist Ukrainy*, no. 11 (1954): 76–80.

Boiko, I., K. Huslysty, B. Datsiuk, and S. Kalashnikova. 'Sbornik dokumentov o vossoedinenii Ukrainy s Rossiei.' *Kommunist*, no. 2 (1954): 108–16.

Braichevsky, Mykhailo. *Pryiednannia chy vozziednannia? Krytychni zauvahy z pryvodu odniiei kontseptsii*. Toronto, 1971. Trans. as *Annexation or Reunification: Critical Notes on One Conception*. Trans. and ed. George P. Kulchycky. Munich, 1974.

Brandenberger, David. *National Bolshevism: Stalinist Mass Culture and the Formation of Modern Russian National Identity, 1931–1956*. Cambridge, Mass., 2002.

Brandenberger, D.L. and A.M. Dubrovsky. '"The People Need a Tsar": The Emergence of National Bolshevism as Stalinist Ideology, 1931–1941.' *Europe-Asia Studies* 50, no. 5 (1998): 873–92.

Brooks, Jeffrey. *Thank You, Comrade Stalin! Soviet Public Culture from Revolution to Cold War*. Princeton, N.J., 2000.

Brudny, Yitzhak M. *Reinventing Russia: Russian Nationalism and the Soviet State, 1953–1991*. Cambridge, Mass., 1999.

Burds, Jeffrey. *The Early Cold War in Soviet West Ukraine, 1944–1948*. Carl Beck Papers in Russian & East European Studies, no. 1505. Pittsburgh, 2001.

Carrère d'Encausse, Hélène. *The End of the Soviet Empire: The Triumph of Nations*. Trans. Franklin Philip. New York, 1993.

– *The Great Challenge: Nationalities and the Bolshevik State, 1917–1930*. Trans. Nancy Festinger. New York, 1992.

Chakrabarty, Dipesh. 'Postcoloniality and the Artifice of History: Who Speaks for "Indian" Pasts?' *Representations* 37 (1992): 1–26.

Chatterjee, Partha. *The Nation and Its Fragments: Colonial and Postcolonial Histories*. Princeton, N.J., 1993.

Conquest, Robert. *The Nation Killers: The Soviet Deportation of the Nationalities*. London, 1970.

Conquest, Robert. *Stalin: Breaker of Nations*. New York, 1991.

Crane, Susan A. 'Writing the Individual Back into Collective Memory.' *American Historical Review* 102, no. 5 (December 1997): 1372–85.

Dakhshleiger, G.F. 'V Institute istorii, arkheologii i ëtnografii Akademii nauk Kazakhskoi SSR.' *Voprosy istorii*, no. 2 (1952): 146–51.

Danyliuk, Iu.Z., ed. *Zberezhemo tuiu slavu: Hromadskyi rukh za uvichnennia istorii ukrainskoho kozatstva v druhii polovyni 50-kh-80-kh rr. XX st.* Kiev, 1997.

Dashkevych, Iaroslav. 'Ivan Krypiakevych – istoryk Ukrainy.' Introduction in Ivan Krypiakevych, *Istoriia Ukrainy*. Lviv, 1990.

Dekada ukrainskoho mystetstva u Moskvi 15–24 chervnia 1951 r.: Zbirka materialiv. Kiev, 1953.

Deutsch, Karl W. *Nationalism and Social Communication: An Inquiry into the Foundations of Nationality*. Cambridge, Mass., 1953; 1966.

Diadychenko, V.A. 'Nauchno-populiarnaia literatura o vossoedinenii Ukrainy s Rossiei.' *Voprosy istorii*, no. 4 (1954): 127–32.

Diadychenko, V.A., O.K. Kasymenko, and F.P. Shevchenko, eds. *Vyzvolna viina 1648–1654 rr. i vozziednannia Ukrainy z Rosiieiu*. Kiev, 1954.

Dmyterko, L. 'Ukrainska radianska literatura pislia postanovy TsK VKP(b) pro zhurnaly "Zvezda" i "Leningrad."' *Bilshovyk Ukrainy*, no. 1 (1949): 72–80.

Dmytrenko, A. *Ukrainskyi radianskyi istorychnyi zhyvopys*. Kiev, 1966.

'Do kintsia likviduvaty burzhuazno-natsionalistychni perekruchennia istorii Ukrainy.' *Bilshovyk Ukrainy*, no. 8 (1947): 1–10.

'Do trydtsiatyrichchia Ukrainskoi Radianskoi Sotsialistychnoi Respubliky.' *Bilshovyk Ukrainy*, no. 12 (1947): 1–9.

'Do ukrainskoho narodu: Zvernennia mitynhu predstavnykiv ukrainskoho narodu 26 lystopada 1941 roku v Saratovi.' In *Naukovi zapysky Instytutu istorii i arkheolohii AN URSR*. Vol. 1. Ufa, 1943.

Dobrenko, Evgenii. 'Sumerki kultury.' *Druzhba narodov*, no. 2 (1991): 249–71.

Dovzhenko, Oleksandr. *Hospody, poshly meni syly: Shchodennyk, kinopovisti, opovidannia, folklorni zapysy, lysty, dokumenty*. Kharkiv, 1994.

Dovzhenok, V.I. *Viiskova sprava v Kyivskii Rusi.* Kiev, 1950.

Duara, Prasenjit. *Rescuing History from the Nation: Questioning Narratives of Modern China.* Chicago, 1995.

Dubenko, S.V. *Taras Shevchenko ta ioho heroi na ekrani.* Kiev, 1967.

Dunham, Vera S. *In Stalin's Time: The Middleclass Values in Soviet Fiction.* Cambridge, 1976.

Dunlop, John B. *The Faces of Contemporary Russian Nationalism.* Princeton, N.J., 1983.

Dziuba, Ivan. *Internationalism or Russification?* 3d ed. New York, 1974.

Editorial untitled, *Voprosy istorii,* no. 1 (1945): 3–5.

Farmer, Kenneth C. *Ukrainian Nationalism in the Post-Stalin Era: Myth, Symbols and Ideology in Soviet Nationalities Policy.* The Hague, 1980.

Fitzpatrick, Sheila. 'Ascribing Class: The Construction of Social Identity in Soviet Russia.' *Journal of Modern History* 65, no. 4 (December 1993): 745–70.

Fitzpatrick, Sheila, 'The Bolshevik Dilemma: Class, Culture, and Politics in the Early Soviet Years.' *Slavic Review* 47, no. 4 (Winter 1988): 599–613.

Fitzpatrick, Sheila. *The Cultural Front: Power and Culture in Revolutionary Russia.* Ithaca, N.Y., 1992.

Funkenstein, Amos. 'Collective Memory and Historical Consciousness.' *History and Memory* 1, no. 1 (Spring/Summer 1989): 5–26.

Gedi, Noa and Yigal Elam. 'Collective Memory – What Is It?' *History and Memory* 8, no. 1 (Spring/Summer 1996): 30–50.

Gellner, Ernest. *Nations and Nationalism.* Oxford, 1983.

Golobutsky [Holobutsky], V.A. 'Rossiia i Osvoboditelnaia voina ukrainskogo naroda 1648–1654 godov.' *Voprosy istorii,* no. 1 (1954): 80–95.

Gorbunova, E. *Dramaturgiia A. Korneichuka.* Moscow, 1952.

Grekov, B.D. Review of *Vossoedinenie ukrainskogo naroda v edinom ukrainskom sovetskom gosudarstve,* by N. Petrovsky. *Istoricheskii zhurnal,* no. 12 (1944): 74–5.

– 'Sudby naseleniia galitskikh kniazheskikh votchin pod vlastiu Polshi.' *Istoricheskii zhurnal,* no. 12 (1944): 37–43.

Grekov, B.D., S.V. Bakhrushin, and V.I. Lebedev, eds. *Istoriia SSSR.* Vol. 1: *S drevneishikh vremen do kontsa XVIII veka.* 2d ed. Moscow, 1948.

Halbwachs, Maurice. *On Collective Memory.* Ed. Lewis A. Coster. Chicago, 1992.

– *The Collective Memory.* Trans. Francis J. Ditter, Jr, and Vida Yazdi Ditter. New York, 1980.

Halfin, Igal and Jochen Hellbeck. 'Rethinking the Stalinist Subject: Stephen Kotkin's *Magnetic Mountain* and the State of Soviet Historical Studies.' *Jahrbücher für Geschichte Osteuropas* 44, no. 3 (1996): 456–63.

Hann, Werner G. *Postwar Soviet Politics: The Fall of Zhdanov and the Defeat of Moderation, 1946–1953.* Ithaca, N.Y., 1982.

H[artley], J[ohn]. 'Nation,' in *Key Concepts in Communication and Cultural Studies,* ed. Tim O'Sullivan et al. 2d ed. New York, 1994.

Hellbeck, Jochen. 'Speaking Out: Languages of Affirmation and Dissent in Stalinist Russia.' *Kritika* 1, no. 1 (Winter 2000): 71–96.

Himka, John-Paul. *Galician Villagers and the Ukrainian National Movement in the Nineteenth Century.* Edmonton, 1988.

Hirsch, Francine. 'The Soviet Union as a Work-in-Progress: Ethnographers and the Category Nationality in the 1926, 1937, and 1939 Censuses.' *Slavic Review* 56, no. 2 (Summer 1997): 251–78.

Hirsch, Francine. 'Toward an Empire of Nations: Border-Making and the Formation of Soviet National Identities.' *Russian Review* 59, no. 2 (April 2000): 201–26.

Hobsbawm, E.J. *Nations and Nationalism since 1780: Programme, Myth, Reality.* Cambridge, 1990.

Hobsbawm, Eric J., and Terence Ranger, eds. *The Invention of Tradition.* New York, 1983.

H[offman], D[avid] L. 'The Soviet Empire: Colonial Practices and Socialist Ideology.' *Russian Review* 59, no. 2 (April 2000): vi–viii.

Holynsky, Iu.F. *Heroichna tema v tvorchosti I.A. Savchenka.* Kiev, 1982.

Hrabovych, Hryhorii [Grabowicz, George]. 'Sovietska albomna shevchenkiana: Kolazh, bricolage i kich.' *Krytyka,* no. 3 (5) (1998): 24–9.

Hrushevsky, Mykhailo. *Istoriia Ukrainy-Rusy.* Vol. 9, parts 1 and 2. Kiev, 1996–7.

Hrynevych, V.A. 'Utvorennia Narkomatu oborony URSR u 1944 r.: Z istorii odniiei politychnoi hry.' *Ukrainskyi istorychnyi zhurnal,* no. 5 (1991): 29–37.

– 'Utvorennia Narodnoho komisariatu zakordonnykh sprav Ukrainskoi RSR: Proekty i realii (1944–1945 rr.).' *Ukrainskyi istorychnyi zhurnal,* no. 3 (1995): 35–46.

Huslysty, K. *Danylo Halytsky.* Nashi velyki predky. Saratov, 1942.

– *Petro Konashevych-Sahaidachny.* Nashi velyki predky. Saratov, 1942.

Iavorsky, M.I. *Istoriia Ukrainy u styslomu narysi.* Kharkiv, 1928.

– *Korotka istoriia Ukrainy.* 5th ed. Kharkiv, 1927.

– *Narysy z istorii revoliutsiinoi borotby na Ukraini.* 2 vols. Kharkiv, 1927–8.

Ienevych, F. 'Amerykanskyi falsyfikator ideinoi spadshchyny Shevchenka.' *Bilshovyk Ukrainy,* no. 8 (1949): 26–40.

– 'Velykyi syn ukrainskoho narodu.' *Bilshovyk Ukrainy,* no. 3 (1951): 20–9.

Ilchenko, Aleksandr [Oleksandr]. *Peterburgskaia osen.* Moscow, 1946.

Ilchenko, Oleksandr. *Peterburzka osin: Dopovnene vydannia.* Kiev, 1952.

Sertse zhde. Kiev, 1939.

Isaievych, Ia. 'Peredmova.' In I.P. Krypiakevych, *Bohdan Khmelnytsky,* 2d ed. Lviv, 1990.

Istoriia Ukrainy. Vol. 1: *Peredkapitalistychna doba.* Kharkiv, 1932.

'Iubileinye nauchnye sessii, posviashchennye 300–letiiu vossoedineniia Ukrainy s Rossiei.' *Voprosy istorii,* no. 5 (1954): 184–6.

Iugov, A. *Daniil Galitskii.* Moscow, 1944.

– *Ratobortsy.* Moscow, 1956.

Iukhymets, H.M. *Ukrainske radianske mystetstvo 1941–1960 rokiv.* Kiev, 1983.

Iurchuk, V.I. *Kulturne zhyttia v Ukraini u povoienni roky: Svitlo i tini.* Kiev, 1995.

Iushkov, S. Review of *Narys istorii Ukrainy. Istoricheskii zhurnal,* no. 7 (1943): 89–90.

Iushkov, S., L. Slavin, M. Petrovsky, and K. Huslysty. *Istoriia Ukrainy.* Vol. 1. Ufa, 1943.

Ivanov, O.O. 'Istorychne znachennia vozziednannia Ukrainy z Rosieiu.' *Radianska shkola,* no. 9 (1953): 19–28.

Kaganovich, Lazar. *Pamiatnye zapiski.* Moscow, 1995.

Kaiser, Robert J. *The Geography of Nationalism in Russia and the USSR.* Princeton, N.J., 1994.

Kasianov, Heorhii. *Nezhodni: Ukrainska intelihentsiia v rusi oporu 1960-80-kh rokiv.* Kiev, 1995.

Kasymenko, O.K., ed. *Istoriia Ukrainskoi SSR.* Lim. ed. Vol. 1. Kiev, 1951.

– ed. *Istoriia Ukrainskoi RSR.* Vol. 1. Kiev, 1953.

– ed. *Vikovichna druzhba rosiiskoho i ukrainskoho narodiv: Zbirnyk statei prysviachenykh 300–richnomu iuvileiu vozziednannia Ukrainy z Rosiieiu (1654–1954).* Kiev, 1954.

Kenez, Peter. *Cinema and Soviet Society, 1917–1953.* Cambridge, 1992.

Kennedy, Michael D., and Ronald Grigor Suny. 'Introduction.' In *Intellectuals and the Articulation of the Nation,* ed. Kennedy and Suny. Ann Arbor, Mich., 1999, 1–51.

Kholmsky [Krypiakevych], Ivan. *Istoriia Ukrainy.* Munich, 1949.

Kholodkovskaia, M. Introduction. *Mikhail Gordeevich Deregus.* Moscow, 1954.

[Khrushchev, N.S.] *Khrushchev Remembers.* Introduction, comments, and notes by Edward Crankshaw. Trans. and ed. Strobe Talbott. Boston, 1970.

– 'Memuary Nikity Sergeevich Khrushcheva.' *Voprosy istorii,* no. 2–3 (1992): 75–102.

Kim, M. Review of *Istoriia Kazakhskoi SSR s drevneishikh vremen do nashikh dnei.* 2d ed. Ed. I.O. Omarov and A.M. Pankratova, *Voprosy istorii,* no. 6 (1949): 130–4.

Klymas, M. 'Ivan Franko – neprymyrennyi borets proty natsionalizmu i kosmo-polityzmu.' *Bilshovyk Ukrainy,* no. 8 (1951): 28–39.

Kobyletsky, Iu. *Kryla krecheta: Zhyttia i tvorchist Oleksandra Korniichuka.* Kiev, 1975.

Kohut, Zenon E. 'History as a Battleground: Russian-Ukrainian Relations and Historical Consciousness in Contemporary Ukraine.' In *The Legacy of History in Russia and the New States of Eurasia,* ed. S. Frederick Starr. Armonk, N.Y., 1994.

Kolesnikov, G.A., and A.M. Rozhkov. *Ordena i medali SSSR.* 2d ed. Moscow, 1978.

Kondratiuk, Kostiantyn, and Ivanna Luchakivska. 'Zakhidnoukrainska intelihentsiia u pershi roky radianskoi vlady (veresen 1939–cherven 1941).' *Visnyk Lvivskoho universytetu: Seriia istorychna,* no. 33 (1998): 178–85.

Kondufor, Iu.Iu., ed. *Kulturne budivnytstvo v Ukrainskii RSR: Cherven 1941–1950: Zbirnyk dokumentiv i materialiv.* Kiev, 1989.

Konstantinov, S.V. 'Nesostoiavshaiasia rasprava (O soveshchanii istorikov v TsK VKP(b) v maie-iiule 1944 goda.' In *Vlast i obshestvennye organizatsii Rossii v pervoi treti XX stoletiia,* ed. A.F. Kisilev. Moscow, 1994.

Korneichik, E.I. 'Ėkonomicheskie predposylki formirovaniia belorusskoi burzhuaznoi natsii.' *Voprosy istorii*, no. 8 (1955): 94–104.

Korniichuk, Oleksandr. *Bohdan Khmelnytsky: Persha chastyna trylohii*. Lviv, 1939.

– *Bohdan Khmelnytsky: Piesa na piat dii*. Kiev, 1954.

Koroliuk, V. Review of *Ocherki po istorii Galitsko-Volynskoi Rusi*, by V.T. Pashuto. *Voprosy istorii*, no. 8 (1951): 132–6.

Koshar, Rudy. *Germany's Transient Pasts: Preservation and National Memory in the Twentieth Century*. Chapel Hill, N.C., 1998.

Kostiuk, Hryhory. *Stalinist Rule in the Ukraine: A Study of the Decade of Mass Terror (1929–39)*. New York, 1960.

Kostiuk, Iu. 'Vysoka patriotychna rol radianskoho mystetstva.' *Bilshovyk Ukrainy*, no. 3 (1949): 40–51.

Kot, S.I. *Okhorona, vykorystannia ta propahanda pamiatok istorii ta kultury v Ukrainskii RSR*. Part 3. Kiev, 1989.

Koval, M.V. 'Flahman ukrainskoi istoriohrafii.' *Ukrainskyi istorychnyi zhurnal*, no. 4 (1997): 11–18.

– 'Sprava Oleksandra Dovzhenka.' *Ukrainskyi istorychnyi zhurnal*, no. 4 (1994): 108–19.

Koval, M.V., and O.S. Rublov. 'Instytut istorii NAN Ukrainy: Pershe dvadtsiatyrichchia (1936–1956 rr.).' *Ukrainskyi istorychnyi zhurnal*, no. 6 (1996): 50–68.

Kovalenko, L. 'Istoricheskie vzgliady revoliutsionera-demokrata T. G. Shevchenko.' *Voprosy istorii*, no. 7 (1951): 26–44.

Kozachenko, A.I. 'Tsennoe sobranie istochnikov po istorii vossoedineniia Ukrainy s Rossiei.' *Voprosy istorii*, no. 5 (1954): 145–51.

Kozhukalo, I.P. 'Vplyv kultu osoby Stalina na ideolohichni protsesy na Ukraini v 40-i-na pochatku 50-kh rokiv.' *Ukrainskyi istorychnyi zhurnal*, no. 2 (1989): 14–26.

Kozlov, Denis. 'The Historical Turn in Late Soviet Culture: Retrospectivism, Factography, Doubt.' *Kritika* 2, no. 3 (2001): 577–600.

Krawchenko, Bohdan. *Social Change and National Consciousness in Twentieth-Century Ukraine*. London, 1985.

K[rut], V. 'Khmelnitsky, Bogdan Zinovii Mikhailovich.' *Bolshaia sovetskaia ėntsiklopediia*. 1st ed. Vol. 59. Moscow, 1935.

Krylova, Anna. 'The Tenacious Liberal Subject in Soviet Studies.' *Kritika* 1, no. 1 (Winter 2000): 119–46.

Krypiakevych, I.P. *Bohdan Khmelnytsky*. Kiev, 1954 (1st ed.); Lviv, 1990 (2d ed.).

– *Mala istoriia Ukrainy*. Feldkirch, 1947.

– *Zviazky Zakhidnoi Ukrainy z Rosiieiu do seredyny XVII st*. Kiev, 1953.

Kubijovyè, V. 'Kholm Region.' *Encyclopedia of Ukraine*. Vol. 2. Toronto, 1988.

Kulish, P.A. *Istoriia vossoedineniia Rusi*. 2 vols. St Petersburg, 1874.

Kulturne budivnytstvo v Ukrainskii RSR: Naivazhlyvishi rishennia Komunistychnoi partii i Radianskoho uriadu: Zbirnyk dokumentiv. Vol. 2. Kiev, 1961.

Kuras, I.F., ed. *Natsionalni vidnosyny v Ukraini u XX st.: Zbirnyk dokumentiv i materialiv.* Kiev, 1994.

Kuromiya, Hiroaki. *Freedom and Terror in the Donbas: A Ukrainian-Russian Borderland.* Cambridge, 1998.

Kuzio, Taras. *Ukraine: State and Nation Building.* New York, 1998.

Kyryliuk, Ievhen, ed., *Istoriia ukrainskoi literatury u vosmy tomakh.* Vols 7 and 8. Kiev, 1971.

Lewytzkyj, Borys. *Die Sowjetukraine 1944–1963.* Cologne, 1964.

Liber, George O. *Alexander Dovzhenko: A Life in Soviet Film.* London, 2002.

– *Soviet Nationality Policy, Urban Growth, and Identity Change in the Ukrainian SSR, 1923–1934.* Cambridge, 1992.

Lieven, Dominic. 'The Russian Empire and the Soviet Union as Imperial Polities.' *Journal of Contemporary History* 30, no. 4 (October 1995): 607–35.

Lindner, Rainer. 'Nationalhistoriker im Stalinismus: Zum Profil der akademischen Intelligentz in Weißrußland, 1921–1946.' *Jahrbücher für Geschichte Osteuropas* 47, no. 4 (1999): 187–209.

Litvin [Lytvyn], K. 'Ob istorii ukrainskogo naroda.' *Bolshevik,* no. 7 (1947): 41–56.

McCagg, William O. *Stalin Embattled, 1943–1948.* Detroit, 1978.

Mace, James E. *Communism and the Dilemmas of National Liberation: National Communism in Soviet Ukraine, 1918–1933.* Cambridge, Mass., 1983.

Magocsi, Paul Robert. *The Shaping of a National Identity: Subcarpathian Rus', 1848–1948.* Cambridge, Mass., 1978.

Maksimov, L. 'O zhurnale "Voprosy istorii."' *Bolshevik,* no. 13 (1952): 60–70.

Manuilsky, D.Z. *Ukrainsko-nemetskie natsionalisty na sluzhbe u fashistskoi Germanii.* Kiev, 1946.

Marples, David R. *Stalinism in Ukraine in the 1940s.* London, 1992.

Martin, Terry. *The Affirmative Action Empire: Nations and Nationalism in the Soviet Union, 1923–1938.* Ithaca, NY, 2001.

– 'Interpreting the New Archival Signals: Nationalities Policy and the Nature of the Soviet Bureaucracy.' *Cahiers du Monde russe* 40, no. 1–2 (janvier–juin 1999): 113–24.

– 'Modernization or Neo-Traditionalism? Ascribed Nationality and Soviet Primordialism.' in *Stalinism: New Directions,* ed. Sheila Fitzpatrick. New York, 2000.

– 'The Soviet Union as Empire: Salvaging a Dubious Analytical Category.' Unpublished paper.

Martyniuk, I. 'Rozvyvaty i kultyvuvaty radianskyi patriotyzm.' *Bilshovyk Ukrainy,* no. 8 (1947): 11–24.

Marx, Karl, and Friedrich Engels. 'Manifesto of the Communist Party.' In *The Marx-Engels Reader,* ed. Robert C. Tucker. 2d ed. New York, 1978.

Mezentseva, G.G. *Muzei Ukrainy.* Kiev, 1959.

Michaels, Paula A. 'Medical Propaganda and Cultural Revolution in Soviet Kazakhstan, 1928–41.' *Russian Review* 59, no. 2 (April 2000): 159–78.

Motyl, Alexander J. 'From Imperial Decay to Imperial Collapse: The Fall of the Soviet Empire in Comparative Perspective.' In *Nationalism and Empire: The Habsburg Empire and the Soviet Union*, ed. Richard L. Rudolph and David F. Good. New York, 1992.

Musiienko, O.H. 'Andrii Patrus-Karpatsky.' In *Z poroha smerti: Pysmennyky Ukrainy – zhertvy stalinskykh represii*, ed. Musiienko. Kiev, 1991.

– ed. *Z poroha smerti: Pysmennyky Ukrainy – zhertvy stalinskykh represii*. Kiev, 1991.

Mykhailov, M. *Konstiantyn Fedorovych Dankevych: Narodnyi artyst SRSR*. Kiev, 1964.

Myshko, D.I. 'Pereiaslavskaia rada 1654 goda.' *Voprosy istorii*, no. 12 (1953): 19–28.

Naulko, I.P. 'Vyvchennia periodu Vyzvolnoi viiny ukrainskoho narodu 1648–1654 rr.' *Radianska shkola*, no. 3 (1954): 13–17.

Nechkina, M.V. 'K itogam diskussii o periodizatsii sovetskoi istoricheskoi nauki.' *Istoriia SSSR*, no. 2 (1962): 57–68.

– 'K voprosu o formule "naimenshee zlo" (Pismo v redaktsiiu).' *Voprosy istorii*, no. 4 (1951): 44–8.

– 'Vopros o M. N. Pokrovskom v postanovleniiakh partii i pravitelstva 1934–1938 gg. o prepodavanii istorii i istoricheskoi nauke.' *Istoricheskie zapiski*, 118 (1990): 233–46.

Nora, Pierre. 'Between History and Memory: Les Lieux de Mémoire.' *Representations* 26 (Spring 1989): 7–25.

– ed. *Les lieux de mémoire*. 7 vols. Paris, 1986–1993.

Northrop, Douglas. 'Languages of Loyalty: Gender, Politics, and Party Supervision in Uzbekistan, 1927–41.' *Russian Review* 59, no. 2 (April 2000): 179–200.

Oberländer, Erwin, ed., *Sowjetpatriotismus und Geschichte: Dokumentation*. Dokumente zum Studium des Kommunismus, Bd. 4. Cologne, 1967.

'Ob itogakh diskussii o periodizatsii istorii SSSR.' *Voprosy istorii*, no. 3 (1951): 53–60.

Osipov, K. *Bogdan Khmelnitsky*. Zhizn zamechatelnykh liudei. Moscow, 1939; 2d ed., 1948.

'Otvet P.K. Ponomarenko na voprosy G.A. Kumaneva 2 noiabria 1978 g.' *Otechestvennaia istoriia*, no. 6 (1998): 133–49.

Panch, Petro. *Homonila Ukraina*. Kiev, 1954.

– *Zaporozhtsi*. Kiev, 1946.

Pankratova, A.M. *Velykyi rosiiskyi narod*. Kiev, 1949; 2d ed., 1952.

– ed. *Istoriia SSSR: Uchebnik dlia VIII klassa srednei shkoly*. 5th ed., Moscow, 1946; 14th ed., Moscow, 1955.

Pashuto, V.T. 'Daniil Galitskii.' *Istoricheskii zhurnal*, no. 3–4 (1943): 37–44.

– *Ocherki po istorii Galitsko-Volynskoi Rusi*. Moscow, 1950.

Pashchenko, O., ed. *IX ukrainskaia khudozhestvennaia vystavka: Katalog*. Kiev, 1948.

Pavlyshyn, Marko. 'Post-Colonial Features in Contemporary Ukrainian Culture.' *Australian Slavonic and East European Studies* 6, no. 2 (1992): 41–55.

Petrone, Karen. *Life Has Become More Joyous, Comrades: Celebrations in the Time of Stalin*. Bloomington, Ind., 2000.

Petrovsky, M.N. *Bogdan Khmelnitsky*. Moscow, 1944.
- *Bohdan Khmelnytsky*. Nashi velyki predky. Saratov, 1942.
- *Narysy istorii Ukrainy XVII-pochatku XVIII stolit*. Vol. 1: *Doslidy nad Litopysom Samovydtsia*. Kharkiv, 1930).
- *Nezlamnyi dukh velykoho ukrainskoho narodu*. Kharkiv, 1943.
- 'Prisoedinenie Ukrainy k Rossii v 1654 godu.' *Istoricheskii zhurnal*, no. 1 (1944): 47–54.
- *Voennoe proshloe ukrainskogo naroda*. Biblioteka krasnoarmeitsa. Moscow, 1939.
- 'Vossoedinenie ukrainskogo naroda v edinom ukrainskom sovetskom gosudarstve.' *Bolshevik*, no. 2 (1944): 42–55.
- *Vossoedinenie ukrainskogo naroda v edinom ukrainskom sovetskom gosudarstve*. Moscow, 1944.
- *Vozziednannia ukrainskoho narodu v iedynii ukrainskii radianskii derzhavi*. Kiev, 1944.
- *Vyzvolna viina ukrainskoho narodu proty hnitu shliakhetskoi Polshchi i pryiednannia Ukrainy do Rosii (1648–1654)*. Kiev, 1940.
- *Zakhidna Ukraina (Istorychna dovidka)*. Biblioteka ahitatora. Kiev, 1945.
Picheta, V. *Osnovnye momenty istoricheskogo razvitiia Zapadnoi Ukrainy i Zapadnoi Belorussii*. Moscow, 1940.
Pilhuk, Ivan. 'Mykola Kostomarov.' *Ukrainska literatura*, no. 4–5 (1945): 122–31.
Pipes, Richard. *The Formation of the Soviet Union: Communism and Nationalism, 1917– 1923*. Rev. ed. Cambridge, MA, 1997.
Platt, Kevin M.F., and David Brandenberger. 'Terribly Romantic, Terribly Progressive, or Terribly Tragic: Rehabilitating Ivan IV under I.V. Stalin. *Russian Review* 58, no. 4 (October 1999): 635–54.
Plokhy, Serhii. 'The Ghosts of Pereiaslav: Russo-Ukrainian Historical Debates in the Post-Soviet Era.' *Europe-Asia Studies* 53, no. 3 (2001): 489–505.
Prystaiko, Volodymyr, and Iurii Shapoval. *Mykhailo Hrushevsky i HPU-NKVD: Trahichne desiatylittia: 1924–1934*. Kiev, 1996.
Pyrih, R.Ia. *Zhyttia Mykhaila Hrushevskoho: Ostannie desiatylittia (1924–1934)*. Kiev, 1993.
Reshetar, John S., Jr. 'The Significance of the Soviet Tercentenary of the Pereiaslav Treaty.' *Annals of the Ukrainian Academy of Arts and Sciences in the U.S.* 4, no. 3 (Winter-Spring 1955): 981–94.
'Rishuche polipshuvaty dobir, rozstanovku i vykorystannia kadriv.' *Partrobitnyk Ukrainy*, no. 8 (1946): 4–11.
Romitsyn, A.A. *Ukrainske radianske kinomystetstvo 1941–1954 rr.* Kiev, 1959.
Rublov, O.S., and Iu.A. Cherchenko. *Stalinshchyna i dolia zakhidnoukrainskoi intelihentsii: 20-50-ti roky XX st.* Kiev, 1994.
Rudenko, Mykola. *Naibilshe dyvo – zhyttia: Spohady*. Kiev, 1998.
Rybak, Natan. *Pereiaslavska rada*. Ed. M.N. Petrovsky. Kiev, 1948.

– *Pereiaslavska rada.* Kiev, 1949.

– *Pereiaslavska rada.* 2 vols. Kiev, 1953.

Safonova, Ie.V. 'Antyfashystski mitynhy predstavnykiv ukrainskoho narodu u roku Velykoi Vitchyznianoi viiny.' In *Druha svitova viina i Ukraina: Materialy naukovoi konferentsii 27–28 kvitnia 1995 r.*, ed. M.V. Koval. Kiev, 1996.

Santsevich [Santsevych], A.V., and N.V. Komarenko, *Razvitie istoricheskoi nauki v Akademii nauk Ukrainskoi SSR: 1936–1986 gg.* Kiev, 1986.

Savchuk, O.V. *Kraieznavchyi rukh v Ukraini (kinets 50-kh-pochatok 90-kh rr. XX st.* Avtoreferat kandydatskoi dysertatsii. Kiev, 1997.

Serhiichuk, Volodymyr, ed. *Desiat buremnykh lit: Zakhidnoukrainski zemli u 1944–1953 rr.: Novi dokumenty i materialy.* Kiev, 1998.

Shakhovsky, S. 'Suspilno-politychni pohliady Lesi Ukrainky.' *Bilshovyk Ukrainy*, no. 4 (1951): 33–45.

Shapoval, Iu.I. *Lazar Kahanovych.* Kiev, 1994.

– *Liudyna i systema: (Shtrykhy do portretu totalitarnoi doby v Ukraini).* Kiev, 1994.

– *Ukraina 20-50-kh rokiv: Storinky nenapysanoi istorii.* Kiev, 1993.

Shelest, P.E. *Da ne sudimy budete: Dnevnikovye zapisi, vospominaniia chlena Politbiuro TsK KPSS.* Moscow, 1995.

Shepilov, D.T. 'Vospominaniia.' *Voprosy istorii*, no. 6 (1998): 3–44.

Shestakov, A.V., ed. *Istoriia SSSR: Kratkii kurs.* Moscow, 1948, 1955.

– ed., *Kratkii kurs istorii SSSR.* Moscow, 1937.

Shevchenko, L.A. 'Kultura Ukrainy v umovakh stalinskoho totalitaryzmu (Druha polovyna 40-kh-pochatok 50-kh rokiv.' In *Ukraina XX st.: Kultura, ideolohiia, polityka*, ed. V.M. Danylenko. Vol. 1. Kiev, 1993.

Shevchenko, L.A. 'Kulturno-ideolohichni protsesy v Ukraini u 40-50-kh rr.' *Ukrainskyi istorychnyi zhurnal*, no. 7/8 (1992): 39–48.

Shevchenko, Taras. *Povne zibrannia tvoriv.* 5 vols. Kiev, 1939.

Shevchuk, H. 'Nauchno-issledovatelskaia rabota Instituta istorii Ukrainy Akademii nauk Ukrainskoi SSR za 1950 god.' *Voprosy istorii*, no. 2 (1951): 156–8.

Shkandrij, Myroslav. *Russia and Ukraine: Literature and the Discourse of Empire from Napoleonic to Postcolonial Times.* Montreal, 2001.

Shovkoplias, I.H. *Arkheolohichni doslidzhennia na Ukraini (1917–1957): Ohliad vyvchennia arkheolohichnykh pamiatok.* Kiev, 1957.

Shteppa, Konstantin F. *Russian Historians and the Soviet State.* New Brunswick, N.J., 1962.

Simon, Gerhard. *Nationalism and Policy toward the Nationalities in the Soviet Union: From Totalitarian Dictatorship to Post-Stalinist Society.* Trans. Karen Forster and Oswald Forster. Boulder, Colo., 1991.

Slezkine, Yuri. 'Imperialism as the Highest Stage of Socialism.' *Russian Review* 59, no. 2 (April 2000): 227–34.

- 'The USSR as a Communal Apartment, or How a Socialist State Promoted Ethnic Particularism.' *Slavic Review* 53, no. 2 (Summer 1994): 414–52.
Slyvka, Iu., ed., *Kulturne zhyttia v Ukraini: Zakhidni zemli: Dokumenty i materially.* Vol. 1: *1939–1953.* Kiev, 1995.
Smirnov, N., and G. Arutiunov. Review of *Istoriia armianskogo naroda*, part 1, ed. B. Arakelian and A. Ioannisian, *Voprosy istorii*, no. 12 (1951): 183–6.
Smith, Anthony. *The Ethnic Origins of Nations.* Oxford, 1986.
- 'The Nation: Invented, Imagined, Reconstructed?' In *Remembering the Nation*, ed. Marjorie Ringrose and Adam J. Lerner. Buckingham, 1993.
Smolii, V.A., ed. *U leshchatakh totalitaryzmu: Pershe dvadtsiatyrichchia Instytutu istorii Ukrainy NAN Ukrainy (1936–1956 rr.): Zbirnyk dokumentiv i materialiv.* 2 parts. Kiev, 1996.
- *Vcheni Instytutu istorii Ukrainy: Biobibliohrafichnyi dovidnyk.* Kiev, 1998.
Sokolovsky, O. *Bohun: Istorychnyi roman z chasiv Khmelnychchyny.* Munich, 1957.
Soroka, M. 'Zinaida Tulub.' In *Z poroha smerti: Pysmennyky Ukrainy – zhertvy stalinskykh represii*, ed. O.H. Musiienko. Kiev, 1991.
Sosiura, Volodymyr. 'Tretia Rota.' *Kyiv*, no. 1 (1988): 63–122; no. 2 (1988): 69–122.
- 'Love Ukraine.' In *The Ukrainian Poets, 1189–1962*, ed. and trans. C.H. Andrusyshen and Watson Kirkconnell. Toronto, 1963.
Stalin, I.V. 'Ob antileninskikh oshibkakh i natsionalisticheskikh izvrashcheniiakh v kinopovesti Dovzhenko "Ukraina v ogne."' *Iskusstvo kino*, no. 4 (1990): 84–96.
- 'Vystuplenie I. V. Stalina na prieme v Kremle v chest komanduiushchikh voiskami Krasnoi armii 24 maia 1945 goda.' In his *O Velikoi Otechestvennoi voine Sovetskogo Soiuza.* Moscow, 1947.
- 'O zadachakh khoziaistvennikov.' In his *Voprosy leninizma* (Moscow, 1934).
Stanishevsky, Iu.O. *Ukrainskyi radianskyi muzychnyi teatr: Narysy istorii (1917–1967).* Kiev, 1970.
'Stenogramma soveshchaniia po voprosam istorii SSSR v TsK VKP(b) v 1944 godu.' *Voprosy istorii*, no. 2 (1966): 55–86; no. 3: 82–112; no. 4: 65–93; no. 5: 77–106; no. 7: 70–87, no. 9: 47–77.
Stoler, Ann Laura, and Frederick Cooper. 'Between Metropole and Colony: Rethinking a Research Agenda.' In *Tensions of Empire: Colonial Cultures in a Bourgeois World*, ed. Cooper and Stoler. Berkeley, Calif., 1997.
Sullivant, Robert S. *Soviet Politics and the Ukraine, 1917–1957.* New York, 1962.
Suny, Ronald Grigor. 'Ambiguous Categories: States, Empires and Nations.' *Post-Soviet Affairs* 11, no. 2 (April-June 1995): 185–96.
- *The Revenge of the Past: Nationalism, Revolution, and the Collapse of the Soviet Union.* Stanford, Calif., 1993.
Syrotiuk, Mykola. *Ukrainska istorychna proza za 40 rokiv.* Kiev, 1958.
- *Ukrainskyi radianskyi istorychnyi roman: Problema istorychnoi ta khudozhnoi pravdy.* Kiev, 1962.

Sysyn, Frank. 'The Changing Image of the Hetman: On the 350th Anniversary of the Khmel'nyts'kyi Uprising.' *Jahrbücher für Geschichte Osteuropas* 46, no. 4 (1998): 531–45.

– 'The Reemergence of the Ukrainian Nation and Cossack Mythology.' *Social Research* 58, no. 4 (Winter 1991): 845–64.

Szporluk, Roman. 'The Fall of the Tsarist Empire and the USSR: The Russian Question and Imperial Overextension.' In his *Russia, Ukraine, and the Breakup of the Soviet Union*. Stanford, Calif., 2000.

– 'National History as a Political Battleground: The Case of Ukraine and Belorussia.' In *Russian Empire: Some Aspects of Tsarist and Soviet Colonial Practices*, ed. Michael S. Pap. Cleveland, 1985.

– 'The Ukraine and Russia.' In *The Last Empire: Nationality and the Soviet Future*, ed. Robert Conquest. Stanford, Calif., 1986.

– 'West Ukraine and West Belorussia: Historical Tradition, Social Communication, and Linguistic Assimilation.' *Soviet Studies* 31, no. 1 (1979): 76–98.

Tadyev, P.E. 'Konferentsiia po voprosam izucheniia istorii Gornogo Altaia.' *Voprosy istorii*, no. 4 (1955): 173–5.

Tezisy o 300–letii vossoedineniia Ukrainy s Rossiei (1654–1954 gg.). Moscow, 1954.

Tillett, Lowell. *The Great Friendship: Soviet Historians on the Non-Russian Nationalities*. Chapel Hill, N.C., 1969.

– 'Ukrainian Nationalism and the Fall of Shelest.' *Slavic Review* 34, no. 4 (1975): 752–68.

Timasheff, Nicholas S. *The Great Retreat: The Growth and Decline of Communism in Russia*. New York, 1946.

Tkachenko, Mykola. 'Kholmshchyna, Hrubeshiv, Iaroslav – odvichni ukrainski zemli.' *Ukrainska literatura*, no. 5–6 (1944): 122–9.

Turianytsia, I. 'Rozvytok kultury v Zakarpatti.' *Bilshovyk Ukrainy*, no. 7 (1949): 40–8.

Velychenko, Stephen. *National History as Cultural Process: A Survey of the Interpretations of Ukraine's Past in Polish, Russian, and Ukrainian Historical Writing from the Earliest Times to 1914*. Edmonton, 1992.

– 'The Origins of the Official Soviet Interpretation of Eastern Slavic History: A Case Study of Policy Formulation.' *Forschungen zur osteuropäischen Geschichte* 46 (1992): 225–53.

– *Shaping Identity in Eastern Europe and Russia: Soviet-Russian and Polish Accounts of Ukrainian History, 1914–1991*. New York, 1993.

Verdery, Katherine. *National Ideology under Socialism: Identity and Cultural Politics in Ceauᵒescu's Romania*. Berkeley, Calif., 1991.

Vershyhora, P. 'Bratia po oruzhiiu (O narodnykh formakh vooruzhennoi borby russkogo i ukrainskogo narodov).' *Oktiabr*, no. 4 (1954): 110–36.

Vladych, Leonid. *Vasyl Kasiian: Piat etiudiv pro khudozhnyka*. Kiev, 1978.

Voblyi, K., K. Huslysty, V. Diadychenko, F. Los, M. Petrovsky, L. Slavin, M. Suprunenko, and F. Sherstiuk. *Narys istorii Ukrainy.* Ufa, 1942.

Voronin, N. Review of *Voennoe delo v Kievskoi Rusi* by V. I. Dovzhenok. *Voprosy istorii,*
no. 1 (1951): 139–40.

Vossoedinenie Ukrainy s Rossiei: Dokumenty i materialy v trekh tomakh. 3 vols. Moscow,
1953.

*Vystavka izobrazitelnogo iskusstva Ukrainskoi SSR posviashchennaia trekhsotletiiu
vossoedineniia Ukrainy s Rossiei: Zhivopis, skulptura, grafika: Katalog.* Kiev, 1954.

Vystavka izobrazitelnogo iskusstva Ukrainskoi SSR: Zhivopis, skulptura, grafika: Katalog.
Kiev, 1951.

Wanner, Catherine. *Burden of Dreams: History and Identity in Post-Soviet Ukraine.*
University Park, Penn., 1998.

Weiner, Amir. *Making Sense of War: The Second World War and the Fate of the Bolshevik
Revolution.* Princeton, N.J., 2001.

Weiner, Amir. 'Nature, Nurture, and Memory in a Socialist Utopia: Delineating the
Soviet Socio-Ethnic Body in the Age of Socialism.' *American Historical Review* 104, no.
4 (October 1999): 1114–55.

Wood, Nancy. 'Memory Remains: *Les lieux de mémoire*.' *History and Memory* 6, no. 1
(Spring-Summer 1994): 123–49.

Yekelchyk, Serhy. 'Creating a Sacred Place: The Ukrainophiles and Shevchenko's Tomb in
Kaniv (1861–ca. 1900).' *Journal of Ukrainian Studies* 20, nos 1–2 (Summer-Winter
1995): 15–32.

– '*Diktat* and Dialogue in Stalinist Culture: Staging Patriotic Historical Opera in Soviet
Ukraine (1936–1954).' *Slavic Review* 59, no. 3 (Fall 2000): 597–624.

Yerushalmi, Yosef. *Zakhor: Jewish History and Jewish Memory.* New York, 1989.

'Za novye uspekhi izobrazitelnogo iskusstva Ukrainy.' *Iskusstvo,* no. 4 (1951): 3–10.

Zak, M., L. Parfenov, and O. Iakubovich-Iasnyi, *Igor Savchenko.* Moscow, 1959.

Zamlynska, O.V. 'Ideolohichni represii u haluzi kultury v Ukraini u 1948–1953 rr.' In
Ukraina XX st.: Kultura, ideolohiia, polityka, ed. V.M. Danylenko. Vol. 2. Kiev, 1996.

– 'Ideolohichnyi teror ta represii proty tvorchoi intelihentsii u pershi povoienni roky
(1945–1947 rr.).' *Kyivska starovyna,* no. 2 (1993): 73–80.

Zimin, A.A., V.D. Mochalov, and A.A. Novoselsky. 'Tsennyi trud po istorii Ukrainskoi
SSR.' *Voprosy istorii,* no. 6 (1954): 128–32.

Zubkova, Elena. *Russia after the War: Hopes, Illusions, and Disappointments, 1945–1957.*
Trans. and ed. Hugh Ragsdale. Armonk, NY, 1998.

Index

www.ingramcontent.com/pod-product-compliance
Lightning Source LLC
Chambersburg PA
CBHW021859020426
42334CB00013B/405